SEVEN
PUCCINI *LIBRETTOS*

WILLIAM WEAVER, a Virginian and a graduate of Princeton, has lived most of his life in Italy (since 1965 on his farm in Tuscany). He is the Arts correspondent for the *Financial Times* (London), a regular contributor to a number of other magazines, and a frequent guest on the Texaco broadcasts from the Metropolitan Opera. He has published *Seven Verdi Librettos* (Norton, 1975), *Verdi: A Documentary Study* (Thames and Hudson, 1977), *Puccini* (Dutton, 1972), and *The Golden Century of Italian Opera* (Thames and Hudson, 1981). With Martin Chusid, he is co-editor of *The Verdi Companion* (Norton, 1979). A well-known translator of contemporary Italian writing, he has been responsible for the English versions of works by Giorgio Bassani, Italo Calvino, Carlo Emilio Gadda, Elsa Morante, and many others. His translations have won the National Book Award and, on two occasions, the John Florio Prize in Great Britain.

SEVEN
PUCCINI *LIBRETTOS*

In new English translations
by William Weaver

WITH THE ORIGINAL ITALIAN

W · W · NORTON & COMPANY
New York · London

For Licia and Pippo Greghi

Library of Congress Cataloging in Publication Data

Puccini, Giacomo, 1858–1924.
    Seven Puccini librettos.

        Contents: La Bohème—Tosca—Madama Butterfly
    —[etc.]
        1. Operas—Librettos.   I. Weaver, William,
    1923–   II. Title.
    ML49.P75W423   782.1′2   81–3916

ISBN 0-393-01221-2 {cloth} AACR2
ISBN 0-393-00930-0 {pbk.}

W. W. Norton & Company, Inc. 500 Fifth Avenue, New York,
N.Y. 10110
W. W. Norton & Company Ltd. 25 New Street Square,
London EC4A 3NT

2 3 4 5 6 7 8 9 0

CONTENTS

AN INTRODUCTORY NOTE

PUCCINI AND HIS LIBRETTOS

"I'm writing this in drama class," Puccini says in a letter to his mother of March 1883, when he was a student at the Milan Conservatory, "which bores me very much . . ."

Though Puccini was a born opera composer — as even his detractors are forced to admit — he was not a born man of the theater; and though he spent a great deal of his time going to plays in his mature years, he had no well-defined literary tastes. One might almost say of him that he not only didn't know much about art, he didn't even know what he liked. In fact, the story of the librettos he *almost* set would be much longer — and even more tormented — than the toilsome story of the selection and composition of his dozen operas. Through most of these operas a linking thread can be traced: the pathetic Anna of *Le Villi*, Puccini's first work for the theater, is, as a character, strikingly similar to the poor slave girl Liù of the posthumous *Turandot*.

The fact is that Puccini, unlike his contemporaries Mascagni and Leoncavallo, for example, knew the nature of his talent, its special qualities and its limitations. At times he toyed with grand themes (for years he dreamed, off and on, of a *Marie Antoinette*); he thought of Shakespeare and of Victor Hugo, but in the end he returned to more congenial if less illustrious authors.

Like Verdi, Puccini drove his librettists crazy. Even when he was hardly more than a student and writing his first opera, he wrote his librettist, Ferdinando Fontana, asking him to make changes in the text. Fontana, several years older than Puccini and already a fairly well-established writer and theatrical figure, was reluctant to make them. Later, when Puccini himself was established, he made his writers revise and recast whole librettos three or four times, and the process continued even after the works had been performed.

But if one reads the correspondence between Verdi and his "poets" and the correspondence between Puccini and his, the differences between the two composers' characters become obvious. Verdi made demands based on his inner certainty of what he wanted. Puccini, a weaker man, had to try things first this way, then that, until he gradually gained confidence in what he was doing. Another evidence of his insecurity is the fact that he most frequently tended to choose for his subjects plays that were already big hits on the legitimate stage (like

Tosca, Madame Butterfly, The Girl of the Golden West) or subjects that other composers had set (*Manon Lescaut*) or wanted to set (*La Bohème*).

In Verdi's day the librettist was often a mere theater employee; one ordered so many pages of drama from him as one ordered so many costumes from the dressmaker. By the last years of Verdi's career (which coincide with the beginning of Puccini's) this was all changed. Creeping Wagnerism and increased sophistication in musical circles had made the librettist a respectable figure. From Fontana on, Puccini dealt with esteemed men-of-letters, editors of literary journals, successful playwrights. Read nowadays, the librettos, as examples of Italian poetry, are not really so superior to the much-maligned texts of Verdi's Francesco Maria Piave and Antonio Somma. At best, Puccini's librettos have a quaint turn-of-the-century, *art nouveau* flavor. But, as the librettist Luigi Illica wrote to Puccini's publisher and mentor Giulio Ricordi: "I still remain of my opinion: the form of a libretto is made by the music, and nothing but the music; It alone . . . is the form! A libretto is merely the outline. And Méry [French librettist of, among other things, Verdi's *Don Carlos*] is right when he says: 'Verses in operas are written only for the convenience of the deaf. . . .'"

In the end the important thing about the librettos of Giacosa and Illica, Adami, Forzano — like those of Piave and Cammarano — is that they inspired the composer to write great operas.

A word about the intentions of this book. Like the translator's volume of *Seven Verdi Librettos,* this book is intended as a guide — the most faithful possible — to the Italian words. The translations, therefore, have absolutely no literary pretensions, and the translator's greatest difficulty was in resisting the almost constant temptation to prettify the English at the expense of literal adherence to the original. He hopes that he has resisted this temptation successfully.

The printed librettos of Puccini's operas generally available are often inaccurate, failing to incorporate changes that the composer made — or had made — in the texts during the course of composition or after the first performances. The Italian texts here have therefore been reconstructed from recent editions of the piano scores of the operas. On the other hand, these scores frequently have condensed versions of the librettists' original stage directions, so for these the editor has had recourse to first editions of the librettos, where the stage directions are more copious. The aim, obviously, is to give the reader the fullest assistance in visualizing the stage picture of the opera as he follows its words and music.

Wherever possible typographically, brackets are used in the Italian text to indicate places where different lines are sung simultaneously.

The translator expresses his gratitude to Tobias Schnee-baum, for his help; to Dorle and Dario Soria, who commissioned several of these translations originally; and to the editor of this new edition, Claire Brook (la sempre cara Signora Fontana).

William Weaver

Rome, 1966
Monte San Savino, 1981

BIBLIOGRAPHICAL NOTE

Puccini, a Critical Biography, by Mosco Carner (Duckworth, London, 1958).

Giacomo Puccini, by Claudio Casini (UTET, Turin, 1978).

Carteggi pucciniani, edited by Eugenio Gara (Ricordi, Milan, 1958).

Come li ho conosciuti, by Giovacchino Forzano (Edizioni Radio Italiana, Turin, 1957).

Puccini, by Howard Greenfeld (Putnam, New York, 1980).

Puccini: Keeper of the Seal, by Edward Greenfeld (Arrow Books, London, 1958).

Opera as Drama, by Joseph Kerman (Knopf, New York, 1956).

Opera as Theater, by George R. Marek (Harper & Row, New York, 1962).

Puccini, by George R. Marek (Simon & Schuster, New York, 1951).

Luigi Illica, by Mario Morini (Ente Provinciale per il Turismo, Piacenza, 1961).

Vita e tempo di Giuseppe Giacosa, by Piero Nardi (Mondadori, Milan, 1949).

Puccini, una vita, by Leonardo Pinzauti (Vallecchi, Florence, 1974).

Puccini Among Friends, by Vincent Seligman (Macmillan, New York, 1938).

Puccini, by William Weaver (Dutton, New York, 1977).

La Bohème

After setting, in his youthful eagerness and inexperience, a pair of uncongenial librettos by the poet Ferdinando Fontana (*Le Villi* in 1884 and *Edgar* in 1889), Puccini turned to other writers for his next work, *Manon Lescaut*. A series of poets and playwrights worked on the libretto at various times, assisted by the composer Paolo Tosti at one point, by the publisher Giulio Ricordi, and to some extent by Puccini himself. In the end the score and libretto were published without any author's name except that of the Abbé Prévost, author of the original novel.

Despite this difficult genesis, *Manon Lescaut* was a considerable success. It not only firmly established Puccini's fame in Italy, but it also brought his name into the opera houses of other countries. And, equally important, it granted him a certain amount of financial independence and, consequently, the ability to compose under less strain.

In fact, the composition of *La Bohème* took almost four years. It might have taken even longer had not Ruggero Leoncavallo, Puccini's rival composer, announced — as Puccini was beginning work — that he too was composing a *Bohème* to a libretto of his own authorship. This competition unquestionably spurred Puccini on. It also created undying bitterness between the two men (exacerbated also by the rivalry of their respective publishers); and by now the story of who thought of *Bohème* first has become swamped in tangled polemics. Puccini's shattering victory has, in any case, made the question academic.

Among the many writers who had a hand in the *Manon Lescaut* libretto were two playwrights, Giuseppe Giacosa and Luigi Illica. These two men — of contrasting temperament but of almost equal talent — were persuaded by Ricordi to prepare the libretto of *La Bohème*. They began sometime early in 1893; their collaboration — often tempestuous — was to continue, through *Tosca* and *Madama Butterfly*, until Giacosa's death in 1906. Virtually a third collaborator in the writing of all three operas was Ricordi himself, and of course, Puccini had a final say, which he exercised very often. The story of the sessions the four men held in Ricordi's office, with the publisher acting as mediator among his three sensitive and touchy artists, is told in all the biographies of the composer.

The adaptation of Henry Murger's once popular book, *Scènes de la vie de bohème*, posed particular problems of condensation and coherence for the librettists, who had to make the sprawling series of sketches into a dramatic whole. The result, even so, is not a well-plotted story, but an effective creation of atmosphere and some subtle characterization.

La Bohème's first performance, conducted by Arturo Toscanini (at twenty-eight already an important figure in Italian musical life), was a success with the audience; but the critics were divided. They were soon overruled, however, and in the space of a few years *La Bohème* had entered — for good — the international repertory.

THE PLOT

ACT ONE

Rodolfo, a poet, and his friend Marcello, a painter, are trying to work in their Paris garret. It is Christmas Eve, and they are cold and hungry — and without money. Colline, another bohemian, comes in, equally discouraged. But then Schaunard, the fourth and luckiest of the group, enters with money and provisions. The friends decide to celebrate by dining out. After a successful skirmish with their landlord, Benoît, they set out for the Café Momus. Only Rodolfo stays behind to finish an article he must write. When he is alone there is a knock at the door. To his surprise, he finds a beautiful young girl on the landing. It is his neighbor, Mimì, who has knocked to ask for a light. Her candle has gone out. Rodolfo relights it for her, but it goes out again, and in the confusion, she loses her key. In the darkness she and Rodolfo search for it. Their hands touch. Rodolfo and Mimì exchange confidences and, finally, declarations of love. Then they go off to join his friends.

ACT TWO

Christmas Eve in the Latin Quarter. The group of friends is separated in the bustling of merrymakers and vendors of every kind. Rodolfo and Mimì go into a milliner's, and he buys her a pink bonnet. Later all are reunited at the Café Momus, where they order a sumptuous supper. As they are enjoying themselves, Musetta — Marcello's beautiful but fickle beloved — enters with Alcindoro, an elderly and strait-laced admirer. Seeing Marcello, Musetta contrives to get rid of her escort. She and Marcello are again in each other's arms. The friends all go off, leaving their bill to the hapless Alcindoro.

ACT THREE

A cold February dawn. Outside a tavern near one of the gates of Paris, Mimì appears and sends for Marcello, who is working in the tavern with Musetta. When he comes out, Mimì tells how Rodolfo's insane jealousy is forcing them apart. Their conversation is cut short when Rodolfo, who was sleeping in the tavern, wakes and comes out. Mimì hides behind a tree. Taxed by Marcello with his fickleness, Rodolfo reveals that he is really concerned for Mimì's health and thinks that another person, less poor than he, could take better care of her. Mimì's presence is discovered, and though she first bids Rodolfo good-by, in the end they agree to stay together at least until spring comes. As Musetta and Marcello quarrel in the background and finally separate, Rodolfo and Mimì go off reconciled, arm in arm.

ACT FOUR

The garret, months later. Rodolfo and Marcello are again trying to work, but this time each is distracted and tormented by the memory of his lost love. Schaunard and Colline come in, and the four friends clown, making light of their poverty, until Musetta interrupts them, bursting in with the news that Mimì is outside, too ill to climb the last stairs. Rodolfo helps her into the room, where she is settled on the bed. Musetta sacrifices her earrings and Colline his coat to buy medicine and a muff for the dying girl. Marcello goes for a doctor. Left alone, the two lovers renew their vows of love and recall their first meeting. Soon the others return. As Musetta prays, Mimì quietly dies, with Rodolfo calling her name in despair.

LA BOHÈME

libretto by Giuseppe Giacosa and Luigi Illica

First performed at the Teatro Regio, Turin
February 1, 1896

CHARACTERS

Rodolfo, a poet	*Tenor*
Marcello, a painter	*Baritone*
Colline, a philosopher	*Bass*
Schaunard, a musician	*Baritone*
Benoît, a landlord	*Bass*
Alcindoro, a councilor of state	*Bass*
Parpignol, a toy vendor	*Tenor*
Customs Sergeant	*Bass*
Mimì	*Soprano*
Musetta	*Soprano*

Students, Working Girls, Bourgeois, Shopkeepers,
Vendors, Soldiers, Waiters, Gamins, etc.

The time is about 1830.
The place is the Latin Quarter, Paris.

QUADRO PRIMO

In soffitta

Ampia finestra dalla quale si scorge una distesa di tetti coperti di neve. A destra un camino. Una tavola, un letto, un armadio, quattro sedie, un cavalletto da pittore con una tela sbozzata ed uno sgabello: libri sparsi, molti fasci di carte, due candelieri. Uscio nel mezzo, altro a sinistra. Rodolfo guarda meditabondo fuori della finestra. Marcello lavora al suo quadro: Il passaggio del Mar Rosso, colle mani intirizzite dal freddo e che egli riscalda alitandovi su di quando in quando, mutando, pel gran gelo, posizione.

MARCELLO   Questo Mar Rosso — mi ammollisce e assidera
come se addosso — mi piovesse in stille.
> (*si allontana dal cavalletto per guardare il suo quadro*)

Per vendicarmi, affogo un Faraon.
> (*torna al lavoro — a Rodolfo*)

Che fai?

RODOLFO   Nei cieli bigi
guardo fumar dai mille
comignoli Parigi,
> (*additando il camino senza fuoco*)

e penso a quel poltrone
d'un vecchio caminetto ingannatore
che vive in ozio come un gran signor!

MARCELLO   Le sue rendite oneste
da un pezzo non riceve.

RODOLFO   Quelle sciocche foreste
che fan sotto la neve?

MARCELLO   Rodolfo, io voglio dirti un mio pensier profondo:
ho un freddo cane.

RODOLFO (*avvicinandosi a Marcello*)
    Ed io, Marcel, non ti nascondo
che non credo al sudor della fronte.

MARCELLO   Ho ghiacciate
le dita . . . quasi ancor le tenessi immollate
giù in quella gran ghiacciaia che è il cuore di Musetta!
> (*lascia sfuggire un lungo sospirone, e tralascia di dipingere, deponendo tavolozza e pennelli*)

RODOLFO   L'amore è un caminetto che sciupa troppo . . .

MARCELLO   . . . e in fretta!

RODOLFO   . . . dove l'uomo è fascina . . .

ACT ONE

In the Garret

A broad window from which an expanse of roofs, covered with snow, is seen. At right, a stove. A table, a bed, a wardrobe, four chairs, a painter's easel with a sketched canvas and a stool: scattered books, many bundles of papers, two candlesticks. A door in the center, another at left. Rodolfo is looking pensively out of the window. Marcello is working at his picture: The Crossing of the Red Sea, with his hands benumbed by the cold. He warms them by breathing on them from time to time, changing his position because of the great chill.

MARCELLO This Red Sea — is soaking and freezing me as
     as if it were raining — upon me in drops.
       (he moves away from the easel to look at
        his picture)
     To avenge myself, I'll drown a Pharaoh.
       (goes back to work — to Rodolfo)
     What are you doing?

RODOLFO In the gray skies
     I'm watching Paris
     smoke from its thousand chimneys,
       (pointing to the stove without fire)
     and I'm thinking of that slacker
     of a deceitful old stove
     which lives in lesiure like a great lord!

MARCELLO For a long time he hasn't received
     his just income.

RODOLFO What are those silly forests
     doing under the snow?

MARCELLO Rodolfo, I want to tell you a deep thought of
      mine:
     I'm cold as hell.

RODOLFO *(approaching Marcello)*
     And I, Marcello, won't conceal from you
     that I don't believe in the sweat of the brow.

MARCELLO I have frozen
     fingers . . . as if I still held them plunged
     down in that great icebox which is Musetta's
      heart!
       (he allows a long sigh to escape him and
       leaves off painting, setting down palette
       and brushes)

RODOLFO Love is a stove that consumes too much . . .

MARCELLO . . . and in haste!

RODOLFO . . . where the man is the kindling-wood . . .

MARCELLO   . . . e la donna è l'alare . . .

RODOLFO   . . . l'uno brucia in un soffio . . .

MARCELLO   . . . e l'altro sta a guardare.

RODOLFO   Ma intanto qui si gela . . .

MARCELLO   . . . e si muore d'inedia . . . !

RODOLFO   Fuoco ci vuole . . .

MARCELLO   (*afferrando una sedia e facendo l'atto di spezzarla*)
              Aspetta . . . sacrifichiam la sedia!

    *Rodolfo impedisce con energia l'atto di Marcello. Ad un
tratto Rodolfo esce in un grido di gioia ad un'idea che gli è
balenata.*

RODOLFO   *Eureka!*
                  (*corre alla tavola e ne leva un voluminoso
                  scartafaccio*)

MARCELLO   Trovasti?

RODOLFO   Sì. Aguzza
              l'ingegno. L'idea vampi in fiamma.

MARCELLO   (*additando il suo quadro*)
              Bruciamo il Mar Rosso?

RODOLFO   No. Puzza
              la tela dipinta. Il mio dramma,
              l'ardente mio dramma ci scaldi.

MARCELLO   (*con comico spavento*)
              Vuoi leggerlo forse? Mi geli.

RODOLFO   No, in cener la carta si sfaldi
              e l'estro rivoli a' suoi cieli.
                  (*con enfasi tragica*)
              Al secol gran danno minaccia . . .
              è Roma in periglio!

MARCELLO   Gran cor!

RODOLFO   (*dà a Marcello una parte dello scartafaccio*)
              A te l'atto primo.

MARCELLO   Qua.

RODOLFO   Straccia.

MARCELLO   Accendi.

    *Rodolfo batte un acciarino, accende una candela, e va al
camino con Marcello: insieme dànno fuoco a quella parte
dello scartafaccio buttato sul focolare, poi entrambi prendono
delle sedie e seggono, riscaldandosi voluttuosamente.*

RODOLFO E MARCELLO
              Che lieto baglior.

    *Si apre con fracasso la porta in fondo ed entra Colline gela-
to, intirizzito, battendo i piedi, gettando con ira sulla tavola un
pacco di libri legato con un fazzoletto.*

COLLINE   Già dell'Apocalisse appariscono i segni.
              In giorno di Vigilia non s'accettano pegni —
                  (*si interrompe sorpreso*)
              Una fiammata!

MARCELLO   . . . and the woman is the andiron . . .

RODOLFO   . . . the one burns up in a flash . . .

MARCELLO   . . . and the other stands and watches.

RODOLFO   But meanwhile here we're freezing . . .

MARCELLO   . . . and we're dying of starvation . . .!

RODOLFO   Fire is needed . . .

MARCELLO   (*seizing a chair and preparing to shatter it*)
            Wait . . . let's sacrifice the chair!

Rodolfo energetically prevents Marcello's action. Suddenly Rodolfo lets out a shout of joy at an idea that has come to him.

RODOLFO   *Eureka!*
                        (*runs to the table and takes a voluminous sheaf of papers from it*)

MARCELLO   You've found it?

RODOLFO   Yes. Sharpen
            your wit. Let the Idea blaze up in flames.

MARCELLO   (*pointing to his picture*)
            Do we burn the Red Sea?

RODOLFO   No. Painted canvas
            stinks. My drama,
            let my burning drama warm us.

MARCELLO   (*with comic fear*)
            Do you want perhaps to read it? You freeze me.

RODOLFO   No, let the paper flake away in ash
            and inspiration fly back to its heavens.
                        (*with tragic vehemence*)
            Great harm threatens our time . . .
            Rome is in danger!

MARCELLO   Magnanimous!

RODOLFO   (*gives Marcello a part of the sheaf*)
            Take the first act.

MARCELLO   Here.

RODOLFO   Tear it up.

MARCELLO   Light it.

Rodolfo strikes a tinderbox, lights a candle, and goes to the stove with Marcello. Together they set fire to the part of the sheaf of papers thrown in the hearth, then both take chairs and sit down, warming themselves voluptuously.

RODOLFO AND MARCELLO
            What a happy glow.

The door in the background is opened with a racket and Colline enters, frozen, numb, stamping his feet, throwing wrathfully on the table a pack of books tied with a handkerchief.

COLLINE   The signs of the Apocalypse are already appearing.
            On Christmas Eve no pawning is allowed —
                        (*breaks off, surprised*)
            A flame!

RODOLFO (*a Colline*)
            Zitto, si dà il mio dramma . . .
MARCELLO   . . . al fuoco.
COLLINE   Lo trovo scintillante.
RODOLFO   Vivo.
    Il fuoco diminuisce.
COLLINE   Ma dura poco.
RODOLFO   La brevità, gran pregio.
COLLINE (*levandogli la sedia*)
            Autore, a me la sedia.
MARCELLO   Quest'intermezzi fan morir d'inedia.
            Presto.
RODOLFO (*prende un'altra parte dello scartafaccio*)
            Atto secondo.
MARCELLO (*a Colline*)
            Non far sussurro.

*Rodolfo straccia parte dello scartafaccio e lo getta sul ca-
mino: il fuoco si ravviva. Colline avvicina ancora più la sedia
e si riscalda le mani: Rodolfo è in piedi presso ai due, col
rimanente dello scartafaccio.*

COLLINE (*con intenzione di critico teatrale*)
            Pensier profondo!
MARCELLO   Giusto color!
RODOLFO   In quell'azzurro — guizzo languente
            sfuma un'ardente — scena d'amor.
COLLINE   Scoppietta un foglio.
MARCELLO   Là c'eran baci!
RODOLFO   Tre atti or voglio — d'un colpo udir.
                (*getta al fuoco il rimanente dello scarta-
                faccio*)
COLLINE   Tal degli audaci — l'idea s'integra.

TUTTI   Bello in allegra — vampa svanir.
                (*applaudono entusiasticamente: la fiamma
                dopo un momento diminuisce*)
MARCELLO   Oh, Dio . . . già s'abbassa la fiamma.
COLLINE   Che vano, che fragile dramma!
MARCELLO   Già scricchiola, increspasi, muor!
COLLINE E MARCELLO
            Abbasso, abbasso l'autor!

*Dalla porta di mezzo entrano due garzoni, portando l'uno
provviste di cibi, bottiglie di vino, sigari, e l'altro un fascio di
legna. Al rumore, i tre innanzi al camino si volgono e con grida
di meraviglia si slanciano sulle provviste portate dal garzone e
le depongono sulla tavola: Colline prende la legna e la porta
presso il caminetto: comincia a far sera.*

RODOLFO   Legna!
MARCELLO   Sigari!

RODOLFO (*to Colline*)
>Hush, my drama is being given . . .

MARCELLO   . . . to the fire.

COLLINE   I find it sparkling.

RODOLFO   Vivid.
The fire dies down.

COLLINE   But it lasts only a short time.

RODOLFO   Brevity — a great merit.

COLLINE (*taking the chair from him*)
>Author, give me the chair.

MARCELLO   These intermissions make you die of boredom.
>Quickly.

RODOLFO (*takes another part of the sheaf*)
>Act Two.

MARCELLO (*to Colline*)
>No whispering.

Rodolfo tears up a part of the papers and throws it in the stove: the fire is revived. Colline draws the chair still closer and warms his hands. Rodolfo is standing near the other two with the rest of the sheaf of papers.

COLLINE (*with the manner of a drama critic*)
>Profound thought!

MARCELLO   Proper color!

RODOLFO   In that blue — languishing flicker
>an ardent love scene — goes up in smoke.

COLLINE   A page crackles.

MARCELLO   There were kisses there!

RODOLFO   Now I want to hear — three acts at one blow.
>(*throws the rest of the sheaf in the fire*)

COLLINE   Thus the thought of the bold becomes integrated.

ALL   It's beautiful to vanish — in a merry flame.
>(*they applaud enthusiastically: after a moment the flame dies down*)

MARCELLO   Oh, God . . . the flame is lowering already.

COLLINE   What a vain, what a fragile drama!

MARCELLO   It's already creaking, curling up, dying!

COLLINE AND MARCELLO
>Down, down with the author!

Two delivery boys enter through the center door, one carrying food supplies, bottles of wine, cigars, and the other a bundle of wood. At the sound, the three in front of the stove turn and, with cries of amazement, throw themselves on the provisions carried by the boy and set them on the table. Colline takes the wood and carries it over to the stove. Evening is beginning to fall.

RODOLFO   Wood!

MARCELLO   Cigars!

COLLINE   Bordò!

RODOLFO   Legna!

MARCELLO   Bordò!

TUTTI   Le dovizie d'una fiera
            il destin ci destinò!

Schaunard entra dalla porta di mezzo con aria di trionfo,
gettando a terra alcuni scudi.

SCHAUNARD   La Banca di Francia
            per voi si sbilancia.

COLLINE (*raccattando gli scudi insieme a Rodolfo e Marcello*)
            Raccatta, raccatta!

MARCELLO (*incredulo*)
            Son pezzi di latta!

SCHAUNARD (*mostrandogli uno scudo*)
            Sei sordo? Sei lippo?
            Quest'uomo chi è?

RODOLFO (*inchinandosi*)
            Luigi Filippo!
            M'inchino al mio re!

TUTTI   Sta Luigi Filippo ai nostri piè!

Schaunard vorrebbe raccontare la sua fortuna: ma gli altri
non lo ascoltano: dispongono ogni cosa sulla tavola e la legna
nel camino.

SCHAUNARD   Or vi dirò: quest'oro, o meglio, argento
            ha la sua brava istoria.

MARCELLO   Riscaldiamo il camino!

COLLINE   Tanto freddo ha sofferto!

SCHAUNARD   Un inglese . . . un signor . . . Lord o Milord
            che sia, voleva un musicista . . .

MARCELLO (*gettando via il pacco di libri di Colline dalla tavola*)
            Via!
            Prepariamo la tavola!

SCHAUNARD   Io? Volo!

RODOLFO   L'esca dov'è?

COLLINE   Là.

MARCELLO   Qua.

SCHAUNARD   E mi presento.
            M'accetta, gli domando —

COLLINE   Arrosto freddo!

MARCELLO (*mettendo a posto le vivande*)
            Pasticcio dolce!

SCHAUNARD   A quando le lezioni?
            Mi presento, m'accetta, gli domando:
            a quando le lezioni?
            Risponde: incominciam!
            Guardare!, e un pappagallo m'addita
            al primo pian, poi soggiunge:
            Voi suonare finchè quello morire!

COLLINE	Bordeaux!
RODOLFO	Wood!
MARCELLO	Bordeaux!
ALL THREE	Destiny destined for us the abundance of a fair!

Schaunard comes in through the center door with an air of triumph, throwing some coins on the ground.

SCHAUNARD   The Bank of France
is going broke for you.

COLLINE   (*picking up the coins along with Rodolfo and Marcello*)
Gather, gather!

MARCELLO   (*incredulous*)
They're pieces of tin!

SCHAUNARD   (*showing him a coin*)
Are you deaf? Are you nearsighted?
Who is this man?

RODOLFO (*bowing*)
Louis Philippe!
I bow to my king!

ALL   Louis Philippe is at our feet!

Schaunard would like to narrate his good luck, but the others don't listen to him. They arrange everything on the table, and the wood in the stove.

SCHAUNARD   Now I'll tell you: this gold, or rather, silver
has its fine story.

MARCELLO   Let's warm up the stove!

COLLINE   It's suffered such cold!

SCHAUNARD   An Englishman...a gentleman...Lord or Milord
as may be, wanted a musician...

MARCELLO   (*throwing Colline's pack of books from the table*)
Away!
Let's prepare the table!

SCHAUNARD   Me? I rush over!

RODOLFO   Where's the tinder?

COLLINE   There.

MARCELLO   Here.

SCHAUNARD   And I present myself.
He accepts me; I ask him —

COLLINE   Cold roast!

MARCELLO   (*arranging the victuals*)
Sweet pastry!

SCHAUNARD   "When are the lessons?"
I present myself, he accepts me, I ask him:
"When are the lessons?"
He answers: "Let's begin!
Look!" And he points out a parrot to me
on the second floor, then adds:
"You play till that dies!"

RODOLFO   Fulgida folgori la sala splendida.

SCHAUNARD   E fu così:
                 Suonai tre lunghi dì . . .

MARCELLO (*accende le candele e le mette sulla tavola*)
                 [Or le candele!
COLLINE   Pasticcio dolce!]

SCHAUNARD   Allora usai l'incanto
                 di mia presenza bella, di mia presenza bella . . .
                 [Affascinai l'ancella . . .

MARCELLO   Mangiar senza tovaglia?]

RODOLFO   Un'idea . . . !

MARCELLO E COLLINE
                 Il *Costituzional!*

RODOLFO (*spiegandolo*)
                 [Ottima carta . . .
                 Si mangia e si divora un'appendice!

SCHAUNARD   Gli propinai prezzemolo . . .]
                 Lorito allargò l'ali,
                 Lorito allargò l'ali,
                 Lorito il becco aprì,
                 Un poco di prezzemolo,
                 da Socrate morì!
                         (*vedendo che nessuno gli bada, afferra
                         Colline che gli passa vicino con un piatto*)

COLLINE   Chi?

SCHAUNARD (*urlando indispettito*)
                 Che il diavolo vi porti tutti quanti!
                         (*poi vedendoli in atto di mettersi a man-
                         giare il pasticcio freddo*)
                 Ed or che fate?
                         (*con gesto solenne stende la mano sul pas-
                         ticcio*)
                 No! Queste cibarie
                 sono la salmeria
                 pei dì futuri
                 tenebrosi e oscuri.
                         (*e nel parlare sgombra la tavola*)
                 Pranzare in casa il dì della vigilia
                 mentre il Quartier Latino le sue vie
                 addobba di salsicce e leccornie?
                 Quando un'olezzo di frittelle
                 imbalsama le vecchie strade?
                 Là le ragazze cantano contente . . .

RODOLFO, MARCELLO, COLLINE
                 La vigilia di Natal!

SCHAUNARD   . . . ed han per eco ognuna uno studente!
                 Un po' di religione, o miei signori:
                 si beva in casa, ma si pranzi fuor!

     *Rodolfo chiude la porta a chiave, poi tutti vanno intorno
alla tavola e versano il vino: s'arrestano stupefatti.*

RODOLFO   Let the splendid hall shine brilliantly.

SCHAUNARD   And so it was:
I played for three long days . . .

MARCELLO (*lights the candles and puts them on the table*)
Now the candles!

COLLINE   Sweet pastry!

SCHAUNARD   Then I used the spell
of my handsome appearance, of my handsome
appearance . . .
I charmed the maid . . .

MARCELLO   Eat without a tablecloth?

RODOLFO   An idea!

MARCELLO AND COLLINE
The *Constitutional!*

RODOLFO (*unfolding it*)
Excellent paper . . .
You eat and you devour a supplement!

SCHAUNARD   I administered parsley to him . . .
Polly spread his wings,
Polly spread his wings,
Polly opened his beak,
a bit of parsley,
he died like Socrates!
(*seeing that no is paying any attention to
him, he seizes Colline, who is going past
him with a dish*)

COLLINE   Who?

SCHAUNARD (*shouting, annoyed*)
The devil take you, one and all!
(*then seeing them about to start eating the
cold pie*)
And now what are you doing?
(*with a solemn gesture he extends his hand
over the pie*)
No! These foodstuffs
are the reserves
for future days,
tenebrous and dark.
(*and as he speaks, he clears the table*)
Dine at home on Christmas Eve
while the Latin Quarter bedecks
its streets with sausages and delicacies?
When an aroma of fritters
perfumes the old streets?
There the girls sing happily . . .

RODOLFO, MARCELLO, COLLINE
Christmas Eve!

SCHAUNARD   . . . and each has a student as her echo!
A bit of religion, O gentlemen:
we drink at home, but we dine out!

*Rodolfo locks the door, then all go around the table and
pour out the wine: they stop, dumbfounded.*

BENOÎT (*di fuori*)
Si può?

MARCELLO   Chi è là?

BENOÎT   Benoît.

MARCELLO   Il padrone di casa!

SCHAUNARD   Uscio sul muso.

COLLINE (*grida*)
Non c'è nessuno.

SCHAUNARD   È chiuso.

BENOÎT   Una parola.

SCHAUNARD (*dopo essersi consultato cogli altri, va ad aprire*)
Sola!

BENOÎT (*entra sorridente: vede Marcello e mostrandogli una
         carta dice:*)
Affitto!

MARCELLO (*con esagerata premura*)
Olà! date una sedia.

RODOLFO   Presto.

BENOÎT (*schermendosi*)
Non occorre. Vorrei . . .

SCHAUNARD (*insistendo con dolce violenza lo fa sedere*)
Segga.

MARCELLO   Vuol bere?
            (*gli versa del vino*)

BENOÎT   Grazie.

RODOLFO   Tocchiamo!

COLLINE   Tocchiamo!

SCHAUNARD   Beva!

RODOLFO   Tocchiam!

*Tutti bevono. Benoît depone il bicchiere e si rivolge a Mar-
cello mostrandogli la carta.*

BENOÎT   Quest'è l'ultimo trimestre . . .

MARCELLO (*con ingenuità*)
Ne ho piacere.

BENOÎT   E quindi . . .

SCHAUNARD (*interrompendolo*)
Ancora un sorso.
(*riempie i bicchieri*)

BENOÎT   Grazie.

RODOLFO   Tocchiam!

COLLINE   Tocchiam!

I QUATTRO (*toccando con Benoît*)
Alla sua salute!

BENOÎT (*riprendendo con Marcello*)
A lei ne vengo
perchè il trimestre scorso
mi promise . . .

BENOÎT (*from outside*)
    May I?

MARCELLO   Who's there?

BENOÎT   Benoît.

MARCELLO   The landlord!

SCHAUNARD   Bolt the door in his face.

COLLINE (*shouts*)
    There's nobody home.

SCHAUNARD   It's locked.

BENOÎT   A word . . .

SCHAUNARD (*after consulting with the others, goes to open*)
    Only one!

BENOÎT (*enters smiling, sees Marcello, and, showing him a a paper, says:*)
    Rent!

MARCELLO (*with exaggerated care*)
    Hola! Give him a chair.

RODOLFO   Quickly.

BENOÎT (*parrying*)
    It's not necessary. I'd like . . .

SCHAUNARD (*insisting, with gentle violence, makes him sit down*)
    Be seated.

MARCELLO   Do you want to drink?
        (*pours him some wine*)

BENOÎT   Thanks.

RODOLFO   Let's touch glasses!

COLLINE   Let's touch glasses!

SCHAUNARD   Drink!

RODOLFO   Let's touch glasses!

All drink. Benoît sets down his glass and addresses Marcello, showing him the paper.

BENOÎT   This is the last quarter . . .

MARCELLO (*naïvely*)
    I'm glad.

BENOÎT   And therefore . . .

SCHAUNARD (*interrupting him*)
    Another sip.
        (*fills the glasses*)

BENOÎT   Thanks.

RODOLFO   Let's touch glasses!

COLLINE   Let's touch glasses!

THE FOUR (*touching Benoît's glass with theirs*)
    To your health!

BENOÎT (*resuming with Marcello*)
    I'm coming to you
    because the last quarter
    you promised me . . .

MARCELLO   Promisi ed or mantengo.
                (*mostrando a Benoît gli scudi che sono
                sulla tavola*)

RODOLFO (*piano a Marcello*)
                Che fai?

SCHAUNARD (*come sopra*)
                Sei pazzo?

MARCELLO (*a Benoît, senza badare ai due*)
                Ha visto? Or via
                resti un momento in nostra compagnia.
                Dica: quant'anni ha,
                caro signor Benoît?

BENOÎT   Gl'anni? Per carità!

RODOLFO   Su e giù la nostra età?

BENOÎT   Di più, molto di più.

    *Mentre fanno chiacchierare Benoît, gli riempiono il bicchiere
appena egli l'ha vuotato.*

COLLINE   Ha detto su e giù.

MARCELLO (*abbassando la voce e con tono di furberia*)
                L'altra sera al Mabil . . .
                l'han colto in peccato d'amor.

BENOÎT (*inquieto*)
                Io?!

MARCELLO   Al Mabil . . . l'altra sera l'han colto.
                Neghi.

BENOÎT   Un caso.

MARCELLO (*lusingandolo*)
                Bella donna!

BENOÎT (*mezzo brillo, con subito moto*)
                Ah! molto!

SCHAUNARD (*gli batte una mano sulla spalla*)
                Briccone!

RODOLFO   Briccone!

COLLINE (*gli batte sull'altra spalla*)
                Seduttore!

SCHAUNARD   Briccone!

RODOLFO   Briccone!

MARCELLO   Una quercia! Un cannone!

RODOLFO   L'uomo ha buon gusto.

BENOÎT   Ah! ah!

MARCELLO   Il crin ricciuto e fulvo.

SCHAUNARD   Briccon!

MARCELLO   Ei gongolava arzillo, pettoruto.

BENOÎT (*ringalluzzito*)
                Son vecchio, ma robusto.

RODOLFO, SCHAUNARD, COLLINE (*con gravità ironica*)
                Ei gongolava arzuto e pettorillo.

MARCELLO   E a lui cedea la femminil virtù.

MARCELLO   I promised and now I keep my promise.
                        (*showing Benoît the coins that are on the
                        table*)

RODOLFO (*softly, to Marcello*)
                        What are you doing?

SCHAUNARD (*same*)
                        Are you crazy?

MARCELLO (*to Benoît, ignoring the other two*)
                        Did you see? Now, come,
                        stay a moment in our company.
                        Tell us: how old are you,
                        dear Monsieur Benoît?

BENOÎT   My age? For heaven's sake!

RODOLFO   More or less our age?

BENOÎT   More, much more.

*As they make Benoît chatter, they fill his glass as soon as he
has emptied it.*

COLLINE   He said more or less.

MARCELLO (*lowering his voice, and in a sly tone*)
                        The other evening at Mabille . . .
                        they caught him, in amorous sin.

BENOÎT (*uneasy*)
                        I?

MARCELLO   At Mabille . . . the other evening they caught
                        him.
                        Deny it.

BENOÎT   By chance.

MARCELLO (*flattering him*)
                        A beautiful woman!

BENOÎT (*half tipsy, with a prompt reaction*)
                        Ah, very!

SCHAUNARD (*slaps him on the shoulder*)
                        Rogue!

RODOLFO   Rogue!

COLLINE (*slaps him on the other shoulder*)
                        Seducer!

SCHAUNARD   Rogue!

RODOLFO   Rogue!

MARCELLO   An oak! A cannon!

RODOLFO   The man has good taste.

BENOÎT   Ha! ha!

MARCELLO   His mane, curly and tawny.

SCHAUNARD   Rogue!

MARCELLO   He swaggered, perky, full-chested.

BENOÎT (*elated*)
                        I'm old, but sturdy.

RODOLFO, SCHAUNARD, COLLINE (*with ironic gravity*)
                        He swaggered, perked, full-chestly.

MARCELLO   And female virtue surrendered to him.

BENOÎT (*in piena confidenza*)
>Timido in gioventù,
>ora me ne ripago!
>Si sa, è uno svago ...
>qualche donnetta allegra ... e un po ...
>(*accenna forme accentuate*)
>Non dico una balena
>o un mappamondo
>o un viso tondo
>da luna piena,
>ma magra, proprio magra, no, poi no!
>Le donne magre sono grattacapi
>e spesso ... sopracapi ...
>e son piene di doglie —
>per esempio mia moglie ...

Marcello dà un pugno sulla tavola e si alza: gli altri lo imitano: Benoît li guarda sbalordito.

MARCELLO (*terribile*)
>Quest'uomo ha moglie
>e sconcie voglie ha nel cor!

SCHAUNARD, COLLINE
>Orror!

RODOLFO
>E ammorba, e appesta
>la nostra onesta magion!

SCHAUNARD, COLLINE
>Fuor!

MARCELLO   Si abbruci dello zucchero!

COLLINE   Si discacci il reprobo!

SCHAUNARD (*maestoso*)
>È la morale offesa ...

BENOÎT (*allibito, tenta inutilmente di parlare*)
>Io di —

MARCELLO   Silenzio!

BENOÎT   Io di —

COLLINE   Silenzio!

SCHAUNARD   ... che vi scaccia!

BENOÎT   Miei signori ...

MARCELLO, SCHAUNARD, COLLINE
>Silenzio! Via signore!

I QUATTRO (*circondando Benoît e spingendolo verso la porta*)
>Via di qua!
>E buona sera a vostra signori ...
>Ah! ah! ah! ah!

Benoît è cacciato fuori.

MARCELLO (*chiudendo l'uscio*)
>Ho pagato il trimestre.

SCHAUNARD   Al Quartiere Latin ci attende Momus.

MARCELLO   Viva chi spende.

SCHAUNARD   Dividiamo il bottin!

Si dividono gli scudi rimasti sulla tavola.

BENOÎT (*confiding completely*)
>> Shy as a young man,
>> now I'm getting my own back!
>> You know, it's a pastime . . .
>> some gay little woman . . . and a bit . . .
>>>> (*indicates accentuated forms*)
>> I don't say a whale
>> or a globe
>> or a round face
>> like a full moon,
>> but thin, downright thin, no, no!
>> Thin women mean headaches
>> and often . . . horns . . .
>> and they're full of complaints —
>> for example my wife . . .

Marcello slams his fist on the table and stands up; the others imitate him. Benoît looks at them, amazed.

MARCELLO (*terrifyingly*)
>> This man has a wife,
>> and he has obscene desires in his heart!

SCHAUNARD, COLLINE
>> Horrors!

RODOLFO
>> And he corrupts and infects
>> our honest dwelling!

SCHAUNARD, COLLINE
>> Out!

MARCELLO
>> Let some sugar be burned!

COLLINE
>> Let the reprobate be driven out!

SCHAUNARD (*majestically*)
>> It is offended morality . . .

BENOÎT (*aghast, tries in vain to speak*)
>> I sa—

MARCELLO
>> Silence!

BENOÎT
>> I sa—

COLLINE
>> Silence!

SCHAUNARD
>> . . . that drives you away!

BENOÎT
>> Gentlemen . . .

MARCELLO, SCHAUNARD, COLLINE
>> Silence! Away, sir!

THE FOUR (*surrounding Benoît and pushing him toward the door*)
>> Away from here!
>> And good evening to Your Lordship.
>> Ha! ha! ha! ha!

Benoît is driven out.

MARCELLO (*shutting the door*)
>> I've paid the quarter.

SCHAUNARD
>> Momus awaits us in the Latin Quarter.

MARCELLO
>> Long live he who spends.

SCHAUNARD
>> Let's share the booty!

They divide the coins left on the table.

RODOLFO   Dividiam!
COLLINE   Dividiam!
MARCELLO (*presentando uno specchio rotto a Colline*)
                    Là ci son beltà scese dal cielo.
                    Or che sei ricco, bada alla decenza!
                    Orso, ravviati il pelo.

COLLINE   Farò la conoscenza
                    la prima volta d'un barbitonsore.
                    Guidatemi al ridicolo
                    oltraggio d'un rasoio.
                    Andiam!
SCHAUNARD   Andiam!
MARCELLO   Andiam!
SCHAUNARD   Andiam!
COLLINE   Andiam!
RODOLFO   Io resto per terminar
                    l'articolo di fondo del *Castoro*.
MARCELLO   Fa presto.
RODOLFO   Cinque minuti. Conosco il mestier.
COLLINE   T'aspetterem dabbasso dal portier.
MARCELLO   Se tardi, udrai che coro!
RODOLFO (*prende un lume ed apre l'uscio: Marcello, Schau-
                    nard, Colline escono e scendono la scala*)
                    Cinque minuti.
SCHAUNARD   Taglia corta la coda al tuo Castor!
MARCELLO (*di fuori*)
                    Occhio alla scala.
                    Tienti alla ringhiera.
RODOLFO (*sempre sull'uscio, alzando il lume*)
                    Adagio!
COLLINE (*di fuori*)
                    È buio pesto!
SCHAUNARD (*di fuori*)
                    Maledetto portier!
      Rumore d'uno che ruzzola.
COLLINE   Accidenti!
RODOLFO   Colline, sei morto?
COLLINE (*dal basso*)
                    Non ancor!
MARCELLO (*dal basso*)
                    Vien presto!
      *Rodolfo chiude l'uscio, depone il lume, sgombra un po' la
tavola, prende calamaio e carta, poi siede e si mette a scrivere
dopo avere spento l'altro lume rimasto acceso: ma non tro-
vando alcuna idea, s'inquieta, straccia il foglio e getta via la
penna.*
RODOLFO   Non sono in vena!
      Bussano timidamente all'uscio.

RODOLFO	Let's share!
COLLINE	Let's share!
MARCELLO	(*presenting a broken mirror to Colline*)
	There, there are beauties descended from heaven.
	Now that you're rich, pay heed to decency!
	Bear, tidy up your fur.
COLLINE	I'll make the acquaintance
	of a beard barber for the first time.
	Lead me to the ridiculous
	outrage of a razor.
	Let's go!
SCHAUNARD	Let's go!
MARCELLO	Let's go!
SCHAUNARD	Let's go!
COLLINE	Let's go!
RODOLFO	I'm staying to finish
	the leading article for *The Beaver*.
MARCELLO	Hurry up.
RODOLFO	Five minutes. I know the trade.
COLLINE	We'll wait for you below, at the concierge's.
MARCELLO	If you delay, what a chorus you'll hear!
RODOLFO	(*takes a light and opens the door: Marcello, Schaunard, Colline go out and descend the stairs*)
	Five minutes.
SCHAUNARD	Cut your Beaver's tail short!
MARCELLO	(*outside*)
	Keep your eye on the steps.
	Hold on to the railing.
RODOLFO	(*still at the door, holding up the light*)
	Slowly!
COLLINE	(*from outside*)
	It's pitch dark!
SCHAUNARD	(*from outside*)
	Damned concierge!

Sound of somebody tumbling down.

COLLINE	Damn it!
RODOLFO	Colline, are you dead?
COLLINE	(*from below*)
	Not yet!
MARCELLO	(*from below*)
	Come quickly!

Rodolfo shuts the door, sets down the light, clears the table a bit, takes inkwell and paper, then sits down and starts writing, after having put out the other light which was left burning. But, finding no idea, he becomes nervous, tears up the paper and throws away the pen.

RODOLFO	I'm not in the mood!

There is a timid knock at the door.

RODOLFO   Chi è là?

MIMÌ (*di fuori*)
             Scusi.

RODOLFO   Una donna!

MIMÌ   Di grazia, mi s'è spento il lume.

RODOLFO (*corre ad aprire*)
             Ecco.

MIMÌ (*sull'uscio, con un lume spento in mano ed una chiave*)
             Vorrebbe?

RODOLFO   S'accomodi un momento.

MIMÌ   Non occorre.

RODOLFO (*insistendo*)
             La prego, entri.

   Mimì entra, è presa da soffocazione.

RODOLFO (*premuroso*)
             Si sente male?

MIMÌ   No . . . nulla.

RODOLFO   Impallidisce!

MIMÌ (*presa da tosse*)
             Il respir . . . Quelle scale . . .

   *Sviene, e Rodolfo è appena a tempo di sorreggerla ed ada-
giarla su di una sedia, mentre dalle mani di Mimì cadono e
candeliere e chiave.*

RODOLFO (*imbarazzato*)
             Ed ora come faccio?
                 (*va a prendere dell'acqua e ne spruzza il
                 viso di Mimì*)
             Così!
                 (*guardandola con grande interesse*)
             Che viso d'ammalata!
                 (*Mimì rinviene*)
             Si sente meglio?

MIMÌ (*con un filo di voce*)
             Sì.

RODOLFO   Qui c'è tanto freddo. Segga vicino al fuoco.
                 (*fa alzare Mimì e la conduce a sedere
                 presso al camino*)
             Aspetti . . . un po' di vino.
                 (*corre alla tavola e vi prende bottiglia e
                 bicchiere*)

MIMÌ   Grazie.

RODOLFO (*le dà il bicchiere e le versa da bere*)
             A lei.

MIMÌ   Poco, poco.

RODOLFO   Così?

MIMÌ   Grazie.
                 (*beve*)

RODOLFO (*ammirandola*)
             (Che bella bambina!)

RODOLFO   Who's there?

MIMÌ (*from outside*)
                    Excuse me.

RODOLFO   A woman!

MIMÌ   Please, my light has gone out.

RODOLFO (*runs to open*)
                    Here.

MIMÌ (*in the doorway, with an extinguished light in her hand
                and a key*)
                    Would you?

RODOLFO   Come in a moment.

MIMÌ   That's not necessary.

RODOLFO (*insisting*)
                    Please, come in.

   Mimì enters, she is seized with choking.

RODOLFO (*concerned*)
                    Do you feel ill?

MIMÌ   No . . . nothing.

RODOLFO   You're pale!

MIMÌ (*seized with coughing*)
                    My breath . . . Those steps . . .

   *She faints, and Rodolfo is just in time to support her and
ease her onto a chair, as from Mimì's hands both candlestick
and key fall.*

RODOLFO (*embarrassed*)
                    And now what shall I do?
                        (*goes and gets some water and sprinkles
                        Mimì's face with it*)
                    Like that!
                        (*looking at her with great interest*)
                    What a sick girl's face!
                        (*Mimì comes to*)
                    Do you feel better?

MIMÌ (*in a faint voice*)
                    Yes.

RODOLFO   It's so cold here. Sit near the fire.
                        (*makes Mimì stand and leads her to sit
                        near the stove*)
                    Wait . . . a bit of wine.
                        (*runs to the table and takes bottle and
                        glass from it*)

MIMÌ   Thanks.

RODOLFO (*gives her the glass and pours her something to drink*)
                    For you.

MIMÌ   Just a little.

RODOLFO   Like this?

MIMÌ   Thanks.
                        (*drinks*)

RODOLFO (*admiring her*)
                    (What a beautiful child!)

MIMÌ (*levandosi, cerca il suo candeliere*)
                 Ora permetta che accenda il lume.
                 Tutto è passato.
RODOLFO   Tanta fretta?
MIMÌ   Sì.

*Rodolfo accende il lume di Mimì e glielo consegna senza far
parola.*

MIMÌ   Grazie. Buona sera.
RODOLFO (*l'accompagna fino sull'uscio, poi ritorna subito al
                 lavoro*)
                 Buona sera.
MIMÌ (*esce, poi riappare sull'uscio*)
                 Oh! sventata, sventata!
                 La chiave della stanza
                 dove l'ho lasciata?
RODOLFO   Non stia sull'uscio;
                 il lume vacilla al vento.

Il lume di Mimì si spegne.

MIMÌ   Oh Dio! Torni ad accenderlo.

*Rodolfo accorre colla sua candela per riaccendere quello di
Mimì, ma avvicinandosi alla porta anche il suo lume si spegne
e la camera rimane buia.*

RODOLFO   Oh Dio! Anche il mio s'è spento!
MIMÌ   Ah! e la chiave ove sarà?
                 (*avanzandosi a tentoni incontra la tavola
                 e vi depone il suo candeliere*)
RODOLFO   Buio pesto!
                 (*si trova presso la porta e la chiude*)
MIMÌ   Disgraziata!
RODOLFO   Ove sarà?
MIMÌ (*confusa*)
                 Importuna è la vicina . . .
RODOLFO   Ma le pare . . .
MIMÌ   Importuna è la vicina . . .
RODOLFO   Cosa dice, ma le pare!
MIMÌ   Cerchi.
RODOLFO   Cerco.

*Mimì cerca la chiave sul pavimento strisciando i piedi:
Rodolfo fa lo stesso e trovata la tavola vi depone egli pure il
candeliere, poi torna a cercare la chiave tastando colle mani
il pavimento.*

MIMÌ   Ove sarà?
RODOLFO (*la trova e la intasca*)
                 Ah!
MIMÌ   L'ha trovata?
RODOLFO   No!
MIMÌ   Mi parve . . .
RODOLFO   In verità!

MIMÌ (*rising, looks for her candlestick*)
                Now allow me to light my light.
                It's all over.

RODOLFO   Such haste?

MIMÌ   Yes.

*Rodolfo lights Mimì's candle and gives it to her without a
word.*

MIMÌ   Thanks. Good evening.

RODOLFO (*accompanies her to the door, then immediately
                comes back to work*)
                Good evening.

MIMÌ (*goes out, then reappears at the door*)
                Oh, foolish, foolish me!
                Where have I left
                the key to my room?

RODOLFO   Don't stand in the doorway;
                the light is flickering in the wind.

Mimì's light goes out.

MIMÌ   Oh, goodness! Light it again.

*Rodolfo runs with his candle to relight Mimì's, but as he
nears the door, his light also goes out, and the room remains
dark.*

RODOLFO   Oh, goodness! Mine has gone out, too!

MIMÌ   Ah! and where can the key be?
                (*groping her way forward, she encounters
                the table and sets her candlestick on it*)

RODOLFO   Pitch darkness!
                (*he is near the door; he closes it*)

MIMÌ   Unlucky me!

RODOLFO   Where can it be?

MIMÌ (*confused*)
                Your neighbor is a nuisance . . .

RODOLFO   Why, not at all . . .

MIMÌ   Your neighbor is a nuisance . . .

RODOLFO   What are you saying? Not at all!

MIMÌ   Search.

RODOLFO   I'm searching.

*Mimì searches for the key on the floor, dragging her feet.
Rodolfo does the same and, having found the table, he also
sets his candlestick on it, then goes back to searching for the
key, touching the floor with his hands.*

MIMÌ   Where can it be?

RODOLFO (*finds it and pockets it*)
                Ah!

MIMÌ   Have you found it?

RODOLFO   No!

MIMÌ   It seemed to me . . .

RODOLFO   Honestly!

MIMÌ   Cerca?

RODOLFO   Cerco!

Guidato dalla voce di Mimì, Rodolfo finge di cercare mentre si avvicina ad essa: Mimì si china a terra e cerca a tastoni; Rodolfo colla sua mano incontra quella di Mimì, e l'afferra.

MIMÌ (*sorpresa, rizzandosi*)
                Ah!

RODOLFO (*tenendo la mano di Mimì*)
                Che gelida manina,
                se la lasci riscaldar.
                Cercar che giova? — Al buio non so trova.

                Ma per fortuna — è una notte di luna,
                e qui la luna l'abbiamo vicina.
                Aspetti signorina,
                le dirò con due parole
                chi son, chi son e che faccio, come vivo.
                Vuole?
                      (*Mimì tace*)
                Chi son? Chi son? — Sono un poeta.
                Che cosa faccio? — Scrivo.
                E come vivo? — Vivo.
                In povertà mia lieta
                scialo da gran signore
                rime ed inni d'amore.
                Per sogni e per chimere
                e per castelli in aria
                l'anima ho milionaria.
                Talor dal mio forziere
                ruban tutti i gioielli
                due ladri: gli occhi belli.
                V'entrar con voi pur ora,
                ed i miei sogni usati
                e i bei sogni miei
                tosto si dileguar!
                Ma il furto non m'accora
                poichè . . . poichè v'ha preso stanza
                la dolce speranza!
                Or che mi conoscete
                parlate voi,
                deh! parlate. Chi siete?
                Vi piaccia dir!

MIMÌ   Sì.
                Mi chiamano Mimì,
                ma il mio nome è Lucia.
                La storia mia
                è breve. A tela o a seta
                ricamo in casa e fuori.
                Son tranquilla e lieta
                ed è mio svago
                far gigli e rose.
                Mi piaccion quelle cose
                che han sì dolce malìa,
                che parlano d'amor, di primavere,

MIMÌ   Are you searching?

RODOLFO   I'm searching!

Led by Mimì's voice, Rodolfo pretends to search as he comes closer to her. Mimì bends to the ground and searches, groping. Rodolfo's hand encounters Mimì's and grasps it.

MIMÌ (*surprised, straightening up*)
                 Ah!

RODOLFO (*holding Mimì's hand*)
                 What an icy little hand,
                 let it be warmed.
                 What's the good of searching? — We can't find
                   it in the dark.
                 But luckily — it's a moonlit night,
                 and here we have the moon near.
                 Wait, miss,
                 I'll tell you in two words
                 who I am, who I am and what I do, how I live.
                 Would you like that?
                     (*Mimì is silent*)
                 Who am I? Who am I? — I'm a poet.
                 What do I do? — I write.
                 And how do I live? — I live.
                 In my merry poverty
                 I squander, like a great lord,
                 rhymes and anthems of love.
                 When it comes to dreams and chimeras
                 and castles in the air
                 I have a millionaire's soul.
                 At times from my coffer
                 two thieves steal all my gems —
                 two beautiful eyes.
                 They entered with you just now,
                 and my familiar dreams
                 and my beautiful dreams
                 quickly disappeared!
                 But the theft doesn't grieve me
                 because . . . because sweet hope
                 has taken their place!
                 Now that you know me,
                 you speak,
                 ah! speak. Who are you!
                 Please tell!

MIMÌ   Yes.
                 They call me Mimì,
                 but my name is Lucia.
                 My story
                 is brief. On canvas or on silk
                 I embroider at home and outside.
                 I'm calm and happy
                 and my pastime
                 is making lilies and roses.
                 I like those things
                 that have such sweet magic,
                 which speak of love, of springtimes,

che parlano di sogni e di chimere,
quelle cose che han nome poesia . . .
Lei m'intende?

RODOLFO   Sì.

MIMÌ   Mi chiamano Mimì,
il perchè non so.
Sola, mi fo
il pranzo da me stessa.
Non vado sempre a messa
ma prego assai il Signor.
Vivo sola, soletta,
là in una bianca cameretta:
guardo sui tetti e in cielo,
ma quando vien lo sgelo
il primo sole è mio,
il primo bacio dell'aprile è mio!
Il primo sole è mio!
Germoglia in un vaso una rosa . . .
Foglia a foglia la spio!
Così gentil è il profumo d'un fior!
Ma i fior ch'io faccio, ahimè! . . .
i fior ch'io faccio, ahimè, non hanno odore!
Altro di me non le saprei narrare:
sono la sua vicina
che la vien fuori d'ora a importunare.

SCHAUNARD   (*dal cortile*)
Ehi! Rodolfo!

COLLINE   Rodolfo!

Alle grida degli amici, Rodolfo s'impazienta.

MARCELLO   Olà! Non senti?
Lumaca!

COLLINE   Poetucolo!

SCHAUNARD   Accidenti al pigro!

*Sempre più impaziente, Rodolfo a tentoni si avvia alla fi-
nestra e l'apre spingendosi un poco fuori per rispondere agli
amici che sono giù nel cortile: dalla finestra aperta entrano i
raggi lunari, rischiarando così la camera.*

RODOLFO   (*alla finestra*)
Scrivo ancor tre righe a volo.

MIMÌ   (*avvicinandosi un poco alla finestra*)
Chi son?

RODOLFO   Amici.

SCHAUNARD   Sentirai le tue.

MARCELLO   Che te ne fai lì solo?

RODOLFO   Non son solo. Siamo in due.
Andate da Momus, tenete il posto,
ci saremo tosto.
(*rimane alla finestra, onde assicurarsi che
gli amici se ne vanno*)

very conversational
no embellishment of notes

which speak of dreams and of chimeras,
those things that are named poetry . . .
Do you understand me?

RODOLFO   Yes.

MIMÌ   They call me Mimì,
I don't know the reason.
Alone, I prepare
dinner by myself.
I don't always go to Mass,
but I pray much to the Lord.
I live alone, all alone,
there in a little white room.
I look out on roofs and into the heavens,
but when the thaw comes
the first sun is mine,
the first kiss of April is mine!
The first sun is mine!
A rose buds in a pot . . .
Leaf by leaf I observe it!
A flower's perfume is so delicate!
But the flowers that I make, alas,
the flowers I make, alas, have no odor!
I wouldn't know what else to tell you about me:
I'm your neighbor
who comes at the wrong hour to bother you.

SCHAUNARD (*from the courtyard*)
Hey! Rodolfo!

COLLINE   Rodolfo!

At his friends' cries, Rodolfo loses his patience.

MARCELLO   Hola! Can't you hear?
Snail!

COLLINE   Poetaster!

SCHAUNARD   Damn that lazy one!

*More and more impatient, Rodolfo gropes his way to the
window and opens it, leaning out a little to answer his friends
who are below in the courtyard. The moon's rays enter through
the open window, thus lighting the room.*

RODOLFO (*at the window*)
I'll write another three lines in haste.

MIMÌ (*coming a little closer to the window*)
Who are they?

RODOLFO   Friends.

SCHAUNARD   You'll get an earful.

MARCELLO   What are you doing up there alone?

RODOLFO   I'm not alone. We're two.
Go to Momus, keep us seats,
we'll be there soon.
(*remains at the window, to make sure that
his friends are going away*)

MARCELLO, SCHAUNARD, COLLINE
> Momus, Momus, Momus,
> zitti e discreti andiamocene via . . .
> (*allontanandosi*)

MARCELLO   Trovò la poesia!

SCHAUNARD, COLLINE
> Momus, Momus, Momus!

Mimì è ancora avvicinata alla finestra per modo che i raggi lunari la illuminano: Rodolfo volgendosi scorge Mimì avvolta come da un nimbo di luce, e la contempla, quasi estatico.

RODOLFO   O soave fanciulla!

MARCELLO   Trovò la poesia . . .

RODOLFO   O dolce viso
            di mite circonfuso alba lunar,
            in te, ravviso
            il sogno ch'io vorrei sempre sognar!

MIMÌ   [Ah! tu sol comandi, Amor!

RODOLFO   Fremon già nell'anima
            le dolcezze estreme.]

MIMÌ   [Oh! come dolce scendono
            le sue lusinghe al core . . .
            Tu sol comandi, amor!

RODOLFO   Fremon dolcezze estreme,
            nel bacio freme amor!]

Rodolfo la bacia.

MIMÌ (*svincolandosi*)
> No, per pietà!

RODOLFO   Sei mia . . . !

MIMÌ   V'aspettan gli amici . . .

RODOLFO   Già mi mandi via?

MIMÌ   Vorrei dir . . . ma non oso . . .

RODOLFO   Di'.

MIMÌ (*con graziosa furberia*)
> Se venissi con voi?

RODOLFO   Che . . . ? Mimì!
            (*con intenzione tentatrice*)
            Sarebbe così dolce restar qui.
            C'è freddo fuori . . .

MIMÌ   Vi starò vicina . . . !

RODOLFO   E al ritorno?

MIMÌ (*maliziosa*)
> Curioso!

RODOLFO   Dammi il braccio, mia piccina . . .

MIMÌ (*dà il braccio a Rodolfo*)
> Obbedisco, signor!

RODOLFO   Che m'ami . . . di' . . .

MIMÌ (*con abbandono*)
> Io t'amo!
> (*escono*)

MARCELLO, SCHAUNARD, COLLINE
Momus, Momus, Momus,
quiet and discreet, let us go away . . .
(*going off*)

MARCELLO He found poetry!

SCHAUNARD, COLLINE
Momus, Momus, Momus!

Mimì is still near the window in such a way that the moon's rays illuminate her. Turning, Rodolfo sees Mimì as if wrapped in a halo of light, and he contemplates her, as if ecstatic.

RODOLFO Oh, sweet maiden!

MARCELLO He found poetry . . .

RODOLFO Oh, gentle face
bathed in a soft lunar dawn,
in you I recognize
the dream I would like to dream forever!

MIMÌ Ah! Love, only you command!

RODOLFO Extreme sweetnesses
already stir in the soul.

MIMÌ Oh! how sweetly his compliments
descend to my heart . . .
Only you command, love!

RODOLFO Extreme sweetnesses stir,
love stirs in a kiss!

Rodolfo kisses her.

MIMÌ (*freeing herself*)
No, please!

RODOLFO You're mine . . .!

MIMÌ Your friends are waiting for you . . .

RODOLFO Are you sending me away already?

MIMÌ I'd like to say . . . but I don't dare . . .

RODOLFO Say it.

MIMÌ (*with charming slyness*)
If I came with you?

RODOLFO What . . . ? Mimì!
(*with enticing intention*)
It would be so sweet to stay here.
It's cold outside . . .

MIMÌ I'll be near you . . .!

RODOLFO And on our return?

MIMÌ (*mischievous*)
Curious!

RODOLFO Give me your arm, my little one . . .

MIMÌ (*gives Rodolfo her arm*)
I obey, sir!

RODOLFO Say that you love me . . .

MIMÌ (*with abandon*)
I love you!
(*they go out*)

MIMÌ, RODOLFO

Amor! Amor! Amor!

QUADRO SECONDO

Al Quartiere latino

La Vigilia di Natale. Un crocicchio di vie che al largo prende forma di piazzale; botteghe, venditori di ogni genere; da un lato il Caffè Momus. Nella folla si aggirano Rodolfo e Mimì, Colline presso alla botte di una rappezzatrice, Schaunard a una bottega di ferravecchi sta comperando una pipa e un corno. Marcello è spinto qua e là dal capriccio della gente. Gran folla e diversa; Borghesi, Soldati, Fantesche, Ragazzi, Bambine, Studenti, Sartine, Gendarmi, ecc. È sera. Le Botteghe sono adorne di lampioncini e fanali accesi; un grande fanale illumina l'ingresso del Caffè Momus. Il Caffè è affollatissimo così che alcuni Borghesi sono costretti a sedere ad una tavola fuori all'aperto.

I VENDITORI (*sul limitare delle loro botteghe*)	
	[Aranci, datteri!
	Caldi i marroni.
	Ninnoli, croci. Torroni!
	Panna montata!
	Oh! la crostata!
	Caramelle!
LA FOLLA	Quanta folla! Che chiasso!
˜ VENDITORI	Fiori alle belle!
	Fringuelli, passeri!
LA FOLLA	Su, corriam! Stringiti a me!
I VENDITORI	Latte di cocco!
	Panna, torroni!
LA FOLLA	Quanta folla! Su, partiam!]
AL CAFFÈ	Presto qua!
	Camerier! Un bicchier! Corri!
	[Birra!
	Da ber!
LA FOLLA	Stringiti a me, ecc.
I VENDITORI	Fringuelli e passeri, ecc.
LA MAMMA	Emma, quando ti chiamo!
AL CAFFÈ	Dunque? Un caffè!
	Da ber, ecc.
I VENDITORI	Voglio una lancia!
	Aranci, ecc.]
SCHAUNARD (*soffia nel corno e ne cava fuori note strane*)	
	Falso questo re! Falso questo re!
	(*tratta col ferravecchi*)
	Pipa e corno quant'è?

Rodolfo e Mimì, a braccio, attraversano la folla avviati al negozio della modista.

MIMÌ, RODOLFO
> Love! Love! Love!

ACT TWO

In the Latin Quarter

Christmas Eve. A crossroads. Where the streets meet a kind of square is formed: shops, vendors of every kind. To one side, the Café Momus. Rodolfo and Mimì stroll in the crowd. Colline is near a rag shop, Schaunard at a junkshop is buying a pipe and a horn. Marcello is pushed here and there at the whim of the throng. The crowd is large and varied: bourgeois, soldiers,   boys, girls, students, seamstresses, gendarmes, etc. It is evening. The shops are decked with lanterns and glowing lights; a large lamp illuminates the entrance of the Café Momus. The café is very crowded so that some bourgeois are forced to sit at a table out in the open.

THE VENDORS *(at the doors of their shops)*
> Oranges, dates!
> Hot chestnuts.
> Trinkets, crosses. Nougat!
> Whipped cream!
> Oh! the pie!
> Sweets!

THE CROWD   What a crowd! What noise!

THE VENDORS   Flowers for the beauties!
> Finches, sparrows!

THE CROWD   Come, let's run! Hold on tight to me!

THE VENDORS   Coconut milk!
> Cream, nougat!

THE CROWD   What a crowd! Come, let's leave!

AT THE CAFÉ   Quickly, here!
> Waiter! A glass! Run!
> Beer!
> Something to drink!

THE CROWD   Hold on tight to me, etc.

THE VENDORS   Finches and sparrows, etc.

THE MAMMA   Emma, when I call you!

AT THE CAFÉ   Well? A coffee!
> Something to drink, etc.

THE VENDORS   I want a lance!
> Oranges, etc.

SCHAUNARD *(blows into the horn and produces some strange notes from it)*
> This re is false! This re is false!
> *(bargains with the junk dealer)*
> How much are pipe and horn?

Rodolfo and Mimì, arm in arm, cross through the crowd, heading for the milliner's shop.

COLLINE (*allo botte della rappezzatrice che gli sta cucendo la*
         falda di uno zimarrone che egli ha appena
         comperato)
         E un poco usato ...

RODOLFO Andiam ...

MIMÌ   Andiam per la cuffietta?

COLLINE ... ma è serio e a buon mercato ...
         (*paga e distribuisce con giusto equilibrio*
         i libri dei quali è carico nelle molte tasche
         del zimarrone)

RODOLFO Tienti al mio braccio stretta ...

MIMÌ   A te mi stringo ...

MIMÌ, RODOLFO
         Andiamo!
         (*entrano dalla modista*)

MARCELLO (*tutto solo in mezzo alla folla, con un involto sotto*
          braccio, occhieggiando le donnine che la
          calca gli getta quasi fra le braccia)
          Io pur mi sento in vena di gridar:
          Chi vuol, donnine allegre, un po' d'amor?

I VENDITORI Datteri! Trote!
             Prugne di Tours!

MARCELLO Facciamo insieme ...
          facciamo a vendere e a comprar!

UN VENDITORE Prugne di Tours!

MARCELLO Io dò ad un soldo il vergine mio cuor!

La folla si espande per le vie adiacenti. Le botteghe sono
piene di compratori che vanno e vengono. Nel Caffè pure
sempre movimento di persone che entrano, escono e si avviano
chi per una strada chi per un'altra. Passato il primo momento
di confusione, il crocicchio diventa luogo di passaggio ani-
matissimo sempre.

SCHAUNARD (*viene a gironzolare avanti al Caffè Momus aspet-*
           tandovi gli amici; intanto armato della enorme
           pipa e del corno da caccia guarda curiosa-
           mente la folla)
           [Fra spintoni e pestate accorrendo affretta
           la folla e si diletta
           nel provar gioie matte ... insoddisfatte ...

LE VENDITRICI Ninnoli, spillette!
               Datteri e caramelle!]

I VENDITORI Fiori alle belle!

COLLINE (*se ne viene al ritrovo avvolto nello zimarrone troppo*
         lungo per lui e che gli fa intorno delle pieghe
         da toga romana, agitando trionfalmente un
         vecchio libro)
         Copia rara, anzi unica,
         la grammatica Runica!

COLLINE (*at the shop of the rag dealer, who is mending for him the lapel of a long coat that he has just bought*)

    It's a bit worn . . .

RODOLFO   Let's go . . .

MIMÌ   Are we going for the bonnet?

COLLINE   . . . but it's sober and cheap . . .

    (*he pays and, with the proper balance, distributes the books he is laden with in the many pockets of the long coat*)

RODOLFO   Hold tight to my arm . . .

MIMÌ   I'm holding tight to you . . .

MIMÌ, RODOLFO

    Let's go!

    (*they enter the milliner's*)

MARCELLO (*all alone in the midst of the crowd, with a package under his arm, ogling the girls who are almost thrown into his arms by the crowd*)

    I also feel in the mood to shout:
    You merry women, who wants a bit of love?

THE VENDORS   Dates! Trout!
    Plums from Tours!

MARCELLO   Let's play together . . .
    let's play together at selling and buying!

A VENDOR   Plums from Tours!

MARCELLO   I'll give for a penny my virgin heart!

    The crowd spreads out along the adjacent streets. The shops are full of customers who come and go. In the café also constant motion of people who enter and go off, some along one street, some another. After the first moment of confusion is past, the crossroads becomes a place of constant, very animated comings and goings.

SCHAUNARD (*comes and saunters in front of the Café Momus, waiting for his friends there; meanwhile, armed with the huge pipe and the hunting horn, he looks at the crowd curiously*)

    Amid shoves and trampling the crowd hastens, running, and enjoys itself
    in experiencing mad . . . unsatisfied . . . pleasures . . .

THE WOMEN VENDORS

    Trinkets, brooches!
    Dates and sweets!

THE VENDORS   Flowers for the beauties!

COLLINE (*comes to the meeting place wrapped in the big coat, which is too long for him and makes folds around him like a Roman toga; triumphantly waving an old book*)

    Rare, indeed unique copy:
    the Runic grammar!

SCHAUNARD (*che giunge in quella alle spalle di Colline, compassionandolo*)
Uomo onesto!

MARCELLO (*arriva al Caffè Momus e vi trova Schaunard e Colline*)
A cena!

SCHAUNARD, COLLINE
Rodolfo?

MARCELLO   Entrò da una modista.

Marcello, Schaunard e Colline entrano nel Caffè Momus, ma ne escono quasi subito, sdegnati da quella gran folla che dentro si stipa chiassosa. Essi portano fuori una tavola e li segue un cameriere per nulla meravigliato di quella loro stramberia di voler cenare fuori: i borghesi alla tavola vicina, infastiditi dal baccano che fanno i tre amici, dopo un po' di tempo s'alzano e se ne vanno. Rodolfo e Mimì escono dalla bottega.

RODOLFO   Vieni, gli amici aspettano.

ALCUNI VENDITORI
Panna montata!

MIMÌ   Mi sta ben questa cuffietta rosa?

MONELLI   Latte di cocco!

I VENDITORI   Oh! la crostata! Panna montata!

AL CAFFÈ   Camerier! Un bicchier!

RODOLFO   Sei bruna e quel color ti dona.

AL CAFFÈ   Presto, olà!
                 Ratafià!

MIMÌ (*guardando con rimpianto verso la bottega della modista*)
Bel vezzo di corallo!

RODOLFO   Ho uno zio milionario.
                 Se fa senno il buon Dio
                 voglio comprarti un vezzo assai più bel!

MONELLI   Ah! ah! ah!

FANTESCHE E STUDENTI
Ah! ah!

BORGHESI   Facciam coda alla gente!
                 Ragazze, state attente!

I VENDITORI   Oh la crostata!

LA FOLLA   Che chiasso! quanta folla!

I VENDITORI   Panna montata!

BORGHESI   Pigliam via Mazzarino!
                 Io soffoco, partiamo!
                 Vedi? Il caffè è vicin!
                 Andiam là da Momus!

I VENDITORI   Aranci, datteri, ecc.

RODOLFO (*a un tratto, vedendo Mimì guardare, si volge egli pure sospettoso*)
Chi guardi?

SCHAUNARD (*who comes up at that moment behind Colline,
                 with compassion for him*)
                 Upright man!

MARCELLO (*arrives at the Café Momus and finds Schaunard
                 and Colline there*)
                 To supper!

SCHAUNARD, COLLINE
                 Rodolfo?

MARCELLO   He went into a milliner's.

*Marcello, Schaunard, and Colline go into the Café Momus,
but they come out almost at once, indignant at that great
crowd that is noisily jammed inside. They carry out a table,
and a waiter follows them, not at all surprised at their bizarre
idea of wanting to sup outdoors. The bourgeois at the nearby
table, irritated by the racket that the three friends are making,
after a little while stand up and go off. Rodolfo and Mimì
come out of the shop.*

RODOLFO   Come, my friends are waiting.

SOME VENDORS Whipped cream!

MIMÌ   Does this pink bonnet become me?

GAMINS   Coconut milk!

THE VENDORS Oh! the pie! Whipped cream!

AT THE CAFÉ Waiter! A glass!

RODOLFO   You're dark and that color becomes you.

AT THE CAFÉ Quickly, hola!
                 Ratafia!

MIMÌ (*looking regretfully towards the milliner's shop*)
                 Beautiful coral necklace!

RODOLFO   I have a millionaire uncle.
                 If the good Lord comes to His senses
                 I want to buy you a much more beautiful neck-
                     lace!

GAMINS   Ha! ha! ha!

SERVANT-GIRLS, STUDENTS
                 Ha! ha!

BOURGEOIS   Let's follow the people!
                 Girls, watch out!

THE VENDORS Oh, the pie!

THE CROWD   What noise! What a crowd!

THE VENDORS Whipped cream!

BOURGEOIS   Let's take Rue Mazarine!
                 I'm suffocating, let's leave!
                 You see? The café is near!
                 Let's go there, to Momus!

THE VENDORS Oranges, dates, etc.

RODOLFO (*suddenly, seeing Mimì looking, he also turns, sus-
                 piciously*)
                 Whom are you looking at?

COLLINE	Odio il profano volgo al par d'Orazio.
MIMÌ	Sei geloso?
RODOLFO	All'uom felice sta il sospetto accanto.
SCHAUNARD	Ed io quando mi sazio vo' abbondanza di spazio . . .
MIMÌ	Sei felice?
MARCELLO (*al cameriere*)	Vogliamo una cena prelibata.
RODOLFO	Ah sì, tanto!
MARCELLO (*al cameriere*)	Lesto!
SCHAUNARD	Per molti!
RODOLFO	E tu?
MIMÌ	Sì, tanto!
FANTESCHE, STUDENTI	Là da Momus! Andiam! Andiam!
MARCELLO, SCHAUNARD, COLLINE	Lesto!

Rodolfo e Mimì raggiungono gli amici.

PARPIGNOL (*da lontano, avvicinandosi*)	Ecco i giocattoli di Parpignol!
RODOLFO (*giunge con Mimì*)	Due posti.
COLLINE	Finalmente!
RODOLFO	Eccoci qui. Questa è Mimì, gaia fioraia. Il suo venir completa la bella compagnia, perchè . . . perchè son io il poeta essa la poesia. Dal mio cervel sbocciano i canti, dalle sue dita sbocciano i fior, dall'anime esultanti sboccia l'amor, sboccia l'amor!
MARCELLO, SCHAUNARD, COLLINE	Ah! ah! ah! ah!
MARCELLO (*ironico*)	Dio che concetti rari!
COLLINE	*Digna est intrari.*
SCHAUNARD	*Ingrediat si necessit.*
COLLINE	Io non dò che un *accessit.*
PARPIGNOL	Ecco i giocattoli di Parpignol!

Rodolfo fa sedere Mimì; seggono tutti: il cameriere ritorna presentando la lista delle vivande.

| COLLINE (*con enfasi romantica al cameriere*) | Salame . . . |

COLLINE	I hate the vulgar crowd as Horace did.
MIMÌ	Are you jealous?
RODOLFO	Suspicion is always near the happy man.
SCHAUNARD	And I, when I sate myself, want an abundance of space ...
MIMÌ	Are you happy?

MARCELLO (*to the waiter*)
We want a choice supper.

RODOLFO	Ah, yes, so much!

MARCELLO (*to the waiter*)
Quickly!

SCHAUNARD	For many!
RODOLFO	And you?
MIMÌ	Yes, so much!

SERVANT-GIRLS, STUDENTS
There, at Momus!
Let's go! Let's go!

MARCELLO, SCHAUNARD, COLLINE
Quickly!

Rodolfo and Mimì join the friends.

PARPIGNOL (*from the distance, approaching*)
Here are Parpignol's toys!

RODOLFO (*arrives, with Mimì*)
Two seats.

COLLINE	At last!
RODOLFO	Here we are. This is Mimì, a gay flower maker. Her coming completes the fine company, because ... because I am the poet, she, poetry. From my brain blossom songs, from her fingers blossom flowers, from exultant souls blossoms love, blossoms love!

MARCELLO, SCHAUNARD, COLLINE
Ha! ha! ha! ha!

MARCELLO (*ironic*)
God, what rare conceits!

COLLINE	*Digna est intrari.*
SCHAUNARD	*Ingrediat si necessit.*
COLLINE	I give only an *accessit.*
PARPIGNOL	Here are Parpignol's toys!

Rodolfo seats Mimì. All sit. The waiter returns, presenting the list of dishes.

COLLINE (*with romantic emphasis to the waiter*)
Salami ...

*Da via Delfino sbocca un carretto tutto a fronzoli e fiori, il-
luminato a palloncini; chi lo spinge è Parpignol.*

RAGAZZI, BAMBINE

>Parpignol! Parpignol! Parpignol! Parpignol!
>Ecco Parpignol! Parpignol! Parpignol!
>Col carretto tutto fior!
>Ecco Parpignol!
>Parpignol! Parpignol! Parpignol!
>Voglio la tromba, il cavallin,
>Il tambur, tamburel,
>voglio il cannon, voglio il frustin,
>dei soldati i drappel.

*Il cameriere presenta ai quattro amici la carta: questa passa
girando nelle mani di tutti guardata con una specie di ammi-
razione ed analizzata profondamente.*

SCHAUNARD   Cervo arrosto!

MARCELLO   Un tacchino!

SCHAUNARD   Vin del Reno!

COLLINE   Vin da tavola!

SCHAUNARD   Aragosta senza crosta!

MAMME (*alle grida dei fanciulli accorrono, tentano inutilmente
            allontanarli da Parpignol e sgridano stizzite*)

>Ah! razza di furfanti indemoniati,
>che ci venite a fare in questo loco?
>A casa, a letto! Via brutti sguaiati,
>gli scappellotti vi parranno poco!
>A casa, a letto, razza di furfanti,
>a letto!

UN RAGAZZO   Vo' la tromba, il cavallin!

*I fanciulli non vogliono andarsene: uno di essi scoppia in
pianto: la mamma lo prende per un orecchio ed esso si mette
a gridare che vuole i giocattoli di Parpignol: le mamme, in-
tenerite, comprano. Parpignol prende giù per via Vecchia
Commedia, seguito dai ragazzi che fanno gran baccano con
tamburi tamburelli e trombette.*

RODOLFO (*piano a Mimì*)

>E tu Mimì, che vuoi?

MIMÌ   La crema.

SCHAUNARD (*al cameriere*)

>È gran sfarzo. C'è una dama!

RAGAZZI, BAMBINE

>Viva Parpignol, Parpignol, Parpignol, Parpignol!
>Il tambur, tamburel,
>dei soldati il drappel!

MARCELLO (*con galanteria a Mimì*)

>Signorina Mimì, che dono raro
>le ha fatto il suo Rodolfo?

From Rue Dauphine a little cart appears, all frills and flowers, illuminated with paper lanterns. The man pushing it is Parpignol.

BOYS, GIRLS   Parpignol! Parpignol! Parpignol! Parpignol!
Here's Parpignol! Parpignol! Parpignol!
With his cart all flowers!
Here's Parpignol!
Parpignol! Parpignol! Parpignol!
I want the trumpet, the little horse,
the drum, the tambourine,
I want the cannon, I want the whip,
the troop of soldiers.

The waiter presents the menu to the four friends; it passes around, through the hands of all, looked at with a kind of wonder and profoundly analyzed.

SCHAUNARD   Roast stag!

MARCELLO   A turkey!

SCHAUNARD   Rhine wine!

COLLINE   Table wine!

SCHAUNARD   Lobster without the shell!

MAMMAS (*run up at the cries of the children, try in vain to take them away from Parpignol and scold angrily*)
Ah! bunch of devilish rascals,
what are you coming to this place for?
Home, to bed! Off, you nasty bawlers,
Slaps will seem little to you!
Home, to bed, you bunch of rascals,
to bed!

A BOY   I want the trumpet, the little horse!

The children don't want to go away. One of them bursts into tears, his mother grabs him by one ear and he starts shouting that he wants Parpignol's toys. The Mammas, weakening, buy. Parpignol goes off down the Rue de l'Ancienne Comédie, followed by the boys who make a great racket with drums, tambourines, and little trumpets.

RODOLFO (*softly, to Mimì*)
And you, Mimì what do you want?

MIMÌ   The custard.

SCHAUNARD (*to the waiter*)
It's great pomp. There's a lady!

BOYS, GIRLS   Long live Parpignol, Parpignol, Parpignol, Parpignol!
The drum, tambourine,
the troop of soldiers!

MARCELLO (*gallantly, to Mimì*)
Miss Mimì, what rare gift
has our Rodolfo made you?

MIMÌ   Una cuffietta
                a pizzi, tutta rosa, ricamata;
                coi miei capelli bruni ben si fonde.
                Da tanto tempo tal cuffietta è cosa desïata!
                Ed egli ha letto quel che il core asconde . . .
                Ora colui che legge dentro a un cuore
                sa l'amore . . . ed è . . . lettore.

SCHAUNARD   Esperto professore . . .
COLLINE   . . . che ha già diplome e non son armi prime
                le sue rime.
SCHAUNARD   Tanto che sembra ver, ciò ch'egli esprime!
MARCELLO (*guardando Mimì*)
                O bella età d'inganni e d'utopie!
                si crede, spera, e tutto bello appare.
RODOLFO   La più divina delle poesie
                è quella, amico, che c'insegna amare!
MIMÌ   Amare è dolce ancora più del miele,
                più del miele!
MARCELLO   Secondo il palato è miele, o fiele!
MIMÌ (*sorpresa a Rodolfo*)
                O Dio! l'ho offeso!
RODOLFO   È in lutto, o mia Mimì.
SCHAUNARD, COLLINE (*per cambiare discorso*)
                Allegri, e un *toast!*
MARCELLO   Qua del liquor!
MIMÌ, RODOLFO, MARCELLO
                E via i pensier,
                alti i bicchier!
TUTTI   Beviam . . . ! Beviam!
MARCELLO (*che da lontano ha veduto Musetta, interrompe
                gridando*)
                Ch'io beva del tossico!
                (*si lascia cadere sulla sedia*)

    *All'angolo di via Mazzarino appare una bellissima signora
dal fare civettuolo e allegro, dal sorriso provocante. Le vien
dietro un vecchio pomposo e lezioso. La signora alla vista della
tavolata degli amici frena la corsa; si direbbe che ella sia
arrivata alla meta del suo viaggio.*

RODOLFO, SCHAUNARD, COLLINE (*alla esclamazione di Marcello
                si volgono ed esclamano*)
                Oh!
MARCELLO   Essa!
RODOLFO, SCHAUNARD, COLLINE
                Musetta!

    *Gli amici guardano con gli occhi pieni di compassione Mar-
cello che si è fatto pallido. Il cameriere comincia a servire;
Schaunard e Colline guardano sempre di sott'occhi dalla parte
di Musetta e parlano di lei; Marcello finge la massima indifferenza. Rodolfo solo non ha occhi e pensieri che per Mimì.*

| MIMÌ | A lace bonnet,
all pink, embroidered;
it goes well with my dark hair.
Such a bonnet is a thing I've wanted for such a
     time!
And he read what the heart hides . . .
Now he who reads in a heart
knows love . . . and he is . . . a reader. |

SCHAUNARD   An expert professor . . .

COLLINE   . . . who already has diplomas and his rhymes
are not novice weapons.

SCHAUNARD   So much so that what he expresses seems true!

MARCELLO (*looking at Mimì*)
Oh, beautiful age of deceits and utopias,
one believes, hopes, and all seems beautiful.

RODOLFO   The most divine of poems,
my friend, is the one that teaches us to love!

MIMÌ   To love is still sweeter than honey,
than honey!

MARCELLO   According to the palate, it's honey, or gall!

MIMÌ (*surprised, to Rodolfo*)
Oh, goodness, I've offended him!

RODOLFO   He's in mourning, my Mimì!

SCHAUNARD, COLLINE (*to change the subject*)
Be happy. And a toast!

MARCELLO   Some liquor here!

MIMÌ, RODOLFO, MARCELLO
Away with thoughts,
glasses high!

ALL   Let's drink . . .! Let's drink!

MARCELLO (*who has seen Musetta in the distance, interrupts,
shouting*)
Let me drink some poison!
(*sinks down on the chair*)

At the corner of Rue Mazarine a very beautiful lady appears, with a merry, flirtatious manner, a provocative smile. After her comes a pompous and affected old man. The lady, at the sight of the friends' table, slows down her pace. One would say that she had arrived at the goal of her journey.

RODOLFO, SCHAUNARD, COLLINE (*at Marcello's exclamation,
turn and exclaim*)
Oh!

MARCELLO   She!

RODOLFO, SCHAUNARD, COLLINE
Musetta!

The friends, their eyes filled with compassion, look at Marcello, who has turned pale. The waiter begins to serve. Schaunard and Colline keep looking discreetly in the direction of Musetta and speak of her. Marcello feigns the maximum indifference. Rodolfo alone has eyes and thoughts only for Mimì.

LE MAMME BOTTEGAIE (*nel ritirarsi a un tratto si soffermano
                    dalla parte delle loro botteghe a riguardare
                    una bella signora: meravigliate nel ricono-
                    scere in lei Musetta, sussurrano fra di loro
                    additandosela:*
                    To'! Lei!
                    Sì! To'!
                    Lei! Musetta! Tornata!
                    Siamo in auge!
                    Che toeletta!

ALCINDORO DE MITONNEAUX (*raggiunge trafelato Musetta*)
                    Come un facchino . . . correr di qua . . . di là . . .
                    No! no! non ci sta . . .

MUSETTA   Vien, Lulù!

ALCINDORO   Non ne posso più . . .

MUSETTA   Vien, Lulù!

ALCINDORO   Non ne posso più!

SCHAUNARD   Quel brutto coso mi par che sudi!

    *La bella signora senza curarsi del vecchio si avvia verso il
Caffè Momus e prende posto alla tavola lasciata libera.*

ALCINDORO   Come! qui fuori? qui?

MUSETTA   Siedi, Lulù!

    Alcindoro siede irritato, rialzando il bavero del pastrano.

ALCINDORO   Tali nomignoli,
                    prego, serbateli
                    al tu per tu!

    Un cameriere s'è avvicinato premuroso e prepara la tavola.

MUSETTA   Non farmi il Barbablù!

COLLINE (*esaminando il vecchio*)
                    È il vizio contegnoso . . .

MARCELLO (*con disprezzo*)
                    Colla casta Susanna!

MIMÌ (*a Rodolfo*)
                    È pur ben vestita!

RODOLFO   Gli angeli vanno nudi.

MIMÌ (*si rivolge curiosa a Rodolfo*)
                    La conosci? Chi è?

MARCELLO   Domandatelo a me.
                    [Il suo nome e Musetta;
                    cognome: Tentazione!
                    Per sua vocazione
                    fa la rosa dei venti;
                    gira e muta sovente
                    d'amanti e d'amore.
                    E come la civetta
                    è uccello sanguinario;
                    il suo cibo ordinario
                    è il cuore . . . ! Mangia il cuore!
                    Per questo io non ne ho più!

THE MAMMAS-SHOPKEEPERS (*as they are retiring suddenly stop
                        near their shops to look at a beautiful lady.
                        Amazed at recognizing her as Musetta, they
                        whisper among themselves, pointing her out
                        to one another*)
                        Well! She!
                        Yes! Well!
                        She! Musetta! Come back!
                        We're flourishing!
                        What a toilette!

ALCINDORO DE MITONNEAUX (*breathless, overtakes Musetta*)
                        Like a porter . . . running here . . . there . . .
                        No! no! It isn't done . . .

MUSETTA   Come, Lulù!

ALCINDORO   I can't stand any more . . .

MUSETTA   Come, Lulù!

ALCINDORO   I can't stand any more!

SCHAUNARD   It seems to me that ugly object is sweating!

*The beautiful lady, not minding the old man, goes toward
the Café Momus and takes a seat at the table left free.*

ALCINDORO   What! Outside here? Here?

MUSETTA   Sit, Lulù

*Alcindoro sits down, irritated, turning up the collar of his
overcoat.*

ALCINDORO   Such pet names,
             please, save them
             for when we're alone!

A waiter has come over eagerly and is preparing the table.

MUSETTA   Don't act like Bluebeard with me!

COLLINE   (*examining the old man*)
             He is sedate Vice . . .

MARCELLO   (*with contempt*)
             . . . with the chaste Susanna!

MIMÌ   (*to Rodolfo*)
             Still, she's well dressed.

RODOLFO   The angels go naked.

MIMÌ   (*addresses Rodolfo, curious*)
             You know her? Who is she?

MARCELLO   Ask me that.
             Her name is Musetta;
             last name: Temptation!
             As her vocation
             she plays the compass card;
             she turns and changes often
             her lovers and her love.
             And like the owl*
             she's a sanguinary bird;
             her ordinary food
             is the heart . . .! She eats the heart!
             That's why I no longer have any!

* Translator's note: the Italian word *civetta* means both "owl"
and "coquette."

MUSETTA (*colpita nel vedere che gli amici non la guardano*)
Marcello mi vide . . .
e non mi guarda, il vile!
Quel Schaunard che ride!
Mi fan tutti una bile!
Se potessi picchiar!
Se potessi graffiar!
Ma non ho sotto man
che questo pellican!
Aspetta!]
          (*chiama il cameriere che si è allontanato*)
Ehi! Camerier!

MARCELLO (*agli amici nascondendo la commozione che lo vince*)
Passatemi il ragù!

Il cameriere accorre: Musetta prende un piatto e lo fiuta.

MUSETTA   Ehi! Camerier! Questo piatto
ha una puzza di rifritto!
          (*getta il piatto a terra; il cameriere si af-fretta a raccogliere i cocci*)

ALCINDORO (*cerca acquetarla*)
No, Musetta . . .
Zitto, zitto!

MUSETTA (*rabbiosa, sempre guardando Marcello*)
(Non si volta!)

ALCINDORO   Zitto, zitto!
Zitto! Modi, garbo!

MUSETTA   (Ah, non si volta!)

ALCINDORO   A chi parli?

COLLINE   Questo pollo è un poema!

MUSETTA   (Ora lo batto, lo batto!)

ALCINDORO   Con chi parli?

MUSETTA (*stizzita*)
Al cameriere! Non seccar!

SCHAUNARD   Il vino è prelibato!

MUSETTA   Voglio fare il mio piacere . . .

ALCINDORO   Parla pian!

MUSETTA   Vo' far quel che mi pare!

ALCINDORO (*prende la nota dal cameriere e si mette ad ordi-nare la cena*)
Parla pian, parla pian!

MUSETTA   Non seccar!

STUDENTI E SARTINE (*attraversando la scena*)
Guarda, guarda chi si vede!
Proprio lei, Musetta!
Con quel vecchio che balbetta,
proprio lei, Musetta! Ah! ah! ah!

MUSETTA   (Che sia geloso di questa mummia?)

ALCINDORO   La convenienza . . . il grado . . . la virtù!

MUSETTA (*struck at seeing that the friends are not looking at her*)

(Marcello saw me . . .
and he isn't looking at me, the coward!
That Schaunard, who laughs!
They all make me cross!
If I could slap!
If I could scratch!
But all I have at hand
is this pelican!
Wait!)
    (*calls the waiter, who has gone off*)
Hey! Waiter!

MARCELLO (*to his friends, hiding the emotion that is overcoming him*)

Pass me the ragout!

The waiter rushes up. Musetta takes a plate and sniffs it.

MUSETTA   Hey! Waiter! This plate
stinks of stale fat!
    (*throws the plate on the ground; the waiter hastens to collect the pieces*)

ALCINDORO (*tries to calm her*)
    No, Musetta . . .
    Hush, hush!

MUSETTA (*angry, still looking at Marcello*)
    (He won't turn around!)

ALCINDORO   Hush, hush!
    Hush! Manners! Tact!

MUSETTA   (Ah, he won't turn around!)

ALCINDORO   To whom are you speaking?

COLLINE   This chicken is a poem!

MUSETTA   (Now I'll hit him, I'll hit him!)

ALCINDORO   With whom are you speaking?

MUSETTA (*irked*)
    To the waiter! Don't bother me!

SCHAUNARD   The wine is choice!

MUSETTA   I want to do what I please . . .

ALCINDORO   Speak softly!

MUSETTA   I want to do as I like!

ALCINDORO (*takes the menu from the waiter and prepares to order the supper*)
    Speak softly, speak softly!

MUSETTA   Don't bother me!

STUDENTS AND SEAMSTRESSES (*crossing the stage*)
    Look, look who's to be seen!
    It's she all right, Musetta!
    With that old man who stammers,
    It's she all right, Musetta! Ha! ha! ha!

MUSETTA   (Could he be jealous of this mummy?)

ALCINDORO   Decorum . . . rank . . . virtue!

MUSETTA   (Vediam se mi resta
               tanto poter su lui da farlo cedere!)

SCHAUNARD   La commedia è stupenda!

MUSETTA (*guardando Marcello, a voce alta*)
               Tu non mi guardi!

ALCINDORO   Vedi bene che ordino!

SCHAUNARD   La commedia è stupenda!

COLLINE   Stupenda!

RODOLFO (*a Mimì*)
               Sappi per tuo governo
               che non darei perdono in sempiterno!

SCHAUNARD (*a Colline*)
               Essa all'un parla
               perchè l'altro intenda.

MIMÌ (*a Rodolfo*)
               Io t'amo tanto,
               a sono tutta tua . . . !
               [Chè mi parli di perdono?

COLLINE (*a Schaunard*)
               E l'altro invan crudel]
               finge di non capir, ma sugge miel!

MUSETTA   Ma il tuo cuore martella.

ALCINDORO   Parla piano.

MUSETTA   Ma il tuo cuore martella!

ALCINDORO   Piano, piano!

MUSETTA (*civettuola, volgendosi con intenzione a Marcello, il
               quale comincia ad agitarsi*)
               Quando me'n vo . . .
               quando me'n vo soletta per la via
               la gente sosta e mira,
               e la bellezza mia
               tutta ricerca in me, ricerca in me
               da capo a piè . . .

MARCELLO (*agli amici*)
               Legatemi alla seggiola.

ALCINDORO   Quella gente che dirà?

MUSETTA   . . . ed assaporo allor la bramosia
               sottil che da gl'occhi traspira
               e dai palesi vezzi intender sa
               alle occulte beltà.
               Così l'effluvio del desìo
               tutta m'aggira,
               felice mi fa . . . felice mi fa!

ALCINDORO   Quel canto scurrile
               [mi muove la bile!
               Mi muove la bile!

MUSETTA   E tu che sai, che memori e ti struggi,
               da me tanto rifuggi?
               So ben: le angoscie tue non le vuoi dir,

               non le vuoi dir, so ben,
               ma ti senti morir!

MUSETTA (Let's see if I still have
    enough power over him to make him give way!)

SCHAUNARD The comedy is stupendous!

MUSETTA (*looking at Marcello, in a loud voice*)
    You aren't looking at me!

ALCINDORO You can see clearly that I'm ordering!

SCHAUNARD The comedy is stupendous!

COLLINE Stupendous!

RODOLFO (*to Mimì*)
    You should know, for your guidance,
    that I would never forgive!

SCHAUNARD (*to Colline*)
    She speaks to the one
    that the other may understand.

MIMÌ (*to Rodolfo*)
    I love you so much,
    and I'm all yours . . .!
    Why do you speak to me of forgiveness?

COLLINE (*to Schaunard*)
    And the other, cruel in vain,
    pretends not to understand, but sucks honey!

MUSETTA But your heart is pounding.

ALCINDORO Speak softly.

MUSETTA But your heart is pounding!

ALCINDORO Softly, softly!

MUSETTA (*flirtatious, turning meaningfully toward Marcello,
    who is beginning to writhe*)
    When I go along . . .
    when I go along, by myself, on the street
    people stop and look,
    and they seek in me, they seek in me
    all my beauty
    from head to foot. . .

MARCELLO (*to his friends*)
    Tie me to the chair.

ALCINDORO What will those people say?

MUSETTA . . . and then I savor the subtle
    longing that breathes from their eyes
    and which knows how to appreciate
    under the obvious charms the hidden beauties.
    And thus the flow of desire
    surrounds me completely,
    it makes me happy . . . it makes me happy!

ALCINDORO That scurrilous song
    rouses my anger!
    It rouses my anger!

MUSETTA And you who know, who remember and suffer,
    do you flee from me so?
    I know well: you don't want to tell your suffer-
     ings,
    you don't want to tell them, I know well,
    but you feel you're dying!

MIMÌ   Io vedo ben . . . che quella poveretta
               tutta invaghita ell'è,
               tutta invaghita di Marcel,
               tutta invaghita ell'è!]

ALCINDORO   Quella gente che dirà!

RODOLFO (*a Mimì*)
               Marcello un dì l'amò,
               [la fraschetta l'abbandonò
               per poi darsi a miglior vita.

SCHAUNARD   Ah Marcello cederà!

COLLINE   Chi sa mai quel che avverrà!]

SCHAUNARD   Trovan dolce al pari il laccio . . .

COLLINE   Santi numi, in simil briga . . .

SCHAUNARD   . . . chi lo tende e chi ci dà.

COLLINE   . . . mai Colline intopperà!

MUSETTA   (Ah! Marcello smania,
               [Marcello è vinto!)

ALCINDORO   Parla pian!

MIMÌ   Quell'infelice mi muove a pietà.

ALCINDORO   Zitta, zitta!]

COLLINE   (Essa è bella, io non son cieco . . .

MIMÌ (*a Rodolfo*)
               T'amo!

RODOLFO   [Mimì!

SCHAUNARD   Quel bravaccio a momenti cederà!
               Stupenda è la commedia!
               Marcello cederà!
                      (*a Colline*)
               Se tal vaga persona
               ti trattasse a tu per tu,
               la tua scienza brontolona
               manderesti a Belzebù!

MUSETTA (*verso Marcello*)
               So ben: le angoscie tue non le vuoi dir.
               Ah! ma ti senti morir.
                      (*ad Alcindoro*)
               Io voglio fare il mio piacere!
               Voglio far quel che mi par . . .
               Non seccar! non seccar!

MIMÌ   Quell'infelice mi muove a pietà!
               L'amor ingeneroso è tristo amor!
               È fiacco amore, ah, ah, mi muove,
               mi muove a pietà!

RODOLFO   È fiacco amor quel che le offese
               vendicar non sa!
               Non risorge spento amor!
               È fiacco amore quel che le offese
               vendicar non sa!

COLLINE   . . . ma piaccionmi assai più
               una pipa e un testo greco,

MIMÌ	I see well . . . that that poor girl is all infatuated, she's all infatuated with Marcello she's all infatuated!
ALCINDORO	What will those people say!
RODOLFO (*to Mimì*)	
	Marcello one day loved her, the coquette abandoned him to devote herself then to a better life.
SCHAUNARD	Ah, Marcello will give way!
COLLINE	Who knows what will happen!
SCHAUNARD	They find the noose equally sweet . . .
COLLINE	Ye gods, in such a fix . . .
SCHAUNARD	. . . the one who extends it and the one who's trapped.
COLLINE	. . . Colline will never fall!
MUSETTA	(Ah, Marcello's raving, Marcello's defeated!)
ALCINDORO	Speak softly!
MIMÌ	That unhappy man moves me to pity.
ALCINDORO	Hush, hush!
COLLINE	(She's beautiful, I'm not blind . . .
MIMÌ (*to Rodolfo*)	
	I love you!
RODOLFO	Mimì!
SCHAUNARD	That swaggerer will give way any minute! The comedy is stupendous! Marcello will give way! (*to Colline*) If such a lovely person were to speak intimately with you, you'd send your grumpy science to Beelzebub!
MUSETTA (*toward Marcello*)	
	I know well: you don't want to tell your suffer- ings. Ah! but you feel you're dying. (*to Alcindoro*) I want to do as I please! I want to do what I like . . . Don't annoy me! Don't annoy me!
MIMÌ	That unhappy man moves me to pity! Ungenerous love is sad love! It's weak love, ah, ah, he moves me, he moves me to pity!
RODOLFO	Weak is that love which cannot avenge its insults! Dead love doesn't rise again! Weak is that love which cannot avenge its insults!
COLLINE	. . . but I like much more a pipe and a Greek text,

mi piaccion assai più!
Essa è bella, non son cieco,
ma piaccionmi assai più
una pipa e un testo greco!)

ALCINDORO   Modi, garbo! Zitta, zitta!]

MUSETTA   Non seccar!
(Or convien liberarsi del vecchio!)
    (*fingendo provare un vivo dolore*)
Ahi!

ALCINDORO   Che c'è?

MUSETTA   Qual dolore, qual bruciore!

ALCINDORO   Dove?

MUSETTA   Al piè!
[Sciogli, slaccia — rompi, straccia!
Te ne imploro . . .
Laggiù c'è un calzolaio.
Corri, presto! Ne voglio un altro paio.
Ahi! che fitta! Corri, va, corri!
presto, va, va!

MARCELLO (*grandemente commosso*)
Gioventù mia, tu non sei morta
nè di te morto è il sovvenir!
Se tu battessi alla mia porta
t'andrebbe il mio core ad aprir . . .
ad aprir!

SCHAUNARD, COLLINE
La commedia è stupenda,
la commedia è stupenda!

MIMÌ   Io vedo ben, ell'è invaghita di Marcello!

RODOLFO   Io vedo ben . . . la commedia è stupenda!

ALCINDORO   Imprudente! Quella gente che dirà?
Ma il mio grado! Vuoi ch'io comprometta?
Aspetta!
    (*disperato, prende la scarpa e rapidamente
    se la caccia nel panciotto, e si abbottona
    maestoso l'abito. Poi per timor di maggior
    scandolo, corre frettolosamente verso la
    bottega del calzolaio*)
Musetta! Vo.]

MUSETTA (*appena partito Alcindoro, si alza e si getta nelle
    braccia di Marcello, che non sa più resistere*)
Marcello!

MARCELLO   Sirena!

SCHAUNARD   Siamo all'ultima scena!

Un cameriere porta il conto.

RODOLFO, SCHAUNARD, COLLINE
Il conto?!

SCHAUNARD   Così presto?

COLLINE   Chi l'ha richiesto?

SCHAUNARD   Vediam!
    (*si fa dare il conto, che fa il giro degli amici*)

	I like them much more!
	She's beautiful, I'm not blind,
	but I like much more
	a pipe and a Greek text!)
ALCINDORO	Manners, tact! Hush, hush!
MUSETTA	Don't bother me!
	(Now it's best to be freed of the old man!)
	(*pretending to feel a sharp pain*)
	Ouch!
ALCINDORO	What is it?
MUSETTA	What pain, what burning!
ALCINDORO	Where?
MUSETTA	In my foot!
	Loosen, unlace — break, tear!
	I implore you . . .
	There's a cobbler over there.
	Run, quickly! I want another pair.
	Ouch! what a pain! Run, go, run!
	Quickly, go, go!

MARCELLO (*greatly moved*)
>   My youth, you're not dead,
>   nor is the memory of you dead!
>   If you knocked at my door,
>   my heart would go to open to you . . .
>   to open!

SCHAUNARD, COLLINE
>   The comedy is stupendous!
>   The comedy is stupendous!

MIMÌ	I see well: she is infatuated with Marcello!
RODOLFO	I see well . . . the comedy is stupendous!
ALCINDORO	Imprudent girl! What will those people say?
	But my rank! You want me to be compromised?
	Wait!

>   (*desperate, he takes the shoe and rapidly
>   stuffs it into his vest, and majestically but-
>   tons up his suit. Then, for fear of greater
>   scandal, he runs hastily toward the cob-
>   bler's shop*)
>   Musetta! I go.

MUSETTA (*as soon as Alcindoro has left, rises and throws her-
>   self into the arms of Marcello, who can resist
>   no longer*)
>   Marcello!

MARCELLO	Siren!
SCHAUNARD	We're at the last scene!

A waiter brings the bill.

RODOLFO, SCHAUNARD, COLLINE
>   The bill?!

SCHAUNARD	So soon?
COLLINE	Who asked for it?
SCHAUNARD	Let's see!

>   (*he has the bill given him; it moves among
>   the friends*)

RODOLFO, COLLINE
        Caro!

RODOLFO, SCHAUNARD, COLLINE
        Fuori il danaro!

SCHAUNARD   Colline, Rodolfo e tu Marcel?

MARCELLO   [Siamo all'asciutto!

SCHAUNARD   Come?

RODOLFO   Ho trenta soldi in tutto!

MARCELLO, SCHAUNARD, COLLINE
        Come? Non ce n'è più?

SCHAUNARD (*terribile*)
        Ma il mio tesoro ov'è?

Portano le mani alle tasche: sono vuote: nessuno sa spiegarsi la rapida scomparsa degli scudi di Schaunard: sorpresi si guardano l'un l'altro. Intanto lontanissima si ode la ritirata militare che poco a poco va avvicinandosi: la gente accorre da ogni parte, guardando e correndo di qua, di là onde vedere da quale parte giunge.

MONELLI   La ritirata!

BORGHESI   La ritirata!

SARTINE, STUDENTI
        La ritirata!]

MONELLI   S'avvicinan per di qua?

MUSETTA (*al cameriere*)
        Il mio conto date a me.

SARTINE, STUDENTI
        No, di là!

MONELLI   S'avvicinan per di là!

SARTINE, STUDENTI
        Vien di qua!

MONELLI   No, vien di là!

MUSETTA (*al cameriere che consegna il conto*)
        Bene!

BORGHESI, VENDITORI
        Largo! largo!

ALCUNI FANCIULLI (*dalle finestre*)
        Voglio veder! voglio sentir!

MUSETTA   Presto sommate quello con questo!

FANCIULLI   Mamma, voglio veder!
        Papà, voglio sentir!

MAMME   Lisetta, vuoi tacer!
        Tonio, la vuoi finir!

MUSETTA   Paga il signor che stava qui con me!

RODOLFO, MARCELLO, SCHAUNARD, COLLINE
        Paga il signor!

MAMME   Vuoi tacer, vuoi finir?

SARTINE, STUDENTI
        S'avvicinano di qua!

LA FOLLA   Sì, di qua!

RODOLFO, COLLINE
    Expensive!

RODOLFO, SCHAUNARD, COLLINE
    Out with the money!

SCHAUNARD   Colline, Rodolfo, and you, Marcello?

MARCELLO   We're broke!

SCHAUNARD   What?

RODOLFO   I have thirty *sous* in all!

MARCELLO, SCHAUNARD, COLLINE
    What? Isn't there any more?

SCHAUNARD (*terrifying*)
    Where is my treasure?

    They put their hands in their pockets; they're empty. Nobody can explain the rapid disappearance of Schaunard's money. Surprised, they look at one another. Meanwhile, very far away, the military tattoo is heard, which is slowly coming nearer. People run in from all sides, looking and running here and there to see from which direction it is coming.

GAMINS   The tattoo!

BOURGEOIS   The tattoo!

SEAMSTRESSES, STUDENTS
    The tattoo!

GAMINS   Are they coming along here?

MUSETTA (*to the waiter*)
    Give me my bill.

SEAMSTRESSES, STUDENTS
    No, from there!

GAMINS   They're coming from there!

SEAMSTRESSES, STUDENTS
    It's coming from here!

GAMINS   No, it's coming from there!

MUSETTA (*to the waiter, who hands her the bill*)
    Very well!

BOURGEOIS, VENDORS
    Make way! Make way!

SOME CHILDREN (*from the windows*)
    I want to see! I want to hear!

MUSETTA   Quickly add that one to this one!

CHILDREN   Mamma, I want to see!
    Papa, I want to hear!

MAMMAS   Lisetta, will you be quiet?
    Tonio, will you stop it?

MUSETTA   The gentleman who was here with me will pay!

RODOLFO, MARCELLO, SCHAUNARD, COLLINE
    The gentleman pays!

MAMMAS   Will you be quiet? Will you stop it?

SEAMSTRESSES, STUDENTS
    They're approaching from here!

THE CROWD   Yes, from here!

MONELLI   Come sarà arrivata
                   la seguiremo al passo!

COLLINE   Paga il signor!

SCHAUNARD   Paga il signor!

MARCELLO   Il signor!

MUSETTA (*ponendo i due conti riuniti al posto di Alcindoro*)
                   E dove s'è seduto
                   ritrovi il mio saluto!

BORGHESI   In quel rullìo tu senti
                   la patria maestà!

RODOLFO, MARCELLO, SCHAUNARD, COLLINE
                   E dove s'è seduto
                   ritrovi il suo saluto!

LA FOLLA   Largo, largo, eccoli qua! In fila!

MONELLI   Ohè! attenti eccoli qua! In fila!

MARCELLO   Giunge la ritirata! Che il vecchio non ci veda
                   fuggir con la sua preda!

COLLINE   Che il vecchio non ci veda
                   fuggir con la sua preda!

RODOLFO   Giunge la ritirata!

MARCELLO, SCHAUNARD, COLLINE
                   Quella folla serrata
                   il nascondiglio appresti!

La ritirata militare attraversa la scena.

LA FOLLA   Ecco il tambur maggiore!
                   Più fier d'un antico guerrier!
                   Il tambur maggior!

MIMÌ, MUSETTA, RODOLFO, MARCELLO, SCHAUNARD, COLLINE
                   Lesti, lesti, lesti!

LA FOLLA   I Zappator, I Zappatori olà!
                   Ecco il tambur maggior!
                   Pare un general!
                   La ritirata è qua!
                   Eccolo là! Il bel tambur maggior!
                   La canna d'or, tutto splendor!
                   Che guarda, passa, va!
                   [Tutto splendor! Di Francia è il più bell'uom!
                   Il bel tambur maggior! Eccolo là!
                   Che guarda, passa, va!

RODOLFO, MARCELLO, SCHAUNARD, COLLINE
                   Viva Musetta! Cuor birichin!
                   Gloria ed onor, onor e gloria
                   del quartier latin!]

*Musetta non potendo camminare perchè ha un solo piede
calzato, è alzata a braccia da Marcello e Colline; la folla vedendo Musetta portata trionfalmente, ne prende pretesto per
farle clamorose ovazioni: Marcello e Colline con Musetta si
mettono in coda alla ritirata: li seguono Rodolfo e Mimì a*

GAMINS   As soon as it's arrived,
                we'll follow it at its pace!

COLLINE   The gentleman pays!

SCHAUNARD   The gentleman pays!

MARCELLO   The gentleman!

MUSETTA (*setting the two bills, added together, at Alcindoro's
                place*)
                And where he was seated
                let him find my farewell!

BOURGEOIS   In that drumming you hear
                the nation's majesty!

RODOLFO, MARCELLO, SCHAUNARD, COLLINE
                And where he was seated
                let him find her farewell!

THE CROWD   Make way, make way, here they are! Line up!

GAMINS   Hey! Watch. here they are! Line up!

MARCELLO   The tattoo's coming! Don't let the old man see us
                flee with his prey!

COLLINE   Don't let the old man see us
                flee with his prey!

RODOLFO   The tattoo's coming!

MARCELLO, SCHAUNARD, COLLINE
                Let that packed crowd
                prepare the hiding place!

The tattoo crosses the stage.

THE CROWD   Here's the drum major!
                Haughtier than an ancient warrior!
                The drum major!

MIMÌ, MUSETTA, RODOLFO,
MARCELLO, SCHAUNARD, COLLINE
                Quickly, quickly, quickly!

THE CROWD   The Pioneers, the Pioneers, hola!
                Here's the drum major!
                He looks like a general!
                The tattoo is here!
                There he is! The handsome drum major!
                The gold baton, all splendor!
                He looks, passes, and goes on!
                All splendor! He's the most handsome man in
                    France!
                The handsome drum major! There he is!
                He looks, passes, and goes on!

RODOLFO, MARCELLO, SCHAUNARD, COLLINE
                Long live Musetta! Roguish heart!
                Glory and honor, honor and glory
                of the Latin Quarter!

*Musetta, unable to walk because only one foot is shod, is
lifted into the arms of Marcello and Colline. The crowd, seeing Musetta borne triumphantly, seizes this excuse to give her
noisy ovations. Marcello and Colline with Musetta take up the
rear of the tattoo. Rodolfo and Mimì, arm in arm, follow them,*

*braccetto e Schaunard col suo corno imboccato; poi studenti
e sartine saltellano allegramente, poi ragazzi, borghesi, donne
che prendono il passo di marcia: tutta questa folla si allontana
dal fondo seguendo e cantando la ritirata militare.—Alcindoro,
con un paio di scarpe bene incartocciate ritorna verso il Caffè
Momus, cerca inutilmente Musetta e s'avvicina alla tavola: il
cameriere che è lì presso, prende i conti lasciati da Musetta e
cerimoniosamente li presenta ad Alcindoro, il quale vedendo
la somma, non trovando più alcuno, cade su una sedia, stupefatto, allibito.*

QUADRO TERZO

La Barriera d'Enfer

*Al di là della barriera il boulevard esterno e, nell'estremo
fondo, la strada d'Orléans che si perde lontana fra le alte case
e la nebbia del febbraio; al di qua, a sinistra, un Cabaret ed il
piccolo largo della barriera, a destra il boulevard d'Enfer; a
sinistra quello di St. Jacques. A destra pure la imboccatura
della via d'Enfer che mette in pieno Quartiere Latino. Il Cabaret ha per insegna il quadro di Marcello "Il passaggio del
Mar Rosso," ma sotto invece, a larghi caratteri, vi è dipinto
"Al porto di Marsiglia." Ai lati della porta sono pure dipinti a
fresco un turco e uno zuavo con una enorme corona d'alloro
intorno al fez. Alla parete del Cabaret, che guarda verso la
barriera, una finestra a pian terreno donde esce un chiarore
rossiccio. I platani che costeggiano il largo della barriera,
grigi, alti e in lunghi filari, dal largo si dipartono diagonal-
mente verso i due boulevards. Fra platano e platano sedili di
marmo. È il febbraio: la neve è dappertutto. All'alzarsi della
tela c'è nel cielo e sulle case il biancheggiare incerto della pri-
missima alba. Seduti avanti ad un braciere stanno sonnecchi-
ando i Doganieri. Dal Cabaret, ad intervalli, grida, cozzi di
bicchieri, risate. Un Doganiere esce dal Cabaret con vino. La
cancellata della barriera è chiusa. Dietro la cancellata chiusa,
battendo i piedi dal freddo e soffiandosi su le mani intirizzite
stanno alcuni Spazzini.*

SPAZZINI Ohè, là, le guardie! Aprite! Ohè, là!
    Quelli di Gentilly! Siam gli spazzini!
     (*I Doganieri rimangono immobili; gli
     Spazzini picchiano colle loro scope e ba-
     dili sulla cancellata, urlando*)
    Fiocca la neve . . . Ohè, là!
    Qui s'agghiaccia!
  I Doganieri si scuotono.

UN DOGANIERE (*sbadigliando e stirandosi le braccia, brontola*)
    Vengo!

*Va ad aprire; gli Spazzini entrano e si allontanano per la via
d'Enfer. Il Doganiere rinchiude la cancellata. Dal cabaret voci
allegre e tintinnii di bicchieri che accompagnano il lieto cantare.*

and Schaunard with his horn to his lips. Then students and seamstresses, gaily leaping, then boys, bourgeois, women, who fall into the marching step. All this crowd goes off in the background, following the tattoo and singing. Alcindoro, with a well-wrapped pair of shoes, comes back toward the Café Momus, looks for Musetta in vain, and approaches the table. The waiter, who is near it, takes the bills left by Musetta and ceremoniously presents them to Alcindoro, who, seeing the sum and no longer finding anyone, falls on a chair, amazed, aghast.

ACT THREE

The Barrière d'Enfer

Beyond the tollgate, the boulevard outside the city, and, in the far background, the Orléans road, which disappears among the tall houses in the February fog. This side, to the left, a tavern and the little square in front of the barrier. At right, the Boulevard d'Enfer; at left, the Boulevard St. Jacques. Also at right the beginning of the Rue d'Enfer, which leads straight to the Latin Quarter. The tavern uses as its sign Marcello's painting "The Crossing of the Red Sea," but below it, instead, in big letters is painted "At the Port of Marseilles." At the sides of the door also are painted frescoes of a Turk and a Zouave with an enormous laurel crown around his fez. In the wall of the tavern that looks toward the tollgate, a ground-floor window from which a rosy light comes. The plane trees that flank the square, gray, tall, and in long rows go from the square, diagonally toward the two boulevards. Between one plane tree and the next, marble benches. It is February: the snow is everywhere. At the rise of the curtain in the sky and over the houses there is the uncertain whitening of very early dawn. Seated before a brazier the customs men are dozing. From the tavern, at intervals, shouts, clink of glasses, laughter. A customs man comes from the tavern with some wine. The gate of the barrier is closed. Beyond the closed gate, stamping their feet with the cold and blowing on their benumbed hands, are some street sweepers.

SWEEPERS   Hey there! Guards! Open! Hey there!
We're the sweepers! Those from Gentilly!
> (*The customs men remain immobile; the sweepers hammer with their brooms and their shovels on the gate, shouting*)

Snow is falling . . . Hey there!
We're freezing here!

The customs men bestir themselves.

A CUSTOMS MAN (*yawning and stretching his arms, grumbles*)
I'm coming!

He goes to open. The sweepers come in and go off along the Rue d'Enfer. The customs man shuts the gate again. From the tavern, gay voices and the clinking of glasses, which accompany merry singing.

VOCI INTERNE Chi nel ber trovò piacer, nel suo bicchier,
nel suo bicchier, ah!
d'una bocca nell'ardor,
trovò l'amor, trovò l'amor!

MUSETTA (*nel cabaret*)
Ah! Se nel bicchiere sta il piacer
in giovin bocca sta l'amor!

VOCI INTERNE Trallerallè, trallerallè, Eva e Noè!

*Suoni di campanelli dallo stradale d'Orléans: sono carri
tirati da muli. Schioccare di fruste e grida di carrettieri: hanno
fra le ruote lanterne accese ricoperte di tela. Passano e si allontanano pel* boulevard *d'Enfer.*

CARRETTIERI Hopp-là!

LATTIVENDOLE Hopp-là!

UN DOGANIERE Son già le lattivendole!

*Dal corpo di guardia esce il Sergente dei Doganieri, il quale
ordina d'aprire la barriera. Le lattivendole passano per la barriera a dorsi di asinelli e si allontanano per diverse strade.*

CARRETTIERI, LATTIVENDOLE
Hopp-là! Hopp-là!

LATTIVENDOLE Buon giorno! Buon giorno! Buon giorno!

CONTADINE (*con ceste a braccio*)
Burro e cacio! Polli ed ova!
(*pagano e i Doganieri le lasciano passare;
giunte al crocicchio*)
Voi da che parte andate?
A San Michele!
Ci troverem più tardi?
A mezzodì!
A mezzodì!

*Si allontanano per diverse strade. I Doganieri ritirano le
panche e il braciere. Mimì dalla via d'Enfer entra guardando
attentamente intorno cercando di riconoscere i luoghi, ma
giunta al primo platano la coglie un violento accesso di tosse:
riavutasi e veduto il sergente, gli si avvicina.*

MIMÌ (*al Sergente*)
Sa dirmi, scusi, qual è l'osteria . . .
(*non ricordandene il nome*)
. . . dove un pittor lavora?

SERGENTE (*indicando il cabaret*)
Eccola.

MIMÌ   Grazie.
(*esce una fantesca dal cabaret. Mimì le si
avvicina*)
O buona donna, mi fate il favore . . .
di cercarmi il pittore Marcello?
Ho da parlargli. Ho tanta fretta.
Ditegli, piano, che Mimì l'aspetta.

La fantesca rientra nel cabaret.

VOICES WITHIN He who in drinking found pleasure, in his glass,
in his glass, ah!
in the ardor of a mouth
found love, found love!

MUSETTA (*in the tavern*)
Ah! if pleasure lies in the glass,
love lies in a young mouth!

VOICES WITHIN Trallerallè, trallerallè, Eve and Noah!

Sounds of little bells from the Orléans road: these are wagons drawn by mules. Cracking of whips and cries of carters. Between the wheels they have lighted lanterns covered with canvas. They go past and go off along the Boulevard d'Enfer.

CARTERS Giddap!

MILK WOMEN Giddap!

A CUSTOMS MAN
The milk women already!

From the guardhouse the customs sergeant comes out. He orders the gate to be opened. The milk women pass the barrier on the backs of little donkeys and go off along different streets.

CARTERS, MILK WOMEN
Giddap! Giddap!

MILK WOMEN Good day! Good day! Good day!

PEASANT WOMEN (*with baskets on their arms*)
Butter and cheese! Chickens and eggs!
(*they pay and the customs men let them
pass. When they reach the crossing*)
Which way are you going?
To St. Michel!
Shall we meet later?
At midday!
At midday!

They go off along different streets. The customs men take away the benches and the brazier. Mimì comes in from the Rue d'Enfer, looking around carefully, trying to recognize the places, but when she has reached the first plane tree a violent fit of coughing seizes her. When she has recovered and seen the sergeant, she goes over to him.

MIMÌ (*to the sergeant*)
Can you tell me, forgive me, which is the tavern . . .
(*not remembering the name*)
. . . where a painter is working?

SERGEANT (*pointing to the tavern*)
There it is.

MIMÌ Thanks.
(*a maidservant comes from the tavern.
Mimì approaches her*)
Oh my good woman, will you do me the favor . . .
of looking for the painter Marcello?
I have to speak to him. I'm in such a hurry.
Tell him, softly, that Mimì is waiting for him.

SERGENTE *(ad uno che passa)*
        Ehi, quel paniere!

DOGANIERE   Vuoto!

SERGENTE   Passi.

Dalla barriera entra altra gente, e chi da una parte, chi dall'altra tutti si allontanano. Le campane dell'ospizio Maria Teresa suonano mattutino. È giorno fatto, giorno d'inverno, triste a caliginoso. Dal cabaret escono alcune coppie che rincasano. Marcello esce dal cabaret e con sorpresa vede Mimì.

MARCELLO   Mimì!

MIMÌ   Speravo di trovarvi qui.

MARCELLO   È ver, siam qui da un mese
        di quell'oste alle spese.
        Musetta insegna il canto ai passeggieri
        io pingo quei guerrieri
        sulla facciata.
                (Mimì tossisce)
        È freddo. Entrate.

MIMÌ   C'è Rodolfo?

MARCELLO   Sì.

MIMÌ   Non posso entrar, no, no!

MARCELLO *(sorpreso)*
        Perchè?

MIMÌ *(scoppia in pianto)*
        Oh! buon Marcello, aiuto! aiuto!

MARCELLO   Cos'è avvenuto?

MIMÌ   Rodolfo, Rodolfo m'ama . . .
        Rodolfo m'ama e mi fugge,
        il mio Rodolfo si strugge per gelosia.
        Un passo, un detto, un vezzo,
        un fior lo mettono in sospetto . . .
        Onde corrucci ed ire.
        Talor la notte fingo di dormire
        e in me lo sento fiso
        spiarmi i sogni in viso.
        Mi grida ad ogni istante:
        Non fai per me,
        ti prendi un altro amante,
        non fai per me!
        Ahimè! ahimè!
        In lui parla il rovello, lo so,
        ma che rispondergli, Marcello?

MARCELLO   Quando s'è come voi
        non si vive in compagnia.

MIMÌ   Dite ben, dite bene.
        Lasciarci conviene.
        Aiutateci, aiutateci voi;
        noi s'è provato più volte, ma invano.

MARCELLO   [Son lieve a Musetta, ell'è lieve a me,
        perchè ci amiamo in allegria . . .
        Canti e risa, ecco il fior
        d'invariabile amor!

SERGEANT (*to a man passing by*)
Hey, that basket!

CUSTOMS MAN
Empty!

SERGEANT Let him pass.

From the barrier more people come in, and some one way, some another, all go off. The bells of the Marie Thérèse Hospice ring matins. It is full day, a winter day, sad and misty. Some couples come from the tavern, going home. Marcello comes from the tavern and, with surprise, sees Mimì.

MARCELLO Mimì!

MIMÌ I was hoping to find you here.

MARCELLO It's true, we've been here for a month
at the expense of that tavern keeper.
Musetta teaches singing to the travelers,
I'm painting those warriors
on the façade.
(*Mimì coughs*)
It's cold. Come in.

MIMÌ Is Rodolfo there?

MARCELLO Yes.

MIMÌ I can't go in, no, no!

MARCELLO (*surprised*)
Why?

MIMÌ (*bursts into tears*)
Oh, good Marcello! Help! Help!

MARCELLO What's happened?

MIMÌ Rodolfo, Rodolfo loves me . . .
Rodolfo loves me and flees from me,
my Rodolfo is consumed with jealousy.
A footstep, a word, a compliment,
a flower arouse his suspicion . . .
Whereupon frowns and wrath.
At times at night I pretend to sleep
and I feel him staring at me,
to observe my dreams in my face.
He shouts at me at every moment:
You're not the one for me,
take another lover for yourself,
you're not the one for me!
Alas! Alas!
Anger is speaking in him, I know,
but what to answer him, Marcello?

MARCELLO When people are like you two
they don't live together.

MIMÌ You're right, you're right.
It's best for us to leave each other.
Help us, you help us;
we've tried several times, but in vain.

MARCELLO I'm easy with Musetta, she's easy with me,
because we love each other gaily . . .
Songs and laughter, there is the flower
of unchanging love!

MIMÌ	Dite ben, dite ben, lasciarci convien!] Fate voi per il meglio.
MARCELLO	Sta ben, sta ben! Ora lo sveglio.
MIMÌ	Dorme?

MARCELLO	È piombato qui
	un'ora avanti l'alba,
	s'assopì sopra una panca.
	Guardate.
	      (*va presso alla finestra e fa cenno a Mimì
	      di guardare. Mimì tossisce*)
	Che tosse!

MIMÌ	Da ieri ho l'ossa rotte. Fuggì da me stanotte dicendomi: È finita. A giorno sono uscita e me ne venni a questa volta.
MARCELLO (*osservando Rodolfo nell'interno del cabaret*)	Si desta . . . s'alza . . . mi cerca . . . viene . . .
MIMÌ	Ch'ei non mi veda!
MARCELLO	Or rincasate Mimì, per carità! Non fate scene qua!

    Spinge dolcemente Mimì verso l'angolo del cabaret di dove però quasi subito sporge curiosa la testa. Marcello corre incontro a Rodolfo.

RODOLFO (*accorrendo verso Marcello*)	Marcello. Finalmente! Qui niun ci sente. Io voglio separarmi da Mimì.
MARCELLO	Sei volubil così?
RODOLFO	Già un'altra volta credetti morto il mio cor, ma di quegl'occhi azzurri allo splendor esso è risorto. Ora il tedio l'assal . . .
MARCELLO	E gli vuoi rinnovare il funeral?

    Mimì non potendo udire le parole, colto il momento opportuno, riesce a ripararsi dietro a un platano, avvicinandosi così ai due amici.

RODOLFO (*con dolore*)	Per sempre!
MARCELLO	Cambia metro. Dei pazzi è l'amor tetro che lacrime distilla. Se non ride e sfavilla l'amore è fiacco e roco. Tu sei geloso.
RODOLFO	Un poco.
MARCELLO	Collerico, lunatico, imbevuto di pregiudizî, noioso, cocciuto!

MIMÌ	You're right, you're right; it's best for us to leave each other! You act for the best.
MARCELLO	All right, all right! Now I'll wake him.
MIMÌ	Is he asleep?

MARCELLO	He rushed in here
	an hour before dawn;
	he dozed off on a bench.
	Look.
	    (*goes to the window and motions to Mimì
	    to look. Mimì coughs*)
	What a cough!

MIMÌ	Since yesterday I've been exhausted. He fled from me last night, saying to me: It's finished. At daybreak I went out and I came in this direction.
MARCELLO	(*observing Rodolfo inside the tavern*) He's waking . . . he's standing up . . . he's look- ing for me . . . he's coming . . .
MIMÌ	Don't let him see me!
MARCELLO	Go home now, Mimì, please! Don't make scenes here!

He gently thrusts Mimì towards the corner of the tavern, from which, however, she almost immediately extends her head, curious. Marcello runs to meet Rodolfo.

RODOLFO	(*running toward Marcello*) Marcello. At last! Here no one hears us. I want to separate from Mimì.
MARCELLO	Are you fickle like that?
RODOLFO	Already another time I believed my heart was dead, but at the glow of those blue eyes it revived. Now boredom assails it . . .
MARCELLO	And you want to repeat its funeral?

Mimì, unable to hear the words, seizing the right moment, manages to take refuge behind a plane tree, thus coming closer to the two friends.

RODOLFO	(*with grief*) Forever!
MARCELLO	Change your tune. The gloomy love that distills tears belongs to madmen. If it doesn't laugh and sparkle love is weak and hoarse. You're jealous.
RODOLFO	A little.
MARCELLO	Choleric, lunatic, steeped in prejudices, boring, stubborn!

MIMÌ (*che ode, fra sè, inquieta*)
          Or lo fa incollerir! Me poveretta!

RODOLFO   Mimì è una civetta
          che frascheggia con tutti. Un moscardino
          di Viscontino
          le fa l'occhio di triglia. Ella sgonnella
          e scopre la caviglia
          con un far promettente e lusinghier ...

MARCELLO   Lo devo dir? Non mi sembri sincer.

RODOLFO   Ebbene, no, non lo son.
          Invan, invan nascondo
          la mia vera tortura.
          Amo Mimì sovra ogni cosa al mondo,
          io l'amo, ma ho paura.
          Ma ho paura.

    Mimì, sorpresa, si avvicina ancora più, sempre nascosta
dietro gli alberi.

RODOLFO   Mimì è tanto malata!
          Ogni dì più declina.
          La povera piccina è condannata!

MARCELLO   Mimì!?

MIMÌ   Che vuol dire?

RODOLFO   Una terribil tosse
          l'esil petto le scuote
          già le smunte gote
          di sangue ha rosse ...

MARCELLO   Povera Mimì!

MIMÌ   Ahimè, morire?!

RODOLFO   La mia stanza è una tana
          squallida ... il fuoco ho spento.
          V'entra e l'aggira il vento
          di tramontana.
          Essa canta e sorride,
          e il rimorso m'assale.
          Me cagion del fatale
          mal che l'uccide.

MARCELLO   Che far dunque?

MIMÌ (*angosciata*)
          O mia vita!

RODOLFO   [Mimì di serra è fiore.
          Povertà l'ha sfiorita,
          per richiamarla in vita
          non basta amor, non basta amor!

MARCELLO   Oh qual pietà! Poveretta!
          Povera Mimì! Povera Mimì!

MIMÌ   Ahimè! Ahimè! È finita!
          O mia vita ... ! È finita!
          Ahimè morir, ahimè morir!]

    La tosse e i singhiozzi violenti rivelano la presenza di Mimì.

RODOLFO (*vedendola e accorrendo a lei*)
          Chè? Mimì! Tu qui?
          [M'hai sentito?

MIMÌ (*who hears; to herself, uneasy*)
> Now he'll make him angry! Poor me!

RODOLFO Mimì is a coquette
who flirts with everyone. A viscount,
a little dandy,
makes sheep's eyes at her. She wiggles
and bares her ankle
with a promising and flattering manner ...

MARCELLO Must I say it? You don't seem sincere to me.

RODOLFO Well, no, I'm not.
In vain, in vain I hide
my real torment.
I love Mimì above everything in the world,
I love her, but I'm afraid.
But I'm afraid.

Mimì, surprised, comes still closer, always hidden behind the trees.

RODOLFO Mimì is so ill!
Every day she declines further.
The poor little thing is doomed!

MARCELLO Mimì!?

MIMÌ What does he mean?

RODOLFO A terrible cough
shakes her fragile bosom,
already her emaciated cheeks
are red with blood ...

MARCELLO Poor Mimì!

MIMÌ Alas, to die?!

RODOLFO My room is a squalid den ...
My fire is out.
The north wind enters there
and moves about.
She sings and smiles,
and remorse assails me.
Me, the cause of the fatal
disease that is killing her.

MARCELLO What to do then?

MIMÌ (*in anguish*)
> Oh, my life!

RODOLFO Mimì's a hothouse flower.
Poverty has blighted her;
to call her back to life
love's not enough, love's not enough!

MARCELLO Oh, what a pity! Poor thing!
Poor Mimì! Poor Mimì!

MIMÌ Alas! Alas! It's finished!
Oh, my life . . .! It's finished!
Alas, to die, alas, to die!

Her cough and her violent sobs reveal Mimì's presence.

RODOLFO (*seeing her and running to her*)
> What? Mimì! You here?
> Did you hear me?

MARCELLO   Ella dunque ascoltava?]

RODOLFO   Facile alla paura
per nulla m'arrovello.
Vien là nel tepor!
    (*vuol farla entrare nel Cabaret*)

MIMÌ   No, quel tanfo mi soffoca.

RODOLFO   Ah, Mimì!

Rodolfo stringe amorosamente fra le sue braccia Mimì. Dal cabaret si ode ridere sfacciatamente Musetta. Marcello corre alla finestra del cabaret.

MARCELLO   È Musetta che ride.
Con chi ride? Ah la civetta!
Imparerai.

MIMÌ (*svincolandosi da Rodolfo*)
    Addio.

RODOLFO (*sorpreso, dolorosamente*)
    Che! Vai?

MIMÌ   Donde lieta uscì
al tuo grido d'amore,
torna sola Mimì
al solitario nido.
Ritorna un'altra volta
a intesser finti fior!
Addio, senza rancor.
Ascolta, ascolta.
Le poche robe aduna che lasciai
sparse. Nel mio cassetto
stan chiusi quel cerchietto
d'or, e il libro di preghiere.
Involgi tutto quanto in un grembiale
e manderò il portiere . . .
Bada, sotto il guanciale
c'è la cuffietta rosa.
Se vuoi . . . se vuoi . . .
Se vuoi serbarla a ricordo d'amor . . .
Addio, addio senza rancor!

RODOLFO   Dunque è proprio finita!
Te ne vai, te ne vai, la mia piccina?
Addio sogni d'amor!

MIMÌ   Addio dolce svegliare alla mattina!

RODOLFO   Addio sognante vita . . .

MIMÌ (*sorridendo*)
    Addio rabbuffi e gelosie!

RODOLFO   . . . che un tuo sorriso acqueta.

MIMÌ   Addio sospetti . . .

RODOLFO   Baci . . .

MIMÌ   . . . pungenti amarezze!

RODOLFO   . . . ch'io da vero poeta
rimavo con: carezze!

MIMÌ, RODOLFO
    Soli l'inverno è cosa da morire!

MARCELLO	She was listening, then?
RODOLFO	Easily frightened, I grow angry over nothing. Come in there, in the warmth! (*wants to make her go into the tavern*)
MIMÌ	No, that moldy smell stifles me.
RODOLFO	Ah, Mimì!

Rodolfo lovingly clasps Mimì in his arms. From the tavern Musetta is heard, laughing shamelessly. Marcello runs to the window of the tavern.

MARCELLO	It's Musetta who's laughing. With whom is she laughing? Ah, the flirt! You'll learn.
MIMÌ (*freeing herself from Rodolfo*)	Good-by.
RODOLFO (*surprised, sorrowfully*)	What! You're going?
MIMÌ	To the place she left happily at your call of love Mimì is returning alone, to the lonely nest. She's going back once again to weave false flowers! Good-by, without bitterness. Listen, listen. Gather up the few things that I left scattered. In my drawer are shut that little gold ring, and the prayer book. Wrap everything in an apron and I'll send the concierge . . . Mind you, under the pillow there's the pink bonnet. If you want . . . if you want . . . If you want to keep it in memory of our love . . . Good-by, good-by without bitterness!
RODOLFO	Then it's really finished! You're going away, you're going away, my little one? Good-by, dreams of love!
MIMÌ	Good-by, sweet wakening in the morning!
RODOLFO	Good-by, dreaming life . . .
MIMÌ (*smiling*)	Good-by, rebukes and jealousies!
RODOLFO	. . . that a smile of yours calms.
MIMÌ	Good-by, suspicions . . .
RODOLFO	Kisses . . .
MIMÌ	. . . poignant bitternesses!
RODOLFO	. . . that I, like a true poet, would rhyme with: caresses!
MIMÌ, RODOLFO	Being alone in winter is a thing to die of!

MIMÌ   Soli!

MIMÌ, RODOLFO
              Mentre a primavera c'è compagno il sol!

MIMÌ   C'è compagno il sol!
   Dal cabaret fracasso di piatti e bicchieri rotti: si odono le
voci concitate di Musetta e Marcello.

MARCELLO   Che facevi? Che dicevi . . . ?

MUSETTA   Che vuoi dir?
MARCELLO   . . . presso al fuoco a quel signore?
MUSETTA   Che vuoi dir?
MIMÌ   Niuno è solo l'april . . .
   Musetta esce stizzita; Marcello la segue fermandosi sulla
porta.

MARCELLO   Al mio venire hai mutato di colore.
MUSETTA   [Quel signore mi diceva:
              Ama il ballo signorina?
MARCELLO   Vana, frivola, civetta!
RODOLFO   Si parla coi gigli e le rose . . .
MIMÌ   Esce dai nidi un cinguettio gentile.
MUSETTA   Arrossendo rispondeva:
              ballerei sera e mattina . . .
              ballerei sera e mattina . . .
MARCELLO   Quel discorso asconde mire disoneste . . .
MUSETTA   Voglio piena libertà!
MARCELLO   (*quasi avventandosi contro Musetta*)
              Io t'acconcio per le feste . . .
MUSETTA   Chè mi canti?
MARCELLO   . . . se ti colgo a incivettire!
MIMÌ, RODOLFO
              Al fiorir di primavera c'è compagno il sol!

MUSETTA   Chè mi gridi? Chè mi canti?
              All'altar non siamo uniti.
MARCELLO   Bada, sotto il mio cappello
              non ci stan certi ornamenti . . .]
MUSETTA   Io detesto quegli amanti
              che la fanno da ah! ah! ah! mariti!
MIMÌ, RODOLFO
              [Chiacchieran le fontane.
              La brezza della sera
              balsami stende sulle doglie umane.
MARCELLO   Io non faccio da zimbello
              ai novizi intraprendenti.
MUSETTA   Fo all'amor con chi mi piace!
              Non ti garba?
              Fo all'amor con chi mi piace!
MARCELLO   Vana, frivola, civetta!

MIMÌ   Alone!

MIMÌ, RODOLFO
            Whereas in the spring there is the sun as companion!

MIMÌ   There is the sun as companion!

From the tavern a racket of broken plates and glasses. The excited voices of Musetta and Marcello are heard.

MARCELLO   What were you doing? What were you saying . . . ?

MUSETTA   What do you mean?

MARCELLO   . . . near the fire to that gentleman?

MUSETTA   What do you mean?

MIMÌ   Nobody's alone in April . . .

Musetta comes out angrily. Marcello follows her, stopping in the doorway.

MARCELLO   When I came in you changed color.

MUSSETA   That gentleman said to me:
            Do you like dancing, miss?

MARCELLO   Vain, frivolous, flirt!

RODOLFO   You speak with lilies and roses . . .

MIMÌ   From the nests comes a sweet twittering.

MUSETTA   Blushing, I answered:
            I would dance evening and morning . . .
            I would dance evening and morning . . .

MARCELLO   That talk conceals dishonest intentions . . .

MUSETTA   I want complete freedom!

MARCELLO (*almost hurling himself against Musetta*)
            I'll fix you . . .

MUSETTA   What's this tune of yours?

MARCELLO   . . . if I catch you flirting!

MIMÌ, RODOLFO
            At spring's blossoming there's the sun as companion!

MUSETTA   What are you shouting at me? What's this tune?
            We're not united at the altar.

MARCELLO   Mind you, under my hat
            certain ornaments don't go . . .

MUSETTA   I hate those lovers
            who behave like ha! ha! ha! husbands!

MIMÌ, RODOLFO
            The fountains chatter.
            The evening's breeze
            spreads balms over human sufferings.

MARCELLO   I'm not a laughingstock
            for enterprising novices.

MUSETTA   I'll make love with whom I please!
            Don't you like that?
            I'll make love with whom I please!

MARCELLO   Vain, frivolous, flirt!

Ve n'andate? Vi ringrazio:
or son ricco divenuto.

MUSETTA   Musetta se ne va, sì, se ne va!

MUSETTA, MARCELLO
Vi saluto!

MIMÌ, RODOLFO
Vuoi che aspettiam la primavera ancor?

MUSETTA   Signor, addio vi dico con piacer!

MARCELLO   Son servo e me ne vo!]

MUSETTA   (*si allontana furiosa; ma poi ad un tratto si sofferma
e gli grida ancora velenosa*)
Pittore da bottega!

MARCELLO   Vipera!

MUSETTA   Rospo!

MARCELLO   Strega!

MIMÌ   Sempre tua per la vita!

MIMÌ, RODOLFO
Ci lascieremo alla stagion dei fior!

Si avviano. Marcello rientra nel cabaret.

MIMÌ   Vorrei che eterno durasse l'inverno!

MIMÌ, RODOLFO
Ci lascierem alla stagion dei fior!

QUADRO QUARTO

In soffitta

*Come nel quadro primo. Marcello sta ancora dinanzi al suo
cavalletto, come Rodolfo sta seduto al suo tavolo: vorrebbero
persuadersi l'un l'altro che lavorano indefessamente, mentre
invece non fanno che chiacchierare.*

MARCELLO   (*continuando il discorso*)
In un coupé?

RODOLFO   Con pariglia e livree.
Mi salutò ridendo.
Tò, Musetta! Le dissi:
e il cuor? "Non batte o non lo sento
grazie al velluto che il copre."

MARCELLO   Ci ho gusto davver, ci ho gusto davver!

RODOLFO   (*fra sè*)
(Loiola va. Ti rodi e ridi).

MARCELLO   (*ruminando*)
Non batte? Bene! — Io pur vidi . . .

RODOLFO   Musetta?

MARCELLO   Mimì.

RODOLFO   (*trasalisce*)
L'hai vista?
(*si ricompone*)
Oh guarda!

Are you going away? I thank you:
now I've become rich.

MUSETTA   Musetta's going away, yes, going away!

MUSETTA, MARCELLO
I bid you good-by!

MIMÌ, RODOLFO
Do you want us to wait until spring again?

MUSETTA   Sir, I say good-by to you with pleasure!

MARCELLO   I'm your servant, and I'm going away!

MUSETTA (*goes off furiously, but then, all of a sudden, she
         stops and shouts at him again, venomously*)
Hack painter!

MARCELLO   Viper!

MUSETTA   Toad!

MARCELLO   Witch!

MIMÌ   Always yours . . . for life!

MIMÌ, RODOLFO
We'll leave each other at the season of flowers!

They start off. Marcello goes back into the tavern.

MIMÌ   I would like winter to last eternally!

MIMÌ, RODOLFO
We'll leave each other at the season of flowers!

ACT FOUR

In the Garret

*As in Act One. Marcello is again before his easel, as Rodolfo
is seated at his table. Each would like to convince the other
that he is working unremittingly, whereas instead they do
nothing but chat.*

MARCELLO (*continuing the conversation*)
In a coupé?

RODOLFO   With a pair and livery.
She greeted me, laughing.
Why, Musetta! I said to her:
and your heart? "It isn't beating or I can't hear it
thanks to the velvet that covers it."

MARCELLO   I'm really delighted; I'm really delighted!

RODOLFO (*aside*)
(Hypocrite, go on! You're consumed and you
    laugh).

MARCELLO (*ruminating*)
It's not beating? Good! — I also saw . . .

RODOLFO   Musetta?

MARCELLO   Mimì.

RODOLFO (*starts*)
You saw her?
      (*recovers himself*)
Just think of that!

MARCELLO   Era in carrozza
                  vestita come una regina.
RODOLFO   Evviva. Ne son contento.
MARCELLO (*fra sè*)
                  (Bugiardo, si strugge d'amor).
RODOLFO   Lavoriam.
MARCELLO   Lavoriam.

Si mettono al lavoro.

RODOLFO (*getta la penna*)
                  Che penna infame!
MARCELLO (*getta il pennello*)
                  Che infame pennello!
RODOLFO   (O Mimì, tu più non torni.
                  O giorni belli,
                  piccole mani, odorosi cappelli . . .
                  [collo di neve!
                  Ah, Mimì, mia breve gioventù!
MARCELLO   (Io non so come sia
                  che il mio pennello lavori
                  e impasta colori
                  contro voglia mia.]
                  Se pingere mi piace o cieli o terre
                  o inverni o primavere,
                  egli mi traccia due pupille nere
                  e una bocca procace,
                  e n'esce di Musetta il viso ancor . . .
                  [e n'esce di Musetta il viso
                  tutto vezzi e tutto frode.
                  Musetta intanto gode
                  e il mio cuor vile la chiama,
                  la chiama e aspetta il vil mio cuor).
RODOLFO   (E tu, cuffietta lieve,
                  che sotto il guancial partendo
                  ascose, tutta sai la nostra felicità
                  vien sul mio cuor morto, ah vien!
                  ah vien sul mio cuor; poichè è morto amor.)]
RODOLFO   Che ora sia?
MARCELLO   L'ora del pranzo . . . di ieri.
RODOLFO   E Schaunard non torna?

Entrano Schaunard e Colline.

SCHAUNARD   Eccoci.
                       (*depone quattro pagnotte sulla tavola*)
RODOLFO   Ebben?
MARCELLO (*con sprezzo*)
                  Ebben? Del pan?
COLLINE (*mostrando un'aringa*)
                  È un piatto degno di Demostene:
                  un'aringa . . .
SCHAUNARD   . . . salata!

MARCELLO   She was in a carriage
                  dressed like a queen.

RODOLFO   Hurrah. I'm pleased.

MARCELLO (*aside*)
                  (Liar, he's consumed with love.)

RODOLFO   Let's work.

MARCELLO   Let's work.

They set to work.

RODOLFO (*throws down his pen*)
                  What a terrible pen!

MARCELLO (*throws down his brush*)
                  What a terrible brush!

RODOLFO   (Oh, Mimì, you return no more.
                  Oh, beautiful days,
                  little hands, perfumed hair . . .
                  snowy neck!
                  Ah, Mimì, my brief youth!)

MARCELLO   (I don't know how it is
                  that my brush works
                  and mixes colors
                  against my will.
                  If I want to paint heavens or lands
                  or winters or springs,
                  it draws for me two black eyes
                  and a saucy mouth,
                  and from it comes Musetta's face again . . .
                  and from it comes Musetta's face
                  all charms and all deceit.
                  Musetta meanwhile enjoys herself
                  and my cowardly heart calls her,
                  my cowardly heart calls her and waits for her.)

RODOLFO   (And you, light bonnet,
                  which she hid under the pillow
                  on leaving, you know all our happiness:
                  come upon my dead heart, ah, come!
                  Ah, come upon my heart, since love is dead.)

RODOLFO   What time can it be?

MARCELLO   Time for dinner . . . yesterday's.

RODOLFO   And Schaunard isn't coming back?

Enter Schaunard and Colline.

SCHAUNARD   Here we are.
                  (*sets four loaves on the table*)

RODOLFO   Well?

MARCELLO (*with contempt*)
                  Well? Bread?

COLLINE (*displaying a herring*)
                  It's a dish worthy of Demosthenes:
                  a herring . . .*

SCHAUNARD   . . . salty!

---

* Translator's note: Colline here makes a pun on the Italian words
aringa (herring) and *arringa* (harangue).

COLLINE   Il pranzo è in tavola.

Siedono attorno alla tavola, fingendo d'essere ad un lauto pranzo.

MARCELLO   Questa è cuccagna
               da Berlingaccio.

SCHAUNARD (*pone il cappello di Colline sulla tavola e vi colloca dentro una bottiglia d'acqua*)
               Or lo sciampagna
               mettiamo in ghiaccio.

RODOLFO (*a Marcello*)
               Scelga, o barone,
               trota o salmone?

MARCELLO (*a Schaunard*)
               Duca, una lingua
               di pappagallo?

SCHAUNARD   Grazie, m'impingua.
               Stassera ho un ballo.

Colline ha mangiato e si alza.

RODOLFO (*a Colline*)
               Già sazio?

COLLINE (*solenne*)
               Ho fretta. Il Re m'aspetta.

MARCELLO   C'è qualche trama?

RODOLFO   Qualche mister?

SCHAUNARD   Qualche mister?

MARCELLO   Qualche mister?

COLLINE   Il Re mi chiama al minister.

SCHAUNARD   Bene!

MARCELLO   Bene!

RODOLFO   Bene!

COLLINE (*con importanza*)
               Però . . . vedrò . . . vedrò . . . Guizot!

SCHAUNARD (*a Marcello*)
               Porgimi il nappo!

MARCELLO (*gli dà l'unico bicchiere*)
               Sì! Bevi, io pappo!

SCHAUNARD (*solenne*)
               Mi sia permesso
               al nobile consesso . . .

RODOLFO, COLLINE (*interrompendolo*)
               Basta!

MARCELLO   Fiacco!

COLLINE   Che decotto!

MARCELLO   Leva il tacco!

COLLINE   Dammi il gotto!

SCHAUNARD (*ispirato*)
               M'ispira irresistibile
               l'estro della romanza!

COLLINE   Dinner is on the table.

They sit around the table, pretending to be at a sumptuous dinner.

MARCELLO   This is an abundance
                 worthy of Shrove Tuesday.

SCHAUNARD (*sets Colline's hat on the table and places a bottle
                 of water inside it*)
                 Now let's put
                 the champagne on ice.

RODOLFO (*to Marcello*)
                 Choose, Baron:
                 trout or salmon?

MARCELLO (*to Schaunard*)
                 Duke, a parrot's
                 tongue?

SCHAUNARD   No thanks, it's fattening.
                 I have a ball tonight.

Colline has eaten, and he stands up.

RODOLFO (*to Colline*)
                 Sated already?

COLLINE (*solemn*)
                 I'm in a hurry. The king awaits me.

MARCELLO   Is there some plot?

RODOLFO   Some mystery?

SCHAUNARD   Some mystery?

MARCELLO   Some mystery?

COLLINE   The king is calling me to the ministry.

SCHAUNARD   Good!

MARCELLO   Good!

RODOLFO   Good!

COLLINE (*importantly*)
                 However . . . I'll see . . . I'll see . . . Guizot!

SCHAUNARD (*to Marcello*)
                 Hand me the goblet!

MARCELLO (*gives him the only glass*)
                 Yes! Drink; I'm feeding!

SCHAUNARD (*solemn*)
                 If the noble company
                 will allow me . . .

RODOLFO, COLLINE (*interrupting him*)
                 Enough!

MARCELLO   Weak!

COLLINE   What a concoction!

MARCELLO   Get out!

COLLINE   Give me the mug!

SCHAUNARD (*inspired*)
                 The genius of song
                 is inspiring me irresistibly!

GLI ALTRI (*urlando*)
        No! No! No!

SCHAUNARD (*arrendevole*)
        Azione coreografica allora?

GLI ALTRI (*applaudendo*)
        Sì! sì!

SCHAUNARD   La danza con musica vocale!

COLLINE   Si sgombrino le sale!

    Portano da un lato la tavola e le sedie e si dispongono a ballare.

COLLINE   Gavotta.

MARCELLO   Minuetto.

RODOLFO   Pavanella.

SCHAUNARD   Fandango.

COLLINE   Propongo la quadriglia.

RODOLFO   Mano alle dame!

COLLINE   Io detto.

SCHAUNARD   Lallera, lallera, lallera, là . . .

RODOLFO (*galante a Marcello*)
        Vezzosa damigella . . .

MARCELLO   Rispetti la modestia.
              La prego.

SCHAUNARD   Lallera, ecc.

COLLINE   *Balancez!*

MARCELLO   Lallera, etc.

SCHAUNARD   Prima c'è il *Rond.*

COLLINE   No, bestia!

SCHAUNARD   Che modi da lacchè.

COLLINE   Se non erro lei m'oltraggia!
              Snudi il ferro!
                 (*prende le molle*)

SCHAUNARD (*prende la paletta*)
        Pronti.
            (*tira un colpo*)
        Assaggia.
        Il tuo sangue io voglio ber.

COLLINE (*battendosi*)
        Un dì di noi qui si sbudella.

SCHAUNARD   Apprestate una barella.

COLLINE   Apprestate un cimiter.

    Mentre si battono, Marcello e Rodolfo ballano loro intorno cantando.

RODOLFO, MARCELLO
        Mentre incalza la tenzone
        gira e balza Rigodone . . .

    Si spalanca l'uscio ed entra Musetta in grande agitazione.

MARCELLO (*colpito*)
        Musetta!

    Tutti rimangono attoniti.

THE OTHERS (*shouting*)
                No! No! No!

SCHAUNARD (*docile*)
                Choreographic action then?

THE OTHERS (*applauding*)
                Yes! Yes!

SCHAUNARD   Dance, with vocal music!

COLLINE   Let the halls be cleared!

    They carry the table and the chairs to one side and take their places for dancing.

COLLINE   Gavotte.

MARCELLO   Minuet.

RODOLFO   Pavanella.

SCHAUNARD   Fandango.

COLLINE   I suggest the quadrille.

RODOLFO   Give your hand to the ladies!

COLLINE   I'll call.

SCHAUNARD   Lallera, lallera, lallera, là . . .

RODOLFO (*gallantly, to Marcello*)
                Charming damsel . . .

MARCELLO   Respect my modesty.
             I beg you.

SCHAUNARD   Lallera, etc.

COLLINE   *Balancez!*

MARCELLO   Lallera, etc.

SCHAUNARD   First there's the *rond.*

COLLINE   No, you animal!

SCHAUNARD   What lackey's manners!

COLLINE   If I'm not mistaken, you insult me!
             Draw your sword!
                (*takes the fire tongs*)

SCHAUNARD (*takes the shovel*)
                Ready.
                (*wields a blow*)
                Taste that.
                I want to drink your blood.

COLLINE (*fighting*)
                One of us here will be disemboweled.

SCHAUNARD   Prepare a litter.

COLLINE   Prepare a cemetery.

    As they fight, Marcello and Rodolfo dance around them, singing.

RODOLFO, MARCELLO
                As the combat rages,
                Rigadoon turns and leaps . . .

    The door is flung open and Musetta enters, greatly upset.

MARCELLO (*struck*)
                Musetta!

    All are stunned.

MUSETTA (*ansimante*)
>C'è Mimì ...
>>(*con viva ansietà attorniano Musetta*)
>C'è Mimì che mi segue e che sta male.

RODOLFO (*atterrito*)
>Ov'è?

MUSETTA   Nel far le scale più non si resse.
Si vede, per l'uscio aperto, Mimì seduta sul più alto gradino della scala.

RODOLFO   Ah!
>>(*si precipita verso Mimì, Marcello accorre anche lui*)

SCHAUNARD (*a Colline*)
>Noi accostiamo quel lettuccio.
Rodolfo coll'aiuto di Marcello porta Mimì fino al letto, sul quale la mette distesa.

RODOLFO   Là.
>(*piano, agli amici*)
>Da bere.

Musetta accorre col bicchiere dell'acqua e ne dà un sorso a Mimì.

MIMÌ (*riavutasi e vedendo Rodolfo presso di sè*)
>Rodolfo!

RODOLFO   Zitta — riposa.

MIMÌ   O mio Rodolfo! Mi vuoi qui con te?

RODOLFO (*amorosamente fa cenno a Mimì di tacere, rimanendo ad essa vicino*)
>Ah! mia Mimì, sempre, sempre!

MUSETTA (*a Marcello, Schaunard, e Colline, piano*)
>Intesi dire che Mimì fuggita
>dal Viscontino era in fin di vita.
>Dove stia? Cerca, cerca ...
>la veggo passar per via ...
>trascinandosi a stento.
>Mi dice: "più non reggo ...
>muoio, lo sento.
>Voglio morir con lui!
>Forse m'aspetta ...!

MIMÌ   Mi sento assai meglio ...

MUSETTA   ... M'accompagni, Musetta?"

MIMÌ   Lascia ch'io guardi intorno.
>Ah come si sta bene qui!
>Si rinasce, si rinasce.
>[Ancor sento la vita qui ...
>No, tu non mi lasci più!

RODOLFO   Benedetta bocca,
>tu ancor mi parli!

MUSETTA (*ai tre*)
>Che ci avete in casa?

MARCELLO   Nulla!]

MUSETTA   Non caffè? Non vino?

MUSETTA (*gasping*)
        There's Mimì . . .
                (*with intense anxiety they surround Musetta*)
        There's Mimì, who's following me and who's ill.

RODOLFO (*terrified*)
        Where is she?

MUSETTA   As she climbed the stairs her strength failed.

Through the open door Mimì is seen, seated on the top step.

RODOLFO   Ah!
                (*he rushes toward Mimì; Marcello also rushes out*)

SCHAUNARD (*to Colline*)
        We'll move that cot closer.

Rodolfo, with the help of Marcello, carries Mimì to the bed, on which he extends her.

RODOLFO   There.
        (*softly, to his friends*)
        Something to drink.

Musetta runs over with the glass of water and gives Mimì a sip.

MIMÌ (*recovering herself and seeing Rodolfo near her*)
        Rodolfo!

RODOLFO   Hush — rest.

MIMÌ   Oh, my Rodolfo! You want me here with you?

RODOLFO (*lovingly motions to Mimì to be silent, remaining near her*)
        Ah, my Mimì! Always, always!

MUSETTA (*softly, to Marcello, Schaunard, and Colline*)
        I heard it said that Mimì, having fled
        from the viscount, was dying.
        Where could she be? I searched and searched...
        I see her passing in the street . . .
        barely dragging herself along.
        She says to me: "I can stand no more . . .
        I'm dying, I feel it.
        I want to die with him!
        Perhaps he's waiting for me . . .!

MIMÌ   I feel much better . . .

MUSETTA   . . . Will you accompany me, Musetta?"

MIMÌ   Let me look around.
        Ah, how comfortable one is here!
        One is reborn, reborn.
        I feel life here again . . .
        No, you won't leave me any more!

RODOLFO   Blessed mouth,
        You're speaking to me again!

MUSETTA (*to the three*)
        What do you have in the house?

MARCELLO   Nothing.

MUSETTA   No coffee? No wine?

MARCELLO   Nulla! Ah! miseria!

SCHAUNARD   (*tristemente a Colline, traendolo in disparte*)
             Fra mezz'ora è morta!

MIMÌ   Ho tanto freddo . . .
             Se avessi un manicotto! Queste mie mani
             riscaldare non si potranno mai?
             (*tossisce*)

RODOLFO   (*le prende le mani nelle sue riscaldandogliele*)
             Qui, nelle mie!
             Taci! Il parlar ti stanca.

MIMÌ   Ho un po' di tosse!
             Ci sono avvezza.
             (*vedendo gli amici di Rodolfo, li chiama
             per nome: essi accorrono premurosi presso
             Mimì*)
             Buon giorno, Marcello,
             Schaunard, Colline, buon giorno.
             Tutti qui, tutti qui sorridenti a Mimì.

RODOLFO   Non parlar, non parlar.

MIMÌ   Parlo pian. Non temere.
             Marcello, date retta:
             è assai buona Musetta.

MARCELLO   Lo so, lo so.
             (*porge la mano a Musetta*)

MUSETTA   (*si leva gli orecchini e li porge a Marcello*)
             A te . . . vendi, riporta
             qualche cordial, manda un dottore!

RODOLFO   Riposa.

MIMÌ   Tu non mi lasci?

RODOLFO   No! No!

MUSETTA   (*a Marcello che si precipita*)
             Ascolta!
             Forse è l'ultima volta
             che ha espresso un desiderio, poveretta!
             Pel manicotto io vo. Con te verrò.

MARCELLO   (*commosso*)
             Sei buona, o mia Musetta.

Musetta e Marcello partono frettolosi.

COLLINE   (*mentre Musetta e Marcello parlavano si è levato il
                 pastrano*)
             Vecchia zimarra, senti,
             io resto al pian, tu ascendere
             il sacro monte or devi.
             Le mie grazie ricevi.
             Mai non curvasti il logoro
             dorso ai ricchi ed ai potenti.
             Passâr nelle tue tasche
             come in antri tranquilli
             filosofi e poeti.
             Ora che i giorni lieti
             fuggir, ti dico addio

MARCELLO   Nothing! Ah, poverty!

SCHAUNARD (*sadly to Colline, drawing him to one side*)
                In half an hour she's dead!

MIMÌ   I'm so cold . . .
                If I had a muff! Can these hands of mine
                never be warmed?
                        (*coughs*)

RODOLFO (*takes her hands in his, warming them*)
                Here, in mine!
                Hush! Talking tires you.

MIMÌ   I have a little cough!
                I'm used to it.
                        (*seeing Rodolfo's friends, she calls them
                        by name; concerned, they rush to Mimì's
                        side*)
                Good day, Marcello,
                Schaunard, Colline, good day.
                All here, all here smiling at Mimì.

RODOLFO   Don't speak, don't speak.

MIMÌ   I'm speaking softly. Don't fear.
                Marcello, pay attention:
                Musetta is very good.

MARCELLO   I know, I know.
                        (*holds out his hand to Musetta*)

MUSETTA (*removes her earrings and hands them to Marcello*)
                Here . . . sell them, bring back
                some cordial, send a doctor!

RODOLFO   Rest.

MIMÌ   You aren't leaving me?

RODOLFO   No! No!

MUSETTA (*to Marcello, who is hurrying off*)
                Listen!
                Perhaps this is the last time
                that she's expressed a wish, poor thing!
                I'm going for the muff. I'll come with you.

MARCELLO (*moved*)
                You're good, Oh, my Musetta.

  Musetta and Marcello leave hurriedly.

COLLINE (*has removed his overcoat while Musetta and Mar-
                cello were talking*)
                Old coat, listen,
                I'm remaining on the plain, you now
                must climb the sacred mountain.*
                Receive my thanks.
                You never bowed your worn
                back to the rich and the mighty.
                In your pockets,
                as in tranquil grottoes,
                passed philosophers and poets.
                Now that the happy days
                have fled, I bid you good-by,

* Translator's note: a reference to the Monte di Pietà, or state-
run Italian pawn shop.

fedele amico mio.
Addio, addio.
> (*fattone un involto, se lo pone sotto il*
> *braccio, ma vedendo Schaunard, gli dice*
> *sottovoce*)

Schaunard, ognuno per diversa via
mettiamo insieme due atti di pietà;
io . . . questo!
> (*gli mostra la zimarra che tiene sotto il*
> *braccio*)

E tu . . .
> (*accennandogli Rodolfo chino su Mimì ad-*
> *dormentata*)

lasciali soli là!

SCHAUNARD (*commosso*)
Filosofo, ragioni!
È ver . . . ! Vo via!

Si guarda intorno, e per giustificare la sua partenza prende
la bottiglia dell'acqua e scende dietro Colline chiudendo con
precauzione l'uscio.

MIMÌ   Sono andati? Fingevo di dormire
perchè volli con te sola restare.
Ho tante cose che ti voglio dire
o una sola, ma grande come il mare,
come il mare profonda ed infinita . . .
Sei il mio amor e tutta la mia vita,
sei il mio amore e tutta la mia vita.

RODOLFO   Ah Mimì, mia bella Mimì!

MIMÌ   Son bella ancora?

RODOLFO   Bella come un'aurora . . .

MIMÌ   Hai sbagliato il raffronto.
Volevi dir: bella come un tramonto.
"Mi chiamano Mimì, mi chiamano Mimì . . .
il perchè non so."

RODOLFO (*intenerito e carezzevole*)
Tornò al nido la rondine e cinguetta.

Si leva di dove l'aveva riposta, in sul cuore, la cuffietta di
Mimì e gliela porge.

MIMÌ (*raggiante*)
La mia cuffietta, la mia cuffietta . . .
> (*tende a Rodolfo la testa, questi le mette*
> *la cuffietta. Mimì rimane colla testa appog-*
> *giata sul petto di lui*)

Ah . . . ! Te lo rammenti quando sono entrata
la prima volta, là?

RODOLFO   Se lo rammento!

MIMÌ   Il lume s'era spento . . .

RODOLFO   Eri tanto turbata!
Poi smarristi la chiave . . .

MIMÌ   E a cercarla tastoni ti sei messo!

RODOLFO   E cerca . . . cerca . . .

my faithful friend.
Good-by, good-by.
> (*making a bundle of it, he places it under
> his arm, but seeing Schaunard, he says to
> him in a whisper*)

Schaunard, let us, each in a different way,
combine two acts of mercy;
I . . . this!
> (*shows him the coat that he holds under
> his arm*)

And you . . .
> (*nodding to Rodolfo, bent over the sleep-
> ing Mimì*)

leave them alone there!

SCHAUNARD (*moved*)
Philosopher, you're reasoning!
It's true . . .! I'm going away!

*He looks around and, to justify his leaving, he takes the
water bottle and goes down after Colline, carefully shutting
the door.*

MIMÌ
Have they gone? I was pretending to sleep
because I wanted to remain alone with you.
I have so many things I want to tell you,
or one alone, but big as the sea,
like the sea, profound and infinite . . .
You're my love and all my life,
You're my love and all my life.

RODOLFO   Ah, Mimì, my beautiful Mimì!

MIMÌ   Am I beautiful still?

RODOLFO   Beautiful as a dawn . . .

MIMÌ
You've mistaken the comparison.
You meant: beautiful as a sunset.
"They call me Mimì, they call me Mimì . . .
I don't know the reason."

RODOLFO (*tender and caressing*)
The swallow returned to the nest and is twittering.

*He takes Mimì's bonnet from where he had placed it, over
his heart, and hands it to her.*

MIMÌ (*radiant*)
My bonnet, my bonnet . . .
> (*holds her head toward Rodolfo, who puts
> the bonnet on it. Mimì remains with her
> head leaning against his chest*)

Ah . . .! You remember when I came in
the first time, there?

RODOLFO   Do I remember!?

MIMÌ   The light had gone out . . .

RODOLFO
You were so upset!
Then you lost the key . . .

MIMÌ   And you started looking for it, groping!

RODOLFO   And I looked . . . and looked . . .

MIMÌ   Mio bel signorino,
posso ben dirlo adesso,
lei la trovò assai presto.

RODOLFO   Aiutavo il destino.

MIMÌ (*ricordando l'incontro suo con Rodolfo la sera della vigilia di Natale*)
Era buio, e il mio rossor non si vedeva . . .
    (*sussurra le parole di Rodolfo*)
"Che gelida manina . . . Se la lasci riscaldar!"
Era buio, e la man tu mi prendevi . . .

Mimì è presa da uno spasimo di soffocazione; lascia ricadere il capo, sfinita.

RODOLFO (*spaventato*)
Oh! Dio! Mimì!

In questo momento Schaunard ritorna: al grido di Rodolfo accorre presso Mimì.

SCHAUNARD   Che avvien?

MIMÌ (*apre gli occhi e sorride per rassicurare Rodolfo e Schaunard*)
Nulla. Sto bene.

RODOLFO   Zitta, per carità.

MIMÌ   Sì, sì, perdona.
Or sarò buona.

Entrano Musetta e Marcello. Musetta porta un manicotto e Marcello una boccetta.

MUSETTA (*a Rodolfo*)
Dorme?

RODOLFO   Riposa.

MARCELLO   Ho veduto il dottore!
Verrà; gli ho fatto fretta.
Ecco il cordial.

Prende una lampada a spirito, la pone sulla tavola e l'accende.

MIMÌ   Chi parla?

MUSETTA (*si avvicina a Mimì e le porge il manicotto*)
Io, Musetta.

MIMÌ   Oh, come è bello e morbido.
Non più, non più le mani allividite.
Il tepore le abbellirà.
    (*a Rodolfo*)
Sei tu che me lo doni?

MUSETTA (*pronta*)
Sì.

MIMÌ   Tu! Spensierato!
Grazie. Ma costerà. Piangi? Sto bene . . .

Pianger così perchè?
    (*assopendosi a poco a paco*)
Qui amor . . . sempre con te . . . !
Le mani . . . al caldo . . . e . . . dormire . . .
    (*silenzio*)

RODOLFO (*a Marcello*)
Che ha detto il medico?

MIMÌ   My fine young gentleman,
              I can readily say it now:
              You found it very quickly.

RODOLFO   I was helping fate.

MIMÌ *(remembering her meeting with Rodolfo on the evening of Christmas Eve)*
              It was dark, and my blushing wasn't seen . . .
              (murmurs Rodolfo's words)
              "What an icy little hand . . . Let it be warmed!"
              It was dark, and you took my hand . . .

Mimì is seized with a choking fit; she lets her head fall back, exhausted.

RODOLFO *(frightened)*
              Oh, God! Mimì!

At this moment Schaunard returns. At Rodolfo's cry he runs over to Mimì.

SCHAUNARD   What's happening?

MIMÌ *(opens her eyes and smiles to reassure Rodolfo and Schaunard)*
              Nothing. I'm well.

RODOLFO   Hush, please.

MIMÌ   Yes, yes, forgive me.
              Now I'll be good.

Musetta and Marcello come in. Musetta is carrying a muff and Marcello, a phial.

MUSETTA *(to Rodolfo)*
              Is she sleeping?

RODOLFO   She's resting.

MARCELLO   I've seen the doctor!
              He'll come; I hurried him.
              Here's the cordial.

He takes a spirit lamp, sets it on the table, and lights it.

MIMÌ   Who's speaking?

MUSETTA *(approaches Mimì and hands her the muff)*
              I, Musetta.

MIMÌ   Oh, how beautiful and soft it is.
              No more, no more, pale hands.
              The warmth will beautify them.
              (to Rodolfo)
              Is it you who gives it to me?

MUSETTA *(prompt)*
              Yes.

MIMÌ   You! Carefree man!
              Thanks. But it must cost. You're crying? I'm well . . .
              Why cry like this?
              (dozing off little by little)
              Here, love . . . always with you . . .!
              My hands . . . in the warmth . . . and . . . to sleep . . .
              (silence)

RODOLFO *(to Marcello)*
              What did the doctor say?

MARCELLO   Verrà.

MUSETTA *(fa scaldare la boccetta alla lampada a spirito, e*
            quasi inconsciamente mormora una preghiera)
            Madonna benedetta,
            fate la grazia a questa poveretta
            che non debba morire.
                (interrompendosi, a Marcello)
            Qui ci vuole un riparo
            perchè la fiamma sventola.
                (Marcello mette un libro ritto sulla tavola
                formando paravento alla lampada)
            Così.
                (ripiglia la preghiera)
            Madonna santa, io sono
            indegna di perdono,
            mentre invece Mimì
            è un angelo del cielo.

Mentre Musetta prega, Rodolfo le si è avvicinato.

RODOLFO   Io spero ancora. Vi pare che sia grave?

MUSETTA   Non credo.

Schaunard si è avvicinato al lettuccio, poi è corso senza
farsi scorgere fino a Marcello.

SCHAUNARD *(piano, a Marcello)*
            Marcello, è spirata . . .

Intanto Rodolfo si è avveduto che il sole della finestra della
soffitta sta per battere sul volto a Mimì e cerca intorno come
porvi riparo; Musetta se ne avvede e gli indica la sua mantig-
lia. Rodolfo la ringrazia con uno sguardo, prende la mantig-
lia, sale su di una sedia e studia il modo di distenderla sulla
finestra. Marcello si avvicina a sua volta al letto e se ne scosta
atterrito; intanto entra Colline che depone del danaro sulla
tavola presso a Musetta.

COLLINE *(a Musetta)*
            Musetta . . . a voi!
                (poi visto Rodolfo che solo non riesce a
                collocare la mantiglia attraverso alla fi-
                nestra, corre ad aiutarlo chiedendogli di
                Mimì)
            Come va?

RODOLFO   Vedi? È tranquilla.

Si volge verso Mimì: in quel mentre Musetta gli fa cenno
che la medicina è pronta. Rodolfo nell'accorrere presso Musetta
si accorge dello strano contegno di Marcello e Schaunard che,
pieni di sgomento, lo guardano con profonda pietà.

RODOLFO   Che vuol dire quell'andare e venire . . .
              quel guardarmi così . . . ?

Marcello non regge più, corre a Rodolfo e abbracciandolo
stretto a sè con voce strozzata gli mormora:

MARCELLO   Coraggio!

RODOLFO *(accorre al lettuccio)*
            Mimì . . . ! Mimì . . . ! Mimì . . . !

MARCELLO   He'll come.

MUSETTA   (*warms the phial at the spirit lamp and, almost un-
                consciously, murmurs a prayer*)
           Blessed Mother,
           be merciful to this poor girl
           who mustn't die.
                (*breaking off, to Marcello*)
           We need a screen here
           because the flame is flickering.
                (*Marcello sets a book upright on the table
                forming a screen for the lamp*)
           Like that.
                (*resumes the prayer*)
           Holy Mother, I'm not worthy
           of forgiveness,
           but Mimì instead
           is an angel from heaven.

As Musetta prays, Rodolfo has come over to her.

RODOLFO   I still hope. Does it seem serious to you?

MUSETTA   I don't believe so.

*Schaunard has gone over to the couch, then without attract-
ing attention, he has run to Marcello.*

SCHAUNARD   (*softly, to Marcello*)
            Marcello, she's dead . . .

*Meanwhile Rodolfo has noticed that the sun from the gar-
ret window is about to strike Mimì's face, and he looks around
for some way to prevent this. Musetta notices and points to
her shawl. Rodolfo thanks her with a look, takes the shawl,
climbs on a chair, and looks for a way to spread the shawl
over the window. Marcello, in turn, goes to the bed and moves
away from it again, frightened. Meanwhile Colline comes in
and places some money on the table near Musetta.*

COLLINE   (*to Musetta*)
          Musetta . . . take this!
                (*then seeing that Rodolfo by himself isn't
                able to arrange the shawl over the window,
                he runs to help him, asking him about
                Mimì*)
          How is she?

RODOLFO   You see? She's calm.

*He turns towards Mimì. At that moment Musetta signals to
him that the medicine is ready. As Rodolfo rushes over to Musetta he notices the strange attitude of Marcello and Schaunard,
who, filled with dismay, look at him with profound pity.*

RODOLFO   What does that going and coming mean . . .
          that looking at me like this . . .?

*Marcello can't restrain himself any more, runs to Rodolfo
and, embracing him hard, murmurs in a choked voice:*

MARCELLO   Courage!

RODOLFO   (*runs to the cot*)
          Mimì . . .! Mimì . . .! Mimì . . .!

Tosca

Puccini first conceived the idea of an opera based on *Tosca* in 1889, at the time of his *Edgar*. The Victorien Sardou play was then less than two years old but already an established success (its first interpreter was Sarah Bernhardt). Then *Manon Lescaut* and *La Bohème* intervened, and it was only in 1896 that Puccini's thoughts returned to this subject. As Puccini's biographer Mosco Carner acutely argues, there were probably three reasons for this revival of interest. First, the new wave of *verismo* opera which was proving popular; second, the fact that another composer, Alberto Franchetti, had the rights to the play and was planning to set it; and finally, the enthusiasm of Verdi for the story. Through a somewhat unscrupulous move, the wily Ricordi persuaded Franchetti to abandon his plan, and the rights passed to Puccini.

Again the Giacosa-Illica-Ricordi-Puccini quartet went to work. This time the job was a bit easier; the extremely well-made play required only some pruning. But things went slowly all the same. Giacosa, who had toured the United States with Bernhardt some years before (where she had performed a play of his), disliked the play intensely. "It is a drama of big actions without poetry," he wrote Ricordi at one point; and Giacosa's task — in the division of labor between the two librettists — was precisely that of turning Illica's prose outline into verse.

Finally the libretto, after many revisions and storms, was completed, and on September 29, 1899, Puccini completed the score. At this point, however, an unexpected obstacle arose. Ricordi — who was, incidentally, a more than amateur composer himself — disapproved of the last act, and in a long letter to Puccini, he went into his objections. With unusual calm, Puccini answered in a long, closely reasoned letter, sticking to his guns. The last act remained unchanged.

For the first performance, the publisher chose the Teatro Costanzi in Rome, since the subject of the opera was Roman. The choice was not an entirely happy one, in view of the strong antagonism which existed — and still exists—between the opera-going audience of the Italian capital and that of La Scala. It was also a period of grave unrest in the country, and on the night of the premiere there were rumors that a bomb was to be planted in the theater (the queen was to be present at the performance). No bomb went off, but there was considerable unrest among the audience and an understandable nervousness on stage.

Again the critics were divided, and of all Puccini's most popular operas, *Tosca* is still the one that arouses most dissension. Some years ago, Joseph Kerman, in his *Opera as Drama,*° singled the work out for special strictures. But, at about the same time, the stirring performances of Maria Callas in the title role demonstrated the work's power when interpreted by a great artist. In any case, even *Tosca's* bitterest opponents cannot deny its popularity.

° (see bibliography)

The libretto of *Tosca* requires a postscript concerning the story's historical background. Sardou based his play on real people and real events, but in cutting his five acts down to libretto dimensions, Giacosa and Illica were forced to eliminate a good deal of exposition. As a result some of the events are obscure (chiefly the "victory" that so excites Mario in Act Two). Audiences have enjoyed the opera for more than half a century without knowing this background, but for the interested reader there is an excellent explanation of it in George R. Marek's *Opera as Theater.*°

THE PLOT

ACT ONE

The interior of the Church of Sant'Andrea della Valle. A political prisoner, Angelotti, enters furtively, having just escaped from the Castel Sant'Angelo through the help of his sister, the Marchesa Attavanti, who has left him some clothes in the church and the key to the Attavanti Chapel, where he can hide and disguise himself. When Angelotti is hidden, the painter Mario Cavaradossi comes in to resume work on a Magdalen. The comic sacristan points out a resemblance between the Magdalen in the painting and a strange lady who has been coming often to the church recently (this is the Marchesa). Cavaradossi ponders the curious harmony of this stranger's beauty with that of his beloved Tosca. Then Angelotti reappears and recognizes Mario, an old friend and political ally. Cavaradossi promises to help, but their talk is interrupted by the arrival of Tosca. Angelotti hides, and Mario has to deal with Tosca's jealous suspicions. Finally they are allayed and the lovers agree to meet again that evening. Once Tosca has left, Angelotti comes out of the chapel again, and — since time is pressing — Mario takes the fugitive away, to conceal him at his villa outside the city.

The sacristan comes in to announce Napoleon's defeat, but Mario has gone. There is a sudden eruption of choristers and acolytes, excitedly preparing the *Te Deum* that is to celebrate the victory of the royalists, but the arrival of Scarpia silences them. Angelotti has been traced to the church. Mario's empty lunch basket is found in the Attavanti Chapel. This discovery throws suspicion on the painter. When Tosca comes back and is disturbed not to find Mario, Scarpia cleverly uses the Marchesa Attavanti's fan — also discovered in the church — to play on the singer's jealousy and to trap her into a false move. In fact, she rushes out to go to the villa, and Scarpia sends his henchman, Spoletta, after her. During the *Te Deum,* Scarpia expresses his desire to have Mario executed and, at the same time, to possess the beautiful Tosca.

° (see bibliography)

ACT TWO

Scarpia's apartments in the Palazzo Farnese. In another part of the building the Queen of Naples is holding her celebration. Spoletta arrives with the news that Angelotti could not be found in Cavaradossi's villa. The painter himself is brought in to be questioned, but he refuses to say anything. Tosca — summoned by a note from Scarpia — also arrives, and Mario, in a whisper, exhorts her to reveal nothing (having been to the villa, she now knows all). Scarpia has Cavaradossi tortured, and though the painter still keeps silent, Tosca, horrified at his sufferings, discloses Angelotti's hiding place. Cavaradossi reproaches her bitterly, but his anger turns to joy when Sciarrone — another of Scarpia's creatures — rushes in with the news that the Battle of Marengo has really been won by Napoleon, not by the royalists, as first reported. Cavaradossi's gloating and taunting infuriate Scarpia, who has him taken off to Castel Sant'Angelo, to be executed at dawn. Tosca pleads for mercy in vain, and Spoletta returns to say that Angelotti, rather than submit to capture, killed himself. Once he is alone with Tosca, Scarpia offers her a revolting bargain: her love in exchange for Mario's life. She is forced to agree, on condition that she and Mario be allowed to flee the country immediately afterward. Scarpia then explains that there will be a mock execution. As he is writing out the safe-conduct for Tosca and Mario, Tosca spies a sharp knife on the table. She conceals it behind her back, and when Scarpia comes to claim his part of the bargain, she plunges the knife into his back, killing him.

ACT THREE

A parapet on top of the Castel Sant'Angelo, just before dawn. A shepherd is heard singing. Mario is brought in and left alone, to think of Tosca and his life, which must now end. But Tosca arrives, gives him the good news of his planned escape, and confesses that she has murdered Scarpia for his sake. They sing of their love and their future. The execution takes place. Tosca calls Mario to rise, then discovers to her horror that Scarpia has cheated her. The firing squad's bullets were real, and Mario is dead. Spoletta, who has found Scarpia's body, now comes rushing up with some soldiers to arrest Tosca. She kills herself by jumping off the ramparts of the fortress.

TOSCA

libretto by Giuseppe Giacosa and Luigi Illica

First performed at the Teatro Costanzi, Rome
January 14, 1900

CHARACTERS

Floria Tosca, a famous singer	*Soprano*
Mario Cavaradossi, a painter	*Tenor*
Baron Scarpia, Chief of Police	*Baritone*
Cesare Angelotti, a political prisoner	*Bass*
The Sacristan	*Baritone*
Spoletta, a police agent	*Tenor*
Sciarrone, a gendarme	*Bass*
A Jailer	*Bass*
A Shepherd	*Boy soprano*

A Cardinal, a Judge, Roberti the Executioner, A Scribe,
An Officer, Soldiers, Police, Ladies, Nobles,
Bourgeois, Populace, etc.

The time is June 1800.
The place is Rome.

ATTO PRIMO

La chiesa di Sant'Andrea della Valle. A destra la Cappella Attavanti. A sinistra un impalcato: su di esso un gran quadro coperto da tela. Attrezzi vari da pittore. Un paniere.

ANGELOTTI *(vestito da prigioniero, lacero, sfatto, tremante dalla paura, entra ansante, quasi correndo, dalla porta laterale. Dà una rapida occhiata intorno)*
Ah . . . ! Finalmente . . . ! Nel terror mio stolto
vedea ceffi di birro in ogni volto.
(torna a guardare attentamente intorno a sè con più calma a riconoscere il luogo. Dà un sospiro di sollievo vedendo la colonna colla pila dell'acqua santa e la Madonna)

La pila . . . la colonna . . .
"A piè della Madonna"
mi scrisse mia sorella . . .
(vi si avvicina, cerca ai piedi della Madonna e ne ritira, con un soffocato grido di gioia, una chiave)
Ecco la chiave . . . ed ecco la cappella!
Addita la Cappella Attavanti; con gran precauzione introduce la chiave nella serratura, apre la cancellata, penetra nella Cappella, rinchiude, e scompare.

IL SAGRESTANO *(entra dal fondo tenendo fra le mani un mazzo di pennelli e parlando ad alta voce come se rivolgesse la parola a qualcuno)*
E sempre lava . . . ! Ogni pennello è sozzo
peggio che il collarin d'uno scagnozzo.
Signor pittore . . . Tò . . . !
(guarda verso l'impalcato dove sta il quadro, e vedendolo deserto, esclama sorpreso)

Nessuno. Avrei giurato
che fosse ritornato
il cavalier Cavaradossi.
(depone i pennelli, sale sull'impalcato, guarda dentro il paniere, e dice)

No, sbaglio. Il paniere è intatto.
(scende dall'impalcato. Suona l'Angelus. Il sagrestano si inginocchia e prega sommesso)
"Angelus Domini nuntiavit Mariae,
et concepit de Spiritu Sancto.
Ecce ancilla Domini;

ACT ONE

*The church of Sant'Andrea della Valle. At right, the Atta-
vanti Chapel. At left, a scaffolding: on it a large painting
covered by a cloth. Various items of painter's equipment. A
basket.*

ANGELOTTI (*dressed as a prisoner, tattered, exhausted, trembling with fear, enters gasping, almost run-
ning, from the side door. He casts a rapid
glance around*)
Ah . . . ! At last . . . ! In my foolish terror
I saw in every face the ugly mug of a cop.
(*he again looks carefully around himself,
with greater calm, to recognize the place.
He heaves a sigh of relief, seeing the column with the holy-water stoup and the
Madonna*)
The stoup . . . the column . . .
"At the foot of the Madonna,"
my sister wrote me . . .
(*he approaches it, searches at the feet of
the Madonna and, with a stifled cry of
joy, withdraws a key*)
Here's the key . . . and here's the chapel!
*He points to the Attavanti Chapel; with great precaution
he puts the key into the lock, opens the gate, goes into the
chapel, shuts the gate again, and vanishes.*

THE SACRISTAN (*enters from the back, holding in his hands a
bunch of brushes and talking in a loud voice
as if he were addressing someone*)
And always wash . . . ! Every brush is dirty,
worse than a poor priest's collar.
Master painter . . . Here . . . !
(*looks toward the scaffolding where the
picture stands and, seeing it deserted, exclaims, surprised:*)
Nobody. I would have sworn
that Cavaliere Cavaradossi
had returned.
(*sets down the brushes, climbs on to the
scaffolding, looks inside the basket, and
says*)
No, I'm mistaken. The basket is untouched.
(*climbs down from the scaffolding. The
Angelus tolls. The sacristan kneels and
prays softly*)
"Angelus Domini nuntiavit Mariae,
et concepit de Spiritu Sancto.
Ecce ancilla Domini;

Fiat mihi secundum verbum tuum.
Et Verbum caro factum est
et habitavit in nobis . . ."

CAVARADOSSI (*dalla porta laterale, vedendo il Sagrestano in*
ginocchio)
Che fai?

IL SAGRESTANO (*alzandosi*)
Recito l'Angelus.

Cavaradossi sale sull'impalcato e scopre il quadro. È una
Maria Maddalena a grandi occhi azzurri con una gran pioggia
di capelli dorati. Il pittore vi sta dinanzi muto attentamente
osservando. Il Sagrestano, volgendosi verso Cavaradossi per
dirigergli la parola, vede il quadro scoperto e dà in un grido di
meraviglia.

IL SAGRESTANO
Sante ampolle! Il suo ritratto!

CAVARADOSSI Di chi?

IL SAGRESTANO
Di quell'ignota
che i dì passati a pregar qui venìa
tutta devota e pia.
(*e accenna verso la Madonna dalla quale*
Angelotti trasse la chiave)

CAVARADOSSI (*sorridendo*)
È vero. E tanto ell'era
infervorata nella sua preghiera
ch'io ne pinsi, non visto,
il bel sembiante.

IL SAGRESTANO (*scandalizzato*)
(Fuori, Satana, fuori!)

CAVARADOSSI Dammi i colori.

Il Sagrestano eseguisce. Cavaradossi dipinge con rapidità e
si sofferma spesso a riguardare: il Sagrestano va e viene, por-
tando una catinella entro la quale continua a lavare i pennelli.
A un tratto Cavaradossi si ristà di dipingere; leva di tasca un
medaglione contenente una miniatura e gli occhi suoi vanno
dal medaglione al quadro.

Recondita armonia
di bellezze diverse . . . ! È bruna Floria,
l'ardente amante mia . . .

IL SAGRESTANO (*brontolando*)
(Scherza coi fanti
e lascia stare i santi . . .)
(*s'allontana per prendere l'acqua onde*
pulire i pennelli)

CAVARADOSSI . . . e te, beltade ignota,
cinta di chiome bionde . . . !
Tu azzurro hai l'occhio,
Tosca ha l'occhio nero!

IL SAGRESTANO (*ritornando dal fondo e sempre scandolezzato*)
Scherza coi fanti
e lascia stare i santi!
(*riprende a lavare i pennelli*)

> *Fiat mihi secundum verbum tuum.*
> *Et Verbum caro factum est*
> *et habitavit in nobis . . ."*

CAVARADOSSI (*from the side door, seeing the sacristan on his knees*)

> What are you doing?

THE SACRISTAN (*standing up*)

> I'm reciting the Angelus.

Cavaradossi climbs onto the scaffolding and uncovers the picture. It is a Mary Magdalen with great blue eyes and a great shower of golden hair. The painter stands before it, mute, observing it carefully. The sacristan, turning toward Cavaradossi to speak to him, sees the uncovered picture, and emits a cry of wonder.

THE SACRISTAN

> Holy cruets! Her portrait!

CAVARADOSSI   Whose?

THE SACRISTAN

> That unknown lady's
> who in these past days came here,
> all devout and pious.
>> (*and he nods towards the Madonna from which Angelotti extracted the key*)

CAVARADOSSI (*smiling*)

> It's true. And she was so
> filled with fervor in her prayer
> that I painted, unseen,
> her lovely face.

THE SACRISTAN (*shocked*)

> (Out, Satan, out!)

CAVARADOSSI   Give me the colors.

The sacristan obeys. Cavaradossi paints rapidly, and pauses often to look: the sacristan comes and goes, bringing a basin in which he continues to wash the brushes. All of a sudden Cavaradossi stops painting: from his pocket he takes a medallion containing a miniature, and his eyes move from the medallion to the picture.

> Obscure harmony
> of different beauties . . . ! Floria,
> my ardent mistress, is dark . . .

THE SACRISTAN (*grumbling*)

> (Joke with soldiers
> and leave saints alone . . .)
>> (*goes off to fetch water with which to clean the brushes*)

CAVARADOSSI   . . . and you, unknown beauty,

> girt with blond tresses!
> You have blue eyes,
> Tosca has black eyes!

THE SACRISTAN (*returning from the back and still shocked*)

> Joke with soldiers
> and leave saints alone!
>> (*resumes washing the brushes*)

CAVARADOSSI L'arte nel suo mistero
le diverse bellezze insiem confonde:
ma nel ritrar costei . . .
il mio solo pensiero,
ah! il mio sol pensier sei tu!
Tosca sei tu!
(*continua a dipingere*)

IL SAGRESTANO
Queste diverse gonne
che fanno concorrenza alle Madonne
mandan tanfo d'inferno.
(*asciuga i pennelli lavati, non senza continuare a borbottare*)
Scherza coi fanti
e lascia stare i santi.
Ma con quei cani di Volteriani
nemici del santissimo governo
non c'è da metter voce . . . !
(*pone la catinella sotto l'impalcato ed i pennelli li colloca in un vaso, presso al pittore*)
Scherza coi fanti
e lascia stare i santi.
Già sono impenitenti tutti quanti!
Facciam piuttosto il segno della croce.
(*a Cavaradossi*)
Eccellenza, vado.

CAVARADOSSI Fa il tuo piacere . . . !
(*continua a dipingere*)

IL SAGRESTANO (*indicando il cesto*)
Pieno è il paniere . . .
Fa penitenza?

CAVARADOSSI Fame non ho.

IL SAGRESTANO (*ironico, stroppicciandosi le mani*)
Oh . . . ! mi rincresce . . . !
(*ma non può trattenere un gesto di gioia e una sguardo d'avidità verso il cesto, che prende ponendolo un po' in disparte. Fiuta due prese di tabacco*)
Badi, quand'esce chiuda.

CAVARADOSSI Va!

IL SAGRESTANO
Vo.

Il Sagrestano s'allontana per il fondo. Cavaradossi, volgendo le spalle alla Cappella, lavora. Angelotti, credendo deserta la chiesa, appare dietro la cancellata e introduce la chiave per aprire.

CAVARADOSSI (*al cigolìo della serratura si volta*)
Gente là dentro!
(*al movimento fatto da Cavaradossi, Angelotti, atterrito, si arresta come per rifugiarsi ancora nella Cappella, ma, alzati gli occhi, un grido di gioia, che egli soffoca*

CAVARADOSSI   Art, in its mystery,
mingles the different beauties together:
but in portraying this woman . . .
my only thought
ah! my only thought is you!
Tosca, it's you!
    (*continues painting*)

THE SACRISTAN
These different skirts
that compete with the Madonnas
emit a stench of hell.
    (*dries the washed brushes, not without
    continuing to grumble*)
Joke with soldiers
and leave saints alone.
But with those dogs of Voltaireans
enemies of the most holy government
you can't raise your voice . . . !
    (*sets the basin below the scaffolding and
    places the brushes in a pot, near the paint-
    er*)
Joke with soldiers
and leave saints alone.
They're impenitent, one and all!
Rather, let us make the sign of the cross.
    (*to Cavaradossi*)
Your Excellency, I'm going.

CAVARADOSSI   Do as you please . . . !
    (*continues painting*)

THE SACRISTAN (*pointing to the basket*)
The basket's full . . .
Are you doing penance?

CAVARADOSSI   I'm not hungry.

THE SACRISTAN (*ironic, rubbing his hands*)
Oh . . . ! I'm sorry . . . !
    (*but he can't restrain a gesture of joy and
    a look of greed towards the basket, which
    he takes and sets a bit to one side. He
    sniffs two pinches of tobacco*)
Mind: when you go out, lock up.

CAVARADOSSI   Go!

THE SACRISTAN
I'm going.

*The sacristan goes off in the background. Cavaradossi,
turning his back to the chapel, works. Angelotti, believing the
church deserted, appears beyond the gate and inserts the key
to open it.*

CAVARADOSSI (*at the creak of the lock turns around*)
Someone in there!
    (*at the movement made by Cavaradossi,
    Angelotti, terrified, stops, as if to take
    refuge in the chapel again, but, as he
    raises his eyes, a cry of joy, which he im-*

> *tosto timoroso, erompe dal suo petto. Egli*
> *ha riconosciuto il pittore e gli stende le*
> *braccia come ad un aiuto insperato)*

ANGELOTTI   Voi! Cavaradossi!
Vi manda Iddio!
(Cavaradossi non riconosce Angelotti e
rimane attonito sull'impalcato. Angelotti
si avvicina di più onde farsi conoscere)
Non mi ravvisate!
Il carcere m'ha dunque assai mutato!

CAVARADOSSI   *(riconoscendolo, depone rapido tavolozza e pen-*
nelli e scende dall'impalcato verso Angelotti,
guardandosi cauto intorno)
Angelotti! Il Console
della spenta repubblica romana.
(corre a chiudere la porta laterale)

ANGELOTTI   Fuggii pur ora da Castel Sant'Angelo . . .
CAVARADOSSI   Disponete di me.
TOSCA *(di fuori)*
Mario!

CAVARADOSSI   *(alla voce di Tosca, fa un rapido cenno ad An-*
gelotti di tacere)
Celatevi!
È una donna . . . gelosa.
Un breve istante e la rimando.

TOSCA *(di fuori)*
Mario!

CAVARADOSSI   *(verso la porticina da dove viene la voce di Tosca)*
Eccomi!

ANGELOTTI   *(colto da un accesso di debolezza, si appoggia al-*
l'impalcato)
Sono stremo di forze,
più non reggo . . .

CAVARADOSSI   *(rapidissimo, sale sull'impalcato, ne discende col*
paniere e incoraggiando Angelotti, lo spinge
verso la Cappella)
In questo panier v'è cibo e vino.

ANGELOTTI   Grazie!
CAVARADOSSI   Presto!
ANGELOTTI   Grazie!
CAVARADOSSI   Presto!
   Angelotti entra nella Cappella.
TOSCA *(di fuori, stizzita)*
Mario! Mario! Mario!
CAVARADOSSI   *(fingendosi calmo apre a Tosca)*
Son qui!

   Tosca entra con una specie di violenza, guardando intorno
sospettosa. Mario si appressa a Tosca per abbracciarla. Tosca
lo respinge bruscamente.

> *mediately stifles fearfully, bursts from his breast. He has recognized the painter and holds out his arms to him, as if toward unhoped-for assistance*)

ANGELOTTI   You! Cavaradossi!
God sends you!
> (*Cavaradossi doesn't recognize Angelotti and remains, dazed, on the scaffolding. Angelotti comes closer to make himself known*)

You don't recognize me!
Prison then has changed me very much!

CAVARADOSSI (*recognizing him, quickly sets down palette and and brushes and comes down from the scaffolding toward Angelotti, looking cautiously around*)
Angelotti! The consul
of the extinct Roman Republic.
> (*runs to shut the side door*)

ANGELOTTI   I fled just now from Castel Sant'Angelo . . .

CAVARADOSSI I'm at your disposal.

TOSCA (*from outside*)
Mario!

CAVARADOSSI (*at Tosca's voice, makes a rapid sign to Angelotti to be silent*)
Hide!
It's a woman . . . a jealous one.
A brief moment and I'll send her away.

TOSCA (*from outside*)
Mario!

CAVARADOSSI (*toward the little door from which Tosca's voice comes*)
Here I am!

ANGELOTTI (*seized with a fit of weakness, leans against the scaffolding*)
I'm at the end of my strength,
I can't stand any more . . .

CAVARADOSSI (*very rapidly climbs onto the scaffolding and comes down with the basket; encouraging Angelotti, he pushes him toward the chapel*)
In this basket there's food and wine.

ANGELOTTI   Thanks!

CAVARADOSSI Quickly!

ANGELOTTI   Thanks!

CAVARADOSSI Quickly!

Angelotti enters the chapel.

TOSCA (*from outside, annoyed*)
Mario! Mario! Mario!

CAVARADOSSI (*pretending to be calm, opens the door to Tosca*)
I'm here!

Tosca enters with a kind of violence, looking around suspiciously. Mario approaches Tosca to embrace her. Tosca rejects him brusquely.

TOSCA   Perchè chiuso?

CAVARADOSSI Lo vuole il Sagrestano . . .

TOSCA   A chi parlavi?

CAVARADOSSI A te!

TOSCA   Altre parole bisbigliavi.
             Ov'è? . . .

CAVARADOSSI Chi?

TOSCA   Colei . . . ! Quella donna . . . ! Ho udito
             i lesti passi e un fruscìo di vesti . . .

CAVARADOSSI Sogni!

TOSCA   Lo neghi?

CAVARADOSSI Lo nego e t'amo!
                    (*tenta di baciarla*)

TOSCA (*con dolce rimprovero*)
             Oh! innanzi la Madonna.
             No, Mario mio, lascia pria
             che la preghi, che l'infiori . . .
                    (*s'avvicina lentamente alla statua della
                    Madonna, dispone con arte intorno ad
                    essa i fiori che ha portato con sè. S'inginoc-
                    chia e prega con grande devozione. Seg-
                    nandosi, si alza. Poi dice a Cavaradossi,
                    che intanto si è avviato per riprendere il
                    lavoro*)
             Ora stammi a sentir . . . stassera canto,
             ma è spettacolo breve. Tu m'aspetti
             sull'uscio della scena
             e alla tua villa andiam soli, soletti.

CAVARADOSSI (*che fu sempre soprapensieri*)
             Stassera?!

TOSCA   È luna piena
             e il notturno effluvio floreal
             inebria il cor.
             Non sei contento?
                    (*si siede sulla gradinata presso a Cavara-
                    dossi*)

CAVARADOSSI (*distratto*)
             Tanto!

TOSCA (*colpita dall'accento freddo*)
             Tornalo a dir!

CAVARADOSSI Tanto!

TOSCA (*stizzita*)
             Lo dici male, lo dici male:
             non la sospiri la nostra casetta
             che tutta ascosa nel verde ci aspetta?
             nido a noi sacro, ignoto al mondo inter,
             pien d'amore e di mister?
             Al tuo fianco sentire
             per le silenziose
             stellate ombre, salir
             le voci delle cose . . . !
             Dai boschi e dai roveti,

TOSCA   Why locked?

CAVARADOSSI   The sacristan wishes it . . .

TOSCA   To whom were you speaking?

CAVARADOSSI   To you!

TOSCA   You were murmuring other words.
Where is she? . . .

CAVARADOSSI   Who?

TOSCA   She . . . ! That woman . . . ! I heard
the hasty footsteps and a rustle of clothes . . .

CAVARADOSSI   You're dreaming!

TOSCA   You deny it?

CAVARADOSSI   I deny it and I love you!
(*tries to kiss her*)

TOSCA (*with gentle reproach*)
Oh! before the Madonna.
No, my Mario, first allow me
to pray to her, to deck her with flowers . . .
(*approaches slowly the statue of the Madonna, artistically arranges around it the flowers she has brought with her. She kneels and prays with great devotion. Blessing herself, she rises. Then she says to Cavaradossi, who in the meanwhile has moved off to resume his work*)
Now listen to me . . . this evening I sing,
but it's a short performance. You wait for me
at the stage entrance
and we'll go to your villa alone, all alone.

CAVARADOSSI (*who has been lost in thought*)
This evening?!

TOSCA   The moon is full
and the nocturnal perfume of the flowers
intoxicates the heart.
Aren't you pleased?
(*sits on the step near Cavaradossi*)

CAVARADOSSI (*absently*)
Very much!

TOSCA (*struck by his cold tone*)
Say it again!

CAVARADOSSI   Very much!

TOSCA (*annoyed*)
You say it badly, you say it badly:
don't you sigh for our little house
which, all hidden in the green, waits us?
Nest to us sacred, unknown to the whole world,
full of love and of mystery?
To hear at your side
through the silent
starry shadows rise
the voices of all things!
From the woods and from the thickets,

                  dall'arse erbe, dall'imo
                  dei franti sepolcreti
                  odorosi di timo,
                  la notte escon bisbigli
                  di minuscoli amori
                  e perfidi consigli
                  che ammolliscono i cuori.
                  Fiorite, o campi immensi, palpitate
                  aure marine, aure marine nel lunare albor,
                  ah! piovete voluttà, volte stellate!
                  Arde in Tosca un folle amor!

CAVARADOSSI   Ah! M'avvinci ne' tuoi lacci
                  mia sirena . . .

TOSCA   Arde a Tosca nel sangue
                  il folle amor . . . !

CAVARADOSSI   Mia sirena, verrò!

TOSCA *(reclinando la testa sulla spalla di Cavaradossi, che*
                quasi subito si allontana un poco guardando
                verso la parte donde uscì Angelotti)
                  O mio amore!

CAVARADOSSI   Or lasciami al lavoro.

TOSCA   Mi discacci?

CAVARADOSSI   Urge l'opra, lo sai!

TOSCA *(stizzita, alzandosi)*
                  Vado . . . vado!
                  (s'allontana un poco da Cavaradossi, vol-
                  tandosi per guardarlo, vede il quadro, ed
                  agitatissima ritorna presso Cavaradossi)
                  Chi è quella donna bionda lassù?

CAVARADOSSI   La Maddalena. Ti piace?

TOSCA   È troppo bella!

CAVARADOSSI *(ridendo ed inchinandosi)*
                  Prezioso elogio.

TOSCA *(sospettosa)*
                  Ridi?
                  Quegl'occhi cilestrini già li vidi . . .

CAVARADOSSI *(con indifferenza)*
                  Ce n'è tanti pel mondo!

TOSCA *(cerca di ricordarsi)*
                  Aspetta . . . aspetta . . .
                  È l'Attavanti . . . !

CAVARADOSSI *(ridendo)*
                  Brava!

TOSCA *(cieca di gelosia)*
                  La vedi? T'ama?
                  Tu l'ami? tu l'ami?

CAVARADOSSI *(procura di calmarla)*
                  Fu puro caso . . .

TOSCA *(non ascoltandolo, con ira gelosa)*
                  Quei passi e quel bisbiglio . . .
                  Ah! qui stava pur ora . . . !

from the burned grasses, from the depth
of the broken tombs
aromatic with thyme,
at night come forth murmurs
of tiny loves
and treacherous counsels
which soften hearts.
Flower, O immense fields, palpitate,
sea breezes, sea breezes in the lunar whiteness,
ah! rain down voluptuousness, starry vaults!
In Tosca a mad love burns!

CAVARADOSSI Ah! You enthral me in your bonds,
my siren . . .

TOSCA In Tosca's blood burns
the mad love . . . !

CAVARADOSSI My siren, I'll come!

TOSCA (*resting her head against Cavaradossi's shoulder; almost
at once he moves away a little, looking toward
the place from which Angelotti emerged*)
O my love!

CAVARADOSSI Now leave me to my work.

TOSCA You drive me away?

CAVARADOSSI The work is urgent, you know!

TOSCA (*annoyed, rising*)
I'm going . . . I'm going!
(*she moves a bit away from Cavaradossi;
turning to look at him, she sees the picture, and highly agitated, she comes back
to Cavaradossi*)
Who is that blond woman up there?

CAVARADOSSI The Magdalen. Do you like her?

TOSCA She's too beautiful!

CAVARADOSSI (*laughing and bowing*)
Precious praise.

TOSCA (*suspicious*)
You laugh?
I've already seen those pale blue eyes . . .

CAVARADOSSI (*with indifference*)
There are so many in the world!

TOSCA (*tries to remember*)
Wait . . . wait . . .
It's la Attavanti . . . !

CAVARADOSSI (*laughing*)
Good for you!

TOSCA (*blind with jealousy*)
You see her? She loves you?
You love her? You love her?

CAVARADOSSI (*tries to calm her*)
It was pure chance . . .

TOSCA (*not listening to him; with jealous wrath*)
Those footsteps and that whispering . . .
Ah! she was here even now . . . !

CAVARADOSSI   Vien via!

TOSCA   Ah! la civetta!
A me! A me!

CAVARADOSSI   (*serio*)
La vidi ieri, ma fu puro caso . . .
A pregar qui venne . . .
non visto la ritrassi . . .

TOSCA   Giura!

CAVARADOSSI   Giuro!

TOSCA   (*sempre cogli occhi rivolti al quadro*)
Come mi guarda fiso!

CAVARADOSSI   Vien via . . .

TOSCA   Di me, beffarda, ride.

CAVARADOSSI   Follia!

Cavaradossi spinge dolcemente Tosca a scendere la gradinata. Essa discende all'indietro tenendo alte le sue mani in quelle di Cavaradossi senza cessare di guardare il quadro.

TOSCA   (*con dolce rimprovero*)
Ah, quegli occhi . . . !

CAVARADOSSI   (*tiene Tosca affettuosamente presso di sè, fissandola negli occhi*)
Qual'occhio al mondo può star di paro
all'ardente occhio tuo nero?
È qui che l'esser mio, che l'esser mio
s'affisa intero . . .
occhio all'amor soave, all'ira fiero
qual altro al mondo può star di paro
all'occhio tuo nero?

TOSCA   (*rapita, appoggiando la testa alla spalla di Cavaradossi*)
Oh come la sai bene
l'arte di farti amare!
(*maliziosamente*)
Ma . . . falle gli occhi neri!

CAVARADOSSI   Mia gelosa!

TOSCA   Sì, lo sento . . .
ti tormento senza posa.

CAVARADOSSI   Mia gelosa!

TOSCA   Certa sono del perdono . . .
certa sono del perdono
se tu guardi al mio dolor!

CAVARADOSSI   Mia Tosca idolatrata,
ogni cosa in te mi piace;
[l'ira audace e lo spasimo d'amor!

TOSCA   Certa sono, ecc.]
Dilla ancora la parola
che consola . . . dilla ancora!

CAVARADOSSI   Mia vita, amante inquieta,
dirò sempre: "Floria, t'amo!"
Ah! L'alma acquieta,
sempre "t'amo!" ti dirò!

CAVARADOSSI	Come away!
TOSCA	Ah! the minx! Leave her to me! to me!
CAVARADOSSI (*serious*)	
	I saw her yesterday, but it was pure chance . . . She came here to pray . . . unseen, I portrayed her . . .
TOSCA	Swear!
CAVARADOSSI	I swear!
TOSCA (*with her eyes still on the picture*)	
	How she stares at me!
CAVARADOSSI	Come away . . .
TOSCA	Mocking, she laughs at me.
CAVARADOSSI	Folly!

Cavaradossi gently pushes Tosca, making her go down the steps. She descends backwards, holding up her hands, in Cavaradossi's, without ceasing to look at the picture.

TOSCA (*with gentle reproof*)	
	Ah, those eyes . . . !
CAVARADOSSI (*holds Tosca affectionately to himself, looking her in the eyes*)	
	What eye in the world can be compared to your black, ardent eye? It is here that my being, that my whole being is fixed . . . eye tender to love, to wrath proud, what other in the world can be compared to your black eye?
TOSCA (*rapt, resting her head against Cavaradossi's shoulder*)	
	Oh, how well you know the art of making yourself loved! (*maliciously*) But . . . make her eyes black!
CAVARADOSSI	My jealous one!
TOSCA	Yes, I feel it . . . I torment you without rest.
CAVARADOSSI	My jealous one!
TOSCA	I'm certain of forgiveness . . . I'm certain of forgiveness if you look at my suffering!
CAVARADOSSI	My worshiped Tosca, I like everything in you: the bold wrath and the pang of love!
TOSCA	I'm certain, etc. Say it again, the word that consoles . . . say it again!
CAVARADOSSI	My life, restless mistress, I will always say: "Floria, I love you!" Ah! calm your soul, always I will say "I love you!"

TOSCA   (*sciogliendosi da Cavaradossi*)
         Dio! quante peccata!
         M'hai tutta spettinata.

CAVARADOSSI   Or va, lasciami!

TOSCA   Tu fino a stassera stai fermo
         al lavoro. E mi prometti
         sia caso o fortuna,
         sia treccia bionda o bruna,
         a pregar non verrà, donna nessuna?

CAVARADOSSI   Lo giuro, amore! Va!

TOSCA   Quanto m'affretti!

CAVARADOSSI   (*con dolce rimprovero vedendo rispuntare la
         gelosia*)
         Ancora?

TOSCA   (*cadendo nelle sue braccia e porgendogli la guancia*)
         No, perdona!

CAVARADOSSI   (*sorridendo*)
         Davanti la Madonna?

TOSCA   È tanto buona!
                   (*Si baciano. Tosca, avviandosi ad uscire,
                   guarda ancora il quadro*)

TOSCA   (*maliziosamente*)
         Ma falle gli occhi neri . . . !

    *Tosca fugge rapidamente. Cavaradossi rimane commosso e
pensieroso, ascoltandone i passi allontanarsi, poi con precauzione socchiude l'uscio e guarda fuori. Visto tutto tranquillo,
corre alla Cappella. Angelotti appare subito dietro la cancellata. Cavaradossi apre la cancellata ad Angelotti e si stringono
affettuosamente la mano.*

CAVARADOSSI   (*ad Angelotti che, naturalmente, ha dovuto udire
         il dialogo precedente*)
         È buona la mia Tosca, ma credente
         al confessor nulla tiene celato,
         ond'io mi tacqui.
         È cosa più prudente.

ANGELOTTI   Siam soli?

CAVARADOSSI   Sì. Qual'è il vostro disegno?

ANGELOTTI   A norma degli eventi,
         uscir di Stato
         o star celato in Roma . . .
         Mia sorella . . .

CAVARADOSSI   L'Attavanti?

ANGELOTTI   Sì . . . ascose un muliebre abbigliamento
         là sotto l'altare . . .
         vesti, velo, ventaglio . . .
                   (*si guarda intorno con paura*)
         Appena imbruni
         indosserò quei panni . . .

CAVARADOSSI   Or comprendo!
         Quel fare circospetto
         e il pregante fervore
         in giovin donna e bella

TOSCA (*releasing herself from Cavaradossi*)
> God! how many sins!
> You've rumpled my hair completely!

CAVARADOSSI Go now, leave me!

TOSCA Until this evening you remain steady
> at your work. And promise me,
> whether by chance or luck,
> whether with blond tresses or dark,
> no woman will come to pray?

CAVARADOSSI I swear it, love! Go!

TOSCA How you hurry me!

CAVARADOSSI (*with gentle reproof, seeing her jealousy crop-*
> *ping up again*)
> Again?

TOSCA (*falling into his arms and extending her cheek to him*)
> No, forgive me!

CAVARADOSSI (*smiling*)
> Before the Madonna?

TOSCA She's so good!

(*They kiss. Tosca, starting to go out, looks at the picture again.*)

TOSCA (*maliciously*)
> But make her eyes black . . . !

Tosca flees rapidly. Cavaradossi remains moved and pensive, listening to her footsteps go off. Then, with precaution, he opens the door slightly and looks out. Having seen that all is calm, he runs to the chapel. Angelotti appears at once behind the gate. Cavaradossi opens the gate for Angelotti and they affectionately shake hands.

CAVARADOSSI (*to Angelotti, who naturally has had to hear the*
> *preceding dialogue*)
> My Tosca is good, but a believer,
> she keeps nothing hidden from her confessor,
> wherefore I was silent.
> It's the more prudent thing.

ANGELOTTI Are we alone?

CAVARADOSSI Yes. What is your plan?

ANGELOTTI According to events,
> to leave the state
> or to remain hidden in Rome . . .
> My sister . . .

CAVARADOSSI Attavanti?

ANGELOTTI Yes . . . hid a woman's dress
> there under the altar . . .
> clothing, veil, fan . . .
> (*looks around with fear*)
> As soon as it grows dark
> I'll put on those clothes . . .

CAVARADOSSI Now I understand!
> That circumspect manner
> and the praying fervor
> in a young and beautiful woman

m'avean messo in sospetto
di qualche occulto amor!
Or comprendo!
Era amor di sorella!

ANGELOTTI   Tutto ella ha osato
onde sottrarmi a Scarpia scellerato!

CAVARADOSSI Scarpia?! Bigotto satiro che affina
colle devote pratiche la foia
libertina e strumento
al lascivo talento
fa il confessore e il boia!
La vita mi costasse,
vi salverò!
Ma indugiar fino a notte è mal sicuro.

ANGELOTTI   Temo del sole!

CAVARADOSSI (*indicando*)
La cappella mette
a un orto mal chiuso, poi c'è un canneto
che va lungi pei campi
a una mia villa . . .

ANGELOTTI   M'è nota . . .

CAVARADOSSI Ecco la chiave . . .
Innanzi sera io vi raggiungo,
portate con voi le vesti femminili . . .

Angelotti va a prendere le vesti nascoste da sua sorella.

ANGELOTTI   Ch'io le indossi?

CAVARADOSSI Per or non monta,
il sentiero è deserto . . .

ANGELOTTI   (*per uscire*)
Addio!

CAVARADOSSI (*accorrendo ancora verso Angelotti*)
Se urgesse il periglio,

correte al pozzo del giardin.
L'acqua è nel fondo,
ma a mezzo della canna un picciol varco
guida ad un antro oscuro,
rifugio impenetrabile e sicuro!

Un colpo di cannone; i due si guardano agitatissimi.

ANGELOTTI   Il cannon del castello!

CAVARADOSSI Fu scoperta la fuga!
Or Scarpia i suoi sbirri sguinzaglia!

ANGELOTTI   Addio!

CAVARADOSSI (*con subita risoluzione*)
Con voi verrò. Staremo all'erta!

ANGELOTTI   Odo qualcun!

CAVARADOSSI (*con entusiasmo*)
Se ci assalgon, battaglia!

had aroused my suspicion
of some secret love!
Now I understand!
It was a sister's love!

ANGELOTTI   She dared everything
to deliver me from wicked Scarpia!

CAVARADOSSI   Scarpia? Bigot-satyr who refines
with devout practices his libertine
lust and instrument
to his lascivious talent
acts as confessor and executioner!
If it costs my life,
I'll save you!
But to delay till night is unsafe.

ANGELOTTI   I'm afraid of the sun!

CAVARADOSSI (*pointing*)
The chapel opens
on to a badly closed garden, then there's a cane-
    brake
which goes along through the fields
to a villa of mine . . .

ANGELOTTI   It is known to me . . .

CAVARADOSSI   Here's the key . . .
Before evening I'll join you . . .
take the woman's clothes with you . . .

Angelotti goes to take the clothes hidden by his sister.

ANGELOTTI   Shall I put them on?

CAVARADOSSI   For now it doesn't matter,
the pathway is deserted . . .

ANGELOTTI (*about to leave*)
Farewell!

CAVARADOSSI (*running again toward Angelotti*)
If danger should press,

THE SACRISTAN (*shouting*)

run to the well in the garden.
The water is at the bottom,
but halfway down the aperture a little opening
leads to a dark cave,
an impenetrable and sure refuge!

*A cannon shot; the two men look at each other, highly agi-
tated.*

ANGELOTTI   The castle's cannon!

CAVARADOSSI   Your flight was discovered!
Now Scarpia is unleashing his police spies!

ANGELOTTI   Farewell!

CAVARADOSSI (*with sudden resolution*)
I'll come with you. We'll be on our guard!

ANGELOTTI   I hear someone!

CAVARADOSSI (*with enthusiasm*)
If they attack us, battle!

Escono rapidamente dalla Cappella. Il Sagrestano entra correndo, tutto scalmanato.

IL SAGRESTANO (*gridando*)
> Sommo giubilo, Eccellenza!
> > (*guarda verso l'impalcato e rimane sorpreso di non trovarvi neppure questa volta il pittore*)
> Non c'è più! Ne son dolente . . . !
> Chi contrista un miscredente
> si guadagna un'indulgenza!

Accorrono da ogni parte chierici, confratelli, allievi e cantori della capella. Tutti costoro entrano tumultuosamente.

IL SAGRESTANO
> Tutta qui la cantoria!
> Presto!

ALLIEVI (*colla massima confusione*)
> Dove?

IL SAGRESTANO (*spingendoli verso la sagrestia*)
> In sagrestia . . .

ALCUNI ALLIEVI
> Ma che avvenne?

IL SAGRESTANO
> Nol sapete? Bonaparte . . .
> scellerato . . . Bonaparte . . .

TUTTI   Ebben? Che fu?

IL SAGRESTANO
> Fu spennato, sfracellato
> e piombato a Belzebù!

ALCUNI ALLIEVI
> Chi lo dice?

ALTRI ALLIEVI È sogno! È fola!

IL SAGRESTANO
> È veridica parola .
> or ne giunge la notizia!

TUTTI   Si festeggia vittoria!

IL SAGRESTANO
> E questa sera gran fiaccolata,
> veglia di gala a Palazzo Farnese,
> ed un'apposita nuova cantata
> con Floria Tosca . . . !
> E nelle chiese inni al Signor!
> Or via a vestirvi,
> non più clamor!
> Via . . . via . . . in sagrestia!

TUTTI (*ridendo e gridando gioiosamente*)
> Ah, ah, ah, ah!
> Doppio soldo . . . *Te Deum . . . Gloria . . . !*
> Viva il Re!
> Si festeggi la vittoria!
> Questa sera gran fiaccolata!

IL SAGRESTANO
> Or via a vestirvi!

They rapidly go out of the chapel. The sacristan enters running, all out of breath.

THE SACRISTAN

Great jubilation, Excellency!
(*looks toward the scaffolding and is surprised not to find the painter there this time either*)
He's not there any more! I'm sorry for it . . . !
He who saddens an unbeliever
earns himself an indulgence!

From all sides altarboys run in, brothers, pupils, and choir boys of the chapel. They all enter in tumult.

THE SACRISTAN

All the choir here!
Quickly!

PUPILS (*in the greatest confusion*)
Where?

THE SACRISTAN (*thrusting them toward the sacristy*)
In the sacristy . . .

SOME PUPILS　　But what happened?

THE SACRISTAN

Don't you know it? Bonaparte . . .
wicked . . . Bonaparte . . .

ALL　　　　　　Well? What was it?

THE SACRISTAN

He was plucked, shattered
and sent plunging to Beelzebub!

SOME PUPILS　　Who says it?

OTHER PUPILS　It's a dream! It's a fable!

THE SACRISTAN

It's truthful word:
the news arrived now!

ALL　　　　　　The victory is to be celebrated!

THE SACRISTAN

And this evening a great torchlight procession,
a gala party at the Farnese Palace,
and an expressly written new cantata
with Floria Tosca . . . !
And in the churches anthems to the Lord!
Now off, to dress yourselves!
No more uproar!
Away . . . away . . . into the sacristy!

ALL (*laughing and shouting joyously*)
Ha, ha, ha, ha!
Double pay . . . *Te Deum* . . . *Gloria* . . . !
Long live the king!
Let the victory be celebrated!
This evening a great torchlight procession!

THE SACRISTAN

Now off, to dress yourselves!

TUTTI   Serata di gala! Si festeggi la vittoria!
               Viva il Re! Viva il Re!
               Te Deum . . . Gloria!
               Si festeggi la vittoria!

*Le loro grida e le loro risa sono al colmo, allorchè una voce
ironica tronca bruscamente quella gazzarra volgare di canti e
risa. È Scarpia, che appare improvvisamente dalla porticina:
dietro a lui Spoletta e alcuni birri. Alla vista di Scarpia tutti
si arrestano allibiti come per incanto.*

SCARPIA   Un tal baccano in chiesa!
               Bel rispetto!

IL SAGRESTANO (*balbettando impaurito*)
               Eccellenza, il gran giubilo . . .

SCARPIA   Apprestate per il *Te Deum.*

*Mogi, mogi s'allontanano tutti e anche il Sagrestano fa per
cavarsela, ma Scarpia bruscamente lo trattiene.*

SCARPIA   Tu resta!

IL SAGRESTANO (*sommessamente impaurito*)
               Non mi muovo!

SCARPIA (*a Spoletta*)
               E tu va, fruga ogni angolo,
               raccogli ogni traccia!

SPOLETTA   Sta bene!
                   (*fa cenno a due sbirri di seguirlo*)

SCARPIA (*ad altri sbirri, che eseguiscono*)
               Occhio alle porte, senza dar sospetti!
                   (*al Sagrestano*)
               Ora a te. Pesa le tue risposte.
               Un prigionier di Stato
               fuggì pur ora da Castel Sant'Angelo . . .
               s'è rifugiato qui . . .

IL SAGRESTANO
               Misericordia!

SCARPIA   Forse c'è ancora.
               Dov'è la cappella degli Attavanti?

IL SAGRESTANO
               Eccola . . . !
                   (*va al cancello e lo trova socchiuso*)
               Aperta! Arcangeli!
               E un'altra chiave!

SCARPIA   Buon indizio. Entriamo.

*Entrano nella Cappella, poi ritornano: Scarpia, assai con-
trariato, ha fra le mani un ventaglio chiuso che agita nervosamente.*

SCARPIA (*fra sè*)
               Fu grave sbaglio quel colpo
               di cannone. Il mariolo
               spiccato ha il volo,
               ma lasciò una preda . . .
               preziosa . . .
                   (*agitandolo in aria*)

ALL   Gala party! Let the victory be celebrated!
                Long live the king! Long live the king!
                Te Deum . . . Gloria!
                Let the victory be celebrated!

Their cries and their laughter are at their peak when an ironic voice abruptly cuts off that vulgar din of songs and laughter. It is Scarpia, who suddenly appears from the little door: behind him are Spoletta and some police spies. At the sight of Scarpia all stop, aghast, as if by magic.

SCARPIA   Such a din in church!
                Fine respect!

THE SACRISTAN (*stammering, frightened*)
                Excellency, the great jubilation . . .

SCARPIA   Make ready for the *Te Deum.*

Crestfallen, they all move away, and the sacristan also starts to slip off, but Scarpia brusquely restrains him.

SCARPIA   You remain!

THE SACRISTAN (*softly, frightened*)
                I'm not moving!

SCARPIA (*to Spoletta*)
                And you go, search every corner,
                collect every clue!

SPOLETTA   Very well!
                    (*motions to two policemen to follow him*)

SCARPIA (*to other policemen, who obey*)
                Keep an eye on the doors, without arousing sus-
                    picions!
                    (*to the sacristan*)
                Now for you. Weigh your answers.
                A state prisoner
                escaped only now from Castel Sant'Angelo . . .
                he took refuge here . . .

THE SACRISTAN
                Mercy!

SCARPIA   Perhaps he's here still.
                Where is the Attavanti Chapel?

THE SACRISTAN
                There it is!
                    (*goes to the gate and finds it open*)
                Open! Ye archangels!
                And another key!

SCARPIA   A good clue. Let us enter.

They enter the Chapel, then they come back: Scarpia, very vexed, has in his hands a closed fan with which he toys nervously.

SCARPIA (*aside*)
                That cannon shot
                was a serious mistake. The rogue
                has taken flight,
                but he left a prey . . .
                a precious one . . .
                    (*waving it in the air*)

un ventaglio.
Qual complice il misfatto preparò!
(*rimane alquanto pensieroso, poi guarda
attentamente il ventaglio; a un tratto vi
scorge uno stemma e vivamente esclama*)
La marchesa Attavanti . . . ! Il suo stemma . . .
(*guarda intorno, scrutando ogni angolo
della chiesa: i suoi occhi si arrestano sull'-
impalcato, sugli arnesi del pittore, sul
quadro . . . e il noto viso dell'Attavanti gli
appare riprodotto nel volto della santa*)
Il suo ritratto!
(*al Sagrestano*)
Chi fe' quelle pitture?

IL SAGRESTANO
Il cavalier Cavaradossi.

SCARPIA   Lui!
Uno dei birri che seguì Scarpia, torna dalla Cappella portando il paniere che Cavaradossi diede ad Angelotti.

IL SAGRESTANO (*vedendolo*)
Numi! Il paniere!

SCARPIA (*seguitando le sue riflessioni*)
Lui! L'amante di Tosca!
Un uom sospetto! Un volterrian!

IL SAGRESTANO (*che andò a guardare il paniere*)
Vuoto? Vuoto!

SCARPIA   Che hai detto?
(*vedendo il birro col paniere*)
Che fu?

IL SAGRESTANO (*prendendo il paniere*)
Si ritrovò nella Cappella
questo panier.

SCARPIA   Tu lo conosci?

IL SAGRESTANO
Certo! È il cesto del pittor . . .
(*esitante e pauroso*)
ma . . . nondimeno . . .

SCARPIA   Sputa quello che sai.

IL SAGRESTANO
Io lo lasciai ripieno
di cibo prelibato . . .
il pranzo del pittor . . . !

SCARPIA (*attento, inquirente per scoprir terreno*)
Avrà pranzato!

IL SAGRESTANO
Nella Cappella?
Non ne avea la chiave
nè contava pranzar . . .
disse egli stesso.
Ond'io l'avea già messo . . . al riparo.
(*mostra dove avea riposto il paniere e ve
lo lascia, poi impressionato dal severo e
silente contegno di Scarpia, fra sè*)

a fan.

What an accomplice prepared the misdeed!
*(he remains quite pensive, then looks
carefully at the fan; suddenly he sees a
coat-of-arms on it and exclaims forcefully)*

The Marchesa Attavanti . . . ! Her arms . . .
*(looks around, examining every corner of
the church: his eyes stop on the scaffolding,
on the painter's equipment, the painting
. . . and the familiar face of the Attavanti
appears to him reproduced in the counten-
ance of the saint)*

Her portrait!
(to the sacristan)

Who made that painting?

THE SACRISTAN

Cavaliere Cavaradossi.

SCARPIA   He!

*One of the spies who followed Scarpia returns from the
chapel carrying the basket that Cavaradossi gave to Angelotti.*

THE SACRISTAN *(seeing it)*

Ye gods! The basket!

SCARPIA *(pursuing his reflections)*

He! Tosca's lover!
A suspect man! A Voltairean!

THE SACRISTAN *(who went to look into the basket)*

Empty? Empty!

SCARPIA   What did you say?
(seeing the spy with the basket)

What was it?

THE SACRISTAN *(taking the basket)*

This basket was found
in the chapel.

SCARPIA   You know it?

THE SACRISTAN

Of course. It's the painter's basket . . .
(hesitating and fearful)

but . . . nonetheless . . .

SCARPIA   Spit out what you know.

THE SACRISTAN

I left it filled
with choice food . . .
the painter's dinner . . . !

SCARPIA *(attentive, inquiring to discover new ground)*

He must have dined!

THE SACRISTAN

In the chapel?
He didn't have the key to it,
nor did he plan to dine . . .
he said so himself.

Wherefore I had already put it . . . in a safe place.
*(shows where he had set the basket and
leaves it there, then, intimidated by Scarpia's severe and silent manner, to himself)*

(Libera me Domine!)

SCARPIA   (Or tutto è chiaro . . .
               la provvista del sacrista
               d'Angelotti fu la preda!)

*Tosca entra, ed è nervosissima: va dritta all'impalcato, ma
non trovandovi Cavaradossi, sempre in grande agitazione va a
cercarlo nella navata centrale della chiesa: Scarpia appena
vista entrare Tosca, si è abilmente nascosto dietro la colonna
ov'è la pila dell'acqua benedetta, facendo imperioso cenno di
rimanere al Sagrestano, il quale, tremante, imbarazzato, si
reca vicino al palco del pittore.*

SCARPIA   Tosca? Che non mi veda.
               (Per ridurre un geloso allo sbaraglio
               Jago ebbe un fazzoletto . . .
               ed io un ventaglio!)

TOSCA (*torna presso l'impalcato, chiamando con impazienza ad
           alta voce*)
               Mario? Mario?

IL SAGRESTANO (*avvicinandosi a Tosca*)
               Il pittor Cavaradossi?
               Chi sa dove sia?
               Svanì, sgattaiolò
               per sua stregoneria.
                   (*se la svigna*)

TOSCA   Ingannata? No . . . no . . .
               tradirmi egli non può,
               tradirmi egli non può.

*Scarpia ha girato la colonna e si presenta a Tosca, sorpresa
dal suo subito apparire. Intinge le dita nella pila e le offre
l'acqua benedetta; fuori suonano le campane che invitano alla
chiesa.*

SCARPIA (*insinuante e gentile*)
               Tosca divina
               la mano mia la vostra aspetta,
               piccola manina,
               non per galanteria, ma . . .
               per offrirvi l'acqua benedetta . . .

TOSCA (*tocca le dita di Scarpia e si fa il segno della croce*)
               Grazie, signor!

*Poco a poco entrano in chiesa, e vanno nella navata prin-
cipale, popolani, borghesi, ciociare, trasteverine, soldati, peco-
rari, ciociari, mendicanti, ecc.: poi un Cardinale, col capitolo,
si reca all'altare maggiore; la folla, rivolta verso l'altare maggiore, si accalca nella navata principale.*

SCARPIA   Un nobile esempio è il vostro.
               Al cielo pieno di santo zelo
               attingete dell'arte il magistero
               che la fede ravviva!

TOSCA (*distratta e pensosa*)
               Bontà vostra . . .

(Libera me Domine!)

SCARPIA   (Now everything is clear . . .
the sacristan's provender
was Angelotti's prey!)

*Tosca enters and is very nervous. She goes straight to the
scaffolding, but, not finding Cavaradossi there, still in great
agitation, she goes to look for him in the central nave of the
church. Scarpia, as soon as he has seen Tosca enter, has deftly
concealed himself behind the column where there is the holy-
water stoup, making an imperious sign to the sacristan to remain. The latter, trembling, embarrassed, moves near the
painter's scaffolding.*

SCARPIA   Tosca? Let her not see me.
(To reduce a jealous man to disaster
Iago had a handkerchief . . .
and I, a fan!)

TOSCA (*comes back to the scaffolding, calling with impatience
in a loud voice*)
Mario? Mario?

THE SACRISTAN (*approaching Tosca*)
The painter Cavaradossi?
Who knows where he is?
He vanished, slipped away
by his witchcraft.
      (*slips away*)

TOSCA   Deceived? No . . . no . . .
He can't betray me,
he can't betray me.

*Scarpia has moved around the column and he presents him-
self to Tosca, who is surprised at his sudden appearance. He
dips his fingers into the stoup and offers her the holy water.
Outside, the bells toll, inviting the people to the church.*

SCARPIA (*insinuating and polite*)
Divine Tosca,
my hand awaits yours,
the tiny little hand,
not out of gallantry, but . . .
to offer you the holy water . . .

TOSCA (*touches Scarpia's fingers and makes the sign of the
cross*)
Thanks, sir!

*Little by little into the church, going into the main nave,
enter men and women of the people, bourgeois, women of
Ciociaria and Trastevere, soldiers, shepherds, men of Ciociaria, beggars, etc. Then a cardinal with the chapter goes to the
main altar. The crowd, facing the main altar, masses in the
central nave.*

SCARPIA   Yours is a noble example.
From heaven, full of holy zeal,
you draw the mastery of art
that enlivens the faith!

TOSCA (*absent and pensive*)
You're too kind . . .

SCARPIA Le pie donne son rare . . .
    Voi calcate la scena . . .
    e in chiesa ci venite per pregar . . .

TOSCA (*sorpresa*)
    Che intendete?

SCARPIA E non fate come certe sfrontate . . .
    (*indica il ritratto*)
    che han di Maddalena viso e costumi . . .
    e vi trescan d'amore!

TOSCA (*scattando*)
    Che? D'amore?
    Le prove! Le prove!

SCARPIA (*mostrandole il ventaglio*)
    È arnese di pittore questo?

TOSCA (*afferrandolo*)
    Un ventaglio? Dove stava?

SCARPIA Là su quel palco.
    Qualcun venne certo a sturbar
    gli amanti ed essa nel fuggir
    perdè le penne . . . !

TOSCA (*esaminando il ventaglio*)
    La corona! Lo stemma!
    È l'Attavanti! Presago sospetto.

SCARPIA (Ho sortito l'effetto!)

TOSCA (*con grande sentimento, trattenendo a stento le lagrime,*
    dimentica del luogo e di Scarpia)
    Ed io venivo a lui tutta dogliosa
    per dirgli: in van stassera
    il ciel s'infosca . . .
    l'innamorata Tosca
    è prigioniera . . .

SCARPIA (Già il veleno l'ha rosa.)

TOSCA . . . dei regali tripudi, prigioniera!

SCARPIA (Già il veleno l'ha rosa.)
    (*mellifluo, a Tosca*)
    O che v'offende, dolce signora?
    Una ribelle lacrima scende
    sovre le belle guancie e le irrora;
    dolce signora, che mai v'accora?

TOSCA Nulla!

SCARPIA (*insinuante*)
    Darei la vita
    per asciugar quel pianto.

TOSCA (*non ascoltandolo*)
    Io qui mi struggo e intanto
    d'altra in braccio
    le mie smanie deride!

SCARPIA (Morde il veleno.)

TOSCA (*con grande amarezza*)
    Dove son?

SCARPIA   Pious women are rare . . .
                 You tread the stage . . .
                 and you come to church to pray . . .

TOSCA (*surprised*)
                 What do you mean?

SCARPIA   And you don't behave like certain shameless
                     women . . .
                         (*points to the portrait*)
                 who have the Magdalen's face and habits . . .
                 and there intrigue about love!

TOSCA (*snapping*)
                 What? Love?
                 The proofs! The proofs!

SCARPIA (*showing her the fan*)
                 Is this a painter's implement?

TOSCA (*seizing it*)
                 A fan? Where was it?

SCARPIA   There on that scaffolding.
                 Someone certainly came to disturb
                 the lovers and, in fleeing,
                 she lost her feathers . . . !

TOSCA (*examining the fan*)
                 The coronet! The coat of arms!
                 It's the Attavanti! Foresighted suspicion.

SCARPIA   (I've achieved the effect!)

TOSCA (*with great feeling, restraining her tears with an effort,
                 forgetting the place and Scarpia*)
                 And I was coming to him, all sorrowful,
                 to say to him: in vain this evening
                 the sky grows dark . . .
                 the loving Tosca
                 is a prisoner . . .

SCARPIA   (Already the poison has eaten her.)

TOSCA   . . . of the royal festivities, a prisoner!

SCARPIA   (Already the poison has eaten her.)
                     (*mellifluously, to Tosca*)
                 Oh, what is offending you, sweet lady?
                 A rebellious tear is descending
                 over the lovely cheeks and bedewing them;
                 sweet lady, whatever is distressing you?

TOSCA   Nothing!

SCARPIA (*insinuating*)
                 I'd give my life
                 to dry that weeping.

TOSCA (*not listening to him*)
                 Here I am pining and in the meanwhile
                 in another woman's arms
                 he mocks my ravings!

SCARPIA   (The poison is biting.)

TOSCA (*with great bitterness*)
                 Where are they?.

Potessi coglierli i traditori.
(*sempre più crucciosa*)
Oh qual sospetto!
Ai doppi amori è la villa ricetto.
Traditor . . . traditor!
Oh mio bel nido insozzato di fango!
(*con pronta risoluzione*)
Vi piomberò inattesa!
(*si rivolge minacciosa al quadro*)
Tu non l'avrai stassera. Giuro!

SCARPIA (*scandolezzato, quasi rimproverandola*)
In chiesa!

TOSCA   Dio mi perdona . . .
Egli vede ch'io piango . . . !

*Tosca parte in grande agitazione: Scarpia l'accompagna,
fingendo di rassicurarla. Appena escita Tosca, la chiesa poco
a poco va sempre più popolandosi. Scarpia ritorna presso la
colonna e fa un cenno: subito si presenta Spoletta.*

SCARPIA   Tre sbirri . . . Una carrozza . . .
Presto . . . seguila dovunque vada . . .
non visto . . . provvedi!

SPOLETTA   Sta bene. Il convegno?

SCARPIA   Palazzo Farnese!
Spoletta esce frettoloso.

SCARPIA (*con un sorriso sardonico*)
Va, Tosca!
Nel tuo cuor s'annida Scarpia.
Va, Tosca!
È Scarpia che scioglie a volo
il falco della tua gelosia.
Quanta promessa nel tuo pronto sospetto!
Nel tuo cuor s'annida Scarpia . . .
Va, Tosca!

*Scarpia s'inchina e prega al passaggio del Cardinale. Il Car-
dinale benedice la folla che reverente s'inchina.*

IL CAPITOLO   *Adjutorum nostrum in nomine Domini . . .*

LA FOLLA   *Qui fecit coelum et terram . . .*

IL CAPITOLO   *Sit nomen Domini benedictum . . .*

LA FOLLA   [*Et hoc nunc et usque in saeculum.*

SCARPIA   A doppia mira tendo il voler,]
nè il capo del ribelle
è la più prezïosa.
Ah di quegli occhi vittoriosi
veder la fiamma illanguidir
con spasimo d'amor . . .
fra le mie braccia illanguidir d'amor.
L'uno al capestro,
l'altra fra le mie braccia . . .

LA FOLLA   *Te Deum laudamus:
te Dominum confitemur!*

If I could catch them, the traitors.
>(*more and more upset*)
Oh, what a suspicion!
The villa is the receptacle of double loves.
Traitor . . . traitor!
Oh, my lovely nest fouled with mud!
>(*with prompt resolution*)
I'll fall on it, unexpected!
>(*turns menacingly to the picture*)
You shan't have him this evening. I swear!

SCARPIA (*shocked, as if reproaching her*)
>In church!

TOSCA
>God forgives me . . .
>He sees that I'm weeping . . . !

Tosca leaves in great agitation; Scarpia sees her out, pretending to reassure her. Once Tosca has left, the church little by little becomes increasingly crowded. Scarpia comes back toward the column and makes a signal. Spoletta presents himself at once.

SCARPIA
>Three policemen . . . A carriage . . .
>Quickly . . . follow her wherever she goes . . .
>unobserved . . . see to it!

SPOLETTA
>Very well. Our meeting place?

SCARPIA
>The Farnese Palace!

Spoletta goes out hastily.

SCARPIA (*with a sardonic smile*)
>Go, Tosca!
>In your heart Scarpia is nesting.
>Go, Tosca.
>It is Scarpia who releases in flight
>the falcon of your jealousy.
>How much promise is in your prompt suspicion!
>In your heart Scarpia is nesting . . .
>Go, Tosca!

Scarpia bows and prays as the cardinal goes past. The cardinal blesses the crowd, which reverently bows.

THE CHAPTER *Adjutorum nostrum in nomine Domini . . .*

THE CROWD *Qui fecit coelum et terram . . .*

THE CHAPTER *Sit nomen Domini benedictum . . .*

THE CROWD *Et hoc nunc et usque in saeculum.*

SCARPIA
>I aim my desire at a double goal,
>nor is the rebel's head
>the more precious.
>Ah, to see the flame
>of those victorious eyes languish
>in a pang of love . . .
>in my arms grow languid with love.
>The one to the noose,
>the other in my arms . . .

THE CROWD *Te Deum laudamus:*
te Dominum confitemur!

Il canto sacro dal fondo della chiesa scuote Scarpia, come svegliandolo da un sogno. Si rimette, fa il segno della croce guardandosi intorno.

SCARPIA   Tosca, mi fai dimenticare Iddio!

SCARPIA, LA FOLLA
        Te aeternum Patrem omnis terra veneratur!

ATTO SECONDO

Palazzo Farnese. La camera di Scarpia al piano superiore. Tavola imbandita. Un'ampia finestra verso il cortile del palazzo. È notte. Scarpia è seduto alla tavola e vi cena. Interrompe a tratti la cena per riflettere. Guarda l'orologio: è smanioso e pensieroso.

SCARPIA   Tosca è un buon falco . . . !
        Certo a quest'ora i miei segugi
        le due prede azzannano!
        Doman sul palco
        vedrà l'aurora
        Angelotti e il bel Mario
        al laccio pendere.
           (*suona il campanello, Sciarrone compare*)
        Tosca è a palazzo?

SCIARRONE   Un ciambellan ne uscia
        pur ora in traccia . . .

SCARPIA (*accennando alla finestra*)
        Apri. Tarda è la notte.

Dal piano inferiore, ove la Regina di Napoli, Maria Carolina, dà una grande festa in onore di Melas, si ode il suonare di un'orchestra.

SCARPIA   Alla cantata ancor manca la Diva,
        e strimpellan gavotte.
           (*a Sciarrone*)
        Tu attenderai la Tosca
        in sull'entrata;
        le dirai ch'io l'aspetto
        finita la cantata . . .
           (*Sciarrone fa per andarsene; richiamandolo*)
        o meglio . . .
           (*si alza, va ad una scrivania e scrive in fretta un biglietto*)
        le darai questo biglietto.
           (*consegnandolo a Sciarrone, che esce*)
        Ella verrà . . .
           (*torna alla tavola e mescendosi da bere dice*)
        per amor del suo Mario;
        Per amor del suo Mario
        al piacer mio s'arrenderà.
        Tal dei profondi amori
        è la profonda miseria.

The sacred chant from the back of the church stirs Scarpia, *as if wakening him from a dream. He recovers himself, makes the sign of the cross, looking around.*

SCARPIA   Tosca, you make me forget God!

SCARPIA, THE CROWD
          Te aeternum Patrem omnis terra veneratur!

ACT TWO

The Farnese Palace. Scarpia's room on the upper floor. A table laid. A broad window onto the courtyard of the palace. It is night. Scarpia is seated at the table, eating his supper. He interrupts his supper at times to ponder. He looks at the clock: he is anxious and pensive.

SCARPIA   Tosca is a good falcon . . . !
          Certainly at this hour my bloodhounds
          have their fangs into the two victims!
          Tomorrow on the gallows
          dawn will see
          Angelotti and the handsome Mario
          hanging from the noose.
                    (*rings the bell. Sciarrone appears*)
          Is Tosca in the palace?

SCIARRONE   A chamberlain went out
          only now to seek her . . .

SCARPIA (*nodding toward the window*)
          Open. The night is late.

From the lower floor, where the Queen of Naples, Maria Carolina, is giving a great party in honor of Melas, the sound of an orchestra is heard.

SCARPIA   The diva is still missing for the cantata,
          and they are strumming gavottes.
                    (*to Sciarrone*)
          You will await Tosca
          at the entrance;
          you will tell her that I await her
          when the cantata is finished . . .
                    (*Sciarrone starts to go; calling him back*)

          or better . . .
                    (*rises, goes to a desk, and hastily writes a
                    note*)
          you will give her this note.
                    (*handing it to Sciarrone, who goes out*)
          She'll come . . .
                    (*returns to the table and, pouring some-
                    thing to drink, says*)
          out of love for her Mario!
          Out of love for her Mario
          she will surrender to my pleasure.
          Such is the profound wretchedness
          of profound loves.

Ha più forte sapore
la conquista violenta
che il mellifluo consenso.
Io di sospiri e di lattiginose
albe lunari poco m'appago.
Non so trarre accordi di chitarra,
nè oròscopo di fior,
nè far l'occhio di pesce,
o tubar come tortora!
  (*s'alza ma non s'allontana dalla tavola*)
Bramo . . . La cosa bramata
perseguo, me ne sazio
e via la getto . . . volto
a nuova esca.
Dio creò diverse beltà,
vini diversi. Io vo' gustar
quanto più posso dell'opra divina!
  (*beve*)

SCIARRONE (*entrando*)
  Spoletta è giunto.
SCARPIA Entri. In buon punto.

*Sciarrone esce per chiamare Spoletta, che accompagna nella
sala, rimanendo poi presso la porta del fondo. Scarpia si siede
e tutt'occupato a cenare, interroga Spoletta senza guardarlo.*

SCARPIA O galantuomo, com'andò la caccia?
SPOLETTA (*avanzandosi un poco ed impaurito*)
  (Sant'Ignazio m'aiuta!)
  Della signora seguimmo la traccia.
  Giunti a un'erma villetta
  tra le fratte perduta
  ella v'entrò.
  N'escì sola ben presto.
  Allor scavalco lesto
  il muro del giardin
  coi miei cagnotti
  e piombo in casa . . .
SCARPIA Quel bravo Spoletta!
SPOLETTA (*esitando*)
  Fiuto . . . ! razzolo . . . ! frugo . . . !

*Scarpia si avvede dell'indecisione di Spoletta e si leva ritto,
pallido d'ira, le ciglia corrugate.*

SCARPIA Ahi! l'Angelotti?
SPOLETTA Non s'è trovato!
SCARPIA (*con rabbia crescente*)
  Ah cane! Ah traditore!
  Ceffo di basilisco, alle forche!
SPOLETTA (*tremante, cerca di scongiurare la collera di Scarpia*)
  Gesù!
   (*timidamente*)
  C'era il pittor . . .
SCARPIA Cavaradossi?

Violent conquest
has a stronger flavor
than mellifluous consent.
I am hardly satisfied
with sighs and milky lunar dawns.
I don't know how to draw chords from a guitar,
or horoscope from flowers,
or assume longing looks,
or coo like a dove!
>   (*rises but doesn't move away from the
>   table*)
I desire . . . I pursue
the thing desired, sate myself with it
and throw it away . . . directed
toward new prey.
God created different beauties,
different wines. I want to savor
as much as I can of the divine work!
>   (*drinks*)

SCIARRONE (*entering*)
Spoletta has arrived.

SCARPIA   Let him enter. At the right moment.

*Sciarrone goes out to call Spoletta, whom he accompanies
into the room, remaining then by the door at the back. Scarpia
sits down and, completely occupied in supping, questions
Spoletta without looking at him.*

SCARPIA   Oh, fine gentleman, how did the hunt go?

SPOLETTA (*advancing a little, and frightened*)
(Saint Ignatius, help me!)
We followed the trail of the lady.
Having reached a solitary little villa,
lost among the thickets,
she entered.
Very soon she came out, alone.
Then I quickly climb
the wall of the garden
with my ruffians
and rush into the house . . .

SCARPIA   That smart Spoletta!

SPOLETTA (*hesitating*)
I sniff . . . ! I rummage . . . ! I search . . . !

*Scarpia notices Spoletta's indecision and stands up erect,
pale with wrath, frowning.*

SCARPIA   Aha! Angelotti?

SPOLETTA   He wasn't found!

SCARPIA (*with mounting anger*)
Ah, dog! Ah, traitor!
Lizard-face, to the gallows!

SPOLETTA (*trembling, tries to allay Scarpia's rage*)
Jesus!
>   (*timidly*)
There was the painter . . .

SCARPIA   Cavaradossi?

SPOLETTA (*accennando di sì col capo, aggiungendo subito*)
Ei sa dove l'altro s'asconde . . .
Ogni suo gesto, ogni accento
tradìa tal beffarda ironia,
ch'io lo trassi in arresto.

SCARPIA (*con sospiro di soddisfazione*)
Meno male!

*Scarpia passeggia meditando: ad un tratto si arresta — dall'-
aperta finestra odesi la cantata eseguita dai cori nella sala della
regina. Dunque Tosca è tornata — è là — sotto di lui.*

CORO   [Sale, ascende l'uman cantico,
                varca spazi, varca cèli
                per ignoti soli empirei,
                profetati dai Vangeli,
                a te giunge o re dei re!

SPOLETTA (*accennando all'anticamera*)
Egli è là.

SCARPIA (*gli balena un'idea e subito dice a Spoletta*)
Introducete il Cavalier.
            (*Spoletta esce*)
            (*a Sciarrone*)
A me Roberti
e il Giudice del Fisco.]

*Sciarrone esce. Scarpia siede ancora a tavola. Spoletta e tre
birri introducono Mario Cavaradossi, poi Roberti, esecutore di
giustizia, il Giudice del Fisco con uno scrivano e Sciarrone.*

CAVARADOSSI (*altero, avanzandosi con impeto*)
Tal violenza!

SCARPIA (*con studiata cortesia*)
Cavalier, vi piaccia accomodarvi . . .

CAVARADOSSI   Vo' saper . . .

SCARPIA (*accennando una sedia al lato opposto della tavola*)
Sedete.

CAVARADOSSI (*rifiutando*)
Aspetto!

SCARPIA   E sia!
                (*guarda fisso mario Cavaradossi, prima di
                interrogarlo*)
                [V'è noto che un prigione . . .

TOSCA, CORO   Questo canto voli a te . . .
                A te . . . quest'inno di gloria
                voli a te,
                sommo Iddio della vittoria,
                Dio che fosti innanzi ai secoli,
                alle cantiche degli angeli,
                or voli quest'umano inno
                di gloria a te!

CAVARADOSSI (*udendo la voce di Tosca, esclama commosso*)
La sua voce!

SPOLETTA (*nodding his head, yes, adding at once*)
    He knows where the other is hiding . . .
    His every gesture, every word
    betrayed such mocking irony
    that I put him under arrest.

SCARPIA (*with a sigh of contentment*)
    So much the better!

Scarpia paces up and down, meditating. All of a sudden he stops — from the open window the cantata is heard, performed by the choruses in the queen's hall. So Tosca has returned — she is there — beneath him.

CHORUS   The human anthem rises, ascends,
    crosses spaces, crosses skies,
    through unknown empyrean suns,
    prophesied by the Gospels,
    it comes to Thee, O King of Kings!

SPOLETTA (*nodding toward the antechamber*)
    He is there.

SCARPIA (*an idea strikes him and he says at once to Spoletta*)
    Show in the Cavaliere.
            (*Spoletta goes out*)
            (*to Sciarrone*)
    Send me Roberti
    and the judge.

Sciarrone goes out. Scarpia sits at the table again. Spoletta and three policemen bring in Mario Cavaradossi, then Roberti, the executioner, the judge with a scribe and Sciarrone.

CAVARADOSSI (*haughty, advancing with vehemence*)
    Such violence!

SCARPIA (*with studied politeness*)
    Cavaliere, would you like to take a seat . . .

CAVARADOSSI   I want to know . . .

SCARPIA (*nodding to a chair at the opposite side of the table*)
    Sit down.

CAVARADOSSI (*refusing*)
    I am waiting!

SCARPIA   So be it!
            (*stares at Mario Cavaradossi, before questioning him*)
    It is known to you that a prisoner . . .

TOSCA, CHORUS
    Let this song fly to Thee . . .
    To Thee . . . this hymn of glory
    fly to Thee,
    great God of victory,
    God who wast before the centuries
    before the canticles of the angels
    now let this human hymn of glory
    fly to Thee!

CAVARADOSSI (*hearing the voice of Tosca, exclaims, moved*)
    Her voice!

SCARPIA (*che si era interrotta all'udire la voce di Tosca, riprende*)
　　　. . . v'è noto che un prigione
　　　oggi è fuggito da Castel Sant'Angelo?

CAVARADOSSI　　Ignoro.

SCARPIA　　　　Eppur si pretende che voi
　　　　　　　l'abbiate accolto in Sant'Andrea,
　　　　　　　provvisto di cibo e di vesti . . .]

CAVARADOSSI (*risoluto*)
　　　　　　　Menzogna!

SCARPIA (*continuando a mantenersi calmo*)
　　　　　　　[. . . e guidato ad un vostro
　　　　　　　podere suburbano . . .

CAVARADOSSI　　Nego. Le prove?

SCARPIA (*mellifluo*)
　　　　　　　Un suddito fedele . . .

CAVARADOSSI　　Al fatto. Chi m'accusa?
　　　　　　　I vostri birri invan frugâr la villa.

SCARPIA　　　　Segno che è ben celato.

TOSCA, CORO　　Sale, ascende l'uman cantico,
　　　　　　　varca spazi, varca cèli!

CAVARADOSSI　　Sospetti di spia!

SPOLETTA (*offeso, interviene*)
　　　　　　　Alle nostre ricerche egli rideva . . .

CAVARADOSSI　　E rido ancor . . . e rido ancor.

SCARPIA (*terribile alzandosi*)
　　　　　　　Questo è luogo di lacrime!
　　　　　　　　　(*minaccioso*)
　　　　　　　Badate!
　　　　　　　Or basta! Rispondete!

TOSCA, CORO　　A te giunge, o re dei re!]

　　*Irritato e disturbato dalle voci della cantata, Scarpia va a
chiudere la finestra.*

SCARPIA (*imperioso, a Cavaradossi*)
　　　　　　　Ov'è Angelotti?

CAVARADOSSI　　Non lo so.

SCARPIA　　　　Negate d'avergli dato cibo?

CAVARADOSSI　　Nego!

SCARPIA　　　　E vesti?

CAVARADOSSI　　Nego!

SCARPIA　　　　E asilo nella villa?
　　　　　　　E che là sia nascosto?

CAVARADOSSI (*con forza*)
　　　　　　　Nego! nego!

SCARPIA (*astutamente, ritornando calmo*)
　　　　　　　Via, Cavaliere, riflettete:
　　　　　　　saggia non è cotesta ostinatezza vostra.
　　　　　　　Angoscia grande,
　　　　　　　pronta confessione eviterà!

SCARPIA (*who had interrupted himself at hearing Tosca's voice, resumes*)

     . . . it is known to you that a prisoner
     fled today from Castel Sant'Angelo?

CAVARADOSSI   I know nothing of it.

SCARPIA   And yet it is claimed that you
                    received him in Sant'Andrea,
                    provided him with food and clothes . . .

CAVARADOSSI (*resolute*)
                    Lie!

SCARPIA (*continuing to remain calm*)
                    . . . and led him to a farm of yours
                    outside the city . . .

CAVARADOSSI   I deny it. The proofs?

SCARPIA (*mellifluous*)
                    A faithful subject . . .

CAVARADOSSI   To the facts. Who accuses me?
                    Your spies searched the villa in vain.

SCARPIA   A sign that he is well hidden.

TOSCA, CHORUS
                    The human anthem rises, ascends,
                    crosses spaces, crosses skies!

CAVARADOSSI   A spy's suspicions!

SPOLETTA (*offended, intervenes*)
                    At our searches he laughed . . .

CAVARADOSSI   And I laugh still . . . and I laugh still.

SCARPIA (*rising, terrible*)
                    This is a place for tears!
                       (*threatening*)
                    Be careful!
                    Enough now! Answer!

TOSCA, CHORUS
                    It comes to Thee, O King of Kings!

Irritated and disturbed by the voices of the cantata, Scarpia goes to shut the window.

SCARPIA (*imperious, to Cavaradossi*)
                    Where is Angelotti?

CAVARADOSSI   I don't know.

SCARPIA   Do you deny having given him food?

CAVARADOSSI   I deny it!

SCARPIA   And clothes?

CAVARADOSSI   I deny it!

SCARPIA   And refuge in the villa?
                    And that he is hidden there?

CAVARADOSSI (*forcefully*)
                    I deny it! I deny it!

SCARPIA (*astutely, becoming calm again*)
                    Come, Cavaliere, reflect:
                    this obstinacy of yours is not wise.
                    A prompt confession
                    will avoid great anguish!

Io vi consiglio, dite:
dov'è dunque Angelotti?

CAVARADOSSI   Non lo so.

SCARPIA   Ancor, l'ultima volta.
Dov'è?

CAVARADOSSI   Nol so!

SPOLETTA   (O bei tratti di corda!)

Tosca entra affannosa: vede Cavaradossi e corre ad abbracciarlo.

SCARPIA (*vedendo Tosca*)
(Eccola!)

TOSCA   Mario, tu qui?

CAVARADOSSI   (*sommessamente a Tosca, che accenna d'aver*
capito)
(Di quanto là vedesti, taci,
o m'uccidi!)

SCARPIA   Mario Cavaradossi, qual testimone
il giudice v'aspetta.
(*fa cenno a Sciarrone di aprire l'uscio che*
dà alla camera della tortura, poi rivolgen-
dosi a Roberti)
Pria le forme ordinaire . . .
Indi . . . ai miei cenni . . .

Sciarrone apre l'uscio. Il Giudice vi entra e gli altri lo segu-
ono, rimanendo Tosca e Scarpia. Spoletta si ritira presso alla
porta in fondo alla sala. Sciarrone chiude l'uscio. Tosca fa un
atto di grande sorpresa: Scarpia, studiatamente gentile, la ras-
sicura.

SCARPIA   Ed or fra noi parliam
da buoni amici.
(*accenna a Tosca di sedere*)
Via quell'aria sgomentata . . .

TOSCA (*siede, con calma studiata*)
Sgomento alcun non ho.

Scarpia passa dietro al canapè sul quale si è seduta Tosca
e vi si appoggia, parlando sempre con galanteria.

SCARPIA   La storia del ventaglio?

TOSCA (*con simulata indifferenza*)
Fu sciocca gelosia.

SCARPIA   L'Attavanti non era dunque
alla villa?

TOSCA   No: egli era solo.

SCARPIA   Solo? Ne siete ben sicura?

TOSCA   Nulla sfugge ai gelosi.
Solo! Solo!

Scarpia prende una sedia, la porta di fronte a Tosca, vi si
siede e la guarda fiso.

SCARPIA   Davver?

TOSCA (*assai stizzita*)
Solo! sì!

I advise you, tell:
where is Angelotti, then?

CAVARADOSSI   I don't know.

SCARPIA   Again, the last time.
Where is he?

CAVARADOSSI   I don't know.

SPOLETTA   (Oh, lovely tugs at the rope!)

Tosca enters breathlessly; she sees Cavaradossi and runs to embrace him.

SCARPIA *(seeing Tosca)*
(There she is!)

TOSCA   Mario, you here?

CAVARADOSSI *(softly, to Tosca, who indicates she has understood)*
(Keep silent about what you saw there,
or you kill me!)

SCARPIA   Mario Cavaradossi, the judge awaits you
as a witness.
       *(motions to Sciarrone to open the door
       that gives on the torture chamber, then,
       speaking to Roberti)*
First the ordinary methods . . .
Then . . . at my signals . . .

Sciarrone opens the door. The judge enters and the others follow him, Tosca and Scarpia remaining. Spoletta withdraws near the door at the back of the room. Sciarrone shuts the door. Tosca makes a gesture of great surprise. Studiously polite, Scarpia reassures her.

SCARPIA   And now let's speak between ourselves
like good friends.
       (motions to Tosca to sit down)
Away with that frightened manner . . .

TOSCA *(sits, with studied calm)*
I have no fright.

Scarpia moves behind the couch on which Tosca is seated; he leans on it, still speaking in a courteous tone.

SCARPIA   The story of the fan?

TOSCA *(with feigned indifference)*
It was foolish jealousy.

SCARPIA   The Attavanti then
wasn't at the villa?

TOSCA   No, he was alone.

SCARPIA   Alone? Are you quite sure?

TOSCA   Nothing escapes the jealous.
Alone! Alone!

Scarpia takes a chair and brings it in front of Tosca. He sits on it and looks hard at her.

SCARPIA   Really?

TOSCA *(very annoyed)*
Alone! Yes!

SCARPIA   Quanto fuoco! Par che abbiate
                 paura di tradirvi.
                          (*rivolgendosi verso l'uscio della camera
                          della tortura chiamando*)
                 Sciarrone: che dice il Cavalier?

SCIARRONE (*apparisce sul limitare*)
                 Nega.

SCARPIA (*a voce più alta*)
                 Insistiamo.

   Sciarrone rientra, chiudendo l'uscio.

TOSCA (*ridendo*)
                 Oh! è inutil!

SCARPIA (*seriissimo: s'alza e passeggia*)
                 Lo vedremo, signora.

TOSCA   Dunque per compiacervi
                 si dovrebbe mentir?

SCARPIA   No: ma il vero potrebbe abbreviargli
                 un'ora assai penosa . . .

TOSCA (*sorpresa*)
                 Un'ora penosa? Che vuol dir?
                 Che avviene in quella stanza?

SCARPIA   È forza che s'adempia la legge.

TOSCA   Oh! Dio! che avvien, che avvien,
                 che avvien?!

SCARPIA (*con espressione di ferocia e con forza crescente*)

                 Legato mani e piè il vostro amante
                 ha un cerchio uncinato alle tempia,
                 che ad ogni niego ne sprizza
                 sangue senza mercè!

TOSCA (*balzando in piedi*)
                 Non è ver, non è ver!
                 Sogghigno di demone . . .
                          (*ascolta con grande ansietà, le mani ner-
                          vosamente avvinghiate alla spalliera del
                          canapè*)

CAVARADOSSI (*gemito prolungato*)
                 Ahimè!

TOSCA   Un gemito? Pietà, pietà!

SCARPIA   Sta in voi salvarlo.

TOSCA   Ebben . . . ma cessate, cessate!

SCARPIA (*volgendosi e avvicinandosi all'uscio*)
                 Sciarrone, sciogliete.

SCIARRONE (*apparendo sul limitare*)
                 Tutto?

SCARPIA   Tutto.

   *Sciarrone rientra nella camera della tortura, chiudendo
l'uscio.*

SCARPIA   Ed or la verità . . .

TOSCA   Ch'io lo veda . . . !

SCARPIA   No!

SCARPIA   How much fire! It seems you're afraid
of giving yourself away.
> (*turning toward the door of the torture
> chamber, calling out*)

Sciarrone, what does the Cavaliere say?

SCIARRONE (*appears on the threshold*)
He denies.

SCARPIA (*in a louder voice*)
Let us insist.

Sciarrone goes back in, shutting the door.

TOSCA (*laughing*)
Oh, it's useless!

SCARPIA (*very serious, stands up and paces up and down*)
We shall see, madam.

TOSCA   So then to satisfy you
one should lie?

SCARPIA   No, but the truth could shorten for him
a very painful hour . . .

TOSCA (*surprised*)
A painful hour? What does that mean?
What is happening in that room?

SCARPIA   The law must be carried out perforce.

TOSCA   Oh, God! What is happening,
what is happening?

SCARPIA (*with an expression of ferocity and with mounting
strength*)
Your lover is bound hand and foot,
he has a spiked circle around his temples,
which at every denial spurts
blood without mercy.

TOSCA (*springing to her feet*)
It's not true, it's not true!
Demon's grin . . .
> (*listens with great anxiety, her hands ner-
> vously clutching the back of the sofa*)

CAVARADOSSI (*prolonged groan*)
Alas!

TOSCA   A moan? Pity! Pity!

SCARPIA   It's up to you to save him.

TOSCA   Very well . . . but stop, stop!

SCARPIA (*turning and approaching the door*)
Sciaronne, untie him.

SCIARRONE (*appearing on the threshold*)
Completely?

SCARPIA   Completely.

*Sciarrone goes back into the torture chamber, closing the
door.*

SCARPIA   And now the truth . . .

TOSCA   Let me see him . . . !

SCARPIA   No!

Tosca poco a poco riesce ad avvicinarsi all'uscio.

TOSCA   Mario!

LA VOCE DI CAVARADOSSI
                         (*dolorosamente*)
                 Tosca!

TOSCA   Ti straziano ancora?

LA VOCE DI CAVARADOSSI
                 No . . . coraggio . . .
                 Taci, taci . . .
                 Sprezzo il dolor!

SCARPIA (*avvicinandosi a Tosca*)
                 Orsù, Tosca, parlate.

TOSCA (*rinfrancata*)
                 Non so nulla!

SCARPIA   Non vale quella prova?
                     (*fa per avvicinarsi all'uscio*)
                 Roberti, ripigliamo . . .

TOSCA (*si frappone fra l'uscio e Scarpia per impedire che dia
         l'ordine*)
                 No! fermate!

SCARPIA   Voi parlerete?

TOSCA   No! no! Ah! mostro!
                 Lo strazi, ah! mostro,
                 lo strazi, l'uccidi . . .
                 ah! l'uccidi!

SCARPIA   Lo strazia quel vostro silenzio
                 assai più.
                     (*ride*)

TOSCA   Tu ridi all'orrida pena?

SCARPIA (*con feroce ironia*)
                 Mai Tosca alla scena
                 più tragica fu!

*Tosca, inorridita, si allontana da Scarpia, che preso da su-
bitaneo senso di ferocia, si rivolge a Spoletta, gridando.*

SCARPIA   Aprite le porte
                 che n'oda i lamenti!

Spoletta apre l'uscio e sta ritto sulla soglia.

LA VOCE DI CAVARADOSSI
                 Vi sfido!

SCARPIA (*gridando a Roberti*)
                 Più forte, più forte!

LA VOCE DI CAVARADOSSI
                 Vi sfido!

SCARPIA (*a Tosca*)
                 Parlate . . .

TOSCA   Che dire?

SCARPIA   Su, via.

TOSCA   Ah! non so nulla!
                     (*disperata*)
                 Ah! dovrei mentir?

SCARPIA   Dite dov'è Angelotti?

TOSCA   No!

Tosca, little by little, manages to move closer to the door.

TOSCA	Mario!
CAVARADOSSI'S VOICE *(painfully)*	
	Tosca!

TOSCA	Are they still torturing you?
CAVARADOSSI'S VOICE	
	No . . . courage . . .
	Be silent, be silent . . .
	I scorn the pain!
SCARPIA *(approaching Tosca)*	
	Now, then, Tosca, speak.
TOSCA *(reassured)*	
	I know nothing!
SCARPIA	Isn't that trial enough?
	(starts to approach the door)
	Roberti, let us resume . . .
TOSCA *(places herself between the door and Scarpia to prevent him from giving the order)*	
	No! Stop!
SCARPIA	You will speak?
TOSCA	No! no! Ah, monster!
	You torture him, ah, monster,
	you torture him, you are killing him . . .
	ah! you are killing him!
SCARPIA	That silence of yours
	is torturing him much more.
	(laughs)
TOSCA	You laugh at the horrible pain?
SCARPIA *(with fierce irony)*	
	Never was Tosca on the stage
	more tragic!

Tosca, horrified, moves away from Scarpia, who, seized by a sudden impulse of ferocity, addresses Spoletta, shouting.

SCARPIA	Open the doors
	that I may hear the moans!

Spoletta opens the door and stands stiffly on the threshold.

CAVARADOSSI'S VOICE	
	I defy you!
SCARPIA *(shouting to Roberti)*	
	Harder, harder!
CAVARADOSSI'S VOICE	
	I defy you!
SCARPIA *(to Tosca)*	
	Speak . . .
TOSCA	What am I to say?
SCARPIA	Come, come.
TOSCA	Ah! I know nothing!
	(desperate)
	Ah! should I lie?
SCARPIA	Tell me: where is Angelotti?
TOSCA	No!

SCARPIA   Dite dov'è Angelotti?
          [Parlate, su, via,
          dove celato sta?
          Su, via, parlate, ov'è?

TOSCA   Ah, ah, più non posso!
          Ah, che orror!]
          Ah, cessate il martir!
          è troppo soffrir!
          Ah! non posso più,
          ah! non posso più!

LA VOCE DI CAVARADOSSI
                    (*lamento forte*)
          Ahimè!

*Tosca si rivolge supplichevole a Scarpia, il quale fa cenno
a Spoletta di lasciare avvicinare Tosca: questa va presso l'uscio
aperto, ed esterrefatta alla vista dell'orribile scena, si rivolge
a Cavaradossi.*

TOSCA (*dolorosamente*)
          Mario . . . consenti
          ch'io parli?

LA VOCE DI CAVARADOSSI
          No! No!

TOSCA   Ascolta, non posso più . . .

LA VOCE DI CAVARADOSSI
          Stolta, che sai?
          che puoi dir?

SCARPIA (*irritatissimo per le parole di Cavaradossi, e temendo
                    che da queste Tosca sia ancora incoraggiata
                    a tacere, grida terribile a Spoletta*)
          Ma fatelo tacere!

*Spoletta entra nella camera della tortura e n'esce poco dopo,
mentre Tosca, vinta dalla terribile commozione, cade prostrata
sul canapè e con voce singhiozzante si rivolge a Scarpia che
sta impassibile e silenzioso. Intanto Spoletta brontola preghiere
sottovoce.*

TOSCA   Che v'ho fatto in vita mia?!
          Son io che così torturate . . . !
          [Torturate l'anima . . . sì . . .

SPOLETTA *Judex ergo cum sedebit
          quidquid latet apparebit.
          Nil inultum remanebit.*]

TOSCA   L'anima mi torturate!

SPOLETTA *Quid sum miser tunc dicturus
          quam patronum rogaturus
          Cum vix justus fit securus.*

*Scarpia, proffittando dell'accasciamento di Tosca, va presso
la camera della tortura e fa cenno di ricominciare il supplizio.*

LA VOCE DI CAVARADOSSI
                    (*straziante grido acuto e prolungato*)
          Ah!

SCARPIA   Tell me: where is Angelotti?
               Speak, come, come,
               where is he hidden?
               Come, speak, where is he?

TOSCA   Ah, ah, I can stand no more!
               Ah, what horror!
               Ah, cease the torment!
               Ah! I can stand no more,
               Ah! I can stand no more!

CAVARADOSSI'S VOICE *(loud moan)*
               Alas!

Tosca turns, pleading, to Scarpia, who motions to Spoletta to allow Tosca to come closer. She goes to the open door and, terrified at the sight of the horrible scene, she speaks to Cavaradossi.

TOSCA *(sorrowfully)*
               Mario . . . do you allow
               me to speak?

CAVARADOSSI'S VOICE
               No! No!

TOSCA   Listen, I can stand no more . . .

CAVARADOSSI'S VOICE
               Foolish woman, what do you know?
               What can you say?

SCARPIA *(highly irritated at the words of Cavaradossi, and*
               fearing that from them Tosca has again been
               encouraged to remain silent, shouts in a ter-
               rible voice to Spoletta)
               But make him shut up!

Spoletta enters the torture chamber and comes out again shortly afterward, as Tosca, overwhelmed by her terrible emotion, falls prostrate on the sofa and in a sobbing voice addresses Scarpia, who remains impassive and silent. Meanwhile Spoletta mutters prayers in a low voice.

TOSCA   What have I done to you in my life?!
               I'm the one you are torturing in this way . . . !
               You torture my soul . . . yes . . .

SPOLETTA *Judex ergo cum sedebit*
               quidquid latet apparebit.
               Nil inultum remanebit.

TOSCA   You torture my soul!

SPOLETTA *Quid sum miser tunc dicturus*
               quam patronum rogaturus
               Cum vix justus fit securus.

Scarpia, taking advantage of Tosca's despondency, goes to the torture chamber and gives the signal to begin the torture again.

CAVARADOSSI'S VOICE
               (shrill and prolonged heart-rending cry)
               Ah!

Al grido di Cavaradossi, Tosca si alza di scatto e subito, con voce soffocata, dice rapidamente a Scarpia.

TOSCA   Nel pozzo . . . nel giardino . . .

SCARPIA   Là è l'Angelotti?

TOSCA   Sì . . .

SCARPIA   (*forte, verso la camera della tortura*)
                   Basta, Roberti.

SCIARRONE   (*apparendo sulla porta*)
                   È svenuto!

TOSCA   (*a Scarpia*)
                   Assassino!
                   Voglio vederlo . . .

SCARPIA   (*a Sciarrone*)
                   Portatelo qui . . . !

Sciarrone rientra e subito appare Cavaradossi svenuto, portato dai birri che lo depongono sul canapè. Tosca corre a lui, ma l'orrore della vista dell'amante insanguinato è così forte, ch'essa sgomentata si copre il volto per non vederlo — poi, vergognosa di questa sua debolezza, si inginocchia presso di lui, baciandolo e piangendo. Sciarrone, il Giudice, Roberti, lo Scrivano escono dal fondo, mentre, ad un cenno di Scarpia, Spoletta e i birri si fermano.

CAVARADOSSI   (*riavendosi*)
                   Floria!

TOSCA   Amore . . .

CAVARADOSSI   Sei tu?

TOSCA   Quanto hai penato, anima mia!
                   Ma il guisto Iddio lo punirà!

CAVARADOSSI   Tosca, hai parlato?

TOSCA   No, amore . . .

CAVARADOSSI   Davvero?

TOSCA   No!

SCARPIA   (*forte, a Spoletta*)
                   Nel pozzo del giardino —
                   Va, Spoletta!
                        (*Spoletta esce*)

CAVARADOSSI   (*si leva minaccioso contro Tosca*)
                   M'hai tradito!

TOSCA   (*supplichevole*)
                   Mario!

CAVARADOSSI   (*si lascia cadere, affranto*)
                   Maledetta!

TOSCA   Mario!

SCIARRONE   (*erompendo affannoso*)
                   Eccellenza, quali nuove!

SCARPIA   (*sorpreso*)
                   Che vuol dir quell'aria afflitta?

SCIARRONE   Un messaggio di sconfitta . . .

SCARPIA   Che sconfitta? Come? Dove?

SCIARRONE   A Marengo . . .

At Cavaradossi's cry, Tosca springs up and at once, in a stifled voice, says rapidly to Scarpia

TOSCA   In the well . . . in the garden . . .

SCARPIA   Angelotti is there?

TOSCA   Yes . . .

SCARPIA (*loud, toward the torture chamber*)
     Enough, Roberti.

SCIARRONE (*appearing at the door*)
     He's fainted!

TOSCA (*to Scarpia*)
     Murderer!
     I want to see him . . .

SCARPIA (*to Sciarrone*)
     Bring him here . . . !

Sciarrone goes back in and at once Cavaradossi appears, unconscious, carried by the policemen, who set him on the sofa. Tosca runs to him, but the horror at the sight of her bloodstained lover is so strong that, aghast, she covers her face so as not to see him — then, ashamed of this weakness of hers, she kneels beside him, kissing him and weeping. Sciarrone, the judge, Roberti, the scribe come out in the background as, at a signal from Scarpia, Spoletta and the policemen stop.

CAVARADOSSI (*coming to*)
     Floria!

TOSCA   Love . . .

CAVARADOSSI   Is it you?

TOSCA   How much you've suffered, my soul!
     But the just God will punish him!

CAVARADOSSI   Tosca, did you speak?

TOSCA   No, love . . .

CAVARADOSSI   Really?

TOSCA   No!

SCARPIA (*loud, to Spoletta*)
     In the well of the garden —
     Go, Spoletta!
     (*Spoletta goes out*)

CAVARADOSSI (*rises, menacing, against Tosca*)
     You've betrayed me!

TOSCA (*pleading*)
     Mario!

CAVARADOSSI (*drops back, shattered*)
     Curse you!

TOSCA   Mario!

SCIARRONE (*bursting in, breathless*)
     Excellency, what news!

SCARPIA (*surprised*)
     What does this afflicted manner mean?

SCIARRONE   A message of defeat . . .

SCARPIA   What defeat? How? Where?

SCIARRONE   At Marengo . . .

SCARPIA (*impaziente, gridando*)
          Tartaruga!
SCIARRONE   Bonaparte è vincitor . . .
SCARPIA   Melas . . .
SCIARRONE   No! Melas è in fuga!

Cavaradossi, che con ansia crescente ha udito le parole di Sciarrone, trova nel proprio entusiasmo la forza di alzarsi minaccioso in faccia a Scarpia.

CAVARADOSSI Vittoria! Vittoria!
             L'alba vindice appar
             che fa gli empi tremar!
             Libertà sorge,
             crollan tirannidi!

TOSCA (*disperata, avvinghiandosi a Cavaradossi cercando cal-
             marlo*)
             Mario, taci,
             pietà di me!

CAVARADOSSI Del sofferto martir
             [me vedrai qui gioir
             il tuo cor trema,
             o Scarpia, carnefice!

SCARPIA (*sorride sarcasticamente*)
             Braveggia, urla!
             T'affretta a palesarmi
             il fondo dell'alma ria!
             Moribondo, il capestro t'aspetta!

TOSCA   Pietà, pietà!

CAVARADOSSI Carnefice, carnefice!]

SCARPIA   Va, va!
                 (*irritato dalla parole di Cavaradossi, grida
                 agli sbirri*)
             Portatemelo via!

*Sciarrone ed i birri s'impossessano di Cavaradossi e lo trasci-
nano verso la porta. Tosca con un supremo sforzo tenta di
tenersi stretta a Cavaradossi, ma invano: essa è brutalmente
respinta.*

TOSCA   Mario . . . con te . . .

SCARPIA   Va, moribondo!

TOSCA   No, no!

SCARPIA   Va, va!

TOSCA   Ah! Mario, Mario!
             Con te . . . con te . . .
                 (*cercando forzare il passo sbarrato da
                 Scarpia*)

SCARPIA (*respingendo Tosca e chiudendo la porta*)
             Voi no!

TOSCA (*con un gemito*)
             Salvatelo!

SCARPIA   Io . . . ? Voi!
                 (*si avvicina alla tavola, vede la sua cena
                 interrotta e ritorna calmo e sorridente*)

SCARPIA (*out of patience, shouting*)
    You tortoise!

SCIARRONE Bonaparte is the victor . . .

SCARPIA   Melas . . .

SCIARRONE No! Melas is in flight!

*Cavaradossi, who has heard Sciarrone's words with mount-
ing anxiety, now in his own enthusiasm finds the strength to
stand up, menacing, facing Scarpia.*

CAVARADOSSI Victory! Victory!
    The avenging dawn appears
    that makes the wicked tremble!
    Liberty rises,
    tyrannies collapse!

TOSCA (*desperate, clinging to Cavaradossi, trying to calm him*)
    Mario, be silent!
    Have pity on me!

CAVARADOSSI You will see me here rejoice
    at the torture suffered;
    your heart is trembling,
    O Scarpia, executioner!

SCARPIA (*smiles sarcastically*)
    Swagger, shout!
    Hasten to expose to me
    the depths of your guilty soul!
    Dying man, the noose awaits you!

TOSCA   Pity, pity!

CAVARADOSSI Executioner, executioner!

SCARPIA   Go, go!
     (*annoyed by Cavaradossi's words, shouts
     to the policemen*)
    Take him away from me!

*Sciarrone and the policemen seize Cavaradossi and drag
him toward the door. With a supreme effort, Tosca tries to
hold tight to Cavaradossi, but in vain. She is brutally thrust
away.*

TOSCA   Mario . . . with you . . .

SCARPIA   Go, dying man!

TOSCA   No, no!

SCARPIA   Go, go!

TOSCA   Ah! Mario, Mario!
    With you . . . with you . . .
     (*trying to force her way, blocked by Scarpia*)

SCARPIA (*repulsing Tosca and shutting the door*)
    You, no!

TOSCA (*with a moan*)
    Save him!

SCARPIA   I . . . ? You!
     (*approaches the table, sees his interrupted
     supper, and becomes calm and smiling
     again*)

La povera mia cena fu interrotta.
> (*vedendo Tosca abbattuta, immobile, an-
> cora presso la porta*)

Così accasciata?
Via, mia bella signora,
sedete qui.
Volete che cerchiamo insieme
il modo di salvarlo?
E allor . . .
> (*si siede, accennando in pari tempo di se-
> dere a Tosca*)

sedete . . . e favelliamo.
> (*forbisce un bicchiere col tovagliolo, quindi
> lo guarda a traverso la luce del cande-
> labro*)

E intanto un sorso.
E vin di Spagna . . .
> (*mescendo, con gentilezza*)

Un sorso per rincorarvi.

*Tosca siede in faccia a Scarpia, guardandolo fissamente;
poi appoggiando i gomiti sul tavolo, colle mani si sorregge il
viso, e coll'accento del più profondo disprezzo chiede a
Scarpia.*

TOSCA   Quanto?

SCARPIA (*imperturbabile, versandosi da bere*)

Quanto?

TOSCA   Il prezzo!

SCARPIA (*ride*)

Già. Mi dicon venal,
mi dicon venal, ma a donna bella
non mi vendo a prezzo di moneta.
No, no!
> (*insinuante*)

A donna bella io non mi vendo
a prezzo di moneta.
Se la giurata fede debbo tradir,
ne voglio altra mercede,
ne voglio altra mercede.
Quest'ora io l'attendeva!
Già mi struggea
l'amor della diva!
Ma poc'anzi ti mirai
qual non it vidi mai!
> (*eccitatissimo, si alza*)

Quel tuo pianto era lava
ai sensi miei
e il tuo sguardo che odio
in me dardeggiava,
mie brame inferociva!
Agil qual leopardo
t'avvinghiasti all'amante.
Ah! In quell'istante
t'ho giurata mia! Mia!

My poor supper was interrupted.
> (*seeing Tosca disheartened, motionless,
> still by the door*)

So crushed?
Come, my lovely lady,
sit here.
Would you like us to look together
for the way to save him?
Well then . . .
> (*sits, motioning at the same time to Tosca
> to sit down*)

. . . sit down . . . and let us talk.
> (*cleans a glass with the napkin, then looks
> at it against the light of the candelabrum*)

And meanwhile a sip.
It's wine from Spain . . .
> (*pouring, politely*)

A sip to cheer you up.

Tosca sits facing Scarpia, looking at him fixedly. Then, setting her elbows on the table, with her hands supporting her face and in the tone of the most profound contempt she asks Scarpia

TOSCA How much?

SCARPIA (*imperturbable, pouring himself something to drink*)
How much?

TOSCA The price!

SCARPIA (*laughs*)
That's right. They say I'm venal;
they say I'm venal, but I don't sell myself
to a beautiful woman at a price in money.
No, no!
> (*insinuating*)

I don't sell myself to a beautiful woman
at a price in money.
If I must betray my sworn faith,
I want another recompense,
I want another recompense.
I was waiting for this hour!
The love of the diva
was already consuming me!
But a little while ago I looked upon you
as I had never seen you!
> (*very excited, stands up*)

That weeping of yours was lava
to my senses,
and your gaze which darted
hatred at me,
made my desires fierce!
Agile as a leopard
you clung to your lover.
Ah! At that moment
I swore you'd be mine! Mine!

Scarpia si avvicina a Tosca, stendendo le braccia: Tosca che aveva ascoltato immobile, impietrita le lascive parole di Scarpia, s'alza di scatto e si rifugia dietro il canapè.

TOSCA   Ah!

SCARPIA   Sì, t'avrò . . . !

TOSCA   Ah!

SCARPIA (*quasi inseguendola*)
                 Sì, t'avrò!

TOSCA (*inorridita corre alla finestra, accennando alla finestra*)
                 Ah! Piuttosto giù m'avvento!

SCARPIA (*freddamente*)
                 In pegno il Mario tuo mi resta!

TOSCA   Ah! miserabile . . .
                 l'orribil mercato!

Le balena l'idea di recarsi presso la Regina e corre verso la porta. Scarpia che ne indovina il pensiero, si tira in disparte.

SCARPIA   Violenza non ti farò.
                 Sei libera. Va pure.

Tosca con un grido di gioia fa per escire: Scarpia con un gesto e ridendo ironicamente la trattiene.

SCARPIA   Ma è fallace speranza:
                 la Regina farebbe grazia
                 ad un cadavere!

Tosca retrocede spaventata e fissando Scarpia si lascia cadere sul canapè: poi stacca gli occhi da Scarpia con un gesto di supremo disgusto e di odio.

SCARPIA (*con accento convinto e con compiacenza*)
                 Come tu m'odii!

TOSCA   Ah! Dio!

SCARPIA (*avvicinandosele*)
                 Così, così ti voglio!

TOSCA (*con ribrezzo*)
                 Non toccarmi, demonio!
                 T'odio, t'odio, t'odio,
                 abbietto, vile!
                         (*fugge da Scarpia, inorridita*)

SCARPIA (*avvicinandosele ancor più*)
                 Che importa?!
                 Spasimi d'ira . . . spasimi d'amore!

TOSCA   Vile!

SCARPIA (*cerca di afferrarla*)
                 Mia!

TOSCA (*si ripara dietro la tavola*)
                 Vile!

SCARPIA (*rincorrendo Tosca*)
                 Mia!

TOSCA   [Aiuto! aiuto! aiuto!

SCARPIA   Mia! mia!]

Al suono lontano dei tamburi si arrestano.

SCARPIA   Odi? È il tamburo.
                 S'avvia. Guida la scorta
                 ultima ai condannati.
                 Il tempo passa!

Scarpia approaches Tosca, holding out his arms. Tosca, who has listened without moving, petrified, to Scarpia's lascivious words, springs up and takes refuge behind the sofa.

TOSCA   Ah!

SCARPIA   Yes, I'll have you . . . !

TOSCA   Ah!

SCARPIA (*almost pursuing her*)
               Yes, I'll have you!

TOSCA (*horrified, runs to the window, indicating the window*)
               Ah! Rather I will throw myself down!

SCARPIA (*coldly*)
               As a pledge your Mario remains with me!

TOSCA   Ah! wretch . . .
               The horrible bargain!

She has the idea of going to the queen and she runs toward the door. Scarpia, who guesses her thought, stands to one side.

SCARPIA   I will not do violence to you.
               You are free. Go ahead.

With a cry of joy Tosca starts to go out: with a gesture, and laughing ironically, Scarpia holds her back.

SCARPIA   But it's a false hope.
               The queen would grant her reprieve
               to a corpse!

Tosca steps back, frightened, and, staring at Scarpia, she sinks onto the sofa, then she removes her eyes from Scarpia with a gesture of supreme disgust and hatred.

SCARPIA (*with a convinced tone and with self-satisfaction*)
               How you hate me!

TOSCA   Ah! God!

SCARPIA (*approaching her*)
               Thus, thus I want you!

TOSCA (*with horror*)
               Don't touch me, demon!
               I hate you, hate you, hate you,
               abject man, coward!
                    (*flees from Scarpia, horrified*)

SCARPIA (*coming still closer to her*)
               What does it matter?
               Transports of wrath . . . transports of love!

TOSCA   Coward!

SCARPIA (*tries to seize her*)
               Mine!

TOSCA (*takes refuge behind the table*)
               Coward!

SCARPIA (*pursuing Tosca*)
               Mine!

TOSCA   Help! Help! Help!

SCARPIA   Mine, mine!

At the distant sound of the drums they stop.

SCARPIA   You hear? It's the drum.
               It's going away. It leads
               the final escort of the condemned men.
               Time is passing!

*Tosca, dopo aver ascoltato con ansia terribile, si allontana
dalla finestra e si appoggia, estenuata, al canapè.*

SCARPIA   Sai quale oscura opra
           laggiù si compia?
           Là si drizza un patibolo.
           Al tuo Mario, per tuo voler,
           non resta che un'ora di vita.

*Tosca affranta dal dolore si lascia cadere sul canapè. Fred-
damente Scarpia va ad appoggiarsi ad un angolo della tavola,
si versa il caffè e lo assorbe mentre continua a guardare Tosca.*

TOSCA (*nel massimo dolore*)
           Vissi d'arte, vissi d'amore,
           non feci mai male ad anima viva!
           Con man furtiva
           quante miserie conobbi, aiutai.
           Sempre con fè sincera
           la mia preghiera
           ai santi tabernacoli salì.
           Sempre con fè sincera,
           diedi fiori agl'altar.
           Nell'ora del dolore
           perchè, perchè Signore,
           perchè me ne rimuneri così?
           Diedi gioelli
           della Madonna al manto,
           e diedi il canto
           agli astri, al ciel,
           che ne ridean più belli.
           Nell'ora del dolor
           perchè, perchè Signor,
           ah, perchè me ne rimuneri così?*

* SCARPIA (*avvicinando di nuovo a Tosca*)
           (A) Risolvi?

TOSCA   Mi vuoi supplice ai tuoi piedi? (B)
           (*s'inginocchia davanti a Scarpia*)
           Vedi . . . le man giunte
           io stendo a te!
           Ecco . . . vedi . . .
           e mercè d'un tuo detto,
           vinta aspetto . . .

SCARPIA   Sei troppo bella, Tosca,
           e troppo amante.
           Cedo. A misero prezzo
           tu, a me una vita,
           io, a te chieggo un'istante!

TOSCA (*alzandosi, con senso di gran disprezzo*)
           Va! va!
           Mi fai ribrezzo! Va! Va!

Bussano alla porta.

SCARPIA   Chi è là?

SPOLETTA (*entrando tutto frettoloso e trafelato*)
           Eccellenza, l'Angelotti
           al nostro giungere s'uccise!

* The lines beginning at (A) and ending at (B) are traditionally
cut.

Tosca, after having listened with terrible anxiety, goes away from the window and leans, exhausted, on the sofa.

SCARPIA   You know what dark deed
is done over there?
There a scaffold rises.
For your Mario, through your wish,
only an hour of life remains.

Tosca, overcome with grief, sinks down on the sofa. Coldly, Scarpia goes and leans on a corner of the table, pours his coffee and sips it as he continues to look at Tosca.

TOSCA (*at the height of grief*)
I lived on art, I lived on love,
I never did harm to a living soul!
With a furtive hand
I assisted such unfortunates as I knew of.
Always with sincere faith
my prayer
rose at the holy tabernacles.
Always with sincere faith
I gave flowers to the altars.
In my hour of grief
why, why, Lord,
why do you repay me thus?
I gave jewels
to the Madonna's mantle,
and I gave my song
to the stars, to heaven
which rejoiced, more beautiful, in them.
In my hour of grief,
why, why, Lord,
ah, why do you repay me thus?*

SCARPIA (*again approaching Tosca*)
(A) Have you made up your mind?

TOSCA   Do you want me imploring at your feet? (B)
(*kneels before Scarpia*)
You see . . . I extend clasped
hands to you!
There . . . you see . . .
and at the mercy of a word from you,
defeated, I wait . . .

SCARPIA   You're too beautiful, Tosca,
and too much in love.
I give in. At a wretched price
you ask a life of me,
I ask of you an instant!

TOSCA (*rising, with a feeling of great contempt*)
Go! Go!
You revolt me! Go! Go!

Knock at the door.

SCARPIA   Who is there?

SPOLETTA (*entering all in haste and breathless*)
Excellency, Angelotti
on our arrival killed himself!

---

* The lines beginning at (A) and ending at (B) are traditionally cut.

SCARPIA   Ebben lo si appenda
               morto alle forche!
               E l'altro prigionier?

SPOLETTA   Il cavalier Cavaradossi?
               È tutto pronto, Eccellenza!

TOSCA   (Dio! m'assisti!)

SCARPIA (*a Spoletta*)
               Aspetta.
                    (*piano a Tosca*)
               Ebbene?

   *Tosca col capo accenna di sì, poi piangendo dalla vergogna
affonda la testa fra i cuscini del canapè.*

SCARPIA (*a Spoletta*)
               Odi . . .

TOSCA (*interrompendo subito Scarpia*)
               Ma libero all'istante
               lo voglio!

SCARPIA (*a Tosca*)
               Occorre simular.
               Non posso far grazia aperta.
               Bisogna che tutti
               abbian per morto il cavalier.
                    (*accenna a Spoletta*)
               Quest'uomo fido provvederà.

TOSCA   Chi m'assicura?

SCARPIA   L'ordin ch'io gli darò
               voi qui presente.
                    (*a Spoletta*)
               Spoletta: chiudi.

   *Spoletta frettolosamente va a chiudere, poi ritorna presso
Scarpia.*

SCARPIA (*fissa con intenzione Spoletta che accenna replica-
               tamente col capo di indovinare il pensiero di
               Scarpia*)
               Ho mutato d'avviso . . .
               Il prigionier sia fucilato.
                    (*Tosca scatta atterrita*)
               Attendi . . .
               Come facemmo del conte Palmieri . . .

SPOLETTA   Un'uccisione . . .

SCARPIA (*subito con marcata intenzione*)
               . . . simulata!
               Come avvenne del Palmieri!
               Hai ben compreso?

SPOLETTA   Ho ben compreso.

SCARPIA   Va.

TOSCA   Voglio avvertirlo io stessa.

SCARPIA   E sia.
                    (*a Spoletta*)
               Le darai passo.
               Bada: all'ora quarta . . .

SCARPIA   Very well, let him be hanged
               dead from the gallows.
               And the other prisoner?

SPOLETTA   Cavaliere Cavaradossi?
               All is ready, Excellency!

TOSCA   (God, assist me!)

SCARPIA (*to Spoletta*)
               Wait.
                    (*softly, to Tosca*)
               Well?

Tosca nods yes, then, weeping with shame, she buries her head amid the cushions of the sofa.

SCARPIA (*to Spoletta*)
               Listen . . .

TOSCA (*immediately interrupting Scarpia*)
               But I want him free
               instantly!

SCARPIA (*to Tosca*)
               We have to simulate.
               I can't grant a reprieve openly.
               Everyone must believe
               the Cavaliere dead.
                    (*nods to Spoletta*)
               This trusted man will provide.

TOSCA   Who guarantees this to me?

SCARPIA   The order that I will give him
               with you here present.
                    (*to Spoletta*)
               Spoletta: shut the door.

Spoletta hastily goes to shut the door, then comes back near Scarpia.

SCARPIA (*fixes Spoletta meaningfully. Spoletta nods repeatedly to follow Scarpia's thoughts*)

               I've changed my mind . . .
               Let the prisoner be shot
                    (*Tosca springs up, terrified*)
               Wait . . .
               As we did with Count Palmieri . . .

SPOLETTA   An execution . . .

SCARPIA (*at once, with marked emphasis*)
                    . . . simulated!
               As it happened with Palmieri!
               Have you understood clearly?

SPOLETTA   I've understood clearly.

SCARPIA   Go.

TOSCA   I want to let him know myself.

SCARPIA   So be it.
                    (*to Spoletta*)
               You will grant her passage.
               Mind you: at four o'clock . . .

SPOLETTA   Sì. Come Palmieri . . .

Spoletta parte. Scarpia, ritto presso la porta, ascolta Spoletta allontanarsi, poi trasformato nel viso e nei gesti si avvicina con grande passione a Tosca.

SCARPIA   Io tenni la promessa . . .

TOSCA (*arrestandolo*)
                    Non ancora.
                    Voglio un salvacondotto
                    onde fuggir dallo stato con lui.

SCARPIA (*con galanteria*)
                    Partir dunque volete?

TOSCA   Sì, per sempre!

SCARPIA   Si adempia il voler vostro.
                    (*va allo scrittoio: si mette a scrivere, in-
                    terrompendosi per domandare a Tosca*)
                    E qual via scegliete?

TOSCA   La più breve!

SCARPIA   Civitavecchia?

TOSCA   Sì.

Mentre Scarpia scrive, Tosca si è avvicinata alla tavola e colla mano tremante prende il bicchiere di vino versato da Scarpia, ma nel portare il bicchiere alle labbra, scorge sulla tavola un coltello affilato ed a punta; dà una rapida occhiata a Scarpia, che in quel momento è occupato a scrivere, e con infinite precauzioni cerca d'impossessarsi del coltello, che poi dissimula dietro di sè, appoggiandosi alla tavola e sempre sorvegliando Scarpia. Questi ha finito di scrivere il salvacon-dotto, vi mette il sigillo, ripiega il foglio: quindi aprendo le braccia si avvicina a Tosca per avvincerla a sè.

SCARPIA   Tosca, finalmente mia! . . .

Ma l'accento voluttuoso si cambia in un grido terribile. Tosca lo ha colpito in pieno petto.

SCARPIA   Maledetta!

TOSCA   Questo è il bacio di Tosca!

SCARPIA   Aiuto! Muoio!
                    (*barcollando cerca d'aggrapparsi a Tosca
                    che indietreggia terrorizzata*)
                    Soccorso! Muoio! Aiuto! Aiuto!

Tosca trovandosi presa fra Scarpia e la tavola e vedendo che sta per essere toccata, respinge inorridita Scarpia, il quale cade, urlando colla voce già soffocata di sangue.

SCARPIA   Ah!

TOSCA (*con odio*)
                    Ti soffoca il sangue?

SCARPIA   Soccorso!

TOSCA   Ti soffoca il sangue?

SCARPIA (*si dibatte inutilmente e cerca di rialzarsi, aggrap-
                    pandosi al canapè*)
                    Aiuto!

TOSCA   Ah!

SPOLETTA   Yes. Like Palmieri . . .

Spoletta leaves. Scarpia, erect near the door, listens to Spoletta going away, then, his face and his movements transformed, he approaches Tosca with great passion.

SCARPIA   I kept my promise . . .

TOSCA (*stopping him*)
            Not yet.
            I want a safe-conduct
            with which to flee from the state with him.

SCARPIA (*gallantly*)
            Then you want to go away?

TOSCA   Yes, forever!

SCARPIA   Let your wish be granted.
                    (*goes to the writing desk; he starts writing, breaking off to ask Tosca*)
            And what route do you choose?

TOSCA   The shortest!

SCARPIA   Civitavecchia?

TOSCA   Yes.

As Scarpia writes, Tosca has gone to the table and with a trembling hand she takes the glass of wine Scarpia poured, but as she raises the glass to her lips, she glimpses a sharp, pointed knife on the table. She casts a rapid glance at Scarpia, who at that moment is busy writing, and with infinite precautions she tries to seize the knife, which she then conceals behind her, leaning against the table and still observing Scarpia. He has finished writing out the safe-conduct; he puts his seal on it, folds the paper. Then, opening his arms, he approaches Tosca to clasp her to himself.

SCARPIA   Tosca, finally mine . . . !

But his voluptuous tone is changed into a terrible cry. Tosca has struck him full in the chest.

SCARPIA   Cursed woman!

TOSCA   This is Tosca's kiss!

SCARPIA   Help! I'm dying!
                    (*staggering, he tries to cling to Tosca, who steps back, terrified*)
            Help! I'm dying! Help! Help!

Tosca, finding herself caught between Scarpia and the table and seeing that she is about to be touched, pushes Scarpia away, horrified. He falls, crying in a voice already choked with blood.

SCARPIA   Ah!

TOSCA (*with hatred*)
            Is the blood choking you?

SCARPIA   Help!

TOSCA   Is the blood choking you?

SCARPIA (*writhes in vain and tries to get up, clinging to the sofa*)
            Help!

TOSCA   Ah!

SCARPIA   Muoio, muoio!

TOSCA   E ucciso da una donna!

SCARPIA   Aiuto!

TOSCA   M'hai assai torturata!

SCARPIA (*affievolendosi*)
               Soccorso! muoio!
               (*fa un ultimo sforzo, poi cade riverso*)

TOSCA   Odi tu ancora? Parla!
               Guardami! Son Tosca! o Scarpia!

SCARPIA   Soccorso, aiuto!

TOSCA   Ti soffoca il sangue?

SCARPIA (*rantolando*)
               Muoio!

TOSCA (*piegandosi sul viso di Scarpia*)
               Muori dannato! Muori!
               Muori! muori!

SCARPIA (*rimanendo rigido*)
               Ah . . . !

TOSCA   È morto. Or gli perdono!

Senza togliere lo sguardo dal cadavere di Scarpia, Tosca
va al tavolo, prende una bottiglia d'acqua e inzuppando un
tovagliolo si lava le dita, poi si ravvia i capelli guardandosi allo
specchio. Si sovviene del salvacondotto, lo cerca sullo scrittoio
ma non lo trova; lo cerca ancora, finalmente vede il salvacon-
dotto nella mano raggrinzata di Scarpia. Solleva il braccio di
Scarpia, che poi lascia cadere inerte, rigido, dopo averne tolto
il foglio, che si nasconde in petto. Si sofferma a guardare il
cadavere di Scarpia.

TOSCA   E avanti a lui tremava tutta Roma!

Spegne il candelabro sulla tavola, va per uscire, ma si pente
e vedendo accesa una delle candele sullo scrittoio, va a pren-
derla ed accende un'altra candela. Colloca una candela accesa
a destra della testa di Scarpia, l'altra candela a sinistra. Cerca
di nuovo intorno a vedendo un crocefisso va a staccarlo dalla
parete e portandolo religiosamente si inginocchia per posarlo
sul petto di Scarpia, poi si alza e con grande precauzione esce
rinchiudendo dietro a sè la porta.

ATTO TERZO

La piattaforma di Castel Sant'Angelo. A sinistra, una casa-
matta: vi è collocata una tavola, sulla quale stanno una lam-
pada, un grosso registro e l'occorrente per scrivere: una panca,
una sedia. Su di una parete della casamatta un crocefisso:
davanti a questo è appesa una lampada. A destra, l'apertura
di una piccola scala per la quale si ascende alla piattaforma.
Nel fondo il Vaticano e S. Pietro. È ancora notte: a poco a
poco la luce incerta e grigia che precede l'alba: le compane
delle chiese suonano mattutino. Odesi il canto di un pastore
che guida un armento.

SCARPIA	I'm dying, I'm dying!
TOSCA	And killed by a woman!
SCARPIA	Help!
TOSCA	You tortured me very much!
SCARPIA (*growing weaker*)	Help! I'm dying!
	(*makes a final effort, then falls on his back*)
TOSCA	Do you still hear? Speak!
	Look at me! I am Tosca, O Scarpia!
SCARPIA	Help, help!
TOSCA	Is the blood choking you?
SCARPIA (*with the death rattle*)	I'm dying!
TOSCA (*bending over Scarpia's face*)	You die damned! Die!
	Die! Die!
SCARPIA (*remaining rigid*)	Ah . . . !
TOSCA	He's dead. Now I forgive him!

Without removing her gaze from Scarpia's corpse, Tosca goes to the table, takes a bottle of water and wetting a napkin, she washes her fingers. Then she adjusts her hair, looking at herself in the mirror. She remembers the safe-conduct, looks for it on the desk, but doesn't find it. She looks for it further, finally sees the safe-conduct in Scarpia's clenched hand. She raises Scarpia's arm, which she then drops again, inert, stiff, after having taken the paper from it, which she hides in her bosom. She stops to look at Scarpia's corpse.

TOSCA	And before him trembled all Rome!

She puts out the candelabrum on the table and starts to leave, but she repents and, seeing one of the candles lighted on the desk, she goes to get it and lights another candle. She sets one lighted candle to the right of Scarpia's head, the other candle to the left. She looks around again and, seeing a crucifix, she goes and removes it from the wall. Carrying it religiously, she kneels to place it on Scarpia's chest, then rises and, with great precaution, goes out, shutting the door after her.

ACT THREE

The platform of Castel Sant'Angelo. To the left, a casemate: a table is placed there, on which there is a lamp, as well as a large ledger and writing materials. A bench, a chair. On one wall of the casemate a crucifix: before this, a lamp is hanging. To the right, the opening of a little stairway which leads to the platform. In the background, the Vatican and St. Peter's. It is still night. Little by little the gray, uncertain light that precedes the dawn. The bells of the churches ring for matins. The song of a shepherd leading his flock is heard.

UN PASTORE   Io de' sospiri,
              Te ne rimanno tanti . . .
              Pe' quante foje
              Ne smoveno li venti.
              Tu mme disprezzi,
              Io me ciaccoro.
              Lampena d'oro,
              Me fai morir!

    *Un Carceriere con una lanterna sale dalla scala, va alla casa-
matta e vi accende la lampada sospesa davanti al crocefisso,
poi quella sulla tavola: siede ed aspetta mezzo assonnato. Più
tardi un picchetto, comandato da un Sergente di guardia, sale
sulla piattaforma accompagnando Cavaradossi: il picchetto si
arresta ed il Sergente conduce Cavaradossi nella casamatta,
consegnando un foglio al Carceriere. Il Carceriere esamina il
foglio, apre il registro e vi scrive mentre interroga.*

CARCERIERE   Mario Cavaradossi?
                    (*Cavaradossi china il capo, assentendo. Il
                    Carceriere porge la penna al Sergente*)
              A voi.
                    (*il Sergente firma il registro, poi parte coi
                    soldati, scendendo per la scala. Il Carceriere
                    si rivolge a Cavaradossi*)
              Vi resta un'ora . . .
              Un sacerdote i vostri cenni attende.

CAVARADOSSI   No. Ma un'ultima grazia
              io vi richiedo . . .

CARCERIERE   Se posso . . .

CAVARADOSSI   Io lascio al mondo
              una persona cara. Consentite
              ch'io le scriva un sol motto.
                    (*togliendosi dal dito un anello*)
              Unico resto di mia ricchezza
              è questo anel . . .
              Se promettete di consegnarle
              il mio ultimo addio,
              esso è vostro . . .

CARCERIERE   (*tituba un poco, poi accetta e fa cenno a Cavara-
                    dossi di sedere alla tavola, andando a sedere
                    sulla panca*)
              Scrivete.

CAVARADOSSI   (*si mette a scrivere, ma dopo tracciate alcune
                    linee è invaso dalle rimembranze e si arresta
                    dallo scrivere*)
              E lucevan le stelle . . .
              e olezzava la terra,
              stridea l'uscio dell'orto . . .
              e un passo sfiorava la rena . . .
              Entrava ella, fragrante,
              mi cadea fra le braccia.
              Oh! dolci baci, o languide carezze,
              mentr'io fremente
              le belle forme disciogliea dai veli!
              Svanì per sempre

A SHEPHERD   I send you
                   So many sighs . . .
                   As many as there are leaves
                   That the winds stir.
                   You scorn me,
                   I suffer for it.
                   Lamp of gold,
                   You make me die!

A jailer with a lantern comes up from the stairway, goes to
the casemate, and lights the lamp hanging before the crucifix,
then the one on the table. He sits down and waits, half asleep.
Later, a squad, commanded by a sergeant of the guard, climbs
up to the platform, escorting Cavaradossi. The picket stops,
and the sergeant leads Cavaradossi into the casemate, handing
a paper to the jailer. The jailer examines the paper, opens the
ledger and writes in it, as he questions.

JAILER   Mario Cavaradossi?
                   (*Cavaradossi nods his head, in assent. The*
                   jailer hands the pen to the sergeant)
                   Here you are.
                   (*the sergeant signs the ledger, then goes*
                   off with the soldiers, descending the steps.
                   The jailer addresses Cavaradossi)
                   You have an hour . . .
                   A priest awaits your instructions.

CAVARADOSSI   No. But I ask of you
                   a last favor . . .

JAILER   If I can . . .

CAVARADOSSI   I am leaving in the world
                   a dear person. Allow
                   me to write her a single word.
                   (*taking a ring from his finger*)
                   The sole remainder of my wealth
                   is this ring . . .
                   If you promise to deliver to her
                   my last farewell,
                   it is yours . . .

JAILER (*hesitates a little, then accepts and motions to Cavara-*
                   dossi to sit at the table, as he goes to sit on
                   the bench)
                   Write.

CAVARADOSSI (*starts to write, but after he has penned a few*
                   lines he is assailed by memories and he
                   stops writing)
                   And the stars were shining . . .
                   and the earth was perfumed,
                   the gate of the garden creaked . . .
                   and a footstep grazed the sand . . .
                   She entered, fragrant,
                   she fell into my arms.
                   Oh! sweet kisses, oh languid caresses,
                   while I impatient
                   freed the beautiful form from its veils!
                   My dream of love

il sogno mio d'amore . . .
l'ora è fuggita
e muoio disperato . . . !
e muoio disperato!
E non ho amato mai tanto la vita,
tanto la vita . . . !
  (*scoppia in pianto cuoprendosi il volto colle
  mani*)

*Dalla scala viene Spoletta accompagnato dal Sergente e
seguito da Tosca: il Sergente porta una lanterna, Spoletta
accenna a Tosca ove trovasi Cavaradossi, poi chiama a sè il
Carceriere: con questi e col Sergente ridiscende, non senza
avere prima dato ad una sentinella, che sta in fondo, l'ordine
di sorvegliare il prigioniero. Tosca, che in questo frattempo è
rimasta agitatissima, vede Cavaradossi che piange: si slancia
presso a lui, e non potendo parlare per la grande emozione,
gli solleva colle due mani la testa, presentandogli in pari tempo
il salvacondotto. Cavaradossi, alla vista di Tosca, balza in
piedi sorpreso, poi legge il foglio che gli presenta Tosca.*

CAVARADOSSI Ah! "*Franchigia a Floria Tosca . . .*

TOSCA, CAVARADOSSI
  . . . e al cavaliere che l'accompagna."

TOSCA (*con un grido d'esultanza*)
  Sei libero!

CAVARADOSSI (*guarda il foglio e ne legge la firma*)
  Scarpia . . . !
  Scarpia che cede?
  (*guardando Tosca con intenzione*)
  La prima sua grazia è questa . . .

TOSCA (*riprende il salvacondotto e lo ripone in una borsa*)
  E l'ultima!

CAVARADOSSI Che dici?

TOSCA Il tuo sangue o il mio amore volea . . .
  Fur vani scongiuri e pianti.
  Invan, pazza d'orror, alla Madonna
  mi volsi e ai Santi . . .
  L'empio mostro dicea:
  Già nei cieli il patibol
  le braccia leva!
  Rullavano i tamburi . . .
  Rideva, l'empio mostro . . .
  rideva . . . già la sua preda
  pronto a ghermir!
  "Sei mia?" — Sì —
  Alla sua brama mi promisi.
  Lì presso luccicava una lama . . .
  Ei scrisse il foglio liberator,
  venne all'orrendo amplesso . . .
  Io quella lama gli piantai nel cor.

CAVARADOSSI Tu? di tua man l'uccidesti!
  tu pia, tu benigna, e per me!

TOSCA N'ebbi le mani
  tutte lorde di sangue!

vanished forever . . .
the hour has fled,
and I die in despair . . . !
and I die in despair!
And I have never loved life so much . . .
life so much . . . !
> (*bursts into tears, covering his face with his hands*)

From the steps comes Spoletta, accompanied by the sergeant and followed by Tosca; the sergeant is carrying a lantern. Spoletta indicates to Tosca where Cavaradossi is, then calls the jailer to him. With the latter and with the sergeant he goes down again, not without first giving orders to a sentry, who is in the background, to watch the prisoner. Tosca, who has remained highly agitated in the meanwhile, sees Cavaradossi weeping. She rushes over to him, and, unable to speak because of her great emotion, she raises his head with both her hands, giving him the safe-conduct at the same time. Cavaradossi, at the sight of Tosca, springs to his feet, surprised, then reads the paper that Tosca hands to him.

CAVARADOSSI Ah! "*Safe-conduct for Floria Tosca . . .*

TOSCA, CAVARADOSSI
> *and for the gentleman who accompanies her.*"

TOSCA (*with a cry of exultation*)
> You are free!

CAVARADOSSI (*looks at the paper and reads the signature on it*)
> Scarpia . . . !
> Scarpia who gives in?
> > (*looking meaningfully at Tosca*)
> This is his first reprieve . . .

TOSCA (*takes back the safe-conduct and puts it in a purse*)
> And the last!

CAVARADOSSI What are you saying?

TOSCA He wanted your blood or my love . . .
Pleas and tears were vain.
In vain, mad with horror, I turned
to the Madonna and to the saints . . .
The wicked monster said:
Already into the heavens the gallows
is raising its arms!
The drums were rolling . . .
He laughed, the wicked monster . . .
he laughed . . . already prepared
to snatch his prey!
"You're mine?" — Yes —
I promised myself to his desire.
There, nearby, a blade gleamed . . .
He wrote the liberating paper,
came toward the horrid embrace . . .
I plunged that blade into his heart.

CAVARADOSSI You? You killed him with your own hand?
You, pious and kind, and for me!

TOSCA I had my hands
all stained with his blood!

CAVARADOSSI (*prendendo amorosamente fra le sue le mani di Tosca*)

O dolci mani mansuete e pure,
o mani elette
a bell'opre e pietose,
a carezzar fanciulli,
a coglier rose,
a pregar, giunte,
per le sventure,
dunque in voi,
fatte dall'amor secure,
giustizia le sue sacre armi depose?
Voi deste morte, o mani vittoriose,
o dolci mani mansuete e pure ... !

TOSCA (*svincolando le mani*)

Senti ... l'ora è vicina;
   (*mostrando la borsa*)
io già raccolsi oro e gioielli ...
una vettura è pronta.
Ma prima — ridi amor —
prima sarai fucilato ...
per finta ... ad armi scariche.
Simulato supplizio.
Al colpo ... cadi.
I soldati sen vanno —
e noi siam salvi, e noi siam salvi!
Poscia a Civitavecchia ... una tartana ...
e via pel mar!

CAVARADOSSI   Liberi!
TOSCA   Liberi!
CAVARADOSSI   Via pel mar!
TOSCA   Chi si duole in terra più?
Senti effluvi di rose?
Non ti par che le cose
aspettan tutte innamorate
il sole?

CAVARADOSSI (*colla più tenera commozione*)

Amaro sol per te
m'era il morire,
Da te la vita prende
ogni splendore,
all'esser mio
la gioia ed il desire ...
nascon di te, come di fiamma ardore.
Io folgorar i cieli e scolorire
vedrò nell'occhio tuo rivelatore,
e la beltà della cose più mire
avrà sol da te voce e colore.

TOSCA   Amor che seppe a te la vita serbare
ci sarà guida in terra,
e in mar nocchier
e vago farà il mondo riguardare.
Finchè congiunti alle celesti sfere
dileguerem, siccome alte sul mare

CAVARADOSSI (*lovingly taking Tosca's hands in his*)

> O sweet hands, gentle and pure,
> O hands destined
> to good and merciful deeds,
> to caressing children,
> to gathering roses,
> to praying, clasped,
> for misfortunes,
> then in you,
> made steady by love,
> justice placed her sacred arms?
> You gave death, O victorious hands,
> O sweet hands, gentle and pure . . . !

TOSCA (*freeing her hands*)

> Listen . . . the hour is near;
> > (*showing the purse*)
> I've already collected gold and jewels . . .
> a carriage is ready.
> But first — laugh, love —
> first you will be shot . . .
> in pretense . . . with blank weapons.
> A simulated punishment.
> At the shot . . . fall.
> The soldiers go away —
> and we are saved, and we are saved!
> Then, at Civitavecchia . . . a vessel . . .
> and away over the sea!

CAVARADOSSI   Free!

TOSCA   Free!

CAVARADOSSI   Away, over the sea!

TOSCA   Who suffers any more on the earth?

> Do you smell perfumes of roses?
> Doesn't it seem to you
> that everything, in love,
> is awaiting the sun?

CAVARADOSSI (*with the most tender emotion*)

> Dying was bitter for me
> only because of you;
> from you life takes on
> all splendor,
> for my being,
> joy and desire
> are born from you, like heat from the flame.
> In your revealing eye
> I will see the heavens flash and fade,
> And the beauty of the most wondrous things
> will have voice and color only from you.

TOSCA   Love, which was able to save your life,

> will be our guide on the earth,
> our helmsman on the sea,
> and will make the world lovely to gaze on.
> Until we shall be dispersed,
> joined to the celestial spheres, like, high over
>   the sea,

a sol cadente, nuvole leggere,
nuvole leggere, nuvole leggere . . . !

*Rimangono commossi, silenziosi, poi Tosca, chiamata dalla
realtà delle cose, si guarda attorno inquieta.*

TOSCA   E non giungono . . .
                  (*a Cavaradossi, con premurosa tenerezza*)
                  Bada . . . !
                  al colpo egli è mestiere
                  che tu subito cada.

CAVARADOSSI   Non temere
                  che cadrò sul momento —
                  e al naturale.

TOSCA (*insistendo*)
                  Ma stammi attento
                  di non farti male!
                  Con scenica scienza
                  io saprei la movenza . . .

CAVARADOSSI (*la interrompe, attirandola a sè*)
                  Parlami ancor . . . come dianzi parlavi,
                  è così dolce il suon della tua voce!

TOSCA (*si abbandona quasi estasiata, poi accalorandosi poco a
                  poco*)
                  Uniti ed esulanti
                  diffonderan pel mondo i nostri amori
                  armonie di colori . . .

TOSCA, CAVARADOSSI
                  . . . armonie di canti diffonderem!
                  Trionfal di nova speme
                  l'anima freme
                  in celestial crescente ardor.
                  Ed in armonico vol
                  già l'anima va all'estasi d'amor.

TOSCA   Gli occhi ti chiuderò con mille baci
                  e mille ti dirò nomi d'amor.

*Frattanto dalla scaletta è salito un drappello di soldati: lo
comanda un Ufficiale, il quale schiera i soldati nel fondo;
seguono Spoletta, il Sergente, il Carceriere. Spoletta dà le nec-
essarie istruzioni. Il cielo si fa più luminoso; è l'alba: suonano
le quattro. Il Carceriere si avvicina a Cavaradossi e togliendosi
il berretto gli indica l'Ufficiale, poi, preso il registro dei condan-
nati scende per la scaletta.*

CARCERIERE   L'ora!

CAVARADOSSI   Son pronto.

TOSCA (*sottovoce a Cavaradossi e ridendo di soppiatto*)
                         (Tieni a mente . . . al primo colpo . . .
                         giù . . .)

CAVARADOSSI (*sottovoce, ridendo esso pure*)
                         (Giù.)

TOSCA   (Nè rialzarti innanzi
                  ch'io ti chiami.)

CAVARADOSSI   (No, amore!)

TOSCA   (E cadi bene.)

> at sunset, the light clouds,
> light clouds, light clouds ... !

They remain moved, silent, then Tosca, recalled to the reality of things, looks around, uneasy.

TOSCA   And they don't come ...
> (*to Cavaradossi, with solicitous tenderness*)
> Remember!
> at the shot it is necessary
> for you to fall at once.

CAVARADOSSI   Don't fear:
> for I'll fall instantly —
> and naturally.

TOSCA (*insisting*)
> But be careful
> not to hurt yourself!
> With stage technique
> I would know the movement ...

CAVARADOSSI (*interrupts her, drawing her to him*)
> Speak to me again ... as you spoke before;
> the sound of your voice is so sweet!

TOSCA (*abandons herself, as if in ecstasy, then, gradually warming*)
> United and exultant,
> our loves will spread through the world
> harmonies of colors ...

TOSCA, CAVARADOSSI
> ... harmonies of songs we will spread!
> Triumphant, with new hope,
> the soul is ecstatic
> in growing, celestial ardor.
> And in harmonous flight
> the soul already goes to the ecstasy of love!

TOSCA   I will close your eyes with a thousand kisses,
> and I will call you a thousand love names.

Meanwhile from the steps a detachment of soldiers has come up. It is commanded by an officer, who lines up the soldiers in the background. Spoletta, the sergeant, the jailer follow. Spoletta gives the necessary instructions. The sky becomes more luminous; it is dawn. Four o'clock strikes. The jailer comes over to Cavaradossi and, removing his cap, points to the officer, then, having taken the ledger of the condemned men, he goes down the steps.

JAILER   The hour!

CAVARADOSSI   I'm ready.

TOSCA (*in a low voice to Cavaradossi, and laughing stealthily*)
> (Remember ...
> at the first shot ... down ...)

CAVARADOSSI (*low voice, also laughing*)
> (Down.)

TOSCA   (Nor are you to rise again before
> I call you.)

CAVARADOSSI   (No, love!)

TOSCA   (And fall well.)

CAVARADOSSI (*sorridendo*)
                (Come la Tosca in teatro.)
TOSCA   (Non ridere . . .)
CAVARADOSSI (*fascendosi cupo*)
                (Così?)
TOSCA   (Così.)

Cavaradossi segue l'Ufficiale dopo aver salutato Tosca, la quale si colloca a sinistra, nella casamatta, in modo però di poter spiare quanto succede sulla piattaforma. Essa vede l'Ufficiale ed il Sergente che conducono Cavaradossi presso al muro di faccia a lei: il Sergente vuol porre la benda agli occhi di Cavaradossi: questi, sorridendo, rifiuta. Tali lugubri preparativi stancano la pazienza di Tosca.

TOSCA   Come è lunga l'attesa!
                Perchè indugiano ancor?
                Già sorge il sole . . .
                Perchè indugiano ancora?
                È una commedia, lo so . . .
                ma questa angoscia eterna pare!

L'Ufficiale e il Sergente dispongono il pelottone dei soldati, impartendo gli ordini relativi.

TOSCA   Ecco . . . ! apprestano l'armi . . .
                Com'è bello il mio Mario . . . !

Vedendo l'Ufficiale che sta per abbassare la sciabola, Tosca si porta le mani agli orecchi per non udire la detonazione, poi fa cenno colla testa a Cavaradossi di cadere. Una scarica dei fucili.

TOSCA   Là! muori!
                    (*vedendolo a terra gli invia colle mani un
                    bacio*)
                Ecco un artista!

Il Sergente si avvicina al caduto e lo osserva attentamente; Spoletta pure si è avvicinato ed allontana il Sergente impedendogli di dare il colpo di grazia. L'Ufficiale allinea i soldati; il Sergente ritira la la sentinella che sta in fondo, poi tutti, preceduti da Spoletta, scendono la scala. Tosca è agitatissima: essa sorveglia questi movimenti temendo che Cavaradossi, per impazienza, si muova o parli prima del momento opportuna.

TOSCA (*a voce repressa verso Cavaradossi*)
                O Mario, non ti muovere . . .
                s'avviano . . . taci!
                vanno . . . scendono . . . scendono . . .

                Ancora non ti muovere . . .

Vista deserta la piattaforma, essa va ad ascoltare presso l'imbocco della scaletta: vi si arresta trepidante, affannosa, parendole ad un tratto che i soldati, anzichè allontanarsi, ritornino sulla piattaforma. Ascolta. Si sono tutti allontanati. Va al parapetto e cautamente sporgendosi, osserva di sotto, poi corre verso Cavaradossi.

TOSCA   Presto, su! Mario! Mario!
                Su, presto! Andiam!
                    (*toccandolo, turbata, poi scuoprendolo*)

CAVARADOSSI (*smiling*)
        (Like Tosca in the theater.)
TOSCA   (Don't laugh . . .)
CAVARADOSSI (*assuming a grim look*)
        (So?)
TOSCA   (So.)

*Cavaradossi follows the officer, after having said good-by
to Tosca, who takes her place to the left, in the casemate, in
such a way, however, that she can observe what happens on
the platform. She sees the officer and the sergeant lead Cavaradossi to the wall opposite her. The sergeant wants to put
the blindfold over Cavaradossi's eyes; smiling, he refuses.
Such lugubrious preparations exhaust Tosca's patience.*

TOSCA   How long the waiting is!
                Why do they delay still?
                The sun is already rising . . .
                Why do they delay still?
                It's a play, I know . . .
                but this anguish seems eternal!

*The officer and the sergeant arrange the platoon of soldiers,
giving the required orders.*

TOSCA   There . . . ! They're readying their weapons . . .
                How handsome my Mario is . . . !

*Seeing the officer about to lower his sabre, Tosca puts her
hands to her ears not to hear the shot, then she signals to
Cavaradossi with her head to fall. A volley of rifles.*

TOSCA   There! die!
              (*seeing him on the ground, she sends him
              a kiss with her hands*)
              There's an artist!

*The sergeant goes over to the fallen man and observes him
carefully. Spoletta has also come over and he sends the sergeant away, preventing him from giving the coup de grace.
The officer lines up the soldiers; the sergeant relieves the
sentry who is in the background, and then all, preceded by
Spoletta, descend the steps. Tosca is very agitated; she observes these movements, fearing that Cavaradossi, out of impatience, will move or speak before the right moment.*

TOSCA (*in a repressed voice, toward Cavaradossi*)
              O Mario, don't move . . .
              they're going away . . . be silent!
              they're going . . . they're going down . . . going
                  down . . .
              Don't move yet . . .

*Seeing the platform deserted, she goes to listen at the top
of the stairs; she stops there, fearful, breathless, as it suddenly
seems to her that the soldiers, instead of going away, are
returning to the platform. She listens. They have all gone
away. She goes to the parapet and, cautiously leaning over,
observes below, then she runs toward Cavaradossi.*

TOSCA   Quickly! Up! Mario! Mario!
              Up, quickly! Let's go!
              (*touching him, upset, then turning him
              over*)

Su, su! Mario! Mario! Ah!
Morto . . . ! morto . . . ! morto . . . . !
O Mario . . . morto . . . ? tu . . . ? così?
Finire così? fiinire così?
> (*con incomposte parole, con sospiri, sin-*
> *ghiozzi si butta sul corpo di Cavaradossi,*
> *quasi non credendo all'orribil destino*)

Tu, morto . . . morto? Mario . . .

Intanto dal cortile al disotto del parapetto e su dalla piccola
scala arrivano prima confuse, poi sempre più vicine le voci di
Sciarrone, di Spoletta e di alcuni soldati.

LA VOCE DI SCIARRONE
     [Vi dico, pugnalato!

VOCI CONFUSE Scarpia?

LA VOCE DI SCIARRONE
     Scarpia.

VOCI CONFUSE Ah!

TOSCA (*piangendo*)
     Mario . . . povera Floria tua!

LA VOCE DI SPOLETTA
     La donna è Tosca!

VARIE VOCI (*più vicine*)
     Che non sfugga!

VOCI DI SPOLETTA E SCIARRONE
     Attenti agli sbocchi delle scale!

ALTRE VOCI Attenti agli sbocchi delle scale!

Spoletta apparisce dalla scala, mentre Sciarrone dietro a
lui gli grida additando Tosca.

SCIARRONE È lei!

SPOLETTA Ah! Tosca, pagherai ben cara
     la sua vita!

Spoletta fa per gettarsi su Tosca, ma essa balzando in piedi
lo respinge così violentemente da farlo quasi cadere riverso
nella bottola della scala, quindi corre al parapetto e dall'alto
grida.

TOSCA Colla mia!
     O Scarpia, avanti a Dio!
     (*si getta nel vuoto*)

Sciarrone ed alcuni soldati, saliti confusamente, corrono al pa-
rapetto e guardano giù. Spoletta rimane esterrefatto, allibito.

Up, up! Mario! Mario! Ah!
Dead . . . ! dead . . . ! dead . . . !
O Mario . . . dead . . . ? you . . . ? like this?
To end like this? To end like this?
> (*with incoherent words, with sighs, sobs,
> she throws herself on Cavaradossi's body,
> as if not believing in his horrible fate*)

You, dead . . . dead? Mario . . .

Meanwhile from the courtyard below the parapet and up from the little staircase come, first confused, then closer and closer, the voices of Sciarrone, Spoletta, and of some soldiers.

SCIARRONE'S VOICE
Stabbed, I tell you!

CONFUSED VOICES
Scarpia?

SCIARRONE'S VOICE
Scarpia.

CONFUSED VOICES
Ah!

TOSCA (*weeping*)
Mario . . . your poor Floria!

SPOLETTA'S VOICE
The woman is Tosca!

VARIOUS VOICES (*closer*)
Let her not escape!

VOICES OF SPOLETTA AND SCIARRONE
Watch the foot of the stairs!

OTHER VOICES Watch the foot of the stairs!

Spoletta appears from the stairs, as Sciarrone, after him, shouts to him, pointing at Tosca

SCIARRONE It's she!

SPOLETTA Ah, Tosca, you will pay very dearly
for his life!

Spoletta starts to throw himself on Tosca, but, springing to her feet, she pushes him away so violently that he almost falls back into the stair well. Then she runs to the parapet and from the top of it shouts

TOSCA With mine!
O Scarpia, before God!
> (*throws herself into the void*)

Sciarrone and some soldiers, who have come up in confusion, run to the parapet and look down. Spoletta remains terrified, aghast.

Madama Butterfly

In the summer of 1900 Puccini was in London, where *Tosca* was being given at Covent Garden for the first time. There some friends took him to see *Madame Butterfly*, a play by David Belasco and John Luther Long (adapted from a story by the latter), which was having a successful run in England after an equally successful presentation on Broadway. Puccini, though he knew little or no English, fell in love at once with the story — or, more specifically, with its heroine. Negotiations with Belasco for the rights took a long time, but in September of 1901 the contract was finally signed; and once again Giacosa and Illica set to work.

The Belasco play was in one act, a long one, however, which Puccini planned to develop into two. Then, characteristically, he changed his mind and decided that a third act must be added. Ricordi objected. At a certain point Giacosa threatened to abandon the whole project (such threats were a recurring event in the relationship of composer, publisher, and librettists), but as usual, he was persuaded to change his mind. When Puccini completed the scoring on December 27, 1903 (a serious automobile accident and a tiresome convalescence had also slowed his progress), *Madama Butterfly* consisted of two long acts, the second divided by the "waiting music" describing the long night during which Butterfly keeps vigil, expecting Pinkerton's return. This vigil was visible to the audience; the curtain was not lowered.

This is the version that the first-night audience saw at La Scala on February 17, 1904. The scandalous reception of the opera is now part of operatic history. Screams, catcalls, whistles interrupted the performance again and again. A number of Puccini's biographers have felt that the fiasco was deliberately planned, and it is true that the composer had many enemies (not the least powerful were several of his fellow-composers). In any case, the opera was withdrawn after that single performance, Puccini made cuts and other revisions, divided the second act into two parts, and presented *Butterfly* to the public again a few months later in Brescia. This time the result was an overwhelming success.

THE PLOT

ACT ONE

Pinkerton, a lieutenant in the U. S. Navy, has arranged with the Nagasaki marriage broker Goro to marry a fifteen-year-old girl, Butterfly (or Cho-cho san). By Japanese law, the groom is free to dissolve the marriage whenever he wants to, and though Pinkerton is clearly fascinated by his child-bride, it is obvious that he doesn't take the marriage seriously. He says as much to Sharpless, the American consul, who warns him that Butterfly is in earnest and tragedy may ensue. But Pinkerton pays no attention. When the brief ceremony is over,

Butterfly's uncle, a Buddhist priest, arrives in a fury, revealing that the girl has renounced her people's ancient faith and taken the white man's god. The family, horrified, deserts Butterfly. She weeps bitterly, but Pinkerton comforts her, and soon all is forgotten as the two express their love.

ACT TWO: PART ONE

Pinkerton has been gone for three years. Everyone — even her faithful maid Suzuki — tells Butterfly that he has forsaken her, but she steadfastly insists that he will come back, as he promised, "when the robins make their nest." Goro keeps urging her to marry his wealthy client Prince Yamadori. And even Sharpless suggests that she accept this offer, since he knows that though Pinkerton is, in fact, coming back he is bringing an American wife with him. Sharpless tries to prepare Butterfly for this blow, but before he can do so, she reveals that she has had a child by Pinkerton, and the consul leaves without delivering his message. The harbor cannon then announces the arrival of a ship. It is Pinkerton's, the *Abraham Lincoln.* With Suzuki's help, Butterfly decorates the little house with flowers. Then, with Suzuki and with the child, Butterfly prepares to await Pinkerton's arrival.

ACT TWO: PART TWO

Dawn. Butterfly has waited all night. Suzuki persuades her to go and rest, and in her absence from the room, Pinkerton and Sharpless arrive. They break the news to Suzuki and try to enlist her help in persuading Butterfly to give up the child to Kate, Pinkerton's new wife, who has also come but is discreetly outside in the garden. Pinkerton then leaves: the memories of the house, his remorse are too much for him. Kate speaks with Suzuki, then goes out again. Butterfly enters and, horror-stricken, learns the truth. When Kate repeats her request, Butterfly answers that she will give the child to his father if Pinkerton will come back for him in a half hour. The visitors leave. Butterfly blindfolds the child, then kills herself. She dies just as Pinkerton rushes in, calling her name.

MADAMA BUTTERFLY

libretto by Giuseppe Giacosa and Luigi Illica

First performed at the Teatro alla Scala, Milan
February 17, 1904

CHARACTERS

Madama Butterfly (Cho-cho san)	*Soprano*
Suzuki, her servant	*Mezzo-soprano*
Kate Pinkerton	*Mezzo-soprano*
B. F. Pinkerton, Lieutenant in the U. S. Navy	*Tenor*
Sharpless, U. S. Consul in Nagasaki	*Baritone*
Goro, a marriage broker	*Tenor*
Prince Yamadori	*Baritone*
The Bonze, Butterfly's uncle	*Bass*
The Imperial Commissioner	*Bass*
The Registry Officer	*Baritone*
Trouble, Butterfly's child	. . .

Butterfly's relatives and friends, servants

Time: the present (i.e., 1904).
Place: Nagasaki

ATTO PRIMO

Collina presso Nagasaki

*Casa giapponese, terrazzo e giardino. In fondo, al basso, la
rada, il porto, la città di Nagasaki. Dalla camera in fondo
alla casetta, Goro, con molti inchini, introduce Pinkerton, al
quale con grande prosopopea, ma sempre ossequente fa am-
mirare in dettaglio la piccola casa. Goro fa scorrere una parete
nel fondo, e ne spiega lo scopo a Pinkerton. Si avanzano un
poco sul terrazzo.*

PINKERTON (*sorpreso per quanto ha visto, dice a Goro*)
      E soffitto . . . e pareti . . .

GORO (*godendo delle sorprese di Pinkerton*)
      Vanno e vengono a prova
      a norma che vi giova
      nello stresso locale
      alternar nuovi aspetti ai consueti.

PINKERTON (*cercando intorno*)
      Il nido nuzïal dov'è?

GORO (*accenna a due locali*)
      Qui, o là . . . secondo . . .

PINKERTON   Anch'esso a doppio fondo!
      La sala?

GORO (*mostra la terrazza*)
      Ecco!

PINKERTON (*stupito*)
      All'aperto?

GORO (*fa scorrere la parete verso la terrazza*)
      Un fianco scorre . . .

PINKERTON (*mentre Goro fa scorrere le pareti*)
      Capisco . . . ! capisco! Un altro . . .

GORO   . . . scivola!

PINKERTON   E la dimora frivola . . .

GORO (*protestando*)
      Salda come una torre
      da terra, fino al tetto.
            (*invita Pinkerton a scendere in giardino*)

PINKERTON   È una casa a soffietto.

*Goro batte tre volte le mani palma a palma; entrano due
uomini ed una donna che umilmente e lenti si genuflettono
sulla terrazza innanzi a Pinkerton.*

GORO (*accennando*)
      Questa è la cameriera
      che della vostra sposa

ACT ONE

Hill near Nagasaki

A Japanese house, terrace, and garden. In the background, below, the roadstead, the port, the city of Nagasaki. From the room in the rear of the house, Goro, with many bows, introduces Pinkerton, to whom with great pomposity, but still obsequious, he is pointing out the details of the little house to be admired. Goro slides a wall in the background and explains its purpose to Pinkerton. They come out a little way onto the terrace.

PINKERTON (*surprised at what he has seen, says to Goro*)
> And the ceiling . . . and the walls . . .

GORO (*enjoying Pinkerton's surprises*)
> They come and go at will
> in order to help you,
> in the same room,
> replace familiar arrangements with new ones.

PINKERTON (*looking around*)
> Where is the nuptial nest?

GORO (*indicating two rooms*)
> Here, or there . . . depending . . .

PINKERTON
> It, too, has a double bottom!
> The living room?

GORO (*shows the terrace*)
> Here!

PINKERTON (*amazed*)
> In the open?

GORO (*slides the wall toward the terrace*)
> One side slides . . .

PINKERTON (*as Goro slides the walls*)
> I understand . . . ! I understand! Another one . . .

GORO
> . . . slips!

PINKERTON
> And the frivolous dwelling . . .

GORO (*protesting*)
> Sound as a tower
> from the ground to the roof.
>> (*invites Pinkerton to come down into the garden*)

PINKERTON
> It's a folding house.

Goro claps his hands three times: two men and a woman enter, then slowly and humbly kneel down on the terrace in front of Pinkerton.

GORO (*pointing*)
> This is the maid
> who has already been

                    fu già serva amorosa.
                    Il cuoco . . . il servitor. Son confusi
                    del grande onore.
PINKERTON (*impaziente*)
                    I nomi?
GORO (*presentando*)
                    Miss *Nuvola leggiera* —
                    Raggio di sol nascente — *Esala aromi.*
SUZUKI (*sempre in ginocchio, ma fatta ardita rialza la testa*)
                    Sorride Vostro Onore?
                    Il riso è frutto e fiore.
                    Disse il savio Ocunama:
                    dei crucci la trama
                    smaglia il sorriso.
                            (*scende nel giardino, seguendo Pinkerton
                            che si allontana sorridendo*)
                    Schiude alla perla il guscio,
                    apre all'uomo l'uscio
                    del Paradiso.
                    Profumo degli Dei . . .
                    Fontana della vita . . .
                    Disse il savio Ocunama:
                    dei crucci la trama
                    smaglia il sorriso.

   *Pinkerton è distratto e seccato. Goro accorgendosi che Pink-
erton comincia ad essere infastidito dalla loquela di Suzuki
batte tre volte le mani. I tre si alzano e fuggono rapidamente
rientrando in casa.*

PINKERTON   A chiacchiere costei
                 mi par cosmopolita.
                        (*a Goro che è andato verso il fondo ad
                        osservare*)
                 Che guardi?
GORO   Se non giunge ancor la sposa.
PINKERTON   Tutto è pronto?
GORO   Ogni cosa.
PINKERTON   Gran perla di sensale!
GORO (*ringrazia con profondo inchino*)
                 Qui verran: l'Ufficiale
                 del registro, i parenti, il vostro Console,
                 la fidanzata. Qui si firma l'atto
                 e il matrimonio è fatto.
PINKERTON   E son molti i parenti?
GORO   La suocera, la nonna, lo zio Bonzo

                 (che non ci degnerà di sua presenza)
                 e cugini, e le cugine . . .
                 Mettiam fra gli ascendenti
                 ed i collaterali, un due dozzine.
                 Quanto alla discendenza . . .
                        (*con malizia ossequiosa*)
                 provederanno assai
                 Vostra Grazia e la bella Butterfly.

> your bride's devoted servant.
> The cook . . . the butler. They're overcome
> by the great honor.

PINKERTON (*impatient*)
> Their names?

GORO (*introducing them*)
> Miss *Light Cloud* —
> *Ray of Rising Sun* — *Exhales-Aromas.*

SUZUKI (*still kneeling, but emboldened, raises her head*)
> Does Your Honor smile?
> Laughter is fruit and flower.
> The sage Okunama said:
> the smile unravels
> the woof of troubles.
>> (*descends into the garden, following Pink-
>> erton, who goes off, smiling*)
> It opens the shell to the pearl,
> opens to man the door
> of paradise.
> Perfume of the gods . . .
> Fountain of life . . .
> The sage Okunama said:
> the smile unravels
> the woof of troubles.

*Pinkerton is distracted and irked. Goro, realizing that
Pinkerton is beginning to be annoyed by Suzuki's garrulity,
claps his hands three times. The three stand up and flee,
rapidly re-entering the house.*

PINKERTON   When it comes to chatter she
> seems a cosmopolitan to me.
>> (*to Goro, who has gone toward the back-
>> ground to look out*)
> What are you looking at?

GORO   To see if the bride isn't coming yet.

PINKERTON   Is all ready?

GORO   Everything.

PINKERTON   Great pearl of a marriage broker!

GORO (*thanks him with a deep bow*)
> Here will come: the registry
> officer, the relatives, your consul,
> the betrothed. Here the act is signed,
> and the marriage is done.

PINKERTON   And are the relatives many?

GORO   The mother-in-law, the grandmother, the Bonze
>   uncle
> (who won't honor us with his presence)
> and male cousins and the female cousins . . .
> Let's say, between ancestors
> and collateral kin, about two dozen.
> As for the descendants . . .
>> (*with obsequious slyness*)
> Your Grace and the beautiful Butterfly
> will provide amply.

PINKERTON   Gran perla di sensale!
Si ode la voce di Sharpless, il Console, che sale il colle.

SHARPLESS   (*dall'interno, un po' lontano*)
                        E suda e arrampica!
                        sbuffa, inciampica!
GORO   (*che è accorso al fondo, annuncia a Pinkerton*)
                        Il Consol sale.

Sharpless appare sbuffando: Goro si prosterna innanzi al Console. Pinkerton va incontro a Sharpless: i due si stringono la mano.

SHARPLESS   Ah . . . ! quei ciottoli
                        mi hanno sfiaccato!
PINKERTON   Bene arrivato.
GORO   Bene arrivato.
SHARPLESS   Ouff!
PINKERTON   Presto Goro
                        qualche ristoro.
                        (*Goro entra in casa frettoloso*)
SHARPLESS   (*sbuffando e guardando intorno*)
                        Alto.
PINKERTON   (*indicando il panorama*)
                        Ma bello!
SHARPLESS   (*contemplando la città ed il mare sottoposti*)
                        Nagasaki, il mare, il porto . . .
PINKERTON   (*accenna alla casa*)
                        . . . e una casetta
                        che obbedisce a bacchetta.

Goro viene frettoloso dalla casa, seguito dai due servi: portano bicchieri e bottiglie che depongono sulla terrazza; i due servi rientrano in casa e Goro si dà a preparare le bevande.

SHARPLESS   Vostra?
PINKERTON   La comperai
                        per novecentonovantanove anni,
                        con facoltà, ogni mese,
                        di rescindere i patti.
                        Sono in questo paese
                        elastici del par, case e contratti.
SHARPLESS   E l'uomo esperto ne profitta.
PINKERTON   Certo.

Pinkerton e Sharpless si siedono sulla terrazza dove Goro ha preparato le bevande.

PINKERTON   (*con franchezza*)
                        Dovunque al mondo lo Yankee vagabondo
                        si gode e traffica
                        sprezzando rischi.
                        Affonda l'áncora alla ventura . . .
                        (*s'interrompe per offrire da bere a Sharpless*)
                        Milk-Punch, o Wisky?
                        (*riprendendo*)

PINKERTON   Great pearl of a marriage broker!

The voice of Sharpless, the consul, is heard, as he climbs the hill.

SHARPLESS (*from within, a bit distant*)
    And sweat and climb!
    Puff and stumble!

GORO (*who has run to the back, announces to Pinkerton*)
    The consul's coming up.

Sharpless appears, panting. Goro prostrates himself before the consul. Pinkerton goes toward Sharpless, the two men shake hands.

SHARPLESS   Ah . . . ! those pebbles
    have exhausted me!

PINKERTON   Welcome!

GORO   Welcome.

SHARPLESS   Ouff!

PINKERTON   Quickly, Goro,
    some refreshment.
     (*Goro hastily enters the house*)

SHARPLESS (*panting and looking around*)
    High.

PINKERTON (*pointing to the view*)
    But beautiful!

SHARPLESS (*gazing at the city and the sea lying below*)
    Nagasaki, the sea, the port . . .

PINKERTON (*pointing to the house*)
    . . . and a little house
    that obeys magically.

Goro comes hastily from the house, followed by the two menservants. They carry glasses and bottles that they set on the terrace. The two servants go back into the house and Goro busily prepares the drinks.

SHARPLESS   Yours?

PINKERTON   I bought it
    for nine hundred ninety-nine years,
    with the right, every month,
    to rescind the agreement.
    In this country
    houses and contracts are equally elastic.

SHARPLESS   And the experienced man profits by it.

PINKERTON   Certainly.

Pinkerton and Sharpless sit down on the terrace where Goro has prepared the drinks.

PINKERTON (*frankly*)
    Everywhere in the world the Yankee vagabond
    enjoys himself and trades,
    scorning risks.
    He lets down the anchor at random . . .
     (*breaks off to offer Sharpless a drink*)

    Milk punch or whisky?
     (*resuming*)

Affonda l'áncora alla ventura
finchè una raffica
scompigli nave e ormeggi, alberatura.
La vita ei non appaga
se non fa suo tesor
i fiori d'ogni plaga . . .

SHARPLESS   È un facile vangelo . . .

PINKERTON   . . . d'ogni bella gli amor.

SHARPLESS   È un facile vangelo
che fa la vita vaga
ma che intristisce il cor.

PINKERTON (*continuando*)
Vinto si tuffa, la sorte racciuffa.
Il suo talento fa in ogni dove.
Così mi sposo all'uso giapponese
per novecentonovantanove anni.
Salvo a prosciogliermi ogni mese.

SHARPLESS   È un facile vangelo.

PINKERTON (*si alza, toccando il bicchiere con Sharpless*)
"America forever!"

SHARPLESS   "America forever!"

Pinkerton e Sharpless si siedono ancora sulla terrazza.

SHARPLESS   Ed è bella la sposa?

GORO (*che ha udito, si avanza premuroso ed insinuante*)
Una ghirlanda di fiori freschi.
Una stella dai raggi d'oro.
E per nulla: sol cento yen.
(*al Console*)
Se Vostra Grazia mi comanda
ce n'ho un assortimento.
(*il Console ridendo, ringrazia e si alza*)

PINKERTON (*con viva impazienza, alzandosi*)
Va, conducila Goro.

*Goro corre in fondo e scompare discendendo il colle: i due
servi rientrano in casa.*

SHARPLESS   Quale smania vi prende!
Sareste addirittura cotto?

PINKERTON   Non so . . . ! non so! Dipende
dal grado di cottura!
Amore o grillo, dir non saprei.
Certo costei
m'ha coll'ingenue arti invescato.
Lieve qual tenue vetro soffiato
alla statura, al portamento
sembra figura da paravento.
Ma dal suo lucido fondo di lacca
cóme con subito moto si stacca,
qual farfalletta svolazza e posa
con tal grazietta silenzïosa
che di rincorrerla furor m'assale
se pure infrangerne dovessi l'ale.

He lets down the anchor at random
until a squall
upsets ship and mooring, masts.
He doesn't satisfy his life
if he doesn't make his treasure
the flowers of every region . . .

SHARPLESS   It's an easy gospel . . .

PINKERTON   . . . the love of every beauty.

SHARPLESS   It's an easy gospel
that makes life charming
but which saddens the heart.

PINKERTON (*continuing*)
Defeated, he plunges, seizes his fate again.
His talent works in every place.
So I'm marrying in the Japanese way
for nine hundred ninety-nine years.
Free to release myself every month.

SHARPLESS   It's an easy gospel.

PINKERTON (*stands up, touching his glass to that of Sharpless*)
"America forever!"

SHARPLESS   "America forever!"

Pinkerton and Sharpless sit down again on the terrace.

SHARPLESS   And is the bride beautiful?

GORO (*who has heard, advances, eager and insinuating*)
A garland of fresh flowers.
A star with golden rays.
And for nothing: only a hundred yen.
         (*to the consul*)
If Your Grace commands me . . .
I have an assortment of them.
         (*the consul, laughing, thanks him and
         stands up*)

PINKERTON (*with lively impatience, rising*)
Go bring her, Goro.

*Goro runs to the back and disappears, descending the hill.
The two servants go back into the house.*

SHARPLESS   What frenzy takes you!
Would you be really infatuated?

PINKERTON   I don't know . . . ! I don't know! It depends
on the degree of infatuation!
Love or whim, I couldn't say.
Certainly she
has ensnared me with her ingenuous arts.
Light as fragile blown glass,
in her stature, in her bearing
she seems a figure from a screen.
But from her shining lacquer background,
how, with a sudden movement, she detaches
     herself,
like a little butterfly she flutters and rests
with such silent gracefulness
that a fury to pursue her assails me
even if I should break her wings.

SHARPLESS (*seriamente e bonario*)
    Ier l'altro, il Consolato
    sen' venne a visitar!
    Io non la vidi, ma l'udii parlar.
    Di sua voce il mistero
    l'anima mi colpì.
    Certo quando è sincer
    l'amor parla così.
    Sarebbe gran peccato
    le lievi ali strappar
    e desolar forse un credulo cuor.

PINKERTON
    Console mio garbato,
    quetatevi! Si sa,
    [la vostra età è di flebile umor.
    Non c'è gran male
    s'io vo' quell'ale
    drizzare ai dolci voli dell'amor!

SHARPLESS
    Sarebbe gran peccato . . .
    Quella divina mite vocina
    non dovrebbe dar note di dolor.]

PINKERTON (*offre di nuovo da bere*)
    Wisky?

SHARPLESS   Un'altro bicchiere.

   Pinkerton mesce del Wisky a Sharpless e colma anche il proprio bicchiere.

SHARPLESS (*leva il calice*)
    Bevo alla vostra famiglia lontana.

PINKERTON (*leva esso pure il bicchiere*)
    E al giorno in cui mi sposerò
    con vere nozze, a una vera sposa americana.

   Goro riappare correndo affannato dal basso della collina.

GORO
    Ecco! Son giunte al sommo del pendìo.
      (*accenna verso il sentiero*)
    Già del femmineo sciame
    qual di vento in fogliame
    s'ode il brusìo.

   Pinkerton e Sharpless si recano in fondo al giardino osservando il sentiero della collina.

VOCI DELLE AMICHE
    Ah! ah! ah! ah!
    Quanto cielo! quanto mar!

VOCE DI BUTTERFLY
    Ancora un passo or via.

VOCI DELLE AMICHE
    Come sei tarda.

VOCE DI BUTTERFLY
    Aspetta.

VOCI DELLE AMICHE
    Ecco la vetta.
    Guarda, guarda quanti fior!

SHARPLESS (*serious and kindly*)
> Day before yesterday, she came
> to visit the consulate.
> I didn't see her, but I heard her speak.
> The mystery of her voice
> struck my soul.
> Certainly, when it's sincere,
> love speaks like that.
> It would be a great pity
> to tear the fragile wings
> and to abandon perhaps a trusting heart.

PINKERTON
> My tactful consul,
> calm yourself. One knows,
> your age is one of mournful mood.
> There's no great harm
> if I want to direct those wings
> to the sweet flights of love!

SHARPLESS
> It would be a great pity . . .
> That divine, mild little voice
> shouldn't utter notes of grief.

PINKERTON (*again offering him a drink*)
> Whisky?

SHARPLESS   Another glass.

Pinkerton pours some whisky for Sharpless and also fills his own glass.

SHARPLESS (*raises the glass*)
> I drink to your family far away.

PINKERTON (*also raises his glass*)
> And to the day when I'll marry,
> in a real wedding, a real American wife.

Goro reappears running, breathless, from the bottom of the hill.

GORO
> There! They've reached the summit of the slope.
>> (*points toward the path*)
> Already the murmur
> of the feminine swarm,
> like wind in foliage, is heard.

Pinkerton and Sharpless go to the end of the garden, looking toward the path of the hill.

VOICES OF THE GIRL FRIENDS
> Ah! ah! ah! ah!
> How much sky! how much sea!

BUTTERFLY'S VOICE
> One more step, come now.

VOICES OF THE GIRL FRIENDS
> How slow you are.

BUTTERFLY'S VOICE
> Wait.

VOICES OF THE GIRL FRIENDS
> Here's the peak.
> Look, look at how many flowers!

VOCE DI BUTTERFLY
    Spira sul mare e sulla terra
    [un primaveril soffio giocondo.

VOCI DELLE AMICHE
    Quanto cielo! quanto mar!

SHARPLESS O allegro cinguettar di gioventù!]

VOCE DI BUTTERFLY
    Io sono la fanciulla
    [più lieta del Giappone, anzi di mondo.
    Amiche, io son venuta
    al richiamo d'amor . . . d'amor
    venni alle soglie
    ove s'accoglie
    il bene di chi vive e di chi muor.
    Amiche, io son venuta, ecc.

VOCI DELLE AMICHE
    Quanti fior! quanto mar!
    Quanto cielo! quanti fior!
    Gioia a te, gioia a te sia
    dolce amica, ma pria
    di varcar la soglia che t'attira
    volgiti e mira, mira
    quanto cielo, quanti fiori, quanto mar!

    Gioia a te, ecc.]

 Appaiono, superato il pendìo della collina, Butterfly colle
amiche, tutte hanno grandi ombrelli aperti, a vivi colori.

BUTTERFLY (*alle amiche*)
    Siam giunte.
     (*vede il gruppo dei tre uomini e riconosce*
     Pinkerton. Chiude subito l'ombrello e
     pronta lo addita alle amiche)

    F. B. Pinkerton.° Giù.
     (*si genuflette*)
LE AMICHE (*chiudono gli ombrelli e si genuflettono*)
    Giù.
     (*poi tutte si alzano e si avvicinano a Pink-*
     erton cerimoniosamente)
BUTTERFLY Gran ventura.
LE AMICHE Riverenza.

PINKERTON (*sorridendo*)
    È un po' dura la scalata?
BUTTERFLY A una sposa costumata
    più penosa è l'impazienza . . .
PINKERTON (*gentilmente, ma un po' derisorio*)
    Molto raro complimento.

 * Translator's note: Pinkerton's initials were inverted out of respect for English audiences, for whom "B.F." stands not so much
for "Benjamin Franklin" as "bloody fool."

BUTTERFLY'S VOICE
>A gay, spring-like breeze
>breathes over the sea and over the earth.

VOICES OF THE GIRL FRIENDS
>How much sky! How much sea!

SHARPLESS   Oh, happy chattering of youth!

BUTTERFLY'S VOICE
>I am the happiest
>maiden in Japan, rather in the world.
>Friends, I have come
>at the summons of love . . . I came
>to love's threshold
>where the good is gathered
>of those who live and those who die.
>Friends, I have come, etc.

VOICES OF THE GIRL FRIENDS
>How many flowers! How much sea!
>How much sky! How many flowers!
>Joy to you, joy be yours,
>sweet friend, but before
>crossing the threshold that attracts you,
>turn and look, look
>at how much sky, how many flowers, how much
>   sea!
>Joy to you, etc.

Having climbed up the slope of the hill, Butterfly and her girl friends appear. All have large, brightly-colored parasols open.

BUTTERFLY (*to the girl friends*)
>We've arrived.
>>(*sees the group of three men and recognizes Pinkerton. She closes her parasol at once and promptly points him out to her friends*)
>F. B. Pinkerton. Down.
>>(*kneels*)

THE GIRL FRIENDS (*close their parasols and kneel*)
>Down.
>>(*then all rise and approach Pinkerton ceremoniously*)

BUTTERFLY   Great fortune.

THE GIRL FRIENDS
>Our respect.

PINKERTON (*smiling*)
>Is the climb a bit hard?

BUTTERFLY   For a well-bred bride
>the impatience is more painful . . .

PINKERTON (*politely, but a bit deridingly*)
>A very rare compliment.

BUTTERFLY (*ingenua*)
    Dei più belli ancor ne so.
PINKERTON (*rincalzando*)
    Dei gioielli!
BUTTERFLY (*volendo sfoggiare il suo repertorio di complimenti*)
    Se vi è caro sul momento . . .
PINKERTON   Grazie — no.

   Sharpless ha osservato prima curiosamente il gruppo delle fanciulle, poi si è avvicinato a Butterfly, che lo ascolta con attenzione.

SHARPLESS   Miss Butterfly . . . Bel nome,
    vi sta a meraviglia.
    Siete di Nagasaki?
BUTTERFLY   Signor sì. Di famiglia
    assai prospera un tempo.
       (*alle amiche*)
    Verità?
LE AMICHE (*approvando premurose*)
    Verità!

BUTTERFLY   Nessuno si confessa mai nato in povertà,
    non c'è vagabondo che a sentirlo non sia
    di gran prosapia. Eppur conobbi la richezza.
    Ma il turbine rovescia le quercie più robuste . . .
    e abbiam fatto la ghescia per sostentarci.
       (*alle amiche*)
    Vero?
LE AMICHE (*confermano*)
    Vero!

BUTTERFLY   Non lo nascondo, nè m'adonto.
       (*vedendo che Sharpless sorride*)
    Ridete? Perchè . . . ? Cose del mondo.

PINKERTON (*ha ascoltato con interesse e si rivolge a Sharpless*)
    (Con quel fare di bambola
    quando parla m'infiamma . . .)
SHARPLESS (*anch'esso interessato dalle chiacchiere di Butter-
    fly, continua ad interrogarla*)
    E ci avete sorelle?
BUTTERFLY   Non signore. Ho la mamma.
GORO (*con importanza*)
    Una nobile dama.
BUTTERFLY   Ma senza farle torto
    povera molto anch'essa.
SHARPLESS   E vostro padre?
BUTTERFLY (*si arresta sorpresa, poi secco secco risponde*)
    Morto.

   Le amiche chinano la testa. Goro è imbarazzato. Tutte si sventolano nervosamente coi ventagli.

SHARPLESS (*ritornando presso Butterfly*)
    Quant'anni avete?
BUTTERFLY (*con civetteria quasi infantile*)
    Indovinate.

BUTTERFLY (*naïvely*)
>I know others even more beautiful.

PINKERTON (*insisting*)
>Gems!

BUTTERFLY (*wanting to show off her repertory of compliments*)
>If you like, here and now . . .

PINKERTON Thanks — no.

>*Sharpless has first observed the group of girls curiously, then he has approached Butterfly, who listens to him with attention.*

SHARPLESS Miss Butterfly . . . Beautiful name,
>it suits you wonderfully.
>Are you from Nagasaki?

BUTTERFLY Yes, sir. From a family
>once very prosperous.
>>(*to the girl friends*)
>Is that the truth?

THE GIRL FRIENDS (*approving eagerly*)
>The truth!

BUTTERFLY Nobody ever confesses he was born in poverty,
>there isn't a vagabond who, to hear him,
>isn't of great lineage. And yet I knew wealth.
>But the hurricane uproots the sturdiest oaks . . .
>and we became Geishas to support ourselves.
>>(*to the girl friends*)
>True?

THE GIRL FRIENDS (*confirm*)
>True!

BUTTERFLY I don't hide it, nor am I ashamed of it.
>>(*seeing that Sharpless smiles*)
>You laugh? Why . . . ? Things that happen in
>the world.

PINKERTON (*has listened with interest and addresses Sharpless*)
>(With that doll-like manner
>when she speaks she sets me afire . . .

SHARPLESS (*also interested in Butterfly's chatter, continues to question her*)
>And do you have sisters?

BUTTERFLY No, sir. I have my mother.

GORO (*self-important*)
>A noble lady.

BUTTERFLY But . . . without wronging her . . .
>also very poor.

SHARPLESS And your father?

BUTTERFLY (*stops, surprised, then answers curtly*)
>Dead.

>*The girl friends bow their heads. Goro is embarrassed. All the girls fan themselves nervously with their fans.*

SHARPLESS (*coming back near Butterfly*)
>How old are you?

BUTTERFLY (*with almost childish coyness*)
>Guess.

SHARPLESS   Dieci.

BUTTERFLY   Crescete.

SHARPLESS   Venti.

BUTTERFLY   Calate. Quindici netti, netti;
                        (*con malizia*)
                    sono vecchia diggià!

SHARPLESS   Quindici anni!

PINKERTON   Quindici anni!

SHARPLESS   L'età dei giuochi . . .

PINKERTON   . . . e dei confetti.

GORO (*che ha veduto arrivare dal fondo altre persone e le ha
          riconosciute, annuncia con importanza*)

                    L'Imperial Commissario,
                    L'Ufficiale del registro,
                    i congiunti.

PINKERTON   Fate presto.

*Goro corre in casa. Dal sentiero in fondo si vedono salire e
sfilare i parenti di Butterfly: questa va loro incontro, insieme
alle amiche: grandi saluti, riverenze: i parenti osservano curiosamente i due americani. Pinkerton ha preso sottobraccio
Sharpless e, condottolo da un lato, gli fa osservare, ridendo, il
bizzarro gruppo dei parenti; il Commissario Imperiale e l'Ufficiale del registro salutano Pinkerton ed entrano in casa, rice-
vuti da Goro.*

PINKERTON   Che burletta la sfilata
                    della nuova parentela,
                    *(A)tolta in prestito, a mesata.

PARENTI, AMICHE (*a Butterfly*)
                    Dov'è? Dov'è?

BUTTERFLY, ALCUNE AMICHE
                    Eccolo là!

UNA CUGINA, ALCUNI PARENTI
                    Bello non è.

BUTTERFLY (*offesa*)
                    Bello è così che non si può sognar di più.

LA MADRE, PARENTI, AMICHE
                    Mi pare un re! Vale un Perù!

ALTRI PARENTI
                    In verità bello non è.

PINKERTON   Certo dietro a quella vela
                    di ventaglio pavonazzo,
                    la mia suocera si cela.

UNA CUGINA (*a Butterfly*)
                    Goro l'offrì pur anco a me.

BUTTERFLY (*sdegnosa, alla Cugina*)
                    Sì, giusto tu!

PINKERTON (*indicando Yakusidé*)
                    E quel coso da strapazzo
                    è lo zio briaco e pazzo.

* The lines beginning at (A) and ending at (B) are traditionally
cut. Though this scene appears complete in the score, it is invari-
ably abbreviated in performance.

SHARPLESS	Ten.
BUTTERFLY	Go higher.
SHARPLESS	Twenty.
BUTTERFLY	Come lower. Exactly fifteen; (*coyly*) I'm already old!
SHARPLESS	Fifteen!
PINKERTON	Fifteen!
SHARPLESS	The age for games . . .
PINKERTON	. . . and wedding cake.

GORO (*who has seen other people arriving from the background
and has recognized them, announces impor-
tantly*)
    The imperial commissioner,
    the registry officer,
    the relatives.

PINKERTON   Hurry up.

    *Goro runs into the house. From the path in the back the
relatives of Butterfly are seen climbing up and passing by.
She goes to them with her friends: great greetings, bows. The
relatives observe the two Americans curiously. Pinkerton has
taken Sharpless by the arm and led him to one side. Laughing,
he makes him observe the bizarre group of relatives. The
imperial commissioner and the registry officer greet Pinkerton
and go into the house, received by Goro.*

PINKERTON   What a farce the parade
    of the new kinfolk,
    borrowed on loan, by the month.

RELATIVES, SOME GIRL FRIENDS (*to Butterfly*)
    Where is he? Where is he?

BUTTERFLY, SOME GIRL FRIENDS
    There he is!

A FEMALE COUSIN, SOME RELATIVES
    He isn't handsome.

BUTTERFLY (*offended*)
    He's more handsome than you can dream of.

MOTHER, RELATIVES, GIRL FRIENDS
    He seems a king to me! He's worth a fortune!

OTHER RELATIVES
    Truly he isn't handsome.

PINKERTON   Surely behind that veil
    of a purple fan,
    my mother-in-law is hidden.

A FEMALE COUSIN (*to Butterfly*)
    Goro also offered him to me.

BUTTERFLY (*indignant, to the cousin*)
    Yes, you, of all people!

PINKERTON (*pointing to Yakusidé*)
    And that outlandish object
    is the drunken, crazy uncle.

AMICHE, PARENTI (*alla Cugina*)
>Ecco, perchè prescelta fu,
>vuol far con te la soprappiù.
>La sua beltà già sfiorì.
>Divorzierà.

CUGINA, ALTRI PARENTI
>Spero di sì. Spero di sì.
>La sua beltà già disfiorì.

Goro esce dalla casa e indispettito dal garrulo cicalìo, va dall'uno all'altro raccomandando di parlare sottovoce.

LO ZIO YAKUSIDÉ (*adocchiando i servi che cominciano a portare vini e liquori*)
>Vino ce n'è?

LA MADRE, LA ZIA (*sbirciando, cercando di non farsi scorgere*)
>Guardiamo un po'.

AMICHE (*con soddisfazione, a Yakusidé*)
>Ne vidi già, color di thè,
>color di thè, e chermisì!

PARENTI, AMICHE
>La sua beltà già disfiorì.

MADRE, ZIA, PARENTI, AMICHE
>Ah! hu! ah! hu! (B)
>[Mi pare un re, ecc.

UNA CUGINA
>Goro l'offri pur anco a me,
>ma s'ebbe un no! Bello non è, ecc.

BUTTERFLY   Sì . . . giusto tu!

LO ZIO YAKUSIDÉ
>Vino ce n'è? Guardiamo un po' . . .

PARENTI, AMICHE
>Bello non è, ecc.]

Goro interviene di nuovo per far cessare il baccano, poi coi gesti fa cenno di tacere.

GORO   Per carità tacete un po' . . .
>Sch . . . ! sch . . . ! sch . . . !

SHARPLESS (*a Pinkerton, a parte*)
>O amico fortunato!
>[O fortunato Pinkerton
>che in sorte v'è toccato
>un fior pur or sbocciato!
>Non più bella e d'assai fanciulla
>io vidi mai di questa Butterfly . . .

PINKERTON   Sì, è vero, è un fiore, un fiore!
>L'esotico suo odore
>m'ha il cervello sconvolto.
>Sì, è vero, è un fiore, un fiore,
>e in fede mia l'ho colto!

AMICHE, LA CUGINA
>Ei l'offrì pur anco a me!
>Ma risposi non lo vo'!
>E risposi no!

GIRL FRIENDS, RELATIVES (*to the cousin*)
  There, because she was the chosen one,
  she wants to act haughty with you.
  Her beauty has already withered.
  She'll be divorced.

FEMALE COUSIN, OTHER RELATIVES
  I hope so. I hope so.
  Her beauty has already withered.

 Goro comes out of the house and, annoyed by the garrulous chatter, he goes from one to another, urging them to speak softly.

UNCLE YAKUSIDÉ (*eyeing the servants who are beginning to
     bring wines and liquors*)
  Is there any wine?

MOTHER, AUNT (*peering, trying not to be noticed*)
  Let's look around a bit.

GIRL FRIENDS (*contented, to Yakusidé*)
  I saw some already, tea-colored,
  tea-colored, and crimson!

RELATIVES, GIRL FRIENDS
  Her beauty has already withered.

MOTHER, AUNT, RELATIVES, GIRL FRIENDS
  Ah! hu! ah! hu!
  He seems a king to me, etc.

A FEMALE COUSIN
  Goro also offered him to me,
  but received a no! He isn't handsome, etc.

BUTTERFLY Yes . . . you, of all people!

UNCLE YAKUSIDÉ
  Is there any wine? Let's look around a bit . . .

RELATIVES, GIRL FRIENDS
  He isn't handsome, etc.

 Goro intervenes again to make the racket stop, then with gestures he signals them to be silent.

GORO For heaven's sake, be quiet a bit . . .
  Shh . . . ! shh . . . ! shh . . . !

SHARPLESS (*to Pinkerton, aside*)
  Oh, lucky friend!
  Oh, lucky Pinkerton,
  since your fate has given you
  a flower that's just blossomed!
  I've never seen any girl more beautiful
  than this Butterfly . . .

PINKERTON Yes, it's true, she's a flower, a flower!
  Her exotic perfume
  has confused my brain.
  Yes, it's true, she's a flower, a flower,
  and, by my faith, I've picked her!

GIRL FRIENDS, THE COUSIN
  He offered him also to me!
  But I answered: I don't want him!
  And I answered no!

Senza tanto ricercar
io ne trovo dei miglior,
e gli dirò un bel no,
e gli dirò di no, di no!

ALTRI PARENTI, LA MADRE
Egli è bel, mi pare un re!
Non avrei risposto no!
Non, mia cara, non mi par,
è davvero un gran signor,
nè mai direi di no, di no!

ALTRI PARENTI
Divorzierà, divorzierà!

BUTTERFLY   Badate, attenti a me!

SHARPLESS   E se a voi sembrano scede
il patto e la sua fede —]
badate . . . ! Ella ci crede.

BUTTERFLY   Mamma, vien qua.
                    (*agli altri*)
                Badate a me:
                attenti, orsù,
                uno, due, tre
                e tutti giù.

*Al cenno di Butterfly tutti si inchinano innanzi a Pinkerton
ed a Sharpless. I parenti si rialzano e si spargono nel giardino;
Goro ne conduce qualcuno nell'interno della casa. Pinkerton
prende per mano Butterfly e la conduce verso la casa.*

PINKERTON   Vieni amor mio!
                Vi piace la casetta?

BUTTERFLY   Signor F. B. Pinkerton . . .
                    (*mostra le mani e le braccia, che sono
                    impacciate dalle maniche rigonfie*)
                perdono . . .
                Io vorrei . . . pochi oggetti da donna . . .

PINKERTON   Dove sono?

BUTTERFLY (*indicando le maniche*)
                Sono qui . . . vi dispiace?

PINKERTON (*un po' sorpreso, sorride, poi acconsente, con ga-
                    lanteria*)
                O perchè mai, mia bella Butterfly?

*Butterfly a mano a mano cava dalle maniche gli oggetti e
li consegna a Suzuki, che è uscita sulla terrazza, e li depone
nella casa.*

BUTTERFLY   Fazzoletti. La pipa. Una cintura. Un piccolo
                fermaglio.
                Uno specchio. Un ventaglio.

PINKERTON (*vede un vasetto*)
                Quel barattolo?

BUTTERFLY   Un vaso di tintura.

PINKERTON   Ohibò!

BUTTERFLY   Vi spiace . . . ? Via!
                    (*getta via il vaso di tintura; trae un astuc-
                    cio lungo e stretto*)

                   Without so much searching
                   I can find better ones,
                   and I'll tell him a round no,
                   and I'll tell him no, no!

OTHER RELATIVES, THE MOTHER
                   He's handsome, he seems a king to me!
                   I wouldn't have answered no!
                   No, my dear girl, it doesn't seem so to me,
                   he's really a great gentlemen,
                   nor would I ever say no, no!

OTHER RELATIVES
                   She'll be divorced, she'll be divorced!

BUTTERFLY   Mind you, pay attention to me!

SHARPLESS   And if the pact and her faith
                   seem jokes to you —
                   mind you . . . ! She believes in it.

BUTTERFLY   Mamma, come here.
                        (*to the others*)
                   Pay attention to me:
                   watch now,
                   one, two, three,
                   and all down!

*At Butterfly's signal all bow before Pinkerton and Sharpless.
The relatives rise again and scatter in the garden. Goro leads
some of them inside the house. Pinkerton takes Butterfly by
the hand and leads her toward the house.*

PINKERTON   Come, my love!
                   Do you like the little house?

BUTTERFLY   Mr. F. B. Pinkerton . . .
                        (*shows her hands and her arms, which are
                        made awkward by her filled sleeves*)
                   forgive me . . .
                   I'd like . . . a few woman's objects . . .

PINKERTON   Where are they?

BUTTERFLY (*pointing to her sleeves*)
                   They're here . . . do you mind?

PINKERTON (*a bit surprised, smiles, then consents, with gal-
                   lantry*)
                   Oh, why should I, my beautiful Butterfly?

*Butterfly, one by one, takes the objects from her sleeves and
hands them to Suzuki, who has come out on the terrace and
sets them in the house.*

BUTTERFLY   Handkerchiefs. My pipe. A sash. A little brooch.

                   A mirror. A fan.

PINKERTON (*sees a little pot*)
                   That jar?

BUTTERFLY   A pot of rouge.

PINKERTON   Aha!

BUTTERFLY   You don't like it . . . ? Away with it!
                        (*throws away the pot of rouge; takes out
                        a long and narrow case*)

PINKERTON   E quello?

BUTTERFLY (*molto seria*)
                Cosa sacra e mia.

PINKERTON (*curioso*)
                E non si può vedere.

BUTTERFLY   C'è troppa gente. Perdonate.
                (*sparisce nella casa portando con sè l'astuc-
                cio*)

GORO (*che si è avvicinato, dice all'orecchio di Pinkerton*)
                È un presente del Mikado a suo padre . . .
                coll'invito . . .
                (*fa il gesto di che s'apre il ventre*)

PINKERTON (*piano a Goro*)
                E . . . suo padre?

GORO   Ha obbedito.

   *Goro s'allontana, rientrando nella casa. Butterfly, che è ri-
tornata, va a sedersi sulla terrazza vicino a Pinkerton e leva
dalle maniche alcune statuette.*

BUTTERFLY   Gli Ottokè.

PINKERTON (*ne prende una e la esamina con curiosità*)
                Quei pupazzi . . . ? Avete detto?

BUTTERFLY   Son l'anime degli avi.
                (*depone le statuette*)

PINKERTON   Ah . . . ! il mio rispetto.

BUTTERFLY (*con rispettosa confidenza, a Pinkerton*)
                Ieri son salita
                tutta sola in secreto alla Missione.
                Colla nuova mia vita
                posso adottare nuova religione.
                Lo zio Bonzo nol sa,
                nè i miei lo sanno.
                Io seguo il mio destino
                e piena d'umiltà
                al Dio del signor Pinkerton m'inchino.
                È mio destino.
                Nella stessa chiesetta in ginocchio con voi,
                pregherò lo stesso Dio.
                E per farvi contento
                potrò forse obliar la gente mia . . .
                (*si getta nella braccia di Pinkerton*)
                Amore mio . . . !*
                (*si arresta come avesse paura d'essere stata
                udita dai parenti*)

   *Intanto Goro ha aperto lo shosi. Nella stanza dove tutto è
pronto pel matrimonio, si trovano Sharpless e le autorità. Butterfly entra nella casa e si inginocchia; Pinkerton è in piedi
vicino a lei. I parenti sono nel giardino, rivolti verso la casa,
inginocchiati.*

GORO   Tutti zitti!

* Translator's note: In some editions this line is still given as
"*E questi via!*" (And away with these!). At which point Butterfly
throws away the statuettes. This version is sung at Covent Garden,
London.

PINKERTON And that?

BUTTERFLY (*very serious*)
Something sacred and mine.

PINKERTON (*curious*)
And can't it be seen?

BUTTERFLY There are too many people. Forgive me.
(*disappears into the house taking the case with her*)

GORO (*who has come over, says in Pinkerton's ear*)
It's a present from the Mikado to her father . . . with the invitation to . . .
(*imitates the gesture of cutting open his stomach*)

PINKERTON (*softly, to Goro*)
And . . . her father?

GORO Obeyed.

Goro goes off, re-entering the house. Butterfly, who has come back, goes to sit on the terrace near Pinkerton and takes some statuettes from her sleeve.

BUTTERFLY The hotoké.

PINKERTON (*takes one and examines it with curiosity*)
Those puppets . . . ? You said?

BUTTERFLY They are the souls of the ancestors.
(*sets down the statuettes*)

PINKERTON Ah . . . ! my respects.

BUTTERFLY (*with respectful familiarity, to Pinkerton*)
Yesterday I went up
all alone, in secret, to the mission.
With my new life
I can adopt a new religion.
My Bonze uncle doesn't know it,
nor do my relatives know.
I follow my destiny
and, full of humility,
I bow to Mr. Pinkerton's God.
It's my destiny.
In the same little church, kneeling with you,
I'll pray to the same God.
And to make you happy
perhaps I'll be able to forget my people . . .
(*throws herself into Pinkerton's arms*)
My love . . . !
(*stops, as if she were afraid of being heard by her relatives*)

Meanwhile Goro has opened the shoji. Sharpless and the authorities are in the room, where all is ready for the marriage. Butterfly enters the house and kneels down; Pinkerton is standing near her. The relatives are in the garden, facing the house, kneeling.

GORO Quiet, all!

COMMISSARIO (*legge*)
 È concesso al nominato
 Benjamin Franklin Pinkerton,
 Luogotenente della cannoniera *Lincoln*,
 marina degli Stati Uniti America del Nord:
 ed alla damigella Butterfly
 del quartiere d'Omara-Nagasaki,
 d'unirsi in matrimonio,
 per dritto il primo, della propria volontà,
 ed ella per consenso dei parenti
 qui testimoni all'atto.
   (*porge l'atto per la firma*)

GORO (*ceremonioso*)
 Lo sposo.
   (*Pinkerton firma*)
 Poi la sposa.
   (*Butterfly firma*)
 E tutto è fatto.

Le amiche si avvicinano, complimentose, a Butterfly, alla quale fanno ripetuti inchini.

LA AMICHE   Madama Butterfly!

BUTTERFLY (*le corregge*)
 Madama F. B. Pinkerton.

Le amiche festeggiano Butterfly, che ne bacia qualcuna intanto l'Ufficiale dello Stato Civile ritira l'atto e le altre carte, poi avverte il Commissario Imperiale che tutto è finito.

COMMISSARIO (*saluta Pinkerton*)
 Auguri molti.

PINKERTON   I miei ringraziamenti.

COMMISSARIO (*a Sharpless*)
 Il signor Console scende?

SHARPLESS   L'accompagno.
   (*saluta Pinkerton*)
 Ci vedrem domani.

PINKERTON   A meraviglia.

UFFICIALE (*congedandosi da Pinkerton*)
 Posterità.

PINKERTON   Mi proverò.

Il Console, il Commissario Imperiale e l'Ufficiale del registro si avviano per scendere alla città.

SHARPLESS (*ritorna indietro e con accento significativo dice a
   Pinkerton:*)
 Giudizio!

Pinkerton con un gesto lo rassicura e lo saluta colla mano. Sharpless scende pel sentiero; Pinkerton che è andato verso il fondo lo saluta di nuovo, ritorna innanzi, stropicciandosi le mani.

PINKERTON (*fra sè*)
   (Ed eccoci in famiglia.)
     (*i servi portano delle bottiglie di saki e
      distribuiscono i bicchieri agli invitati*)

COMMISSIONER (*reads*)
>It is permitted to the said
>Benjamin Franklin Pinkerton,
>Lieutenant of the gunboat *Lincoln,*
>United States Navy, North America,
>and to the spinster Butterfly,
>of the Omara quarter, Nagasaki,
>to be united in matrimony,
>the former by right of his own free will,
>and she by agreement of her relatives,
>here witnesses to the contract . . .
>>(*holds out the contract for the signature*)

GORO (*ceremoniously*)
>The groom.
>>(*Pinkerton signs*)
>Then the bride.
>>(*Butterfly signs*)
>And all is done.

The girl friends come over, formally, to Butterfly, to whom they make repeated bows.

THE GIRL FRIENDS
>Madame Butterfly!

BUTTERFLY (*corrects them*)
>Madame F. B. Pinkerton

The girl friends congratulate Butterfly, who kisses some of them. Meanwhile the registry officer collects the contract and the other papers, then informs the imperial commissioner that all is finished.

COMMISSIONER
>Congratulations.

PINKERTON My thanks.

COMMISSIONER (*to Sharpless*)
>Is the consul going down?

SHARPLESS I'll accompany you.
>>(*says good-by to Pinkerton*)
>We'll see each other tomorrow.

PINKERTON Splendid.

OFFICER (*taking leave of Pinkerton*)
>I wish you many descendants.

PINKERTON I'll do my best.

The consul, the imperial commissioner, and the registry officer start off, to go down to the city.

SHARPLESS (*comes back and says to Pinkerton in a meaningful tone*)
>Discretion!

Pinkerton reassures him with a gesture and waves good-by to him. Sharpless goes down the path. Pinkerton, who has gone toward the back, waves again, then comes back to the foreground, rubbing his hands.

PINKERTON (*to himself*)
>(And here we are, just the family).
>>(*the servants bring some bottles of sake and distribute glasses to the guests*)

Sbrighiamoci al più presto . . . in modo onesto.
(*brindando cogli invitati*)

Hip! hip . . . !
INVITATI   O Kami! O Kami!
PINKERTON   Beviamo ai novissimi legami.
TUTTI   O Kami! O Kami!
                       Beviamo ai novissimi legami.

Grida terribili dal sentiero della collina interrompono i brindisi: ad un tratto appare dal fondo uno strano personaggio, la cui vista fa allibire tutti. E il Bonzo che si fa innanzi furibondo e vista Butterfly, stende le mani minacciose verso di lei, gridando.

BONZO   Cio-cio san . . . ! Cio-cio san . . . !
                       Abbominazione!

A questo grido tutti i parenti e gli amici allibiscono e si raccolgono impauriti; Butterfly rimane isolata in un angolo.

BUTTERFLY, INVITATI
                       Lo zio Bonzo!
GORO (*infastidito dalla venuta del Bonzo*)
                       Un corno al guastafeste!
                       Chi ci leva d'intorno le persone moleste?
BONZO   Cio-cio san . . . ! Cio-cio san . . . ! Cio-cio san!
                       Che hai tu fatto alla Missione?
INVITATI   Rispondi, Cio-cio san!
PINKERTON (*seccato per la scenata del Bonzo*)
                       Che mi strilla quel matto?
BONZO   Rispondi, che hai tu fatto?
INVITATI   Rispondi, Cio-cio san!
BONZO   Come, hai tu gli occhi asciutti?
                       Son dunque questi i frutti?
                            (*urlando*)
                       Ci ha rinnegato tutti!
INVITATI (*scandolezzati*)
                       Hou! Cio-cio san!
BONZO   Rinnegato, vi dico,
                       il culto antico.
INVITATI   Hou! Cio-cio san!
BONZO (*imprecando contro Butterfly, che si copre il volto colle mani: la madre si avanza per difenderla, ma il Bonzo duramente la respinge*)
                       Kami sarundasico!*
                       All'anima tua guasta
                       qual supplizio sovrasta!
PINKERTON (*infastidito*)
                       Ehi, dico: basta, basta!

Alla voce di Pinkerton, il Bonzo si arresta stupefatto, poi con subita risoluzione invita i parenti e le amiche a partire.

---

* Translator's note: This is apparently the Japanese word *warugashicoè* ("cunning").

> Let's get it over as fast as possible . . . in a decent way.
> *(toasting with the guests)*
> Hip! hip!

GUESTS   O Kami! O Kami!

PINKERTON   Let's drink to the new bonds.

ALL   O Kami! O Kami!
     Let's drink to the new bonds.

Terrible cries from the hill path interrupt the toasts. Suddenly, from the background, there appears a strange personage the sight of whom frightens all. It is the Bonze, who comes forward in a fury and, seeing Butterfly, extends his hands menacingly toward her, shouting.

BONZE   Cho-cho san . . . ! Cho-cho san . . . !
     Abomination!

At this cry all the relatives and friends are dismayed and huddle together in fear; Butterfly remains isolated in one corner.

BUTTERFLY, GUESTS
     The Bonze uncle!

GORO *(annoyed by the coming of the Bonze)*
     Damn the spoilsport!
     Who'll rid us of annoying people?

BONZE   Cho-cho san . . . ! Cho-cho san . . . ! Cho-cho san!
     What have you done at the mission?

GUESTS   Answer, Cho-cho san!

PINKERTON *(annoyed at the Bonze's scene)*
     What's that madman yelling at me?

BONZE   Answer: what have you done?

GUESTS   Answer, Cho-cho san!

BONZE   What, you have dry eyes?
     Are these then the fruits?
     (shouting)
     She has rejected us all!

GUESTS *(shocked)*
     Oh! Cho-cho san!

BONZE   Rejected, I tell you,
     the ancient religion.

GUESTS   Oh! Cho-cho san!

BONZE *(railing at Butterfly, who covers her face with her hands. Her mother advances to defend her, but the Bonze harshly pushes her away)*
     Kami! Cunning one!
     What punishment threatens
     your ruined soul!

PINKERTON *(annoyed)*
     Hey, I say: enough, enough!

At the sound of Pinkerton's voice, the Bonze stops, amazed, then with prompt determination, he invites the relatives and the girl friends to leave.

BONZO   Venite tutti. Andiamo!
                 (*a Butterfly*)
                 Ci hai rinnegato e noi . . .

BONZO, INVITATI
                      . . . ti rinneghiamo!

Tutti si ritirano frettolosamente al fondo e stendono le brac-
cia verso Butterfly.

PINKERTON (*autorevolmente*)
                 Sbarazzate all'istante. In casa mia
                 niente baccano e niente bonzeria.

Alle parole di Pinkerton, tutti corrono precipitosamente
verso il sentiero che scende alla città: la madre tenta di nuovo
di andare presso Butterfly, ma viene travolta dagli altri. Il
Bonzo sparisce pel sentiero che va al tempio.

INVITATI (*nell'uscire*)
                 Hou! Cio-cio san! Hou! Cio-cio san!

Le voci poco a poco si allontanano. Butterfly sta sempre
immobile e muta colla faccia nelle mani, mentre Pinkerton si
è recato alla sommità del sentiero per assicurarsi che tutti quei
seccatori se ne vanno.

BONZO, INVITATI
                 Kami sarundasico!
                 Hou! Cio-cio san!
                 Ti rinneghiamo!
                 Hou! Cio-cio san!

Comincia a calare la sera. Butterfly scoppia in pianto infan-
tile. Pinkerton l'ode e va premuroso presso di lei, sollevandola
dall'abbattimento in cui è caduta e togliendole con delicatezza
le mani dal viso piangente.

PINKERTON   Bimba, bimba, non piangere
                 per gracchiar di ranocchi.

VOCI (*lontanissimo*)
                 Hou! Cio-cio san!

BUTTERFLY (*turandosi le orecchie, per non udire le grida*)
                 Urlano ancor!

PINKERTON (*rincorandola*)
                 Tutta la tua tribù
                 e i Bonzi tutti del Giappone non valgono
                 il pianto di quegli occhi
                 cari e belli.

BUTTERFLY (*sorridendo infantilmente*)
                 Davver? Non piango più.
                 E quasi del ripudio non mi duole
                 per le vostre parole
                 che mi suonan così dolci nel cor.
                      (*si china per baciare la mano a Pinkerton*)

PINKERTON (*dolcemente impedendo*)
                 Che fai . . . ? la man?

BUTTERFLY   M' han detto
                 che laggiù fra le gente costumata
                 è questo il segno del maggior rispetto.

BONZE   Come, all. Let us go!
                 (*to Butterfly*)
                 You have rejected us and we . . .

BONZE, GUESTS
                 . . . reject you!

All withdraw hastily to the rear and stretch out their arms toward Butterfly.

PINKERTON (*with authority*)
                 Clear out this minute. In my house
                 no racket and no bonze stuff.

At Pinkerton's words, all run hastily toward the path that goes down to the city. The mother tries again to go toward Butterfly, but she is overrun by the others. The Bonze disappears along the path that goes to the temple.

GUESTS (*going out*)
                 Oh! Cho-cho san! Oh! Cho-cho san!

Little by little the voices go away. Butterfly is still motionless and silent, her face in her hands, while Pinkerton has gone to the top of the path to make sure that all those bores leave.

BONZE, GUESTS
                 Kami! Cunning one!
                 Oh! Cho-cho san!
                 We reject you!
                 Oh! Cho-cho san!

Evening begins to fall. Butterfly bursts into childish weeping. Pinkerton hears her and, concerned, goes to her, raising her from the dejection into which she has fallen and delicately removing her hands from her weeping face.

PINKERTON   Child, child, don't cry
                 because of frogs' croaking.

VOICES (*very far away*)
                 Oh! Cho-cho san!

BUTTERFLY (*covering her ears so as not to hear the cries*)
                 They're still shouting!

PINKERTON (*comforting her*)
                 Your whole tribe
                 and all the Bonzes of Japan aren't worth
                 the weeping of those eyes,
                 dear and beautiful.

BUTTERFLY (*smiling childishly*)
                 Really? I'm not crying any more.
                 And I almost don't suffer at their rejection,
                 thanks to your words
                 which ring so sweetly in my heart.
                      (*bends to kiss Pinkerton's hand*)

PINKERTON (*gently preventing her*)
                 What are you doing . . . My hand?

BUTTERFLY   They told me
                 that over there, among well-bred people,
                 this is the mark of greatest respect.

SUZUKI (*internamente*)
 E Izaghi ed Izanami sarundasico,
 e Kami, e Izaghi ed Izanami, sarundasico,

 e Kami.
PINKERTON (*sorpreso per tale sordo bisbiglio*)
 Chi brontola lassù?
BUTTERFLY È Suzuki che fa la sua preghiera seral.
PINKERTON (*conduce Butterfly verso la casetta*)
 Viene la sera . . .
BUTTERFLY . . . e l'ombra e la quiete.
PINKERTON E sei qui sola.
BUTTERFLY Sola e rinnegata!
 Rinnegata . . . e felice!
 *Pinkerton batte tre volte le mani: i servi e Suzuki accorrono
subito.*
PINKERTON (*ordina ai servi*)
 A voi, chiudete.
 *I servi chiudono le pareti che danno sul terrazzo poi si
ritirano.*
BUTTERFLY Sì, sì, noi tutti soli . . .
 E fuori il mondo . . .
PINKERTON (*ridendo*)
 E il Bonzo furibondo.
BUTTERFLY (*a Suzuki, che è venuta coi servi e sta aspettando
 gli ordini*)
 Suzuki, le mie vesti.
 *Suzuki fruga in un cofano e dà a Butterfly gli abiti per la
notte ed un cofanetto coll'occorrente per la toeletta.*
SUZUKI (*inchinandosi a Pinkerton*)
 Buona notte.
 *Pinkerton batte le mani: i servi corrono via. Butterfly entra
nella casa ed aiutata da Suzuki fa cautelosamente la sua toelet-
ta da notte, levandosi la veste nuziale ed indossandone una
tutta bianca; poi siede su di un cuscino e mirandosi in uno
specchietto si ravvia i capelli: Suzuki esce.*
BUTTERFLY Quest'obi pomposa
 di scioglier mi tarda . . .
 [si vesta la sposa di puro candor.
 Tra motti sommessi
 sorride e mi guarda.
 Celarmi potessi! ne ho tanto rossor!
 E ancor l'irata voce mi maledice . . .
 Butterfly . . . rinnegata . . .
 rinnegata e felice.
PINKERTON (*guardando amorosamente Butterfly*)
 Con moti di scojattolo
 i nodi allenta e scioglie! . . .
 Pensar che quel giocattolo
 è mia moglie. Mia moglie!
 Ma tal grazia dispiega
 ch'io mi struggo per la febbre
 d'un subito desìo.]

SUZUKI (*inside*)
> And Izanagi and Izanami, Cunning One,
> and Kami, and Izanagi and Izanami, Cunning
> One,
> and Kami.

PINKERTON (*surprised at this dull murmuring*)
> Who's grumbling up there?

BUTTERFLY   It's Suzuki, who's saying her evening prayer.

PINKERTON (*leads Butterfly toward the house*)
> Evening is coming . . .

BUTTERFLY   . . . and the darkness and peace.

PINKERTON   And you're here alone.

BUTTERFLY   Alone and rejected!
> Rejected . . . and happy!

Pinkerton claps his hands three times; the servants and Su-zuki run out at once.

PINKERTON (*orders the servants*)
> You, close up.

The servants close the walls that give on the terrace, then they withdraw.

BUTTERFLY   Yes, yes, we all alone . . .
> And the world outside . . .

PINKERTON (*laughing*)
> And the furious Bonze.

BUTTERFLY (*to Suzuki, who came with the menservants and is awaiting orders*)
> Suzuki, my garments.

Suzuki digs into a case and gives Butterfly her night clothes and a little coffer with what is necessary for her toilet.

SUZUKI (*bowing to Pinkerton*)
> Good night.

Pinkerton claps his hands. The servants run away. Butterfly goes into the house and, assisted by Suzuki, carefully makes her toilet for the night, taking off her nuptial garment and put-ting on an all white one. Then she sits on a pillow and, looking at herself in a little mirror, combs her hair. Suzuki leaves.

BUTTERFLY   Undoing this pompous obi
> delays me . . .
> let the bride be dressed in pure whiteness.
> Amid murmured words
> he smiles and looks at me.
> If I could hide! I blush so at him!
> And still the wrathful voice curses me . . .
> Butterfly . . . rejected . . .
> rejected and happy.

PINKERTON (*looking lovingly at Butterfly*) ....
> With a squirrel's movements
> she loosens and unties the knots . . . !
> To think that that toy
> is my wife. My wife!
> But she displays such grace
> that I am consumed by the fever
> of a sudden desire.

(*stende le mani a Butterfly che sta per scendere dalla terrazza*)
Bimba dagli occhi pieni di malìa
ora sei tutta mia.
Sei tutta vestita di giglio.
Mi piace la treccia tua bruna
fra candidi veli.

BUTTERFLY (*scendendo dal terrazzo*)
Somiglio la Dea della luna,
la piccola Dea della luna che scende
la notte dal ponte del ciel . . .

PINKERTON . . . e affascina i cuori . . .

BUTTERFLY . . . e li prende,
e li avvolge in un bianco mantel.
E via se li reca negli alti reami.

PINKERTON Ma intanto finor non m'hai detto,
ancor non m'hai detto che m'ami.
Le sa quella Dea le parole
che appagan gli ardenti desir?

BUTTERFLY Le sa. Forse dirle non vuole

per tema d'averne a morir,
per tema d'averne a morir.

PINKERTON Stolta paura, l'amor non uccide
ma dà vita, e sorride
per gioie celestiali
come ora fa nei tuoi lunghi occhi ovali.
(*avvicinandosi a Butterfly e carezzandole il viso*)

BUTTERFLY Adesso voi siete per me
l'occhio del firmamento.
E mi piaceste dal primo momento
che vi ho veduto. Siete
alto, forte. Ridete
con modi sì palesi!
E dite cose che mai non intesi.
Or son contenta, or son contenta.
(*avvicinandosi lentamente a Pinkerton seduto sulla panca nel giardino, si inginocchia
ai suoi piedi e lo guarda con tenerezza,
quasi supplichevole*)
Vogliatemi bene,
un bene piccolino,
un bene da bambino
quale a me si conviene.
Vogliatemi bene.
Noi siamo gente avvezza
alle piccole cose
umili e silenziose,
ad una tenerezza
sfiorante e pur profonda
come il ciel, come l'onda del mare.

PINKERTON Dammi ch'io baci le tue mani care.
(*prorompe con grande tenerezza*)

(*holds out his hands to Butterfly, who is
about to come down from the terrace*)
Child with your eyes full of magic,
now you're all mine.
You're all dressed in lily white.
I like your dark hair
amid white veils.

BUTTERFLY (*coming down from the terrace*)
I resemble the moon goddess,
the little moon goddess who descends
at night from the bridge of heaven . . .

PINKERTON   . . . and captivates hearts . . .

BUTTERFLY   . . . and takes them,
and folds them in a white cloak.
And she takes them away into the lofty realms.

PINKERTON   But meanwhile you still haven't told me,
you still haven't told me that you love me.
Does that goddess know the words
that satisfy ardent desires?

BUTTERFLY   She knows them. Perhaps she doesn't want to
                   say them
for fear of having to die of them,
for fear of having to die of them.

PINKERTON   Foolish fear, love doesn't kill
but gives life, and smiles
in celestial joys
as it's doing now in your long oval eyes.
          (*approaching Butterfly and caressing her
          face*)

BUTTERFLY   Now you are for me
the eye of the firmament.
And I liked you from the first moment
that I saw you. You are
tall, strong. You laugh
in such an open manner!
And you say things I never heard.
Now I'm happy, now I'm happy.
          (*slowly approaching Pinkerton, now seated
          on the garden bench, she kneels at his feet
          and looks at him with tenderness, almost
          pleadingly*)
Love me,
a little love,
a childlike love
as is suited to me.
Love me.
We are people accustomed
to little things,
humble and silent,
to a tenderness,
barely grazing and yet deep
as the sky, as the sea's wave.

PINKERTON   Give me your dear hands that I may kiss them.
          (*bursts out, with great tenderness*)

Mia Butterfly . . . ! come t'han ben nomata
tenue farfalla.

BUTTERFLY (*a queste parole si rattrista e ritira le mani*)

Dicon ch'oltre mare
se cade in man dell'uom, ogni farfalla
da uno spillo è trafitta
ed in tavola infitta!

PINKERTON (*riprendendole dolcemente le mani e sorridendo*)
Un po' di vero c'è.
E tu lo sai perchè?
Perchè non fugga più.
(*abbracciandola*)
Io t'ho ghermita . . .
Ti serro palpitante. Sei mia.

BUTTERFLY (*abbandonandosi*)
Sì, per la vita.

PINKERTON   Vieni, vieni . . .
Via dall'anima in pena
l'angoscia paurosa.
È notte serena!
Guarda: dorme ogni cosa!

BUTTERFLY (*guardando il cielo, estatica*)
Ah! dolce notte . . . !

PINKERTON   Vieni, vieni . . .

BUTTERFLY   [Quante stelle!
Non le vidi mai sì belle!
Trema, brilla ogni favilla
col baglior d'una pupilla. Oh!

PINKERTON   È notte serena!
Guarda: dorme ogni cosa!
Vieni, vieni, sei mia!]

Compaiono le lucciole, che brillano attorno agli amanti, tra
i fiori e tra il fogliame degli alberi.

PINKERTON (*con cupido amore*)
[Via l'angoscia dal tuo cor!
Ti serro palpitante. Sei mia!
Ah vien . . . ecc.

BUTTERFLY   Oh! quanti occhi fisi, attenti
d'ogni parte a riguardar!
Pei firmamenti, via pei lidi,
via pel mare . . .
Ah! quanti occhi fisi, attenti!
Quanti sguardi . . . ride il ciel!
Ah! dolce notte! Tutto estatico d'amor
ride il ciel!]

Butterfly e Pinkerton entrano nella camera nuziale.

My Butterfly . . . how well they named you,
light butterfly.

BUTTERFLY (*is saddened at these words and withdraws her
hands*)
They say that across the sea,
if it falls into a man's hands, any butterfly
is pierced with a pin
and stuck in a board!

PINKERTON (*gently taking her hands again and smiling*)
There's a bit of truth in it.
And do you know why?
So that it won't flee any more.
(*embracing her*)
I've caught you . . .
I hold you, fluttering. You're mine.

BUTTERFLY (*abandoning herself*)
Yes, for life.

PINKERTON Come, come . . .
Away with the fearing anguish
from the suffering soul.
The night is calm!
Look: everything's asleep!

BUTTERFLY (*looking at the sky, ecstatic*)
Ah! sweet night . . . !

PINKERTON Come, come . . .

BUTTERFLY How many stars!
I never saw them so beautiful!
Every spark trembles, shines
with the glow of an eye. Oh!

PINKERTON The night is calm!
Look: everything's asleep!
Come, come, you're mine!

*The fireflies appear, shining around the lovers, amid the
flowers and the foliage of the trees.*

PINKERTON (*with greedy love*)
Away with the anguish from your heart!
I hold you, fluttering. You're mine!
Ah, come . . . etc.

BUTTERFLY Oh! how many eyes, staring, intently
watching from every side!
Through the firmaments, away along the shores,
away over the sea . . .
Ah! how many eyes, staring, intently!
How many gazes . . . the sky is laughing!
Ah! sweet night! All ecstatic with love,
the sky is laughing!

Butterfly and Pinkerton go into the nuptial chamber.

ATTO SECONDO

parte prima

Interno della casetta di Butterfly

Le pareti sono chiuse lasciando la camera in una semioscurità. Suzuki prega, raggomitolata davanti all'immagine di Budda: suona di quando in quando la campanella delle preghiere. Butterfly è stesa a terra, appoggiando la testa nelle palme delle mani.

SUZUKI (*pregando*)
    E Izaghi ed Izanami
    Sarundasico e Kami . . .
      (*interrompendosi*)
    Oh! la mia testa!
      (*suona la campanella per richiamare l'attenzione degli Dei*)
    E tu Ten-Sjoo-daj
      (*guardando Butterfly*)
    fate che Butterfly
    non pianga più, mai più,
    mai più.

BUTTERFLY Pigri ed obesi
    son gli Dei Giapponesi.
    L'americano Iddio son persuasa
    ben più presto risponde a chi l'implori.

    Ma temo ch'egli ignori
    che noi stiam qui di casa.
      (*rimane pensierosa, poi si rivolge a Suzuki che si è alzata in piedi ed ha aperto la parete verso il giardino*)
    Suzuki, è lungi la miseria?

Suzuki va ad un piccolo mobile ed apre un cassetto cercando delle monete, poi va presso Butterfly e le mostra poche monete.

SUZUKI Questo è l'ultimo fondo.

BUTTERFLY Questo? Oh! troppe spese!

Suzuki ripone il danaro nel piccolo mobile e lo chiude.

SUZUKI (*sospirando*)
    S'egli non torna e presto,
    siamo male in arnese.

BUTTERFLY (*decisa, alzandosi*)
    Ma torna.

SUZUKI (*crollando la testa*)
    Tornerà.

BUTTERFLY (*indispettita, avvicinandosi a Suzuki*)
    Perchè dispone

ACT TWO

Part One

Interior of Butterfly's House

The walls are shut, leaving the room in a semidarkness. Su-
zuki is praying, huddled before the image of Buddha. From
time to time she rings the little prayer bell. Butterfly is lying
on the floor, her head resting in the palms of her hands.

SUZUKI (*praying*)
> And Izanagi and Izanami,
> Cunning One and Kami . . .
> > (*breaking off*)
>
> Oh! my head!
> > (*rings the bell to attract the gods' atten-*
> > *tion*)
>
> And you, Tenshō-daijin,
> > (*looking at Butterfly*)
>
> grant that Butterfly
> shall weep no more, nevermore, nevermore.

BUTTERFLY
> Lazy and obese
> are the Japanese gods.
> The American God, I'm convinced,
> answers those who implore him much more
> > quickly.
>
> But I'm afraid he doesn't know
> that we live here.
> > (*remains pensive, then addresses Suzuki,*
> > *who has risen and has opened the wall to-*
> > *ward the garden*)
>
> Suzuki, is poverty far away?

Suzuki goes to a little cabinet and opens a drawer, looking
for some coins, then she goes to Butterfly and shows her a few
coins.

SUZUKI   These are our last funds.

BUTTERFLY   These? Oh! too many expenditures!

Suzuki puts the money back in the little cabinet and closes
it.

SUZUKI (*sighing*)
> If he doesn't come back, and quickly,
> we're in a bad way.

BUTTERFLY (*determined, rising*)
> But he is coming back.

SUZUKI (*shaking her head*)
> He may come back.

BUTTERFLY (*irked, approaching Suzuki*)
> Why does he arrange

che il Console provveda alla pigione,
rispondi, su!
Perchè con tante cure
la casa rifornì di serrature,
s'ei non volesse ritornar mai più?

SUZUKI   Non lo so.

BUTTERFLY (*meravigliata a tanta ignoranza*)
Non lo sai?
(*con orgoglio*)
Io te lo dico. Per tener ben fuori
le zanzare, i parenti ed i dolori
e dentro, con gelosa
custodia, la sua sposa,
la sua sposa che son io: Butterfly.

SUZUKI (*poco convinta*)
Mai non s'è udito
di straniero marito
che sia tornato al suo nido.

BUTTERFLY (*furibonda, afferrando Suzuki*)
Ah! Taci, o t'uccido.
(*insistendo nel persuadere Suzuki*)
Quell'ultima mattina:
tornerete signor? — gli domandai.
Egli, col cuore grosso,
per celarmi la pena
sorridendo rispose:
O Butterfly
piccina mogliettina,
tornerò colle rose
alla stagion serena
quando fa la nidiata il pettirosso.
(*calma e convinta*)
Tornerà.

SUZUKI (*con incredulità*)
Speriam.

BUTTERFLY (*insistendo*)
Dillo con me: tornerà.

SUZUKI (*per compiacerla ripete*)
Tornerà . . .
(*poi si mette a piangere*)

BUTTERFLY (*sorpresa*)
Piangi? Perchè? Perchè?
Ah la fede ti manca!
(*fiduciosa e sorridente*)
Senti. Un bel dì, vedremo
levarsi un fil di fumo sull'estremo
confin del mare.
E poi la nave appare.
Poi la nave bianca
entra nel porto, romba il suo saluto.
Vedi? È venuto!
Io non gli scendo incontro. Io no. Mi metto
là sul ciglio del colle e aspetto,
e aspetto gran tempo e non mi pesa,

                    for the consul to take care of our rent?
                    Answer! Come!
                    Why, with such care,
                    did he supply the house with locks,
                    if he didn't want ever to return?

SUZUKI   I don't know.

BUTTERFLY (*amazed at such ignorance*)
                    You don't know?
                          (*with pride*)
                    I'll tell you. To keep firmly outside
                    mosquitoes, relatives, and sorrows,
                    and inside, with jealous
                    safekeeping, his bride,
                    his bride who am I: Butterfly.

SUZUKI (*unconvinced*)
                    Nobody's ever heard
                    of a foreign husband
                    who has come back to his nest.

BUTTERFLY (*furious, seizing Suzuki*)
                    Ah! Be silent, or I'll kill you.
                          (*insisting on persuading Suzuki*)
                    That last morning:
                    "Will you return, sir?" I asked him.
                    He, with swollen heart,
                    smiling to conceal
                    his suffering, answered:
                    "Oh, Butterfly,
                    tiny little wife,
                    I'll return with the roses
                    in the serene season
                    when the robin makes his nest."
                          (*calm and convinced*)
                    He'll return.

SUZUKI (*with disbelief*)
                    Let's hope so.

BUTTERFLY (*insisting*)
                    Say it with me: he'll return.

SUZUKI (*to please her, repeats*)
                    He'll return . . .
                          (*then she starts weeping*)

BUTTERFLY (*surprised*)
                    You weep? Why? Why?
                    Ah, you lack faith!
                          (*trusting and smiling*)
                    Listen. One lovely day we'll see
                    a thread of smoke rise at the farthest
                    edge of the sea.
                    And then the ship appears.
                    Then the white ship
                    enters the port, thunders its greeting.
                    You see? He's come!
                    I don't go down toward him. Not I. I stand
                    there, at the edge of the hill, and wait,
                    and I wait a long time and the long waiting

la lunga attesa.
E . . . uscito dalla folla cittadina
un uomo, un picciol punto
s'avvia per la collina.
Chi sarà? chi sarà?
E come sarà giunto
che dirà? che dirà?
Chiamerà Butterfly dalla lontana.
Io senza dar risposta
me ne starò nascosta
un po' per celia e un po' per non morire
al primo incontro, ed egli alquanto in pena
chiamerà, chiamerà:
Piccina mogliettina
olezzo di verbena,
i nomi che mi dava al suo venire.
        (*a Suzuki*)
Tutto questo avverrà, te lo prometto.
Tienti la tua paura, io con sicura
fede l'aspetto.

Butterfly e Suzuki si abbracciano commosse. Butterfly con-
geda Suzuki, che esce dall'uscio di sinistra. Butterfly la segue
mestamente collo sguardo. Nel giardino compaiono Goro e
Sharpless. Goro guarda entro la camera, scorge Butterfly.

GORO (*a Sharpless*)
        C'è. Entrate.

Goro introduce Sharpless, poi torna subito fuori, e spia di
quando in quando dal giardino. Sharpless, affacciandosi, bussa
discretamente contro la porta di destra.

SHARPLESS   Chiedo scusa . . .
                (*vede Butterfly che udendo entrare alcuno*
                si è mossa)
                Madama Butterfly . . .

BUTTERFLY (*senza volgersi, ma correggendo*)
                Madama Pinkerton. Prego.

Si volge e riconoscendo il Console batte le mani per alle-
grezza. Suzuki entra premurosa e prepara un tavolino coll'-
occorrente per fumare, alcuni cuscini ed uno sgabello.

BUTTERFLY   Oh! il mio signor Console, signor Console!
SHARPLESS (*sorpreso*)
                Mi ravvisate?
BUTTERFLY (*facendo gli onori di casa*)
                Benvenuto in casa americana.
SHARPLESS   Grazie.

Butterfly invita il Console a sedere presso il tavolino: Sharp-
less si lascia cadere grottescamente su di un cuscino: Butterfly
si siede dall'altra parte e sorride con malizia dietro il ventaglio
vedendo l'imbarazzo del Console: poi con molta grazia gli
chiede:

BUTTERFLY   Avi, antenati tutti bene?
SHARPLESS (*sorride ringraziando*)
                Ma spero.

                    doesn't weigh on me.
                    And . . . coming from the city's crowd,
                    a man, a little dot,
                    starts up the hill.
                    Who will it be? Who will it be?
                    And when he has arrived,
                    what will he say? What will he say?
                    He will call Butterfly from the distance.
                    I, without giving an answer,
                    will stay hidden
                    a bit to tease and a bit so as not to die
                    at the first meeting, and he, quite worried,
                    will call, he will call:
                    "Tiny little wife,
                    verbena perfume,"
                    the names he gave me when he came.
                         (*to Suzuki*)
                    All this will happen, I promise you.
                    Keep your fear; I, with firm
                    faith, wait for him.

*Butterfly and Suzuki embrace, moved. Butterfly dismisses
Suzuki, who goes out the door at left. Butterfly sadly follows
her with her eyes. In the garden Goro and Sharpless appear.
Goro looks inside the room, sees Butterfly.*

GORO (*to Sharpless*)
                    She's there. Go in.

*Goro leads in Sharpless, then goes out again at once, and
peers in from time to time from the garden. Sharpless, looking
in, knocks discreetly at the door to the right.*

SHARPLESS   I beg your pardon . . .
                         (*sees Butterfly, who, hearing somebody
                         enter, has moved*)
                    Madame Butterfly . . .

BUTTERFLY (*without turning, but correcting him*)
                    Madame Pinkerton. Please.

*She turns and, recognizing the consul, claps her hands for
happiness. Suzuki enters eagerly and prepares a little table
with smoking materials, some pillows, and a stool.*

BUTTERFLY   Oh! my dear consul, my dear consul!
SHARPLESS (*surprised*)
                    You recognize me?
BUTTERFLY (*acting as hostess*)
                    Welcome in an American house.
SHARPLESS   Thank you.

*Butterfly invites the consul to sit down near the table. Sharp-
less sinks grotesquely down on a pillow. Butterfly sits on the
other side and smiles slyly behind her fan, seeing the consul's
embarrassment. Then, with great charm, she asks him:*

BUTTERFLY   Forebears, ancestors — all well?
SHARPLESS (*smiles, thanking her*)
                    Why, I hope so.

BUTTERFLY (*fa cenno a Suzuki che prepari la pipa*)
                    Fumate?
SHARPLESS Grazie.
                    (*desideroso di spiegare lo scopo per cui è
                    venuto, cava una lettera di tasca*)
                    Ho qui . . .
BUTTERFLY (*gentilmente interrompendolo*)
                    Signore — io vedo il cielo azzurro.
                    (*dopo aver tirato una boccata dall pipa
                    che Suzuki ha preparata l'offre al Console*)
SHARPLESS (*rifiutando*)
                    Grazie . . .
                    (*tentando ancora di riprendere il discorso*)
                    Ho . . .
BUTTERFLY (*depone la pipa sul tavolino e assai premurosa dice:*)

                    Preferite forse le sigarette americane?
                    (*ne offre*)
SHARPLESS (*ne prende una*)
                    Grazie.
                    (*si alza e tenta continuare il discorso*)

                    Ho da mostrarvi . . .
BUTTERFLY (*porge un fiammifero acceso*)
                    A voi.
SHARPLESS (*accende la sigaretta, ma poi la depone subito e
                    presentando la lettera si siede sullo sgabello*)
                    Mi scrisse Benjamin Franklin Pinkerton . . .
BUTTERFLY (*premurosissima*)
                    Davvero! È in salute?
SHARPLESS Perfetta.
BUTTERFLY (*alzandosi, lietissima*)
                    Io son la donna più lieta del Giappone.
                    Potrei farvi una domanda?
                    (*Suzuki è in faccende per preparare il thè*)
SHARPLESS Certo.
BUTTERFLY (*torna a sedere*)
                    Quando fanno il lor nido
                    in America i pettirossi?
SHARPLESS (*stupito*)
                    Come dite?
BUTTERFLY Sì . . . prima o dopo di qui?
SHARPLESS Ma . . . perchè . . . ?
            *Goro sale dal terrazzo del giardino ed ascolta, non visto,
            quanto dice Butterfly.*
BUTTERFLY Mio marito m'ha promesso
                    di ritornar nella stagion beata
                    che il pettirosso rifà la nidiata.
                    Qui l'ha rifatta per ben tre volte, ma
                    può darsi che di là
                    usi nidiar men spesso.
                    (*Goro s'affaccia e fa una risata*)

BUTTERFLY (*motions to Suzuki to prepare the pipe*)
   Do you smoke?

SHARPLESS Thank you.
   (*anxious to explain the reason why he has
   come, he takes a letter from his pocket*)
   I have here . . .

BUTTERFLY (*politely interrupting*)
   Sir — I see the sky clear blue.
   (*after taking a puff on the pipe that Suzuki has prepared, she offers it to the consul*)

SHARPLESS (*refusing*)
   No, thanks . . .
   (*trying again to resume the conversation*)
   I have . . .

BUTTERFLY (*sets down the pipe on the table and says very
   solicitously:*)
   Perhaps you prefer American cigarettes?
   (*offers some*)

SHARPLESS (*takes one*)
   Thanks.
   (*rises and tries to go on with the conversation*)
   I have to show you . . .

BUTTERFLY (*holds out a lighted match*)
   Here.

SHARPLESS (*lights the cigarette, but then puts it down at once
   and, holding out the letter, sits on the stool*)
   Benjamin Franklin Pinkerton wrote me . . .

BUTTERFLY (*very eagerly*)
   Really! Is he in good health?

SHARPLESS Perfect.

BUTTERFLY (*rising, very happy*)
   I'm the happiest woman in Japan.
   Could I ask you a question?
   (*Suzuki is busy preparing the tea*)

SHARPLESS Certainly.

BUTTERFLY (*sits down again*)
   When do the robins
   make their nest in America?

SHARPLESS (*amazed*)
   What did you say?

BUTTERFLY Yes . . . earlier or later than here?

SHARPLESS But . . . why . . . ?

 *Goro comes from the garden to the terrace and listens, un-
seen, to what Butterfly is saying.*

BUTTERFLY My husband promised me
   to return in the blissful season
   when the robin remakes his nest.
   Here he's remade it fully three times, but
   it may be that, there,
   he's accustomed to nest less often.
   (*Goro looks in and lets out a laugh*)

BUTTERFLY   Chi ride?
                  (*vede Goro*)
             Oh, c'è il *nakodo*.
                  (*piano a Sharpless*)
             Un uom cattivo.

GORO (*ossequioso, inchinandosi*)
             Godo . . .

BUTTERFLY (*a Goro, che s'inchina di nuovo e si allontana nel
                  giardino*)
             Zitto.
                  (*a Sharpless*)
             Egli osò — No, prima rispondete
             alla dimanda mia.

SHARPLESS (*imbarazzato*)
             Mi rincresce, ma ignoro.
             Non ho studiato ornitologia . . .

BUTTERFLY   Orni . . . ?

SHARPLESS   . . . tologia.

BUTTERFLY   Non lo sapete insomma.

SHARPLESS   No.
                  (*ritenta di tornare in argomento*)
             Dicevamo . . .

BUTTERFLY (*lo interrompe seguendo la sua idea*)
             Ah, sì. Goro,
             appena F. B. Pinkerton fu in mare
             mi venne ad assediare
             con ciarle e con presenti
             per ridarmi ora questo, or quel marito.
             Or promette tesori
             per uno scimunito . . .

GORO (*intervenendo per giustificarsi, entra nella stanza e si
                  rivolge a Sharpless*)
             Il ricco Yamadori.
             Ella è povera in canna. I suoi parenti
             l'han tutti rinnegata.

   *Al di là della terrazza si vede giungere il Principe Yama-
dori in un palanchino, attorniato dai servi. Butterfly vede
Yamadori e lo indica a Sharpless sorridendo.*

BUTTERFLY   Eccolo. Attenti.

   *Yamadori entra con grande imponenza, fa un graziosissimo
inchino a Butterfly poi saluta il Console. Due servi consegnano
dei fiori a Suzuki e si ritirano nel fondo. Goro, servilissimo,
porta uno sgabello a Yamadori, fra Sharpless e Butterfly, ed
è dappertutto durante la conversazione. Sharpless e Yamadori
siedono.*

BUTTERFLY (*a Yamadori*)
             Yamadori — ancor — le pene
             dell'amor, non v'han deluso?
             Vi tagliate ancor le vene
             se il mio bacio vi ricuso?

YAMADORI (*a Sharpless*)
             Tra le cose più moleste
             è l'inutil sospirar.

BUTTERFLY   Who's laughing?
                 (*sees Goro*)
              Oh, there's the *nakodo*.
                 (*softly, to Sharpless*)
              A bad man.

GORO (*obsequious, bowing*)
              I'm delighed . . .

BUTTERFLY (*to Goro, who bows again and goes off into the
                 garden*)
              Quiet!
                 (*to Sharpless*)
              He dared to — No, first answer
              my question.

SHARPLESS (*embarrassed*)
              I'm sorry, but I don't know.
              I haven't studied ornithology.

BUTTERFLY   Orni . . . ?

SHARPLESS   . . . thology.

BUTTERFLY   You don't know, in short.

SHARPLESS   No.
                 (*tries again to return to the subject*)
              We were saying . . .

BUTTERFLY (*interrupts him, following her own idea*)
              Ah, yes. Goro,
              as soon as F. B. Pinkerton was at sea,
              came to besiege me
              with chatter and with presents
              to give me again this or that husband.
              Now he is promising treasures
              for a fool . . .

GORO (*intervening, to justify himself, enters into the room and
                 addresses Sharpless*)
              The rich Yamadori.
              She's extremely poor. Her relatives
              have all rejected her.

*Beyond the terrace Prince Yamadori is seen arriving in a
palanquin, surrounded by servants. Butterfly sees Yamadori
and points him out to Sharpless, smiling.*

BUTTERFLY   Here he is. Watch.

*Yamadori comes in with great pomp, makes a very graceful
bow to Butterfly, then greets the consul. Two servants hand
some flowers to Suzuki and withdraw to the background.
Goro, very servile, brings a stool to Yamadori, between Sharpless and Butterfly, and is everywhere during the conversation.
Sharpless and Yamadori sit down.*

BUTTERFLY (*to Yamadori*)
              Yamadori — still — the sufferings
              of love haven't disappointed you?
              Will you still cut open your veins
              if I refuse you my kiss?

YAMADORI (*to Sharpless*)
              Among the most troubling of things
              is sighing in vain.

BUTTERFLY (*con graziosa malizia*)
    Tante mogli omai toglieste,
    vi doveste abituar.

YAMADORI   L'ho sposate tutte quante
    e il divorzio mi francò.

BUTTERFLY   Obbligata.

YAMADORI   A voi però giurerei fede costante.

SHARPLESS (*sospirando, rimette in tasca la lettera*)
    (Il messaggio, ho gran paura,
    a trasmetter non riesco).

GORO (*con enfasi indicando Yamadori a Sharpless*)
    Ville, servi, oro, ad Omara
    un palazzo principesco.

BUTTERFLY (*con serietà*)
    Già legata è la mia fede . . .

GORO, YAMADORI (*a Sharpless*)
    Maritata ancor si crede.

BUTTERFLY (*alzandosi di scatto*)
    Non mi credo: sono, sono.

GORO   Ma la legge . . .

BUTTERFLY   Io non la so.

GORO   . . . per la moglie, l'abbandono
    al divorzio equiparò.

BUTTERFLY (*crollando vivamente il capo*)
    La legge giapponese . . .
    non già del mio paese.

GORO   Quale?

BUTTERFLY   Gli Stati Uniti.

SHARPLESS   (Oh, l'infelice!)

BUTTERFLY (*nervosissima, accalorandosi*)
    Si sa che aprir la porta
    e la moglie cacciar per la più corta
    qui divorziar si dice.
    Ma in America questo non si può.
        (*a Sharpless*)
    Vero?

SHARPLESS (*imbarazzato*)
    Vero . . . Però . . .

BUTTERFLY (*lo interrompe rivolgendosi a Yamadori ed a Goro,
        trionfante*)
    Là un bravo giudice
    serio, impettito
    dice al marito:
    "Lei vuol andarsene?
    Sentiam perchè . . ."
    "Sono seccato
    del coniugato!"
    E il magistrato:
    "Ah, mascalzone,
    presto in prigione!"
        (*per troncare il discorso si alza ed ordina:*)

BUTTERFLY (*with charming malice*)
> You've taken so many wives by now,
> you should become accustomed.

YAMADORI I married every last one of them,
> and divorce freed me.

BUTTERFLY Much obliged.

YAMADORI To you, however, I'd swear constant faith.

SHARPLESS (*sighing, puts the letter in his pocket*)
> (I'm greatly afraid that I won't succeed
> in delivering the message.)

GORO (*emphatically, indicating Yamadori to Sharpless*)
> Villas, servants, gold, at Omara
> a princely palace.

BUTTERFLY (*seriously*)
> My word is already given . . .

GORO, YAMADORI (*to Sharpless*)
> She still believes herself married.

BUTTERFLY (*springing up abruptly*)
> I don't believe myself: I am, I am.

GORO But the law.

BUTTERFLY I don't know it.

GORO . . . for the wife, being abandoned
> is equivalent to divorce.

BUTTERFLY (*briskly shaking her head*)
> The Japanese law . . .
> not that of my country.

GORO Which?

BUTTERFLY The United States.

SHARPLESS (Oh, the unhappy girl!)

BUTTERFLY (*very nervous, warming*)
> We know that to open the door
> and drive out the wife in the curtest way
> here is called divorce.
> But in America this can't be done.
>> (*to Sharpless*)
> True?

SHARPLESS (*embarrassed*)
> True . . . however . . .

BUTTERFLY (*interrupts him, addressing Yamadori and Goro, triumphantly*)
> There a fine judge,
> serious, dignified,
> says to the husband:
> "You want to go away?
> Let's hear why . . . "
> "I'm bored
> with married life!"
> And the magistrate:
> "Ah, rascal,
> in prison quickly!"
>> (*to cut off the subject, she stands up and orders:*)

Suzuki, il thè.
(*va anche lei presso Suzuki*)

YAMADORI (*sottovoce a Sharpless, mentre Butterfly prepare il thè*)
Udiste?

SHARPLESS   Mi rattrista una sì piena cecità.

GORO (*sottovoce a Sharpless e Yamadori*)
Segnalata è già la nave di Pinkerton.

YAMADORI (*disperato*)
Quand'essa lo riveda . . .

SHARPLESS (*sottovoce ai due*)
Egli non vuol mostrarsi. Io venni appunto

per levarla d'inganno . . .
(*vedendo che Butterfly, seguita da Suzuki, si avvicina per offrire il thè, tronca il discorso*)

BUTTERFLY (*con grazia, servendo a Sharpless una tazza di thè*)
Vostra Grazia permette . . .
(*poi apre il ventaglio e dietro a questo accenna ai due, ridendo*)
Che persone moleste!
(*offre il thè a Yamadori, che rifiuta*)

YAMADORI (*sospirando si alza e si inchina a Butterfly, mettendo la mano sul cuore*)
Addio. Vi lascio il cuor pien di cordoglio:
ma spero ancor . . .

BUTTERFLY   Padrone.

YAMADORI (*s'avvia, poi torna presso Butterfly*)
Ah! se voleste . . .

BUTTERFLY   Il guaio è che non voglio . . .

Yamadori sospira di nuovo: saluta Sharpless, poi se ne va, seguito dai servi. Butterfly fa cenno a Suzuki di spreparare il thè: Suzuki esegue, poi va in fondo alla camera. Goro segue premurosamente Yamadori. Sharpless assume un fare grave, serio, però con gran rispetto e con una certa commozione invita Butterfly a sedere, e torna a tirar fuori di tasca la lettera.

SHARPLESS   Ora a noi. Sedete qui.
Legger con me volete questa lettera?

BUTTERFLY (*prendendo la lettera, baciandola*)
Date. Sulla bocca, sul cuore . . .
Siete l'uomo migliore del mondo.
(*rende la lettera e si mette ad ascoltare colla massima attenzione*)
Incominciate.

SHARPLESS (*legge*)
"Amico, cercherete
quel bel fior di fanciulla . . ."

BUTTERFLY (*interrompendolo con gioia*)
Dice proprio così?

SHARPLESS   Sì, così dice,
ma se ad ogni momento . . .

Suzuki, the tea.
> (*she also goes over to Suzuki*)

YAMADORI (*softly, to Sharpless, as Butterfly prepares the tea*)
> You heard?

SHARPLESS   Such complete blindness grieves me.

GORO (*softly to Sharpless and Yamadori*)
> Pinkerton's ship has already been reported.

YAMADORI (*desperate*)
> When she sees him again . . .

SHARPLESS (*softly, to the two men*)
> He doesn't want to show himself. I came pre-
> cisely
> to undeceive her . . .
>> (*seeing that Butterfly, followed by Suzuki,
>> is approaching to serve the tea, he breaks
>> off the conversation*)

BUTTERFLY (*gracefully, serving Sharpless a cup of tea*)
> If Your Grace permits me . . .
>> (*then she opens her fan and, behind it,
>> points to the two, laughing*)
> What tiresome people!
>> (*offers the tea to Yamadori, who refuses*)

YAMADORI (*sighing, rises and bows to Butterfly, putting his
> hand on his heart*)
> Good-by. I leave you my heart full of sorrow;
> but I still hope . . .

BUTTERFLY   You're free to do so.

YAMADORI (*goes off, then returns to Butterfly*)
> Ah! if you wanted . . .

BUTTERFLY   The trouble is that I don't want . . .

*Yamadori sighs again, says good-by to Sharpless, then goes
off, followed by the servants. Butterfly motions to Suzuki to
clear away the tea. Suzuki obeys, then goes to the back of the
room. Goro solicitously follows Yamadori. Sharpless assumes a
grave, serious manner, but with great respect and with a certain emotion, he invites Butterfly to be seated and once again
takes the letter from his pocket.*

SHARPLESS   Now to our business. Sit here.
> Will you read this letter with me?

BUTTERFLY (*taking the letter, kissing it*)
> Give it to me. On my mouth, on my heart . . .
> You are the best man in the world.
>> (*gives back the letter and prepares to lis-
>> ten with the greatest attention*)
> Begin.

SHARPLESS (*reads*)
> "*My friend, you must seek out
> that beautiful flower of a girl . . .*"

BUTTERFLY (*interrupting him, with joy*)
> Does he really say that?

SHARPLESS   Yes, that's what he says;
> but if, at every moment . . .

BUTTERFLY (*rimettendosi tranquilla*)
Taccio, taccio — più nulla.

SHARPLESS "*Da quel tempo felice*
tre anni son passati . . ."

BUTTERFLY (*non può trattenersi*)
Anche lui li ha contati!

SHARPLESS "*E forse Butterfly*
non mi rammenta più . . ."

BUTTERFLY (*sorpresa*)
Non lo rammento?
(*rivolgendosi a Suzuki*)
Suzuki, dillo tu.
(*ripete come scandolezzata le parole della*
lettera)
" 'Non mi rammenta più'!"

Suzuki accenna affermando, poi esce per la porta di sinistra
asportando il thè.

SHARPLESS (*fra sè*)
(Pazienza!)
(*seguita a leggere*)
"*Se mi vuol bene ancor,*
se m'aspetta . . ."

BUTTERFLY (*assai commossa*)
Oh le dolci parole!
(*prende la lettera e la bacia*)
Tu, benedetta!

SHARPLESS (*riprende la lettera e segue a leggere imperterrito,*
ma con voce commossa)
"*A voi mi raccomando*
perchè vogliate con circospezione
prepararla . . ."

BUTTERFLY (*ansiosa e raggiante*)
Ritorna . . .

SHARPLESS "*. . . al colpo . . .*"

BUTTERFLY (*salta di gioia e batte le mani*)
Quando? Presto! Presto!

SHARPLESS (*rassegnato piega la lettera e la ripone in tasca*)
(Benone. Qui troncarla conviene . . .
(*crollando il capo arrabbiato*)

Quel diavolo d'un Pinkerton!)
(*guarda Butterfly negli occhi, serissimo*)
Ebbene, che fareste Madama Butterfly
s'ei non dovesse ritornar più mai?

BUTTERFLY (*immobile, come colpita a morte, china la testa e*
dice con sommessione infantile:)
Due cose potrei far:
tornar a divertir la gente col cantar . . .
oppur . . . meglio . . . morire.

SHARPLESS (*vivamente commosso passeggia agitatissimo, poi*
torna verso Butterfly, le prende le due mani
e con paterna tenerezza le dice:)
Di strapparvi assai mi costa
dai miraggi ingannatori.

BUTTERFLY (*becoming calm again*)
> I'll be silent, I'll be silent — not another sound.

SHARPLESS   *"Since that happy time*
> *three years have passed . . ."*

BUTTERFLY (*can't restrain herself*)
> He's counted them too!

SHARPLESS   *"And perhaps Butterfly*
> *no longer remembers me . . ."*

BUTTERFLY (*surprised*)
> I don't remember him?
>   (*addressing Suzuki*)
> Suzuki, you tell him.
>   (*repeats, as if shocked, the letter's words*)

> " 'No longer remembers me'!"
Suzuki nods, confirming, then goes out through the door at left, taking away the tea.

SHARPLESS (*to himself*)
>   (Patience!)
>   (*continues to read*)
> *"If she still loves me,*
> *if she's waiting for me . . ."*

BUTTERFLY (*very moved*)
> Oh, the sweet words!
>   (*takes the letter and kisses it*)
> You, blessed letter!

SHARPLESS (*takes back the letter and goes on reading, unper-
> turbed, but with a moved voice*)
> *"I'm relying on you*
> *to prepare her,*
> *with tact . . ."*

BUTTERFLY (*eager and radiant*)
> He's returning . . .

SHARPLESS   *" . . . for the blow . . ."*

BUTTERFLY (*leaping with joy and clapping her hands*)
> When? Soon! Soon!

SHARPLESS (*resigned, folds the letter and puts it back in his
> pocket*)
>   (Splendid. It's best to break off here . . .
>   (*shaking his head angrily*)
> That devil of a Pinkerton!)
>   (*looks Butterfly very seriously in the eye*)
> Well, Madame Butterfly, what would you do
> if he were never to return again?

BUTTERFLY (*motionless, as if mortally stricken, bows her head
> and says with childish submission*)
> I could do two things:
> go back to entertaining people by singing . . .
> or else . . . better . . . die.

SHARPLESS (*deeply moved, paces up and down, agitated, then
> comes back to Butterfly, takes both her hands
> and says to her with paternal tenderness:*)
> It costs me a great deal to tear you away
> from your deceiving mirages.

Accogliete la proposta
di quel ricco Yamadori.

BUTTERFLY (*ritirando le mani*)
Voi . . . voi, signor . . . mi dite questo . . . ! Voi?

SHARPLESS (*imbarazzato*)
Santo Dio, come si fa?

BUTTERFLY (*batte le mani; Suzuki accorre*)
Qui, Suzuki, presto, presto,
che Sua Grazia se ne va.

SHARPLESS (*fa per avviarsi ad uscire*)
Mi scacciate?

BUTTERFLY (*pentita, corre a Sharpless e singhiozzando lo trattiene*)
Ve ne prego, già l'insistere non vale.
(*congeda Suzuki, la quale va nel giardino*)

SHARPLESS (*scusandosi*)
Fui brutale, non lo nego.

BUTTERFLY (*dolorosamente, portandosi la mano al cuore*)
Oh, mi fate tanto male, tanto male,
tanto, tanto!

*Butterfly vacilla, Sharpless fa per sorreggerla ma Butterfly si
domina subito.*

BUTTERFLY   Niente, niente!
Ho creduto morir. Ma passa presto
come passan le nuvole sul mare . . .
Ah! m'ha scordata?
(*corre nella stanza di sinistra, rientra trionfalmente tenendo il suo bambino seduto
sulla spalla e lo mostra a Sharpless glori-
andosene*)
E questo . . . ? e questo . . . ? e questo
egli potrà pure scordare?
(*depone il bambino a terra e lo tiene stretto a sè*)

SHARPLESS (*con emozione*)
Egli è suo?

BUTTERFLY (*indicando mano, mano*)
Chi vide mai a bimbo del Giappon occhi azzur-
rini?
E il labbro? E i ricciolini d'oro schietto?

SHARPLESS (*sempre più commosso*)
È palese. E Pinkerton lo sa?

BUTTERFLY   No. No. È nato quand'egli stava
in quel suo gran paese.
(*accarrezza il suo bambino*)
Ma voi . . . gli scriverete che l'aspetta
un figlio senza pari!
e mi saprete dir s'ei non s'affretta
per le terre e pei mari
(*mettendo il bimbo a sedere sul cuscino e
inginocchiandosi vicino a lui*)
Sai cos'ebbe cuore

> Accept the proposal
> of that rich Yamadori.

BUTTERFLY (*withdrawing her hands*)
> You . . . you, sir . . . say this to me . . . ! You?

SHARPLESS (*embarrassed*)
> Good God, what's to be done?

BUTTERFLY (*claps her hands; Suzuki runs in*)
> Come here, Suzuki, quickly, quickly,
> since His Grace is leaving.

SHARPLESS (*starts to leave*)
> You drive me away?

BUTTERFLY (*repentant, runs to Sharpless and, sobbing, restrains him*)
> Please, insisting is no use.
>> (*dismisses Suzuki, who goes into the garden*)

SHARPLESS (*apologizing*)
> I was brutal, I don't deny it.

BUTTERFLY (*sorrowfully, putting her hand to her heart*)
> Oh, you cause me so much pain, so much pain,
> so much, so much!

Butterfly staggers, Sharpless starts to support her, but Butterfly controls herself at once.

BUTTERFLY Nothing, nothing!
> I thought I would die. But it passes quickly
> as the clouds pass over the sea . . .
> Ah! has he forgotten me?
>> (*runs into the room at left, re-enters triumphantly carrying her child seated on her shoulder, and shows him to Sharpless, proud of him*)
> And this . . . ? and this . . . ? and can he
> also forget this?
>> (*sets the child on the ground and holds him tight to herself*)

SHARPLESS (*with emotion*)
> He's his?

BUTTERFLY (*pointing, one by one*)
> Who ever saw pale blue eyes in a child of Japan?
>
> And lips? And little curls of pure gold?

SHARPLESS (*more and more moved*)
> It's obvious. And Pinkerton knows it?

BUTTERFLY No. No. He was born when he was
> in that great country of his.
>> (*caresses her child*)
> But you . . . you'll write him
> that a son without equal awaits him!
> And you can tell me if he won't hasten
> over lands and over the seas . . .
>> (*putting the child in a sitting position on the pillow and kneeling next to him*)
> You know what that gentleman

di pensare quel signore?
> (*indicando Sharpless*)

Che tua madre dovrà
prenderti in braccio ed alla pioggia e al vento

andar per la città
a guadagnarti il pane e il vestimento.
Ed alle impietosite
genti, la man tremante stenderà,
gridando: Udite, udite
la triste mia canzon.
A un' infelice madre la carità,
muovetevi a pietà!
> (*si alza, mentre il bimbo rimane seduto sul cuscino giocando con una bambola*)

E Butterfly — orribile destino — danzerà
per te . . . ! E come fece già
la Ghescia canterà!
E la canzon giuliva e lieta
in un singhiozzo finirà!
> (*buttandosi a' ginocchi davanti a Sharpless*)

Ah no . . . ! no . . . ! questo mai!
questo mestier che al disonore porta!
Morta! morta!
Mai più danzar!
Piuttosto la mia vita vo' troncar!
> (*cade a terra vicino al bimbo che abbraccia strettamente ed accarezza con moto convulsivo*)

Ah! morta!

SHARPLESS (*non può trattenere le lagrime*)
> (Quanta pietà!)
> (*vincendo la propria emozione*)

Io scendo al piano. Mi perdonate?

Butterfly si alza in piedi e con atto gentile dà la mano a Sharpless che la stringe con ambo le mani con effusione.

BUTTERFLY (*al bimbo*)
A te, dagli la mano.

SHARPLESS I bei capelli biondi!
> (*lo bacia*)

Caro: come ti chiamano?

BUTTERFLY Rispondi:
Oggi il mio nome è *Dolore.*
Però dite al babbo, scrivendogli, che il giorno
del suo ritorno
Gioia, Gioia mi chiamerò.

SHARPLESS Tuo padre lo saprà, te lo prometto.
> (*fa un saluto a Butterfly, ed esce rapidamente dalla porta di destra*)

SUZUKI (*di fuori, gridando*)

had the heart to say?
> (*pointing to Sharpless*)

That your mother will have
to take you in her arms and, in the rain and the
    wind,
go about the city
to earn your bread and clothing.
And, toward the pitying
people, she'll hold out her trembling hand,
crying: "Hear, hear
my sad song.
Charity for an unhappy mother,
be moved to pity!"
> (*stands up, as the child remains seated on
> the pillow, playing with a doll*)

And Butterfly — horrible fate — will dance
for you . . . ! And as she did before,
the Geisha will sing!
And the merry, happy song
will end in a sob!
> (*throwing herself down on her knees be-
> fore Sharpless*)

Ah, no . . . ! no . . . ! Never this!
This profession that leads to dishonor!
Dead! Dead!
Never to dance again!
Rather I want to end my life!
> (*she falls on the floor beside the child,
> whom she embraces tightly and caresses
> with a convulsive gesture*)

Ah! dead!

SHARPLESS (*can't restrain his tears*)
> (What a pity!)
> (*overcoming his own emotion*)

I'm going down to the plain. Do you forgive me?

*Butterfly stands up and, with a polite movement, gives
Sharpless her hand. He clasps it in both of his, with emotion.*

BUTTERFLY (*to the child*)
Here, give him your hand.

SHARPLESS   The beautiful blond hair!
> (*kisses him*)

Dear, what is your name?

BUTTERFLY   Answer:
Today my name is *Trouble*.
However, tell Papa, writing him, that the day
of his return
I'll be called *Joy, Joy!*

SHARPLESS   Your father will know it, I promise you.
> (*says good-by to Butterfly and goes rapid-
> ly out of the door at right*)

SUZUKI (*from outside, shouting*)

---

* *Dolore* would more correctly be translated *Sorrow*, but *Trouble*
was the name given to the child by John Luther Long, author of
the original story.

Vespa! Rospo maledetto!
(poi entra trascinando con violenza Goro
che tenta inutilmente di sfuggirle)

BUTTERFLY *(a Suzuki)*
Che fu?

SUZUKI   Ci ronza intorno
il vampiro! e ogni giorno
ai quattro venti spargendo va
che niuno sa
chi padre al bimbo sia!
(lascia Goro)

GORO *(protestando, con voce di paura)*
Dicevo . . . solo . . . che là in America
quando un figlio è nato maledetto
trarrà sempre reietto
la vita fra le genti.

Butterfly, furente, corre al reliquiario e prende il coltello
che servì per l'hari-kari — suicidio per condanna — di suo padre,
gridando:

BUTTERFLY   Ah! tu menti! menti! menti!
Ah! menti!
(afferra Goro, che cade a terra, e minac-
cia d'ucciderlo: Goro grida disperatamente)

Dillo ancora e t'uccido!

SUZUKI *(intromettendosi)*
No!
(spaventata a tale scena prende il bimbo
e lo porta nella stanza a sinistra)

BUTTERFLY *(presa da disgusto, respinge Goro col piede)*

Va via!

Goro fugge: poi Butterfly si scuote, va a riporre il coltello e
volgendo il pensiero al suo bambino, esclama:

BUTTERFLY   Vedrai, piccolo amor,
mia pena e mio conforto,
mio piccolo amor . . .
Ah! vedrai che il tuo vendicator
ci porterà lontano, lontan,
nella sua terra, lontan ci porterà . . .
(un colpo di cannone)

SUZUKI *(entrando affannosamente)*
Il cannone del porto!
(corre verso il terrazzo: Butterfly la segue)

Una nave da guerra.

BUTTERFLY   Bianca . . . bianca . . . il vessillo americano
delle stelle . . . Or governa
per ancorare.
(prende sul tavolino un cannocchiale e
corre sul terrazzo: tutta tremante per
l'emozione, appunta il cannocchiale verso
il porto e dice a Suzuki:)

Wasp! Accursed toad!
> (*then she comes in, violently dragging
> Goro, who tries in vain to escape her*)

BUTTERFLY (*to Suzuki*)
What was it?

SUZUKI   The vampire is buzzing
around us! And every day
to the four winds he spreads the word
that nobody knows
who's the child's father!
> (*lets go of Goro*)

GORO (*protesting, in a frightened voice*)
I was saying . . . only . . . that there in America
when a child is born, accursed,
he will always lead the life
of an outcast among the people.

*Butterfly, in a rage, runs to the reliquary and takes the
dagger that was used for hara-kiri — sentenced suicide — by
her father, shouting:*

BUTTERFLY   Ah! you're lying! lying! lying!
Ah! you're lying!
> (*seizes Goro, who falls to the ground, and
> threatens to kill him; Goro screams desper-
> ately*)

Say it again and I'll kill you!

SUZUKI (*coming between them*)
No!
> (*frightened by such a scene, she takes the
> child and carries him into the room at left*)

BUTTERFLY (*overcome with disgust, thrusts Goro away with
her foot*)
Go away!

*Goro flees. Then Butterfly stirs, goes and replaces the dag-
ger, and thinking of her child, exclaims:*

BUTTERFLY   You'll see, little love,
my sorrow and my comfort,
my little love . . .
Ah! you'll see that your avenger
will carry us far away, far away,
in his country, he'll carry us far away . . .
> (*a cannon shot*)

SUZUKI (*entering breathlessly*)
The cannon of the port!
> (*runs toward the terrace; Butterfly follows
> her*)

A warship.

BUTTERFLY   White . . . white . . . the American flag
with the stars . . . Now it's putting about
to anchor.
> (*takes a spyglass from the table and runs
> onto the terrace. All trembling with emo-
> tion, she turns the spyglass toward the port
> and says to Suzuki:*)

Reggimi la mano
ch'io ne discerna il nome, il nome, il nome.
Eccolo: *Abramo Lincoln!*
> (*dà il cannocchiale a Suzuki e rientra nella
> stanza in preda a una grande esaltazione*)

Tutti han mentito! tutti! tutti . . . !
sol io lo sapevo . . . sol io che l'amo.
> (*a Suzuki*)

Vedi lo scimunito
tuo dubbio? È giunto! è giunto!
proprio nel punto
che ognun diceva: piangi e dispera.
Trionfa il mio amor!
il mio amor; la mia fè trionfa intera:
Ei torna e m'ama!
> (*giubilante corre sul terrazzo, dicendo a
> Suzuki:*)

Scuoti quella fronda
di ciliegio e m'innonda
di fior. Io vo' tuffar
nella pioggia odorosa l'arsa fronte.
> (*singhiozzando per tenerezza*)

SUZUKI (*calmandola*)
> Signora, quetatevi . . . quel pianto . . .

BUTTERFLY   No: rido, rido! Quanto lo dovrem aspettar?

Che pensi? Un'ora?

SUZUKI   Di più.

BUTTERFLY   Due ore forse.
> (*aggirandosi per la stanza*)

Tutto . . . tutto sia pien di fior,
come la notte è di faville.
> (*accenna a Suzuki di andare nel giardino*)

Va pei fior!

SUZUKI (*dal terrazzo*)
> Tutti i fior?

BUTTERFLY   Tutti i fior . . . tutti . . . tutti.
Pesco, viola, gelsomin,
quanto di cespo, o d'erba, o d'albero fiorì.

SUZUKI (*nel giardino ai piedi del terrazzo*)
> Uno squallor d'inverno sarà tutto il giardin.

BUTTERFLY   Tutta la primavera voglio che olezzi qui.

SUZUKI   Uno squallor d'inverno sarà tutto il giardin.
> (*appare sul terrazzo e sporge un fascio di
> fiori e di fronde*)

A voi signora.

BUTTERFLY (*prendendo il fascio*)
> Cogline ancora.

*Butterfly sparge i fiori nella stanza, mentre Suzuki ritorna
nel giardino.*

Support my hand
so I can make out the name, the name, the name.
There is it: *Abraham Lincoln!*
> (*gives the spyglass to Suzuki and goes
> back into the room, in the grip of great
> excitement*)
They all lied! all! all . . . !
Only I knew . . . only I, who love him.
> (*to Suzuki*)
You see your foolish
doubt? He's come! he's come!
just at the moment
when everyone was saying: weep and despair.
My love triumphs!
My love, my faith triumphs completely:
he's coming back and he loves me!
> (*jubilant, runs to the terrace, saying to
> Suzuki:*)
Shake that branch
of the cherry tree and bathe me
in flowers. I want to plunge
my burning brow into the perfumed rain.
> (*sobbing in her tenderness*)

SUZUKI (*calming her*)
Madame, be calm . . . that crying . . .

BUTTERFLY   No: I'm laughing, I'm laughing! How long will
we have to await him?
What do you think? An hour?

SUZUKI   More.

BUTTERFLY   Two hours perhaps.
> (*moving about the room*)
Everything . . . let everything be full of flowers,
as the night is full of sparks.
> (*motions Suzuki to go into the garden*)
Go for the flowers!

SUZUKI (*from the terrace*)
All the flowers?

BUTTERFLY   All the flowers . . . all . . . all . . .
Peach blossom, violet, jasmine,
anything that's bloomed on bush, or stem or
tree.

SUZUKI (*in the garden at the foot of the terrace*)
The whole garden will be a wintry squalor.

BUTTERFLY   I want all springtime to be fragrant here.

SUZUKI   The whole garden will be a wintry squalor.
> (*appears on the terrace and holds out a
> bunch of flowers and branches*)
Here, madame.

BUTTERFLY (*taking the bunch*)
Pick some more.

*Butterfly scatters the flowers in the room, as Suzuki goes
back into the garden.*

SUZUKI (*dal giardino*)
> Soventi a questa siepe veniste a riguardare
> lungi, piangendo nella deserta immensità.

BUTTERFLY   Giunse l'atteso, nulla più chiedo al mare;

> diedi pianto alla zolla, essa i suoi fior mi dà!

SUZUKI (*appare nuovamente sul terrazzo colle mani piene di fiori*)
> Spoglio è l'orto.

BUTTERFLY   Spoglio è l'orto?
> Vien, m'aiuta.

Butterfly e Suzuki spargono fiori ovunque.

SUZUKI   Rose al varco della soglia.

BUTTERFLY, SUZUKI
> Tutta la primavera voglio che olezzi qui.
> Seminiamo intorno april.
> Tutta la primavera, ecc.

SUZUKI   Gigli? viole?

BUTTERFLY   Intorno, intorno spandi.

SUZUKI, BUTTERFLY
> Seminiamo intorno april.

BUTTERFLY   [Il suo sedil s'inghirlandi,
> di convolvi s'inghirlandi;
> gigli e viole intorno spandi,
> seminiamo intorno april.

SUZUKI   Gigli, rose spandi,
> tutta la primavera, ecc.]

BUTTERFLY, SUZUKI
> Gettiamo a mani piene
> mammole e tuberose,
> corolle di verbene,
> petali d'ogni fior!
> . . . corolle di verbene,
> petali d'ogni fior!

Suzuki dispone due lampade vicino alla toeletta dove si accoscia Butterfly.

BUTTERFLY (*a Suzuki*)
> Or vienmi ad adornar.
> Nol pria portami il bimbo.
>> (*Suzuki va nella stanza a sinistra e porta il bambino che fa sedere vicino a Butterfly, la quale, intanto, si guarda in un piccolo specchio e dice tristamente:*)
> Non son più quella!
> Troppi sospiri la bocca mandò,
> e l'occhio riguardò
> nel lontan troppo fiso.
>> (*a Suzuki*)
> Dammi sul viso un tocco di carminio . . .
>> (*prende un pennello e mette del rosso sulle guancie del suo bimbo*)
> ed anche a te piccino
> perchè la veglia non it faccia vôte
> per pallore le gote.

SUZUKI (*from the garden*)
>Often you came to this hedge to look
>far out, weeping, into the deserted immensity.

BUTTERFLY
>The man awaited has come; I ask no more of
>>the sea;
>I gave tears to the earth, it gives me its flowers!

SUZUKI (*appears again on the terrace with her hands full of
>flowers*)
>The garden is stripped.

BUTTERFLY
>The garden is stripped?
>Come, help me.

Butterfly and Suzuki scatter flowers everywhere.

SUZUKI
>Roses on the threshold.

BUTTERFLY, SUZUKI
>I want all springtime to be fragrant here.
>We are sowing April around.
>I want all springtime, etc.

SUZUKI
>Lilies? Violets?

BUTTERFLY
>Spread them around.

SUZUKI, BUTTERFLY
>We are sowing April around.

BUTTERFLY
>Let his seat be garlanded,
>garlanded with morning glories;
>spread lilies and violets around,
>we are sowing April around.

SUZUKI
>Spread lilies, roses,
>I want all springtime, etc.

BUTTERFLY, SUZUKI
>Let us throw with full hands
>shrinking violets and tuberoses,
>corollas of verbena,
>petals of every flower!
>. . . corollas of verbena,
>petals of every flower!

*Suzuki sets two lamps near the toilet table, where Butterfly
crouches down.*

BUTTERFLY (*to Suzuki*)
>Now come to adorn me.
>No! first bring me the baby.
>>(*Suzuki goes into the room at left and
>>brings the child, which she seats beside
>>Butterfly, who in the meanwhile looks at
>>herself in a little mirror and says sadly:*)
>I'm no longer that girl!
>My mouth emitted too many sighs,
>and my eye stared
>too fixedly into the distance.
>>(*to Suzuki*)
>Give me a touch of carmine on my face . . .
>>(*takes a brush and puts some rouge on her
>>baby's cheeks*)
>and also for you, little one,
>so that the vigil won't make
>your cheeks hollow with pallor.

SUZUKI (*a Butterfly*)
>Non vi movete
>che v'ho a ravviare i capelli.

BUTTERFLY (*seguendo una sua idea*)
>Che ne diranno! E lo zio Bonzo?
>già del mio danno tutti contenti . . . !
>E Yamadori coi suoi languori!
>Beffati, scornati, beffati,
>spennati gli ingrati!

SUZUKI (*ha terminato la toeletta*)
>È fatto.

BUTTERFLY
>L'obi che vestii da sposa.
>Qua . . . ch'io lo vesta.
>
>>(*mentre Butterfly indossa la veste, Suzuki mette l'altra al bambino, avvolgendolo quasi tutto nelle pieghe ampie e leggiere*)
>
>Vo' che mi veda indosso
>il vel del primo dì.
>
>>(*a Suzuki, che ha finito d'abbigliare il bambino*)
>
>E un papavero rosso
>nei capelli . . .
>
>>(*Suzuki punta il fiore nei capelli di Butterfly, che se ne compiace*)
>
>Così.
>
>>(*con grazia infantile fa cenno a Suzuki di chiudere lo shosi*)
>
>Nello *shosi* or farem tre forellini
>per riguardar,
>e starem zitti come topolini
>ad aspettar.

Butterfly porta il bambino presso lo shosi, nel quale fa tre fori: uno alto per sè, uno più basso per Suzuki e il terzo ancor più basso pel bimbo, che fa sedere su di un cuscino, accennandogli di guardare attento fuori del foro preparatogli. Suzuki si accoscia e spia essa pure all'esterno. Butterfly si pone innanzi al foro più alto e spia da quello. Dopo qualche tempo Suzuki ed il bambino si addormentano. Intanto si è fatta notte ed i raggi lunari illuminano dall'esterno lo shosi. Butterfly rimane immobile, rigida come una statua.

ATTO SECONDO

parte seconda

Passa la notte angosciosa. Dal porto al basso della collina salgono voci confuse di marinai e rumori diversi. All'alzarsi del sipario è già l'alba: Butterfly spia sempre al di fuori.

VOCI DI MARINAI (*dalla baia, lontanissimi*)
>Oh eh! oh eh! oh eh!

SUZUKI (*to Butterfly*)
>Don't move
>because I have to arrange your hair.

BUTTERFLY (*following an idea of hers*)
>What will they say to it! And the Bonze uncle?
>All pleased already with my trouble . . . !
>And Yamadori with his languors!
>Mocked, ridiculed, mocked,
>plucked clean, the ingrates!

SUZUKI (*has finished the toilet*)
>It's done.

BUTTERFLY
>The obi that I wore as a bride.
>Here . . . let me put it on.
>>(*as Butterfly puts on the garment, Suzuki puts the other on the child, wrapping him almost entirely in the broad, light folds*)
>I want him to see on me
>the veil of the first day.
>>(*to Suzuki, who has finished dressing the child*)
>And a red poppy
>in my hair . . .
>>(*Suzuki puts the flower in Butterfly's hair; Butterfly is pleased*)
>Like that.
>>(*with childish grace she motions to Suzuki to close the shoji*)
>In the shoji now we'll make three little holes
>to look out,
>and we'll be quiet as mice
>to wait.

Butterfly carries the child over to the shoji, in which she makes three holes: a high one for herself, a lower one for Suzuki and the third, still lower, for the baby, whom she seats on a pillow, motioning to him to look carefully through the hole prepared for him. Suzuki crouches down and also peers out. Butterfly places herself before the highest hole and looks through it. After a while Suzuki and the child fall asleep. Meanwhile night has fallen, and the moon's rays illuminate the shoji from outside. Butterfly remains motionless, rigid as a statue.

ACT TWO

Part Two

The anguished night passes. From the harbor at the foot of the hill rise the vague voices of sailors and various sounds. At the rise of the curtain it is already dawn: Butterfly is still peering out.

SAILORS' VOICES (*from the bay, very distant*)
>Oh eh! Oh eh! Oh eh!

SUZUKI (*svegliandosi di soprassalto*)
>   Già il sole . . .
>   (*si alza e batte dolcemente sulla spalla a
>   Butterfly*)
>   Cio-cio san . . .

BUTTERFLY (*si scuote e fidente dice:*)
>   Verrà . . . verrà vedrai.
>   (*vede il bimbo addormentato e lo prende
>   sulle braccia*)

SUZUKI   Salite a riposare, affranta siete . . .
>   al suo venire . . . vi chiamerò.

BUTTERFLY (*s'avvia*)
>   Dormi amor mio,
>   dormi sul mio cor.
>   Tu sei con Dio
>   ed io col mio dolor.
>   A te i rai
>   degli astri d'or:
>   Bimbo mio dormi!

SUZUKI (*mestamente, crollando la testa*)
>   Povera Butterfly . . .

BUTTERFLY (*entra nella camera a sinistra*)
>   Dormi amor mio,
>   dormi sul mio cor.
>   Tu sei con Dio
>   ed io col mio dolor . . .

SUZUKI (*si inginocchia innanzi al simulacro di Budda*)
>   Povera Butterfly!

Si batte lievemente all'uscio d'ingresso.

SUZUKI   Chi sia?
>   (*va ad aprire e rimane grandemente sor-
>   presa*)
>   Oh . . . !

SHARPLESS (*facendole cenno di non far rumore*)
>   Stz!

PINKERTON   Zitta! zitta!

SHARPLESS   Zitta . . . zitta!

Pinkerton e Sharpless entrano cautamente in punta di piedi.

PINKERTON (*premurosamente a Suzuki*)
>   Non la destar.

SUZUKI   Era stanca sì tanto! Vi stette ad aspettare
>   tutta la notte col bimbo.

PINKERTON   Come sapea?

SUZUKI   Non giunge
>   da tre anni una nave nel porto, che da lunge
>   Butterfly non ne scruti il color, la bandiera.

SHARPLESS (*a Pinkerton*)
>   Ve lo dissi!

SUZUKI (*per andare*)
>   La chiamo . . .

PINKERTON (*fermandola*)
>   No: non ancor.

SUZUKI (*waking with a start*)
> The sun already . . .
>> (*stands and gently taps Butterfly on the shoulder*)
>
> Cho-cho san . . .

BUTTERFLY (*stirs and says confidently:*)
> He'll come . . . he'll come, you'll see.
>> (*sees the child, asleep, and takes him in her arms*)

SUZUKI
> Go up and rest, you're exhausted . . .
> at his coming . . . I'll call you.

BUTTERFLY (*starts off*)
> Sleep, my love,
> sleep upon my heart.
> You're with God,
> and I'm with my sorrow.
> For you the rays
> of the golden stars:
> My baby, sleep!

SUZUKI (*sadly, shaking her head*)
> Poor Butterfly . . .

BUTTERFLY (*goes into the room at left*)
> Sleep, my love,
> sleep upon my heart.
> You're with God,
> and I'm with my sorrow . . .

SUZUKI (*kneels before the image of Buddha*)
> Poor Butterfly!

There is a light knock at the front door.

SUZUKI
> Who can it be?
>> (*goes to open and remains greatly surprised*)
>
> Oh . . . !

SHARPLESS (*motioning to her to make no noise*)
> Ssh!

PINKERTON   Hush! hush!

SHARPLESS   Hush . . . ! hush!

Pinkerton and Sharpless enter cautiously on tiptoe.

PINKERTON (*solicitously to Suzuki*)
> Don't waken her.

SUZUKI
> She was so tired! She remained waiting
> for you all night with the baby.

PINKERTON   How did she know?

SUZUKI
> For three years
> a ship hasn't entered the port, that Butterfly
> from afar doesn't examine its color, its flag.

SHARPLESS (*to Pinkerton*)
> I told you!

SUZUKI (*about to go*)
> I'll call her . . .

PINKERTON (*stopping her*)
> No, not yet.

SUZUKI   Lo vedete, ier sera, la stanza
                  volle sparger di fiori.

SHARPLESS (*commosso*)
                  Ve lo dissi . . . ?

PINKERTON (*turbato*)
                  Che pena!

SUZUKI (*sente rumore nel giardino, va a guardare fuori ed es-*
clama con meraviglia:)
                  Chi c'è là fuori nel giardino?
                  Una donna!

PINKERTON (*la riconduce sul davanti*)
                  Zitta!

SUZUKI (*agitata*)
                  Chi è? chi è?

SHARPLESS (*a Pinkerton*)
                  Meglio dirle ogni cosa . . .

SUZUKI (*sgomenta*)
                  Chi è? chi è?

PINKERTON (*imbarazzato*)
                  È venuta con me.

SUZUKI   Chi è? chi è?

SHARPLESS (*deliberatamente*)
                  È sua moglie.

SUZUKI (*sbalordita, alza le braccia al cielo, poi si precipita in*
ginocchio colla faccia a terra)
                  Anime sante degli avi! Alla piccina
                  s'è spento il sol, s'è spento il sol!

SHARPLESS (*calma Suzuki e la solleva da terra*)
                  Scegliemmo quest'ora mattutina
                  per ritrovarti sola, Suzuki, e alla gran prova
                  un aiuto, un sostegno cercar con te.

SUZUKI (*desolata*)
                  Che giova? che giova?

Sharpless prende a parte Suzuki e cerca colla preghiera e
colla persuasione di averne il consenso: Pinkerton, sempre più
agitato, si aggira per la stanza ed osserva.

SHARPLESS (*a Suzuki*)
                  Io so che alle sue pene
                  non ci sono conforti!
                  Ma del bimbo conviene
                  assicurar le sorti!
                  [La pïetosa
                  che entrar non osa
                  materna cura del bimbo avrà.
                  Suvvia, parla, suvvia parla
                  con quella pia
                  e conducila qui . . . S'anche la veda
                  Butterfly, non importa.
                  Anzi — meglio se accorta
                  del vero si facesse alla sua vista.
                  Suvvia, parla ecc.

SUZUKI   You see: yesterday evening, she wanted
                  to scatter the room with flowers.

SHARPLESS (*moved*)
                  Didn't I tell you . . . ?

PINKERTON (*upset*)
                  How sad!

SUZUKI (*hears a sound in the garden, goes to look out, and
        exclaims with amazement:*)
                  Who is out there in the garden?
                  A woman!

PINKERTON (*leads her forward again*)
                  Hush!

SUZUKI (*disturbed*)
                  Who is she? Who is she?

SHARPLESS (*to Pinkerton*)
                  Better to tell her everything . . .

SUZUKI (*alarmed*)
                  Who is she? Who is she?

PINKERTON (*embarrassed*)
                  She's come with me.

SUZUKI   Who is she? Who is she?

SHARPLESS (*deliberately*)
                  She's his wife.

SUZUKI (*stunned, raises her arms to heaven, then sinks to her
        knees, with her face to the ground*)
                  Sainted souls of the ancestors! For the little one
                  the sun has gone out, the sun has gone out!

SHARPLESS (*calms Suzuki and raises her from the ground*)
                  We chose this early-morning hour
                  to find you alone, Suzuki, and, in the great trial,
                  to seek in you aid, support.

SUZUKI (*desolate*)
                  What's the use? What's the use?

*Sharpless takes Suzuki to one side and, with pleading and
persuasion, tries to win her assent. Pinkerton, more and more
agitated, paces about the room and observes.*

SHARPLESS (*to Suzuki*)
                  I know that for her sufferings
                  there are no comforts!
                  But it's best to guarantee
                  the fate of the baby!
                  The pitying woman
                  who doesn't dare come in
                  will take maternal care of the baby.
                  Come, speak, come speak
                  with that kind woman
                  and bring her here . . . Even if
                  Butterfly sees her, it doesn't matter.
                  Indeed — better if she were to become aware
                  of the truth at the sight of her.
                  Come, speak, etc.

PINKERTON   Oh! l'amara fragranza
             di questi fior,
             velenosa al cor me va.
             Immutata è la stanza
             dei nostri amor . . .
             ma un gelo di morte vi sta.
                  (*vede il proprio ritratto*)
             Il mio ritratto . . .
             Tre anni son passati — e noverati
             n'ha i giorni e l'ore!

SUZUKI   Oh me trista! E volete
             ch'io chieda ad una madre . . .
             e volete ch'io chieda ad una madre . . .
             Oh! me trista! Oh! me trista!
             Anime sante degli avi . . . !
             Alla piccina s'è spento il sol!
             Oh! me trista ecc.]

SHARPLESS   Vien, Suzuki, vien!

SUZUKI (*spinta da Sharpless va nel giardino a raggiungere Mis-
             tress Pinkerton*)
             Oh! me trista!

PINKERTON (*vinto dall'emozione e non potendo trattenere il
             pianto si avvicina a Sharpless e gli dice reso-
             lutamente:*)
             Non posso rimaner. — Sharpless, v'aspetto
             per via . . .

SHARPLESS   Non ve l'avevo detto?

PINKERTON (*consegna danari al Console*)
             Datele voi qualche soccorso . . .
             Mi struggo dal rimorso,
             mi struggo dal rimorso.

SHARPLESS   Vel dissi . . . vi ricorda?
             quando la man vi diede:
             Badate, ella ci crede
             e fui profeta allor!
             Sorda ai consigli, sorda
             ai dubbî — vilipesa
             nell'ostinata attesa
             raccolse il cor.

PINKERTON   Sì, tutto in un istante
             io vedo il fallo mio e sento
             che di questo tormento
             tregua mai non avrò,
             mai non avrò, no!

SHARPLESS   Andate — il triste vero
             da sola apprenderà . . .

PINKERTON   Addio fiorito asil
             di letizia e d'amor.
             Sempre il mite suo sembiante
             con strazio atroce vedrò . . .

SHARPLESS   Ma or quel cor sincero
             presago è già . . .
             [Vel dissi ecc.

PINKERTON   Oh! the bitter fragrance
of these flowers,
goes to my heart like poison.
The room of our loves
is unchanged . . .
but a deathly chill is in it.
     (*sees his own portrait*)
My portrait . . .
Three years have passed — and she's counted
their days and their hours!

SUZUKI   Oh, unhappy me! And you want
me to ask a mother . . .
and you want me to ask a mother . . .
Oh! unhappy me! Oh! unhappy me!
Sainted souls of the ancestors . . . !
For the little one the sun has gone out!
Oh! unhappy me! etc.

SHARPLESS   Come, Suzuki, come!

SUZUKI (*thrust by Sharpless, goes into the garden to join Mrs.
Pinkerton*)
Oh! unhappy me!

PINKERTON (*overcome with emotion and unable to restrain
his tears, approaches Sharpless and says resolutely:*)
I can't stay. — Sharpless, I'll wait for you
along the way . . .

SHARPLESS   Didn't I tell you?

PINKERTON (*gives the consul some money*)
Give her some assistance . . .
I'm destroyed by remorse,
I'm destroyed by remorse.

SHARPLESS   I told you . . . you remember?
when she gave you her hand:
Mind you, she believes in it,
and I was a prophet then!
Deaf to advice, deaf
to doubts — insulted,
she gathered her heart
in her stubborn waiting.

PINKERTON   Yes, all in one moment
I see my wrongdoing, and I feel
that I'll never have peace
from this torment,
I'll never have it, no!

SHARPLESS   Go — she'll learn
the sad truth alone . . .

PINKERTON   Good-by, flowered refuge
of happiness and of love.
I'll always see her gentle face
with atrocious torment . . .

SHARPLESS   But now that sincere heart
is already foreseeing . . .
I told you, etc.

PINKERTON   Addio fiorito asil . . .
             Non reggo al tuo squallor,
             ah! non reggo al tuo squallor!
             Fuggo, fuggo, son vil!
             Addio, non reggo al tuo squallor,]
             ah! son vil, ah! son vil . . . !

Pinkerton, strette le mani al Console, esce rapidamente men-
tre Kate e Suzuki vengono dal giardino.

KATE (*con dolcezza a Suzuki*)
             Glielo dirai?

SUZUKI (*a testa bassa risponde senza scomporsi dalla sua rigi-*
             dezza)
             Prometto.

KATE   E le darai consiglio d'affidarmi . . . ?

SUZUKI   Prometto.

KATE   Lo terrò come un figlio.

SUZUKI   Vi credo. Ma bisogna ch'io le sia sola accanto . . .
             Nella grande ora — sola! Piangerà tanto!
             Piangerà tanto!

BUTTERFLY (*voce lontana dalla camera a sinistra, chiamando*)
             Suzuki . . . ! Suzuki . . . !
             (*più vicina*)
             Dove sei? Suzuki . . . !

Butterfly appare alla porta socchiusa; Kate per non essere
vista si allontana nel giardino.

SUZUKI   Son qui . . . pregavo e rimettevo a posto . . .
             (*si precipita per impedire a Butterfly di*
             entrare)
             No . . . no . . . no . . . non scendete . . .
             (*gridando*)
             No . . . no . . . no . . .

Butterfly entra precipitosa, svincolandosi da Suzuki che
cerca invano trattenerla.

BUTTERFLY (*aggirandosi per la stanza con grande agitazione,*
             ma giubilante)
             È qui . . . è qui . . . dove è nascosto?
             è qui . . . è qui . . .
             (*scorgendo Sharpless*)
             Ecco il Console . . .
             (*sgomenta, cercando Pinkerton*)
             e . . . dove . . . ? dove . . . ?
             (*dopo aver guardato da per tutto, in ogni*
             angolo, nella piccola alcova e dietro il pa-
             ravento, sgomenta si guarda attorno)
             Non c'è.
             (*vede Kate nel giardino e guarda fissamente*
             Sharpless)
             Quella donna? Che vuol da me?
             Niuno parla . . . !

Suzuki piange silenziosamente.

BUTTERFLY (*sorpresa*)
             Perchè piangete?

PINKERTON   Good-by, flowered refuge . . .
         I can't bear your squalor,
         Ah! I can't bear your squalor!
         I flee, I flee, I'm cowardly!
         Good-by, I can't bear your squalor,
         ah! I'm cowardly, ah! I'm cowardly . . . !

Pinkerton, having clasped the consul's hands, goes out rapidly, as Kate and Suzuki come in from the garden.

KATE   (*sweetly, to Suzuki*)
         You'll tell her?

SUZUKI   (*hanging her head, answers without relaxing her stiffness*)
         I promise.

KATE   And you'll advise her to entrust him to me . . . ?

SUZUKI   I promise.

KATE   I'll keep him like a son.

SUZUKI   I believe you. But I must be alone with her . . .
         In the great hour — alone! She'll weep so much!
         She'll weep so much!

BUTTERFLY (*voice distant, from the room at left, calling*)
         Suzuki . . . ! Suzuki . . . !
         (*closer*)
         Where are you? Suzuki . . . !

Butterfly appears at the half-opened door; in order not to be seen, Kate goes off into the garden.

SUZUKI   I'm here . . . I was praying and tidying up . . .
         (*hastens to prevent Butterfly from entering*)
         No . . . no . . . no . . . don't come down . . .
         (*shouting*)
         No . . . no . . . no . . .

Butterfly enters hastily, freeing herself from Suzuki, who tries in vain to hold her back.

BUTTERFLY (*rushing about the room in great agitation, but jubilant*)
         He's here . . . he's here . . . Where is he hidden?
         He's here . . . he's here . . .
         (*noticing Sharpless*)
         Here's the consul . . .
         (*alarmed, looking for Pinkerton*)
         and . . . where . . . ? where . . . ?
            (*after having looked everywhere, in every corner, in the little alcove and behind the screen, she looks around in alarm*)
         He isn't here.
            (*sees Kate in the garden and looks hard at Sharpless*)
         That woman? What does she want of me?
         No one speaks . . . !

Suzuki weeps silently.

BUTTERFLY (*surprised*)
         Why are you weeping?

(*Sharpless si avvicina a Butterfly per par-
larle; questa teme di capire e si fa piccina
come una bimba paurosa*)

No: non ditemi nulla . . . nulla . . .
forse potrei cader morta sull'attimo . . .
(*con bontà affettuosa ed infantile a Suzuki*)

Tu Suzuki che sei tanto buona,
non piangere, e mi vuoi tanto bene —
un sì, un no, di' piano . . . Vive?

SUZUKI   Sì.

BUTTERFLY (*come se avesse ricevuto un colpo mortale: irrigi-
dita*)
Ma non viene più. Te l'han detto . . . !
(*irritata al silenzio di Suzuki*)
Vespa! Voglio che tu risponda.

SUZUKI   Mai più.

BUTTERFLY Ma è giunto ieri?

SUZUKI   Sì.

BUTTERFLY (*guarda Kate, quasi affascinata*)
Ah! quella donna mi fa tanta paura!
tanta paura!

SHARPLESS È la causa innocente d'ogni vostra sciagura.
Perdonatele.

BUTTERFLY (*comprendendo*)
Ah! è sua moglie!
Tutto è morto per me!
tutto è finito! ah!

SHARPLESS Coraggio.

BUTTERFLY Voglion prendermi tutto! Il figlio mio!

SHARPLESS Fatelo pel suo bene il sacrifizio . . .

BUTTERFLY Ah! triste madre! triste madre!
Abbandonar mio figlio!
(*calma*)
E sia! A lui devo obbedir!

KATE (*che si è avvicinata timidamente al terrazzo, senza entrare nella stanza*)
Potete perdonarmi, Butterfly?

BUTTERFLY Sotto il gran ponte del cielo non v'è
donna di voi più felice.
Siatelo sempre, non v'attristate per me.

KATE (*a Sharpless che le si è avvicinato*)
Povera piccina!

SHARPLESS (*assai commosso*)
È un'immensa pietà!

KATE E il figlio lo darà?

BUTTERFLY (*che ha udito*)
A lui lo potrò dare
se lo verrà a cercare.
Fra mezz'ora salite la collina.

(Sharpless approaches Butterfly to speak to her; she is afraid she understands and she makes herself tiny like a frightened child)
No: tell me nothing . . . nothing . . .
perhaps I might fall dead on the spot . . .
(with affectionate and childish goodness to Suzuki)
You, Suzuki, who are so good,
don't weep, and who love me so —
say softly a "yes," a "no" . . . Is he alive?

SUZUKI   Yes.

BUTTERFLY *(as if she had received a mortal blow: rigid)*
But he's not coming any more. They've told you . . . !
(irritated at Suzuki's silence)
Wasp! I want you to answer.

SUZUKI   Never again.

BUTTERFLY   But he arrived yesterday?

SUZUKI   Yes.

BUTTERFLY *(looks at Kate, as if fascinated)*
Ah! that woman frightens me so!
She frightens me so!

SHARPLESS   She's the innocent cause of all your woe.
Forgive her.

BUTTERFLY *(understanding)*
Ah! she's his wife!
All is dead for me!
All is finished, ah!

SHARPLESS   Courage.

BUTTERFLY   They want to take everything from me! My son!

SHARPLESS   Make the sacrifice for his good . . .

BUTTERFLY   Ah! sad mother! sad mother!
To abandon my son!
(calm)
So be it! I must obey him!

KATE *(who has timidly approached the terrace, without enter-ing the room)*
Can you forgive me, Butterfly?

BUTTERFLY   Under the great bridge of heaven there is
no woman happier than you.
May you always be so; don't be sad for me.

KATE *(to Sharpless, who has come over to her)*
Poor little one!

SHARPLESS *(very moved)*
It's a huge pity!

KATE   And will she give up the son?

BUTTERFLY *(who has heard)*
I can give him to him
if he will come for him.
In half an hour climb the hill.

Suzuki accompagna Kate e Sharpless che escono dal fondo.
Butterfly cade a terra, piangendo. Suzuki s'affretta a soccor-
rerla.

SUZUKI (*mettendo una mano sul cuore a Butterfly*)
            Come una mosca prigioniera
            l'ali batte il piccol cuor!

Butterfly si rinfranca poco a poco: vedendo che è giorno
fatto, si scioglie da Suzuki, e le dice:

BUTTERFLY   Troppa luce è di fuor,
            e troppa primavera. Chiudi.

Suzuki va a chiudere lo shosi, in modo che la camera rimane
quasi in completa oscurità, poi ritorna verso Butterfly.

BUTTERFLY   Il bimbo ove sia?
SUZUKI   Giuoca . . . Lo chiamo?
BUTTERFLY   Lascialo giuocar . . . lascialo giuocar . . .
            Va a fargli compagnia.
SUZUKI (*piangendo*)
            Resto con voi.
BUTTERFLY (*risolutamente batte le mani*)
            Va — va. Te lo comando.

Fa alzare Suzuki e la spinge fuori dell'uscio di sinistra, poi
Butterfly accende un lume davanti al reliquiario, si inchina e
rimane immobile assorta in doloroso pensiero: va allo stipo, ne
leva un gran velo bianco che getta sul paravento; poi prende
il coltello che, chiuso in un astuccio di lacca, sta appeso alla
parete presso il simulacro di Budda, lo impugna e ne bacia
religiosamente la lama tenendola colle due mani per la punta
e per l'impugnatura: quindi legge le parole che sono incise
sulla lama.

BUTTERFLY   "Con onor muore
            chi non può serbar vita con onore."

Si appunta il coltello alla gola; s'apre la porta di sinistra e
si vede il braccio di Suzuki che spinge il bambino verso la
madre; il bimbo entra correndo colle mantne alzate; Butterfly
lascia cadere il coltello, si precipita verso il bambino, lo ab-
braccia soffocandolo di baci.

BUTTERFLY   Tu? tu? tu? tu?
            piccolo Iddio!
            Amore, amore mio,
            fior di giglio e di rosa.
            Non saperlo mai
            per te, pei tuoi puri occhi,
            muor Butterfly
            perchè tu possa andar
            di là dal mare
            senza che ti rimorda ai dì maturi
            il materno abbandono.
            O a me, sceso dal trono
            dell'alto Paradiso,
            guarda ben fiso, fiso
            di tua madre la faccia . . . !
            che te'n resti una traccia,
            guarda ben!

Suzuki accompanies Kate and Sharpless, who leave at the rear. Butterfly falls to the ground, weeping. Suzuki hastens to succor her.

SUZUKI (*putting a hand on Butterfly's heart*)
> Like an imprisoned fly
> the little heart is beating its wings!

Butterfly little by little is reanimated. Seeing that it is broad daylight, she frees herself from Suzuki and says:

BUTTERFLY Too much light is outside,
> and too much spring. Close.

Suzuki goes to close the shoji, so that the room remains almost in complete darkness, then she comes back to Butterfly.

BUTTERFLY Where is the baby?

SUZUKI He's playing . . . Shall I call him?

BUTTERFLY Let him play . . . let him play . . .
> Go and keep him company.

SUZUKI (*weeping*)
> I'll stay with you.

BUTTERFLY (*resolutely claps her hands*)
> Go -- go. I command you.

She makes Suzuki rise and pushes her out through the door at left, then Butterfly lights a lamp in front of the reliquary, bows, and remains motionless, absorbed in sorrowful thought. She goes to the cabinet, takes a white veil from it which she throws over the screen. Then she takes the dagger, which, closed in a lacquer case, is hanging on the wall near the image of Buddha. She grasps it and kisses the blade religiously, holding it in both hands by the tip and by the hilt. Then she reads the words that are engraved on the blade.

BUTTERFLY "He dies with honor
> who cannot continue living with honor."

She aims the knife at her throat. The door at left opens, and Suzuki's arm is seen, thrusting the baby towards his mother. The child runs in with his little hands upraised; Butterfly drops the dagger, rushes towards the child, and embraces him, smothering him with kisses.

BUTTERFLY You? you? you? you?
> little God!
> Love, my love,
> flower of lily and of rose.
> Never know:
> for you, for your pure eyes,
> Butterfly dies,
> so that you may go
> beyond the sea
> without your mother's abandonment
> tormenting you in your grown-up days.
> O you, descended to me from the throne
> of lofty paradise,
> look very hard, hard
> at your mother's face . . . !
> that a trace of it may remain with you,
> look hard!

Amore, addio! addio! piccolo amor ... !
    (*guarda lungamente il suo bimbo e lo*
    bacia ancora)
Va. Gioca, gioca.

*Butterfly prende il bambino, lo mette su di una stuoia col
viso voltato verso sinistra, gli dà in mano una banderuola
americana ed una puppattola e lo invita a trastullarsi mentre
delicatamente gli benda gli occhi. Poi afferra il coltello, chiude
la porta di sinistra e collo sguardo sempre fisso sul figlio, va
dietro il paravento. Si ode cadere a terra il coltello, mentre il
gran velo bianco sparisce come tirato da una mano invisibile.
Butterfly scivola a terra, mezza fuori del paravento: il velo le
circonda il collo. Con un debole sorriso saluta colla mano il
bambino e si trascina presso di lui, avendo ancora forza suffi-
ciente per abbracciarlo, poi gli cade vicino. In questo momento si ode fuori, a destra, la voce affannosa di Pinkerton.*

VOCE DI PINKERTON
    Butterfly ... ! Butterfly ... ! Butterfly ... !

*La porta di destra è violentemente aperta. Pinkerton e
Sharpless si precipitano nella stanza accorrendo presso Butterfly che con debole gesto indica il bambino e muore. Pinkerton
si inginocchia, mentre Sharpless prende il bimbo e lo bacia
singhiozzando.*

Love, good-by! good-by! little love . . . !
> (*she looks long at her child and kisses him
> again*)

Go. Play, play.

*Butterfly takes the child, puts him on a mat with his face
turned toward the left. She puts in his hand a little American
flag and a doll and tells him to amuse himself, while she delicately blindfolds him. Then she seizes the danger, shuts the
door at left, and with her eyes always on her son, she goes
behind the screen. The dagger is heard falling to the ground,
as the great white veil vanishes, as if pulled by an invisible
hand. Butterfly slips to the floor, half outside the screen. The
veil is wrapped around her neck. With a weak smile, she
waves to the child and drags herself over to him, still having
enough strength to embrace him. Then she falls beside him.
At this moment, outside, at right, the breathless voice of Pinkerton is heard.*

PINKERTON'S VOICE (*shouting*)
Butterfly . . . ! Butterfly . . . ! Butterfly . . . !

*The door at right is opened violently. Pinkerton and Sharp-
less rush into the room, running to Butterfly, who with a weak
gesture points to the child and dies. Pinkerton kneels, as
Sharpless picks up the child and kisses him, sobbing.*

Il trittico

After the death of Giuseppe Giacosa, there began for Puccini a particularly unhappy period, both in his private life (his wife's almost insane jealousy was soon to lead to tragedy) and in his career. The search for a libretto—and for new librettists—became more frenetic than ever. Dozens of ideas were suggested to him; some reached an advanced stage before being dropped. Finally another Belasco play—*The Girl of the Golden West*—furnished him with his next subject, though the opera that resulted did not win the acclaim of its predecessors. And the work that followed the *Girl*—his half-hearted attempt at operetta, *La rondine*—was even less successful.

The librettist of *La rondine* was the playwright Giuseppe Adami, a young man in his thirties. Sometime in 1915, Puccini set him to work on another text, a one-act work, *Il tabarro*, based on a French play by Didier Gold which the composer had seen at the Théâtre Marigny in Paris in 1912. Working closely with the composer, Adami prepared the libretto, and Puccini set promptly to work. At that time, he was thinking of composing a trilogy (the over-all title *Il trittico* had not yet been conceived), with two other librettos to be supplied perhaps by D'Annunzio and Tristan Bernard.

On November 26, 1916, Puccini wrote to Tito Ricordi: "I have finished *Houppelande* [the original title of the French play] completely." Since there was no sign of the other two librettos to complete the evening, for a while Puccini thought of giving *Il tabarro* alone, or with his youthful *Le villi*. But before anything could be arranged, another librettist came into his life: the energetic, garrulous young Tuscan Giovacchino Forzano. This newcomer promptly suggested ideas for the two one-act operas needed to make a complete evening.

The ideas couldn't have been happier. Puccini had long wanted to write an opera for women's voices only; Forzano conceived the idea of *Suor Angelica*. And another of the composer's dreams was a text drawn from Dante; Forzano's *Gianni Schicchi* was inspired by three verses of Canto xxx of the *Inferno*. In addition, the latter proposal offered Puccini the chance to write a comic opera, a new and challenging field for him.

Puccini composed *Suor Angelica* between March and September of 1917, occasionally calling on his sister, Suor Enrichetta, mother superior of a convent, for advice. He also consulted his "pretino," the "little priest" Don Pietro Panichelli, whom he had known for years. When the score was complete, Puccini visited his sister's little convent at Vicopelago, near their native Lucca, and played and sang the work for the nuns, who—according to biographers—were moved to tears.

During the composition of *Suor Angelica*, Puccini had worked simultaneously on *Gianni Schicchi*. It, too, was completed fairly rapidly, by April 20, 1918. Even before it was finished, opera houses were vying for the privilege of presenting the triple-bill. Giulio Gatti-Casazza won out, and *Il trittico* was first heard at the Metropolitan Opera. Its European premiere—at the Teatro Costanzi in Rome—came a few weeks later.

The initial reception of the work was mixed. *Schicchi* was an immediate success, but the other two operas appealed less to public and critics. Much to the composer's regret, the trio was dismembered, and the comic opera was often performed without the other two works. In recent years, there has been a growing tendency to present the three operas as Puccini conceived them: first the dark *Tabarro*, then the tender *Angelica*, and—as happy ending—the boisterous *Schicchi*.

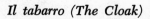

Il tabarro (The Cloak)

THE PLOT

A barge is tied up at a Paris quay. As the stevedores un-
load it, the boss Michele talks briefly with his young wife
Giorgetta, complaining of her coldness. Then, as work ends,
Giorgetta offers wine to the men; and when a strolling musician stops and plays, she dances with Luigi, the youngest of
the stevedores. With him, too, she tells of the joys of living in
Paris, instead of the cramped, unsettled life on the barge.
When they are alone, it becomes clear that they are lovers;
they arrange to meet that same night, after Michele has gone
to sleep. Giorgetta will strike a match as the signal that the
coast is clear. Luigi leaves. Again Michele tries to stir Giorgetta from her frustrating estrangement, even reminding her
of their dead child. Giorgetta goes into the cabin. Now convinced that she has a lover, Michele remains on deck, musing
bitterly. He strikes a match to light his pipe. Thinking this is
the signal, Luigi steals aboard. Michele catches him, forces a
confession from him, and strangles him, concealing the body
in his cloak. When Giorgetta, uneasy, comes out of the cabin,
Michele opens his cloak and Luigi's body rolls at her feet.

IL TABARRO

libretto by Giuseppe Adami

First performed at the Metropolitan Opera House, New York

December 14, 1918

CHARACTERS

Michele, barge-owner	*Baritone*
Luigi, a stevedore	*Tenor*
Il Tinca (the Tench), a stevedore	*Tenor*
Il Talpa (the Mole), a stevedore	*Bass*
Giorgetta, Michele's wife	*Soprano*
La Frugola (the Rummager), Talpa's wife	*Mezzosoprano*

Stevedores, a Song-Vendor, Midinettes, an Organ-Grinder and
His Assistant, Two Lovers

The time is the present.
The place is Paris, a quay along the Seine.

Un angolo della Senna, dove è ancorato il barcone di Michele.

La barca occupa quasi tutto il primo piano della scena ed è congiunta al molo con una passerella.

La Senna si va perdendo lontana. Nel fondo il profilo della vecchia Parigi e principalmente la mole maestosa di Notre-Dame staccano sul cielo di un rosso meraviglioso.

Sempre nel fondo, a destra, sono i caseggiati che fiancheggiano il lungo-Senna e in primo piano alti platani lussureggianti.

Il barcone ha tutto il carattere delle consuete imbarcazioni da trasporti che navigano la Senna. Il timone campeggia in alto della cabina. E la cabina è tutta linda e ben dipinta con le sue finestrelle verdi, il fumaiolo e il tetto piano, a mo' d'altana, sul quale sono alcuni vasi di geranii. Su una corda sono distesi i panni ad asciugare. Sulla porta della cabina, la gabbia dei canarini.

È il tramonto.

_____

Quando si apre il velario, Michele—il padrone del barcone—è seduto presso il timone, gli occhi fissi a contemplare il tramonto. La pipa gli pende dalle labbra, spenta.

Dalla stiva al molo vanno e vengono gli scaricatori trasportando faticosamente i sacchi. Sulla Senna, di tratto in tratto, la sirena d'un rimorchiatore lancia il suo grido lugubre. Qualche cornetta d'automobile lontano.

Giorgetta esce dalla cabina senza avvedersi di Michele. Accudisce alle sue faccende; ritira alcuni panni stesi ad asciugare; cava una secchia d'acqua dal fiume e innaffia i suoi fiori; ripulisce la gabbia dei canarini.

Finalmente si accorge che il suo uomo è laggiù, e facendo schermo con la mano agli occhi, tanto è vivo il riflesso del sole che tramonta, lo chiama.

GIORGETTA   O Michele? . . . Michele? . . . Non sei stanco
             d'abbacinarti al sole che tramonta?
             Ti sembra un gran spettacolo?

MICHELE   Sicuro!

GIORGETTA   Lo vedo bene: dalla tua pipa
             il fumo bianco non sbuffa più!

MICHELE (*accennando agli scaricatori*)
             Han finito laggiù?

GIORGETTA (*premurosamente*)
             Vuoi che discenda?

MICHELE   No. Resta. Andrò io stesso.

GIORGETTA   Han lavorato tanto! . .

A curve in the Seine, where Michele's barge is anchored.

The boat occupies almost the entire foreground of the stage and is connected with the quay by a gangplank.

The Seine flows by and is lost in the distance. At the back, the silhouette of old Paris and, in particular, the majestic mass of Nôtre Dame stand out against the sky, a marvelous red.

Also in the back, to the right, are the apartment buildings that flank the quay, and in the foreground, tall, flourishing plane-trees.

The barge has the typical appearance of the usual transport boats that navigate the Seine. The wheel is set high up, above the cabin. And the cabin is all neat and freshly painted with its little green window-frames, its chimney, and its flat roof, like a terrace, on which some pots of geraniums are set. On a line clothes are hung out to dry. At the door of the cabin, the canaries' cage.

It is sunset.

When the curtain parts, Michele—the owner of the barge—is seated near the wheel, his eyes staring, contemplating the sunset. His pipe hangs from his lips; it has gone out.

From the hold to the quay the stevedores come and go, painfully carrying the sacks. On the Seine, from time to time, the siren of a tugboat lets out its lugubrious cry. Some automobile horns honk in the distance.

Giorgetta comes out of the cabin without noticing Michele. She tends to her chores; she collects some clothes hung out to dry; draws a bucket of water from the river and waters her flowers; cleans the canaries' cage.

Finally she becomes aware that her man is over there, and shielding her eyes with her hand—the glare of the setting sun is so bright—she calls him.

GIORGETTA	O Michele! . . . Michele? . . . Aren't you tired of blinding yourself in the setting sun? Does it seem a great show to you?
MICHELE	Certainly!
GIORGETTA	I can see that clearly: from your pipe the white smoke no longer puffs!
MICHELE (*indicating the stevedores*)	Have they finished down there?
GIORGETTA (*eagerly*)	You want me to go down?
MICHELE	No. Stay. I'll go myself.
GIORGETTA	They've worked so much! . . .

Come avean promesso,
la stiva sarà sgombra,
[e per doman . . .

SCARICATORI (*dal disotto del barcone*)
Oh! Issa! oh!]

GIORGETTA   . . . si potrà caricare.
Bisognerebbe compensare
questa loro fatica: un buon bicchiere.

MICHELE   Ma certo. Pensi a tutto,
cuore d'oro!

SCARICITORI (*dalla stiva*)
Oh! Issa! oh! Un giro ancor!
Se lavoriam senza ardore,
si resterà ad ormeggiare, e Margot . . .

MICHELE   Porta loro da bere.

SCARICATORI . . . con altri andrà!

GIORGETTA   Sono alla fine: prenderanno forza.

MICHELE   Il mio vinello smorza
la sete, e li ristora.

SCARICATORI Oh! Issa! oh! Un giro ancor!
Non ti stancar, battelliere;
dopo potrai riposare,
e Margot felice sarà!

MICHELE (*avvicinandosi a Giorgetta affettuosamente*)
E a me, non hai pensato?

GIORGETTA (*scostandosi un poco*)
A te? . . Che cosa?

MICHELE (*cingendola con un braccio*)
Al vino ho rinunciato;
ma, se la pipa è spenta,
[non è spento il mio ardore . . .

SCARICATORI Oh! Issa! oh! Un giro ancor!]
Ora la stiva è vuota,
chiusa è la lunga giornata,
e Margot l'amor ti darà!

MICHELE   Un tuo bacio, o mio amore . . .
(*la bacia: essa si scansa, voltando il
viso. Michele un po' contrariato s'avvia
verso la stiva e discende*)

LUIGI (*passando dalla banchina sul barcone*)
Si soffoca, padrona!

GIORGETTA   Lo pensavo.
Ho quel che ci vuole.
Sentirete che vino!
(*Si avvia verso la cabina, dopo aver lan-
ciata un'occhiata espressiva a Luigi.*)

IL TINCA (*salendo dalla stiva*)
Sacchi dannati! Mondo birbone!
Spicciati, Talpa! Si va a mangiare!

As they had promised,
the hold will be empty,
and for tomorrow . . .

STEVEDORES (*from below the barge*)
Oh! Heave ho!

GIORGETTA   . . . it'll be possible to load.
We should reward
this toil of theirs: a nice glass.

MICHELE   Why, of course. You think of everything,
heart of gold!

STEVEDORES (*from the hold*)
Oh! Heave ho! One more turn!
If we work without enthusiasm,
we'll stay moored, and Margot . . .

MICHELE   Take them something to drink.

STEVEDORES   . . . will go with others!

GIORGETTA   They're at the end: they'll gain strength.

MICHELE   My little wine dulls
thirst, and refreshes them.

STEVEDORES   Oh! Heave ho! One more round!
Don't tire, boatman;
afterwards you'll be able to rest,
and Margot will be happy!

MICHELE (*approaching Giorgetta affectionately*)
And me? Haven't you thought?

GIORGETTA (*moving away slightly*)
Of you? . . What?

MICHELE (*putting an arm around her*)
I've given up wine;
but, though my pipe is burnt out,
my passion is not burnt out . . .

STEVEDORES   Oh! Heave ho! One more turn!
Now the hold is empty,
the long day is concluded,
and Margot will give you love!

MICHELE   A kiss of yours, O my love . . .
(*he kisses her; she moves away, turning
her face aside. Michele, somewhat vexed,
heads for the hold and goes down*)

LUIGI (*moving from the dock onto the barge*)
It's stifling, mistress!

GIORGETTA   I thought so.
I have what's needed.
You'll taste what wine this is!
(*she goes towards the cabin, after having
given Luigi an expressive glance*)

IL TINCA (*coming up from the hold*)
Damned sacks! Rascally world!
Hurry up, Talpa! We're going to eat!

IL TALPA (*salendo dalla stiva con un carico sulle spalle*)
>
> Non aver fretta, non mi seccare!
>
> Ah! questo sacco spacca il groppone!
>> (*scotendo la testa e tergendosi
>> il sudore col rovescio della mano*)
>
> Dio! che caldo! . . O Luigi,
>
> ancora una passata.

LUIGI (*indicando Giorgetta che reca la brocca del vino e i bicchieri*)
>
> Eccola la passata! . . Ragazzi, si beve!
>
> Qui, tutti insiem, lesti!
>
> Lesti! Pronti!
>> (*tutti accorrono alla chiamata, facendosi
>> intorno a Giorgetta che distribuisce bic-
>> chieri e verrà mescendo*)

LUIGI
>
> Nel vino troverem
>
> l'energia per finir!
>> (*e beve*)

GIORGETTA (*ridendo*)
>
> Come parla difficile! . . Ma certo:
>
> vino alla compagnia! Qua, Talpa!
>
> Al Tinca! . . A voi! Prendete!

IL TALPA
>
> Alla salute vostra il vino si beva!
>> (*il carrettiere se ne va con il suo carico di
>> cemento, dopo di aver bevuto un bic-
>> chiere di vino*)

IL TALPA
>
> S'alzi il bicchier!
>
> Bevo! Viva!
>
> Tanta felicità
>
> per la gioia che dà!
>> (*si asciuga la bocca con il dorso della
>> mano*)

GIORGETTA
>
> Se ne volete ancora! . .
>> (*mesce di nuovo al Talpa*)

IL TALPA
>
> Non si rifiuta mai!

GIORGETTA (*agli altri*)
>
> Avanti coi bicchieri!

LUIGI (*indicando un suonatore di organetto che passa sulla
>
> banchina*)
>
> Guarda là l'organetto!
>
> È arrivato in buon punto.
>> (*chiama il suonatore ambulante*)

IL TINCA (*alzando il bicchiere*)
>
> In questo vino affogo i tristi pensieri.
>
> Bevo al padron! Viva!
>> (*a Giorgetta che mesce ancora*)
>
> Grazie, grazie!
>
> L'unico mio piacer
>
> sta qui in fondo al bicchier!

LUIGI (*al suonatore*)
>
> Ei, là! Professore! Vien qua!
>> (*agli amici*)
>
> Sentirete che artista!

IL TALPA (*coming up from the hold with a load on his back*)
> Don't be in a hurry, don't bother me!
> Ah! this sack breaks the back!
> > (*shaking his head and wiping away
> > the sweat with the back of his hand*)
>
> God! what heat! . . . O Luigi,
> one more round.

LUIGI (*pointing to Giorgetta, who is carrying the pitcher of
> wine and the glasses*)
> Here's the round! . . . Boys, we drink!
> Here, all together, lively!
> Lively! Promptly!
> > (*all rush at the summons, gathering around
> > Giorgetta, who passes out the glasses, then
> > will continue pouring*)

LUIGI
> In the wine we'll find
> the energy to finish!
> > (*and he drinks*)

GIORGETTA (*laughing*)
> How he talks fancy! . . . Why, of course:
> wine for all! Here, Talpa!
> For Tinca! . . . For you! Take it!

IL TALPA
> Let the wine be drunk to your health!
> > (*the wagon-driver goes off with his load of
> > cement, after having drunk a glass of
> > wine*)

IL TALPA
> Let the glass be raised!
> I drink! Long life!
> So much happiness
> for the joy it gives!
> > (*he wipes his mouth with the back of
> > his hand*)

GIORGETTA
> If you want some more! . . .
> > (*she pours for Talpa again*)

IL TALPA
> It's never refused!

GIORGETTA (*to the others*)
> Hold out your glasses!

LUIGI (*pointing to a hurdy-gurdy man passing on the quay*)

> Look there: the hurdy-gurdy!
> It's come at a good time.
> > (*calls the wandering musician*)

IL TINCA (*raising his glass*)
> In this wine I drown sad thoughts.
> I drink to the boss! Long life!
> > (*to Giorgetta, who pours again*)
>
> Thanks, thanks!
> My only pleasure
> lies here, at the bottom of the glass!

LUIGI (*to the musician*)
> Hey, there, Professor! Come here!
> > (*to his friends*)
>
> You'll hear what an artist he is!

GIORGETTA (*a Luigi, come per sedurlo a ballare con lei*)
          Io capisco una musica sola:
          quella che fa ballare.
IL TINCA (*si fa avanti per il primo*)
          Ma sicuro!
          Ai suoi ordini sempre,
          e gamba buona!
GIORGETTA (*ridendo*)
          To'! Io ti prendo in parola.
IL TINCA (*lusingatissimo*)
          Ballo con la padrona!

*Si ride. Ma si ride anche di più perchè il Tinca non riesce a
prendere il passo e a mettersi d'accordo con Giorgetta. Luigi
e il Talpa si tappano le orecchie alle stonature dell'organetto.*
LUIGI (*ridendo*)
                    La musica e la danza van d'accordo.
                    (*al Tinca che balla strisciando i piedi*)

                    Sembra che tu pulisca il pavimento!
GIORGETTA   Ahi! M'hai pestato un piede!
LUIGI (*allontanando il Tinca con una spinta e sostituendolo*)

                    Va'! Lascia! Son qua io!
*E serra Giorgetta fra le braccia. Essa s'abbandona langui-
damente. La danza continua mentre dalla stiva appare Michele.*
IL TALPA   Ragazzi, c'è il padrone!

*Luigi e Giorgetta si staccano. Luigi getta qualche moneta
al suonatore, poi assieme agli altri s'avvia verso la stiva,
mentre Michele procede verso Giorgetta. Essa, dopo essersi ri-
composta e ravviati i capelli, s'avvicina a Michele, con sten-
tata naturalezza.*
GIORGETTA   Dunque, che cosa credi? Partiremo
             la settimana prossima?
MICHELE (*vagamente*)
             Vedremo.
GIORGETTA   Il Talpa e il Tinca restano?
MICHELE   Resterà anche Luigi.
GIORGETTA   Ieri non lo pensavi.
MICHELE   Ed oggi, penso.
GIORGETTA   Perchè?
UN VENDITORE DI CANZONETTE (*interno, un poco lontano*)
             Chi vuol l'ultima canzonetta?
MICHELE   Perchè non voglio
             ch'egli crepi di fame.
GIORGETTA   Quello s'arrangia sempre.
VENDITORE   [Chi la vuole?
MICHELE   Lo so: s'arrangia, è vero.]
             Ed è per questo
             che non conclude mulla.

GIORGETTA (*to Luigi, as if to lure him to dance with her*)
I understand only one music:
that which makes you dance.

IL TINCA (*presenting himself first*)
Why, certainly!
At your orders always,
and shake a leg!

GIORGETTA (*laughing*)
Well! I'll take you at your word.

IL TINCA (*highly flattered*)
I'm dancing with the mistress!

All laugh. But they laugh even more because Tinca cannot grasp the pace and keep up with Giorgetta. Luigi and Talpa cover their ears at the wrong notes of the hurdy-gurdy.

LUIGI (*laughing*)
The music and the dancing go together.
(*to Tinca, who dances, dragging his feet*)
It seems you're cleaning the floor!

GIORGETTA   Ouch! You stepped on my foot!

LUIGI (*sending away Tinca with a shove and taking his place*)
Go! Leave her! I'm here!

And he clasps Giorgetta in his arms. She abandons herself languidly. The dance continues as Michele appears from the hold.

IL TALPA   Boys, the boss is here!

Luigi and Giorgetta break apart. Luigi throws some coins to the musician, then along with the others heads for the hold, as Michele comes forward towards Giorgetta. After composing herself and adjusting her hair, she approaches Michele, with forced naturalness.

GIORGETTA   Well, what do you think? Will we leave
next week?

MICHELE (*vaguely*)
We'll see.

GIORGETTA   Are Talpa and Tinca staying on?

MICHELE   Luigi will stay on, too.

GIORGETTA   Yesterday you didn't think so.

MICHELE   And today I think so.

GIORGETTA   Why?

A SONG PEDDLER (*offstage, a bit distant*)
Who wants the latest song?

MICHELE   Because I don't want
him to die of hunger.

GIORGETTA   That one always manages.

PEDDLER   Who wants it?

MICHELE   I know: he manages, true.
And that's why
he never achieves anything.

GIORGETTA (*seccata*)
Con te non si sa mai
[chi fa male o fa bene!

VENDITORE (*più vicino*)
Chi la vuole?]

MICHELE (*semplicemente*)
Chi lavora si tiene.
(*sirena lontana di rimorchiatore*)

GIORGETTA   Già discende la sera . . .
Oh che rosso tramonto di settembre!
Che brivido d'autunno!
Non sembra un grosso arancio
questo sole che muore nella Senna?
Guarda laggiù la Frugola!

VENDITORE   Chi la vuole?

GIORGETTA   La vedi?

VENDITORE   Con musica e parole?

GIORGETTA   Cerca di suo marito e non lo lascia!

MICHELE   È giusto. Beve troppo!

GIORGETTA   Non lo sai che è gelosa?
(*scrutando Michele*)
O mio uomo, non sei di buon umore!
Che hai? . . Che guardi? . . .
E perchè taci?

Michele non risponde. Nel frattempo il cantastorie è apparso sulla strada al di là della Senna, seguito da un gruppo di midinettes che escono da una casa di mode e che si fermano ad ascoltarlo. Il venditore è seguito da un uomo che porta una piccola arpa ad armacollo.

VENDITORE   Chi la vuole l'ultima canzonetta?

LE MIDINETTES
Bene! bene! Sì! sì!

L'arpista ha deposto lo strumento, si è seduto su un piccolo sgabello portatile e si accinge a suonare; il venditore di canzonette è pronto a candare e le midinettes ad ascoltare.

MICHELE   T'ho mai fatto scenate?

GIORGETTA   Lo so bene: tu non mi batti!

VENDITORE   Primavera, primavera,
non cercare più i due amanti
[là fra l'ombre della sera.

MICHELE   Che? lo vorresti?

GIORGETTA   Ai silenzi talvolta, sì, preferirei]
lividi di percosse!

Michele, senza rispondere, risale il barcone e si mette a fissar meglio una corda d'amarra.

VENDITORE   Primavera, primavera!
Chi ha vissuto per amore,
per amore si morì.
È la storia di Mimì!

GIORGETTA With you there's never any knowing
who does wrong or does well!

PEDDLER (*closer*)
Who wants it?

MICHELE (*simply*)
You keep on a man who works.
(*tugboat's distant siren*)

GIORGETTA Evening is already falling . . .
Oh, what a red September sunset!
What a shiver of autumn!
Doesn't it look like a big orange,
this sun dying in the Seine?
Look at Frugola over there!

PEDDLER Who wants it?

GIORGETTA You see her?

PEDDLER With words and music?

GIORGETTA She's hunting her husband and won't leave
him!

MICHELE That's right. He drinks too much.

GIORGETTA Don't you know she's jealous?
(*examining Michele*)
O, my man, you're not in a good humor!
What's wrong? . . . What are you looking at? . . .
And why are you silent?

*Michele doesn't answer. In the meanwhile the street-singer
has appeared in the street beyond the Seine, followed by a
group of midinettes who are coming out of a dressmaker's es-
tablishment and who stop to listen to him. The peddler is followed by a man carrying a little harp over his shoulder.*

PEDDLER Who wants the latest song?

THE MIDINETTES
Fine, fine! Yes! Yes!

*The harpist has set down his instrument and sat on a little
portable stool; he prepares to play. The song peddler is ready
to sing, and the midinettes to listen.*

MICHELE Have I ever made scenes with you?

GIORGETTA Yes, I know: you don't beat me!

PEDDLER Springtime, springtime,
don't look any more for the two lovers
there among the shadows of the evening.

MICHELE What? Would you want that?

GIORGETTA At times, yes, I would prefer to silences
the bruises of beatings!

*Michele, without answering, goes back up the barge and
starts tightening a mooring rope.*

PEDDLER Springtime, springtime!
Who lived for love,
died for love.
It's the story of Mimì!

Le raggazze comprano la canzonetta e due se ne vanno leg-
gendola.

GIORGETTA (*che ha seguito Michele, con insistenza*)
            Dimmi almeno che hai!

MICHELE   Nulla! . . Nulla! . .

VENDITORE   Chi aspettando sa che muore
            [conta ad ore le giornate
            con i battiti del cuore.

GIORGETTA   Quando siamo a Parigi
            io mi sento felice.]

MICHELE   Si capisce.

GIORGETTA   Perchè?

VENDITORE   Conta ad ore le giornate.
            Ma l'amante non tornò
            e i suoi battiti finì
            anche il cuore di Mimì!

Il venditore di canzonette s'allontana seguito dall'arpista; le
ragazze, leggendo sui foglietti comperati, sciamano, ripetendo
l'ultima strofa della canzonetta.

LE MIDINETTES (*interno lontano*)
            Conta ad ore le giornate,
            ma l'amante non tornò
            e i suoi battiti finì
            larà, larà, larà,
            anche il cuore di Mimì.

La Frugola è apparsa sulla banchina, attraversa la passer-
ella e sale sul barcone. Ha sulle spalle una vecchia sacca gon-
fia di ogni sorta di roba raccattata.

LA FRUGOLA O eterni innamorati,
            buona sera.

GIORGETTA   Oh buona sera, Frugola!

Michele, dopo aver salutato con un gesto la Frugola, si al-
lontana ed entra nella cabina.

LA FRUGOLA Il mio uomo ha finito il lavoro?
            Stamattina son ne poteva più
            dal mal di reni.
            Faceva proprio pena.
            Ma l'ho curato io: una buona frizione
            e il mio rum l'ha bevuto la sua schiena!

Sghignazza forte, poi getta a terra la sacca e vi fruga den-
tro con voluttà, cavandone vari oggetti.

LA FRUGOLA Ah! Giorgetta, guarda:
            un pettine fiammante!
            Se lo vuoi, te lo dono,
            È quanto di più buono
            ho raccolto in giornata.

GIORGETTA (*prendendo il pettine*)
            Hanno ragione di chiamarti Frugola;
            tu rovisti ogni angolo
            ed hai la sacca piena.

The girls buy the song, and two of them go off, reading it.

GIORGETTA *(who has followed Michele, insisting)*
Tell me at least what's wrong with you!

MICHELE   Nothing! . . . Nothing! . . .

PEDDLER   She who, waiting, knows she's dying
counts days by the hours
with the beats of her heart.

GIORGETTA   When we're in Paris
I feel happy.

MICHELE   That's clear.

GIORGETTA   Why?

PEDDLER   She counts days by the hours.
But her lover didn't return,
and Mimì's heart also
finished its beats.

The song-peddler goes off, followed by the harpist; the girls, reading the sheets they have bought, swarm off, repeating the last verse of the song.

THE MIDINETTES *(offstage, distant)*
She counts days by the hours,
but her lover didn't return,
and it finished its beats,
larà, larà, larà,
Mimì's heart also.

La Frugola has appeared on the quay. She comes up the gangplank and climbs onto the barge. On her back she has an old sack swollen with every kind of gathered object.

LA FRUGOLA   O eternal lovers,
good evening.

GIORGETTA   Oh, good evening, Frugola!

Michele, after greeting Frugola with a wave, goes off and enters the cabin.

LA FRUGOLA   Has my man finished his work?
This morning he couldn't take it any more,
his backache.
He was really pathetic.
But I treated him: a good massage,
and his back drank up my rum!

She guffaws loudly, then flings her sack on the ground, and rummages in it with delight, extracting various objects from it.

LA FRUGOLA   Ah, Giorgetta! Look:
a brand-new comb!
If you want it, I give it to you.
It's the best thing
I've picked up all day.

GIORGETTA *(taking the comb)*
They're right to call you Rummager;
you ransack every corner
and you have your sack full.

LA FRUGOLA (*mostrando la sacca*)
    Se tu sapessi gli oggetti strani
    che in questa sacca sono racchiusi!
    Guarda! guarda! è per te
    questo ciuffo di piume. Trine e velluti,
    stracci, barattoli. Vi son confusi
    gli oggetti strani. Strane reliquie,
    i documenti di mille amori.
    Gioie e tormenti quivi raccolgo,
    senza distinguere fra i ricchi e il volgo!

GIORGETTA E in quel cartoccio?

LA FRUGOLA (*tira fuori dalla sacca un cartoccio*)
    Cuore di manzo per *Caporale*,
    il mio soriano
    dal pelo fulvo,
    dall'occhio strano,
    che non ha uguale!

GIORGETTA (*ridendo*)
    Gode dei privilegi il tuo soriano!

LA FRUGOLA Li merita! Vedessi!
    (*sghignazza*)
    È il più bel gatto,
    il mio più bel romanzo.
    Quando il mio Talpa è fuori,
    mi tiene compagnia
    e insieme noi filiamo,
    noi filiam i nostri amori,
    senza puntigli e senza gelosia.
    Vuoi saperla la sua filosofia?
    Ron, ron, ron: meglio padrone
    in una catapecchia
    che servo in un palazzo.
    Ron, ron, ron, ron:
    meglio cibarsi
    con due fette di cuore
    che logorare il proprio nell'amor!

 Il Talpa appare dalla stiva, seguito da Luigi.

IL TALPA To'! guarda la mia vecchia! . .
    Che narravi?

LA FRUGOLA Parlavo con Giorgetta del soriano.

MICHELE (*uscendo dalla cabina, si avvicina a Luigi*)
    O Luigi, domani
    si carica del ferro.
    Vieni a darci una mano?

LUIGI   Verrò, padrone.

 *Il Tinca viene dalla stiva, seguito dagli altri scaricatori che
se ne vanno per la banchina dopo di avere salutato Michele.*

IL TINCA Buona notte a tutti.

IL TALPA (*al Tinca*)
    Hai tanta fretta?

LA FRUGOLA (*displaying the sack*)
    If you knew the curious objects
    that are contained in this sack!
    Look, look! It's for you,
    this bunch of feathers. Laces and velvets,
    rags, tins. The strange objects
    are jumbled together. Odd relics,
    the documents of a thousand loves.
    Joys and torments I gather here,
    without distinguishing between rich and plebs!

GIORGETTA And in that package?

LA FRUGOLA (*takes a package from the sack*)
    Beef heart for *Corporal*,
    my tabby cat,
    with tawny coat,
    with strange eyes,
    who has no equal!

GIORGETTA (*laughing*)
    Your tabby enjoys privileges!

LA FRUGOLA He deserves them! You should see!
    (*snickers*)
    He's the most beautiful cat,
    my most beautiful romance.
    When my Talpa is out,
    he keeps me company,
    and together we conduct,
    we conduct our loves,
    without sulks and without jealousy.
    You want to know his philosophy?
    Purr, purr, purr: better boss
    in a hovel
    than servant in a palace.
    Purr, purr, purr, purr:
    better to feed
    on two slices of heart
    than to wear out one's own, in love!

Talpa appears from the hold, followed by Luigi.

IL TALPA Well! Look at my old woman! . . .
    What were you telling?

LA FRUGOLA I was talking with Giorgetta about the tabby.

MICHELE (*coming out of the cabin, approaches Luigi*)
    Oh, Luigi, tomorrow
    we load on some iron.
    Are you coming to lend us a hand?

LUIGI I'll come, boss.

Tinca comes from the hold, followed by the other steve-dores, who go off along the quay, after having said goodnight to Michele.

IL TINCA Good night to all.

IL TALPA (*to Tinca*)
    Are you in such a hurry?

LA FRUGOLA (*al Tinca*)
Corri ad ubbriacarti?
Ah! se fossi tua moglie!

IL TINCA   Che fareste?

LA FRUGOLA   Ti pesteri finchè non la smettessi
di passar le notti all'osteria.
Non ti vergogni?

IL TINCA   No, no, no! Fa bene il vino!
Si affogano i pensieri di rivolta:
ché se bevo non penso,
e se penso non rido!
Ah! ah! ah! ah! ah! ah! ah!
(*s'incammina sghignazzando, mentre
Michele discende nella stiva*)

LUIGI (*fermando il Tinca*)
Hai ben ragione; meglio non pensare,
piegare il capo ed incurvar la schiena.
Per noi la vita non ha più valore,
ed ogni gioia si converte in pena.
I sacchi in groppa e giù la testa a terra!

Se guardi in alto, bada alla frustata.
(*con amarezza*)
Il pane lo guadagni col sudore,
e l'ora dell'amore va rubata!
Va rubata fra spasimi e paure
che offuscano l'ebbrezza più divina.
Tutto è conteso, tutto ci è rapito . . .

la giornata è già buia alla mattina.
Hai ben ragione; meglio non pensare.
Piegare il capo ed incurvar la schiena!

IL TINCA   Segui il mio esempio: bevi!

GIORGETTA   Basta!

IL TINCA (*fissandola*)
Non parlo più!
A domani, ragazzi, e state bene!
(*s'incammina e scompare per la banchina*)

IL TALPA (*alla Frugola*)
Ce n'andiamo anche noi?
Son stanco morto.

LA FRUGOLA   Ah! quando mai potremo
comprarci una bicocca?
Là ci riposeremo.

GIORGETTA   È la tua fissazione, la campagna!

LA FRUGOLA   Ho sognato una casetta
con un piccolo orticello.
Quattro muri, stretta stretta,
e due pini per ombrello.
Il mio vecchio steso al sole,
ai miei piedi *Caporale*,

LA FRUGOLA (*to Tinca*)
>You're running to get drunk?
>Ah! if I were your wife!

IL TINCA   What would you do?

LA FRUGOLA   I'd beat you until you stopped
>spending your nights in the tavern.
>Aren't you ashamed?

IL TINCA   No, no, no! Wine is good for you!
>Thoughts of rebellion are drowned:
>for if I drink, I don't think,
>and if I think, I don't laugh!
>Ha! ha! ha! ha! ha! ha! ha!
>>(*goes off, snickering, as Michele goes
>>down into the hold*)

LUIGI (*stopping Tinca*)
>You're quite right; better not to think,
>to bow the head and bend the back.
>For us life has no more value,
>and every joy is turned into sorrow.
>Sacks on the back, and the head down, to the
>ground!
>If you look up, watch out for the whiplash.
>>(*with bitterness*)
>You earn your bread with sweat,
>and the hour of love has to be stolen.
>It has to be stolen between sufferings and fears
>that cloud the most divine ecstasy.
>Everything is fought for, everything is stolen
>from us . . .
>the day is already dark at morning.
>You're quite right; better not to think.
>To bow the head and bend the back!

IL TINCA   Follow my example: drink!

GIORGETTA   Enough!

IL TINCA (*looking hard at her*)
>I'll speak no more!
>Till tomorrow, boys, and be well!
>>(*goes off and disappears along the quay*)

IL TALPA (*to Frugola*)
>Shall we go away, too?
>I'm dead tired.

LA FRUGOLA   Ah! when will we ever be able
>to buy ourselves a shanty?
>There we'll rest.

GIORGETTA   It's your obsession, the country!

LA FRUGOLA   I've dreamed of a little house
>with a little garden.
>Four walls, very narrow,
>and two pines as umbrella.
>My old man lying in the sun,
>*Corporal* at my feet,

e aspettar così la morte
ch'è rimedio d'ogni male!

GIORGETTA (*vivamente*)
~ È ben altro il mio sogno!
Son nata nel sobborgo, e solo l'aria
di Parigi m'esalta, m'esalta e mi nutrisce!
Oh! se Michele, un giorno, abbandonasse
questa logora vita vagabonda!
Non si vive là dentro, fra il letto e il fornello!
Tu avessi visto la mia stanza, un tempo!

LA FRUGOLA   Dove abitavi?

GIORGETTA   Non lo sai?

LUIGI (*avanzando d'improvviso*)
                Belleville!

GIORGETTA   Luigi lo conosce!

LUIGI   Anch'io ci son nato!

GIORGETTA   Come me. Come me, l'ha nel sangue!

LUIGI   Non ci si può staccare!

GIORGETTA   Bisogna aver provato!
                (*con crescente entusiasmo*)
                Belleville è il nostro suolo
                e il nostro mondo!
                Noi non possiamo vivere sull'acqua!
                Bisogna calpestare il marciapiede! . .
                Là c'è una casa, là ci sono amici,
                festosi incontri e piene confidenze . . .

LUIGI   Ci si conosce tutti!
                S'è tutti una famiglia!

GIORGETTA   Al mattino, il lavoro che ci aspetta.
                Alla sera, i ritorni in comitiva . . .
                Botteghe che s'accendono
                di luci e di lusinghe,
                vetture che s'incrociano,
                domeniche chiassose . . .
                Piccole gite in due
                al bosco di Boulogne!
                Balli all'aperto,
                intimità amorose . . .
                È difficile dire cosa sia
                quest'ansia, questa strana nostalgia.

LUIGI, GIORGETTA (*con esaltazione*)
                Ma chi lascia il sobborgo
                vuol tornare,
                e chi ritorna, chi ritorna
                non si può staccare.
                C'è là in fondo Parigi, che ci grida
                con mille voci liete
                il suo fascino immortal!

*I due amanti restano per un attimo assorti, la mano nella
mano, come se lo stesso pensiero e la stessa anima li trasci-
nasse. Poi, riprendono istantaneamente la coscienza che gli
altri li guardano, e si staccano.*

and waiting, like that, for death,
which is the cure for every ailment!

GIORGETTA (*with animation*)
My dream is quite different!
I was born in a suburb, and the very air
of Paris excites me, excites and nourishes me!
Oh! if Michele, one day, would abandon
this drab, vagabond life!
You can't live in there, between bed and stove!
You should have seen my room, once!

LA FRUGOLA   Where did you live?

GIORGETTA   Don't you know?

LUIGI (*suddenly stepping forward*)
Belleville!

GIORGETTA   Luigi knows it!

LUIGI   I was born there, too!

GIORGETTA   Like me. Like me, he has it in his blood!

LUIGI   You can't tear yourself away from it!

GIORGETTA   You have to have experienced it!
(*with growing enthusiasm*)
Belleville is our terrain
and our world!
We can't live on the water!
You have to tramp the pavement! . . .
There is a house, there are friends there,
festive meetings and complete trust . . .

LUIGI   Everybody knows everybody else!
It's all one family!

GIORGETTA   In the morning, the job awaits us.
In the evening, the coming home in a group . . .
Shops that turn bright
with lights and lures,
carriages criss-crossing,
rowdy Sundays . . .
Little excursions, in couples,
to the Bois de Boulogne!
Dances in the open,
amorous liberties . . .

It's hard to say what it is,
this anxiety, this odd homesickness.

LUIGI, GIORGETTA (*with elation*)
But whoever leaves the neighborhood
wants to go back,
and whoever goes back, whoever goes back
cannot tear himself away.
There in the distance is Paris, that cries to us
with a thousand happy voices
its immortal spell!

*The two lovers remain for a moment, lost in thought, hands
clasped, as if the same thought and the same spirit carried
them away. Then, in a moment, they regain the awareness
that the others are looking at them; and they part.*

LA FRUGOLA   Adesso ti capisco:
             qui la vita è diversa . . .

IL TALPA (*che s'è poco interessato dello sfogo di Giorgetta*)

             Se s'andasse a mangiare?
             (*a Luigi*)
             Che ne dici?

LUIGI   Io resto: ho da parlare col padrone.

IL TALPA   Quando è così, a domani.

GIORGETTA   Miei vecchi, buona notte!

    *Il Talpa e la Frugola s'incamminano a braccetto, canterel-
lando. Le loro voci si perdono.*

LA FRUGOLA, IL TALPA
             Ho sognato una casetta,
             con un piccolo orticello.
             Quattro muri, stretta stretta,
             e due pini per ombrello.
             Il mio vecchio steso al sole,
             ai miei piedi *Caporale*,
             e aspettar così la morte
             che è rimedio d'ogni male!

VOCE DI SOPRANO (*interno*)
             Ah! Ah! Ah!

VOCE DI TENORINO (*interno lontano*)
             La la la la la . . .

    *Suono prolungato di sirena di rimorchiatore lontanissimo.
Luigi s'avvicina a Giorgetta che con un gesto lo ferma.*

GIORGETTA (*con ardore, ma sommesso*)
             O Luigi! Luigi!
             Bada a te! Può salir fra un momento!
             Resta pur là, lontano!

LUIGI   Perchè dunque inasprisci il tormento?
             Perchè mi chiami invano?

GIORGETTA   Vibro tutta se penso a ier sera,
             all'ardor dei tuoi baci! . .

LUIGI   In quei baci tu sai cosa c'era . . .

GIORGETTA   Sì, mio amore, mio amore.
             Ma taci!

LUIGI   Quale folle paura ti prende?

GIORGETTA   Se ci scopre, è la morte!

LUIGI (*scattando*)
             Preferisco morire, alla sorte
             che ti tiene legata!

GIORGETTA   Ah! se fossimo soli, lontani . . .

LUIGI   E sempre uniti! . .

GIORGETTA   E sempre innamorati! . .
             Dimmi . . . che non mi manchi! . .

LUIGI (*facendo per correre a lei*)
             Mai! . .

LA FRUGOLA   Now I understand you:
              here life is different . . .

IL TALPA   *(who hasn't been very interested in Giorgetta's*
              unburdening herself)
              What if we went to eat?
              (to Luigi)
              What do you say?

LUIGI   I'm staying: I have to talk with the boss.

IL TALPA   In that case: till tomorrow.

GIORGETTA   My old friends, good night!

Talpa and Frugola go off, arm in arm, singing softly. Their
voices die away.

LA FRUGOLA, IL TALPA
              I've dreamed of a little house
              with a little garden.
              Four walls, very narrow,
              and two pines as umbrella.
              My old man lying in the sun,
              Corporal at my feet,
              and waiting, like that, for death,
              which is the cure for every ailment!

SOPRANO'S VOICE *(offstage)*
              Ah! Ah! Ah!

LIGHT TENOR'S VOICE *(offstage, distant)*
              La la la la la . . .

Prolonged sound of a very distant tugboat's siren. Luigi ap-
proaches Giorgetta, who stops him with a gesture.

GIORGETTA   *(ardent, but softly)*
              O Luigi! Luigi!
              Be careful! He can come up in a moment!
              Stay there, at a distance!

LUIGI   Why make the torment worse then?
              Why do you call me in vain?

GIORGETTA   I throb all over if I think of last night,
              of the passion of your kisses! . . .

LUIGI   You know what there was in those kisses . . .

GIORGETTA   Yes, my love, my love.
              But hush!

LUIGI   What mad fear is gripping you?

GIORGETTA   If he discovers us, it's death!

LUIGI   *(sharply)*
              I prefer to die, to the fate
              that keeps you bound!

GIORGETTA   Ah! if we were alone, far away . . .

LUIGI   And always together! . . .

GIORGETTA   And always in love! . .
              Tell me . . . that you won't fail me! . . .

LUIGI   *(about to run to her)*
              Never! . . .

GIORGETTA (*paurosa*)
                    Sta' attento!
Apparisce Michele dalla stiva.
MICHELE (*a Luigi*)
                    Come? Non sei andato?
LUIGI   Padrone, v'ho aspettato,
                    perchè volevo dirvi
                    quattro parole sole:
                    intanto ringraziarvi
                    d'avermi tenuto . . .
                    Poi volevo pregarvi,
                    se lo potete fare,
                    di portarmi a Rouen
                    e là farmi sbarcare . . .
MICHELE   A Rouen? Ma sei matto?
                    Là non c'è che miseria:
                    ti troveresti peggio.
LUIGI   Sta bene. Allora resto.

Michele sensa rispondere si avvia verso la cabina.
GIORGETTA (*a Michele*)
                    Dove vai?
MICHELE   A preparare i lumi.
LUIGI   Buona notte, padrone . . .
MICHELE   Buona notte.

Michele entra nella cabina. Luigi è quasi presso la passerella. Giorgetta lo raggiunge lestamente. Il dialogo che segue è rapido, concitato, sommesso, ma pieno di intensità amorosa.
GIORGETTA   Dimmi: perchè gli hai chiesto
                    di sbarcarti a Rouen?
LUIGI   Perchè non posso
                    dividerti con lui! . .
GIORGETTA   Hai ragione: è un tormento.
                    Anch'io ne son presa,
                    anch'io la sento
                    ben più forte di te questa catena!
                    Hai ragione: è un tormento,
                    è un'angoscia, una pena;
                    ma quando tu mi prendi,
                    è pur grande, è pur grande il compenso!
LUIGI   Par di rubar insieme
                    qualche cosa alla vita!
GIORGETTA   La voluttà è più intensa!
LUIGI   È la gioia rapita
                    fra spasimi e paure . . .
GIORGETTA   In una stretta ansiosa . . .
LUIGI   Fra grida soffocate . . .
                    E baci senza fine . . .
GIORGETTA   E parole sommesse . . .
LUIGI   E baci senza fine!

GIORGETTA (*afraid*)
  Be careful!

Michele appears from the hold.

MICHELE (*to Luigi*)
  What? You haven't gone?

LUIGI
  Boss, I've waited for you,
  because I wanted to say to you
  only a few words:
  first of all to thank you
  for having kept me on . . .
  Then I wanted to ask you,
  if you can do it,
  to take me to Rouen
  and there let me go ashore . . .

MICHELE
  To Rouen? Why, are you mad?
  There's nothing but poverty there:
  you'd be worse off.

LUIGI
  All right. Then I'll stay on.

Michele, without answering, goes towards the cabin.

GIORGETTA (*to Michele*)
  Where are you going?

MICHELE
  To prepare the lanterns.

LUIGI
  Good night, boss . . .

MICHELE
  Good night.

Michele goes into the cabin. Luigi is almost at the gang-plank. Giorgetta quickly joins him. The following dialogue is rapid, urgent, in a low voice, but full of amorous intensity.

GIORGETTA
  Tell me: why did you ask him
  to put you ashore at Rouen?

LUIGI
  Because I can't
  share you with him! . . .

GIORGETTA
  You're right: it's a torment.
  I'm overcome by it, too;
  I, too, feel,
  stronger than you do, this chain!
  You're right: it's a torment,
  it's an anguish, a suffering;
  but when you take me,
  the reward is yet great, yet great!

LUIGI
  It's like stealing together
  something from life!

GIORGETTA
  The pleasure is more intense!

LUIGI
  It is joy stolen
  amid sufferings and fears . . .

GIORGETTA
  In an anxious embrace . . .

LUIGI
  Amid stifled cries . . .
  And kisses without end . . .

GIORGETTA
  And soft words . . .

LUIGI
  And kisses without end!

GIORGETTA   Giuramenti e promesse . . .

LUIGI   D'esser soli noi . . .

GIORGETTA   Noi soli, via, via, lontani!

LUIGI   Noi tutti soli, lontani dal mondo! . . .
             (*poi sussultando come se avesse
                 sentito dei passi*)
             È lui?

GIORGETTA (*rassicurandolo*)
             No, non ancora.
             Dimmi che tornerai più tardi . . .

LUIGI   Sì, fra un'ora . . .

GIORGETTA   Ascolta: come ieri
             lascerò la passerella.
             Sono io che la tolgo . . .
             Hai le scarpe di corda?

LUIGI   Sì . . . Fai lo stesso segnale?

GIORGETTA   Sì . . . il fiammifero acceso!
             Come tremava sul braccio mio teso
             la piccola fiammella!
             Mi pareva d'accendere una stella,
             fiamma del nostro amore,
             stella senza tramonto! . .

LUIGI   Io voglio la tua bocca,
             voglio le tue carezze!

GIORGETTA   Dunque anche tu lo senti
             il folle desiderio! . .

LUIGI (*con grande intensità*)
             Folle di gelosia!
             Vorrei tenerti stretta
             come una cosa mia!
             Vorrei non più soffrir,
             non più soffrir che un altro ti toccasse,
             e, sottrarre a tutti
             il corpo tuo divino,
             io te lo giuro, lo giuro,
             non tremo a vibrare il coltello,
             e con gocce di sangue
             fabbricarti un gioiello!

   Giorgetta cerca frenare Luigi e impaurita lo allontana guardando verso la cabina. Luigi fugge rapidamente spinta da Giorgetta.

GIORGETTA (*si passa penosamente una mano sulla fronte*)
             Come è difficile esser felici!

   Ora l'oscurità è completa. Michele, recando i fanali accesi, viene dalla cabina.

MICHELE   Perchè non vai a letto?

GIORGETTA   E tu?

MICHELE   No, non ancora . . .

   Un silenzio. Michele ha collocato i fanali sul barcone.

GIORGETTA   Penso che hai fatto bene a trattenerlo.

GIORGETTA   Vows and promises . . .

LUIGI   To be us, alone . . .

GIORGETTA   Us alone, away, away, far!

LUIGI   Us all alone, far from the world! . .
             (*then starting, as if he had
             heard footsteps*)
             Is that him?

GIORGETTA (*reassuring him*)
             No, not yet.
             Tell me you'll come back later . . .

LUIGI   Yes, in an hour . . .

GIORGETTA   Listen: like yesterday
             I'll leave the gangplank down.
             I'm the one who removes it . . .
             Do you have on rope-soled shoes?

LUIGI   Yes . . . You'll make the same signal?

GIORGETTA   Yes . . . the lighted match!
             How it trembled, on my outstretched arm,
             the little flame!
             It seemed I was lighting a star,
             flame of our love,
             star that never sets! . . .

LUIGI   I want your mouth,
             I want your caresses!

GIORGETTA   Then you also feel
             the mad desire! . . .

LUIGI (*with great intensity*)
             Mad with jealousy!
             I would like to hold you close,
             like something that is mine!
             I would like to suffer no more,
             suffer no more that another touch you,
             and, take away from everyone
             your divine body,
             I swear it to you, I swear it;
             I do not tremble at wielding the knife,
             and with drops of blood
             creating a jewel for you!

*Giorgetta tries to restrain Luigi, and, frightened, she sends
him away, looking towards the cabin. Luigi flees rapidly,
pushed by Giorgetta.*

GIORGETTA (*painfully running her hand over her brow*)
             How hard it is to be happy!

*Now the darkness is complete. Michele, carrying the
lighted lamps, comes from the cabin.*

MICHELE   Why don't you go to bed?

GIORGETTA   And you?

MICHELE   No, not yet . . .

A silence. Michele has set the lamps down on the barge.

GIORGETTA   I think you were right to keep him.

MICHELE   Chi mai?

GIORGETTA   Luigi.

MICHELE   Forse ho fatto male.
            Basteranno due uomini:
            non c'è molto lavoro.

GIORGETTA   Il Tinca lo potresti licenziare . . .
            beve sempre . . .

MICHELE   S'ubriaca
            per calmare i suoi dolori.
            Ha per moglie una bagascia!
            Beve per non ucciderla . . .

Giorgetta non risponde. Ma appare turbata e nervosa.

MICHELE   Che hai?

GIORGETTA   Son tutte queste storie . . .
            che a me non interessano . . .

MICHELE   (*improvvisamente avvicinandosi a lei con angoscia e
                con commozione*)
            Perchè, perchè non m'ami più? Perchè?

GIORGETTA   (*con freddezza*)
            Ti sbagli; t'amo . . .
            Tu sei buono e onesto . . .
                (*come per troncare il discorso*)
            Ora andiamo a dormire . . .

MICHELE   (*fissandola*)
            Tu non dormi! . .

GIORGETTA   Lo sai perchè non dormo . . .
            E poi . . . là dentro soffoco . . .
            Non posso! . . non posso!

MICHELE   Ora le notti son tanto fresche . . .
            E l'anno scorso là in quel nero guscio
            eravamo pur tre . . . c'era il lettuccio

            del nostro bimbo . . .

GIORGETTA   (*sconvolta*)
            Il nostro bimbo! Taci, taci!

MICHELE   (*insistendo, commosso*)
            Tu sporgevi la mano e lo cullavi
            dolcemente,
            lentamente,
            e poi sul braccio mio t'addormentavi . . .

GIORGETTA   (*con affanno*)
            Ti supplico, Michele:
            non dir niente.

MICHELE   Erano sere come queste . . .
            Si spirava la brezza,
            vi raccoglievo insieme nel tabarro
            come in una carezza . . .
            Sento sulle mie spalle
            le vostre teste bionde . . .
            Sento le vostre bocche
            vicino alla mia bocca . . .
            Ero tanto felice, ah! tanto felice!

MICHELE   Who do you mean?

GIORGETTA   Luigi.

MICHELE   Maybe I was wrong.
Two men will be enough:
there isn't much work.

GIORGETTA   You could fire Tinca . . .
he's always drinking . . .

MICHELE   He gets drunk
to allay his pains.
He has a tramp for a wife!
He drinks so as not to kill her . . .

Giorgetta doesn't answer. But she seems upset and nervous.

MICHELE   What's the matter?

GIORGETTA   It's all these stories . . .
that don't interest me . . .

MICHELE   (*suddenly, going over to her, with anguish and
            emotion*)
Why, why don't you love me any more? Why?

GIORGETTA   (*coldly*)
You're wrong; I love you . . .
You are good and honest . . .
            (*as if to cut short the subject*)
Now let's go and sleep . . .

MICHELE   (*looking hard at her*)
You don't sleep! . . .

GIORGETTA   You know why I don't sleep . . .
And besides . . . I stifle in there . . .
I can't! . . . I can't!

MICHELE   Now the nights are so cool . . .
And last year, there in that black shell
there were even three of us . . . there was the
crib
of our baby . . .

GIORGETTA   (*distraught*)
Our baby! Hush, hush!

MICHELE   (*insisting, moved*)
You stretched out your hand and rocked him
gently,
slowly,
and then on my arm you fell asleep . . .

GIORGETTA   (*with suffering*)
I beseech you, Michele:
don't say anything.

MICHELE   They were evenings like these . . .
The breeze wafted,
I gathered you both into my cloak
as in a caress . . .
I feel on my shoulders
your blond heads . . .
I feel your mouths
next to my mouth . . .
I was so happy, ah! so happy!

                         Ora che non c'è più
                         [i miei capelli grigi
                         mi sembrano un insulto
                         alla tua gioventù!
GIORGETTA   Ah! ti supplico, Michele,
                         non dir niente! Ah no!]
MICHELE   Ah! mi sembrano un insulto
                         alla tua gioventù!
GIORGETTA   No ... calmati, Michele ... sono stanca ...
                         Non reggo ... Vieni ...
MICHELE *(aspro)*
                         Ma non puoi dormire!
                         Sai bene che non devi addormentarti!
GIORGETTA *(atterrita)*
                         Perchè mi dici questo?
MICHELE   Non so bene ...
                         Ma so che è molto tempo che non dormi!
                             *(cerca di attirare Giorgetta
                             vicino a sè)*
                         Resta vicino a me! .. Non ti ricordi
                         altre notti, altri cieli ed altre lune?
                         Perchè chiudi il tuo cuore?
                         Ti rammenti le ore
                         che volavan via su questa barca
                         trascinate dall'onda? ...
GIORGETTA   Non ricordare ...
                         Oggi è maliconia ...
MICHELE   Ah! Ritorna, ritorna come allora,
                         ritorna ancora mia!
                         quando tu m'amavi
                         e ardentemente mi cercavi
                         e mi baciavi ...
                         quando tu m'amavi!
                         Resta vicino a me!
                         La notte è bella!
GIORGETTA *(conciliante)*
                         Che vuoi! S'invecchia!
                         Non son più la stessa.
                         Tu pure sei cambiato ...
                         Diffidi ... Ma che credi?

Da una chiesa lontana giungono i rintocchi delle ore.

MICHELE   Non lo so nemmen io!
GIORGETTA *(per tagliar corto)*
                         Buona notte, Michele ... Casco dal sonno ...
MICHELE   E allora va pure; ti raggiungo ...

*Michele cerca di baciarla, ma Giorgetta si schermisce e
s'avvia. Michele, guardandola allontanarsi, mormora cupamente:*

MICHELE   Sgualdrina!

*Michele dispone i fanali rosso, verde e bianco, ai posti fis-
sati sul barcone. Sulla strada due ombre d'amanti passano.*

> Now that he is no more,
> my gray hair
> seems to me an insult
> to your youthfulness!

GIORGETTA   Ah! I beseech you, Michele,
> don't say anything! Ah, no!

MICHELE   Ah! it seems to me an insult
> to your youthfulness!

GIORGETTA   No . . . calm down, Michele . . . I'm tired . . .
> I can't bear it . . . Come . . .

MICHELE *(harsh)*
> But you can't sleep!
> You know well that you must not sleep!

GIORGETTA   *(terrified)*
> Why do you say this to me?

MICHELE   I don't really know . . .
> But I know that you haven't slept for a long
> time!
>   *(tries to draw Giorgetta towards himself)*
> Stay near me! . . . Don't you remember
> other nights, other skies and other moons?
> Why do you close your heart?
> You remember the hours
> that flew away on this boat,
> drawn away by the wave? . . .

GIORGETTA   Don't remember . . .
> Today it's sadness . . .

MICHELE   Ah! Come back, come back as you were then,
> come back and be mine again!
> when you loved me
> and ardently sought me
> and kissed me . . .
> when you loved me!
> Stay near me!
> The night is beautiful!

GIORGETTA *(conciliatory)*
> What do you expect? We grow old!
> I'm no longer the same.
> You too have changed . . .
> You suspect . . . But what do you think?

The tolling of the hour arrives from a distant church.

MICHELE   I myself don't know!

GIORGETTA *(to cut it short)*
> Good night, Michele . . . I'm dropping with
> sleep . . .

MICHELE   Then go along; I'll join you . . .

Michele tries to kiss her, but Giorgetta parries and goes off. Michele, watching her move away, murmurs grimly:

MICHELE   Slut!

Michele arranges the red, green, and white lanterns at the set places on the barge. The shadows of two lovers pass on the street.

TENORE   Bocca di rosa fresca . . .

SOPRANO   E baci di rugiada . . .

TENORE   Labbra profumate . . .

SOPRANO   O profumata sera . . .
              C'è la luna . . .

TENORE   La luna che ci spia . . .

SOPRANO   A domani, mio amore . . .

TENORE   Domani, amante mia! . . .

SOPRANO   A domani, mio amore . . .

TENORE   Domani, amante mia!

Una cornetta lontana suona il silenzio da una caserma.
Michele lentamente, cautamente, si avvicina alla cabina.
Tende l'orecchio.

MICHELE   Nulla! Silenzio!
                    (*strisciando verso la parete e*
                    spiando nell'interno)
              È là! . . Non s'è spogliata . . .
              non dorme . . . Aspetta . . .
                    (*con un brivido*)
              Chi? . . . Che cosa aspetta?
                    (*risalendo, cupo, tutto chiuso nel*
                    suo dubbio)
              Chi? . . . chi? Forse il *mio* sonno ! . .
                    (*dal centro del barcone*)
              Chi l'ha trasformata?
              Qual ombra maledetta
              è discesa fra noi? Chi l'ha insidiata? . . .

                    (*e riandando col pensiero ai*
                    suoi uomini)
              Il Talpa? . . . Troppo vecchio! . .
              Il Tinca forse?
              No . . no . . . non pensa . . . beve. E dunque
              chi?
              Luigi . . . no . . . se proprio questa sera
              voleva abbandonarmi . . .
              e m'ha fatto preghiera
              di sbarcarlo a Rouen!
              Ma chi dunque? Chi dunque? Chi sarà?
              Squarciare le tenebre! . . Vedere!
              E serrarlo così, fra le mie mani!
              E gridargli: Sei tu! Sei tu!
              E gridargli: Sei tu! Sei tu! Il tuo volto
              livido sorrideva alla mia pena!
              Sei tu! Sei tu! Su! su! su!
              Dividi con me questa catena!
              Travolgimi con te nella tua sorte . . .
              giù insiem nel gorgo più profondo!
              Dividi con me questa catena! . .
              Accomuna la tua con la mia sorte . . .
              La pace è nella morte!

TENOR	Mouth like a fresh rose . . .
SOPRANO	And kisses like dew . . .
TENOR	Perfumed lips . . .
SOPRANO	O perfumed evening . . . There's the moon . . .
TENOR	The moon watching us . . .
SOPRANO	Till tomorrow, my love . . .
TENOR	Tomorrow, my lover! . .
SOPRANO	Till tomorrow, my love . . .
TENOR	Tomorrow, my lover!

A distant bugle sounds Taps from a barracks. Michele slowly, cautiously moves towards the cabin. He pricks up his ear.

MICHELE   Nothing! Silence!°
       (crawling towards the wall and peer-
       ing inside)
   She's there! . . She hasn't undressed . . .
   she's not sleeping . . . She's waiting . . .
       (with a shudder)
   Who? . . . What is she waiting for?
       (moving away, grim, all sealed in
       his suspicion)
   Who? . . . who? Perhaps *my* sleep! . .
       (from the center of the barge)
   Who has transformed her?
   What accursed shadow
   has fallen between us? Who has seduced
   her? . . .
       (and returning in his mind to
       his men)
   Talpa? . . . Too old! . .
   Tinca perhaps?
   No . . . no . . . he doesn't think . . . he drinks.
   Then who?
   Luigi . . . no . . . not if this very evening
   he wanted to leave me . . .
   and asked me
   to put him ashore at Rouen!
   But who then? Who then? Who can it be?
   To dispel the shadows! . . To see!
   And clutch him like this, in my hands!
   And shout at him: It's you! It's you!
   And shout at him: It's you! It's you! Your face,
   livid, smiled at my suffering!
   It's you! It's you! Come! come! come!
   Share with me this chain!
   Sweep me away with you, in your fate . . .
   down together into the deepest abyss!
   Share with me this chain!
   Unite your fate with mine . . .
   Peace is in death!

° See note on p. 303

*S'accascia sfibrato: la notte è buia. Macchinalmente leva di
tasca la pipa e l'accende. Dopo qualche momento, Luigi, che
stava in attesa del segnale sulla banchina, attraversa di corsa
la passerella e balza sul barcone. Michele vede l'ombra, sus-
sulta, si mette in agguato; riconosce Luigi e di colpo si precipita afferrandolo per la gola.*

MICHELE   T'ho colto!

LUIGI (*dibattendosi*)
              Sangue di Dio! Son preso!

MICHELE   Non gridare!
              Che venivi a cercare?
              Volevi la tua amante?

LUIGI   Non è vero!

MICHELE   Mentisci!
              Confessa, confessa!

LUIGI   Non è vero!

MICHELE   Volevi la tua amante?

LUIGI (*tirando fuori il coltello*)
              Ah! perdio!

MICHELE (*afferrando il braccio di Luigi e forzandolo a las-
              ciare il coltello*)
              Giù il coltello!
              Non mi sfuggi, canaglia!
              Anima di forzato! . . Verme!
              Volevi andare giù, a Rouen, non è vero?
              Morto ci andrai, nel fiume!

LUIGI   Assassino! Assassino!

MICHELE   Confessami che l'ami!
              confessa! confessa!

LUIGI   Lasciami, lasciami, lasciami!

MICHELE   No! Infame! infami!
              Se confessi, ti lascio!

LUIGI   Sì . . .

MICHELE   Ripeti! Ripeti!

LUIGI (*con voce fioca*)
              Sì . . . l'amo!

MICHELE   Ripeti! Ripeti!

LUIGI (*come un gemito*)
              L'amo!

MICHELE   Ripeti!

LUIGI (*più debole ancora*)
              L'amo!

MICHELE   Ancora!

LUIGI (*rantolando*)
              L'amo . . . Ah! . .
                            (*resta aggrappato a Michele in una
                            suprema contorsione di morte*)

He slumps down, exhausted: the night is dark. Automatically he takes his pipe from his pocket and lights it. After a few moments, Luigi, who was waiting on the quay for the signal, crosses the gangplank, running, and leaps onto the barge. Michele sees the shadow, starts, waits in ambush; he recognizes Luigi and abruptly rushes, grabbing him by the throat.

MICHELE   I've caught you!

LUIGI (*struggling*)
    God's blood! I'm caught!

MICHELE   Don't shout!
    What have you come looking for?
    You wanted your mistress?

LUIGI   That's not true!

MICHELE   You're lying!
    Confess, confess!

LUIGI   It's not true!

MICHELE   You wanted your mistress?

LUIGI (*pulling out his knife*)
    Ah, by God!

MICHELE (*seizing Luigi's arm and forcing him to let go of the knife*)
    Drop the knife!
    You won't escape me, bastard!
    Gallows-bird! . . . Worm!
    You wanted to go down to Rouen, did you?
    You'll go there dead, in the river!

LUIGI   Murderer! Murderer!

MICHELE   Confess to me that you love her!
    Confess! confess!

LUIGI   Let go of me, let go, let go!

MICHELE   No! Villain! villains!
    If you confess, I'll let go of you!

LUIGI   Yes . . .

MICHELE   Repeat it! repeat it!

LUIGI (*in a faint voice*)
    Yes . . . I love her!

MICHELE   Repeat it! Repeat it!

LUIGI (*like a groan*)
    I love her!

MICHELE   Repeat it!

LUIGI (*weaker still*)
    I love her!

MICHELE   Again!

LUIGI (*with the death-rattle*)
    I love her . . . Ah! . .
     (*remains clinging to Michele in an
     extreme contortion of death*)

GIORGETTA (*dalla cabina*)
            Michele?

Un silenzio. Michele, sentendo la voce di Giorgetta, rapidamente ravvolge nel tabarro il cadavere di Luigi aggrappato a lui, e si siede. Giorgetta appare sulla porta, indagando con lo sguardo smarrito.

GIORGETTA (*a mezza voce*)
            Ho paura, Michele . . .

Giorgetta s'avvicina lentamente a Michele, guardando intorno con ansia.

MICHELE (*calmissimo*)
            Avevo ben ragione: non dovevi dormire . . .
GIORGETTA   Son presa dal rimorso
            d'averti dato pena . . .
MICHELE   Non è nulla . . . i tuoi nervi . . .
GIORGETTA   Ecco . . . è questo . . . hai ragione . . .
            Dimmi che mi perdoni.
                (*insinuante*)
            Non mi vuoi più vicina? . . .
MICHELE (*terribile*)
            Dove? . . . Nel mio tabarro?
GIORGETTA   Sì, vicina, vicina . . .
            Sì . . . Mi dicevi un tempo:
            "Tutti quanti portiamo
            un tabarro che asconde
            qualche volta una gioia,
            qualche volta un dolore . . ."
MICHELE (*selvaggiamente*)
            Qualche volta un delitto!
            Vieni nel mio tabarro! . .
            Vieni!
            [Vien!
GIORGETTA   Ah!]

Michele si erge terribile, apre il tabarro; il cadavere di Luigi rotola ai piedi di Giorgetta che lancia un grido terribile e indietreggia con orrore. Ma Michele le è sopra, l'afferra, e la trascina, e la piega violentemente contro il volto dell'amante morto.

MICHELE   Scorri, fiume eterno!
            Come il tuo mistero è fondo!
            L'ansia che mi strugge non ha fine!
            L'ansia che mi strugge non ha fine!
            Passa, fiume eterno, passa!
            E me pure travolgi!
            Quante sono state le rovine
            che calmò la tua onda?
            Tu della miseria
            hai segnata la fine!
            E sempre calmo passi
            e non ti ferma nè paura
            nè tormento, nè volgere d'anni!
            Continui la tua corsa,

GIORGETTA *(from the cabin)*
> Michele?

A silence. Michele, hearing Giorgetta's voice, rapidly wraps in the cloak Luigi's corpse, clinging to him; and he sits down. Giorgetta appears at the door, her bewildered gaze searching.

GIORGETTA *(in a low voice)*
> I'm afraid, Michele . . .

Giorgetta slowly comes to Michele, looking around anxiously.

MICHELE *(very calm)*
> I was quite right: you were not to sleep . . .

GIORGETTA
> I'm seized with remorse
> at having caused you suffering . . .

MICHELE
> It's nothing . . . your nerves . . .

GIORGETTA
> There . . . it's that . . . you're right . . .
> Tell me you forgive me.
> > *(seductive)*
>
> Don't you want me near you any more? . . .

MICHELE *(terrifying)*
> Where? . . . In my cloak?

GIORGETTA
> Yes, near, near . . .
> Yes . . . You used to say to me once:
> "All of us wear
> a cloak that hides
> sometimes a joy,
> sometimes a sorrow . . ."

MICHELE *(savagely)*
> Sometimes a crime!
> Come into my cloak!
> Come!
> Come!

GIORGETTA
> Ah!

Michele stands up, awful, opens the cloak; Luigi's corpse rolls out at the feet of Giorgetta, who emits a terrible cry and steps back, with horror. But Michele is upon her, grabs her, and drags her, and bends her violently against the face of her dead lover.

MICHELE
> Flow, eternal river!
> As your mystery is deep,
> so the anguish destroying me is endless!
> The anguish destroying me is endless!
> Pass by, eternal river, pass by!
> And sweep me away too!
> How many ruins have there been
> that your wave calmed?
> You have marked
> the end of wretchedness!
> And you pass by, always calm,
> and neither fear stops you
> nor torment, nor the passing of years!
> You continue your way,

continui il tuo lamento!
Passa, passa, fiume eterno!
Sono i lamenti, forse, dei tuoi morti,
che portasti l'un dopo l'altro
verso il gran destino,
sulle tue braccia lugubri e forti?
Sono i dolori che tu soffocasti
chiudendo l'urlo estremo in un gorgoglio?
Sono forse i lamenti dei tuoi morti?
Acqua misteriosa e cupa,
passa sul mio triste cuore!
Lava via la pena e il mio dolore,
fa pur tua la mia sorte!
E se non puoi la pace,
allor dammi la morte!
dammi la morte!

you continue your lament!
Pass by, pass by, eternal river!
Are they perhaps the laments of your dead,
whom you carried, one after the other,
towards the great destiny,
in your arms, lugubrious and strong?
Are they the sorrows you stifled,
shutting off the final cry in a gurgle?
Are they perhaps the laments of your dead?
Mysterious and grim water,
pass over my sad heart!
Wash away the suffering and my grief,
make my fate yours also!
And if you cannot give me peace,
then give me death!
Give me death!

Translator's note: This aria for Michele appears in the original version of *Il tabarro*; Puccini then replaced it with the more dramatic solioquy "Nulla Silenzio!" (page 297). The original, more formal aria has been recorded on several occasions.

Suor Angelica (Sister Angelica)

THE PLOT

In a little convent, daily life seems to flow peacefully: the nuns pray, do penance, perform their simple tasks, even dream briefly of unfulfilled, innocent desires. Only Sister Angelica seems profoundly restless: for seven years, ever since she has been here, she has had no news of the outside world. But then a visitor arrives, and Sister Angelica is summoned to the parlatory. The visitor is her aunt, a stern, austere aristocrat, who has come chiefly to settle a matter of inheritance. Almost marginally, she informs Angelica that her child—the child of sin and the reason why the family put Angelica in the convent—has died. The Princess leaves, and Angelica—half-crazed with grief—prepares a poisonous drink from some herbs and drinks it. Realizing her crime, she begs the Madonna to save her; and as the other sisters look on, the miracle occurs: the Madonna appears with Angelica's child, who will lead her to Paradise.

SUOR ANGELICA

libretto by Giovacchino Forzano

First performed at the Metropolitan Opera House, New York

December 14, 1918

CHARACTERS

Sister Angelica	*Soprano*
The Princess-Aunt	*Contralto*
The Abbess	*Mezzosoprano*
The Sister Zelatrice	*Mezzosoprano*
The Novice Mistress	*Mezzosoprano*
Sister Genovieffa	*Soprano*
Sister Osmina	*Soprano*
Sister Dolcina	*Soprano*
The Sister Infirmaress	*Mezzosoprano*
The Alms-Collectors	*Sopranos*
The Novices	*Sopranos*
The Lay Sisters	*Soprano and Mezzosoprano*

The time is towards the end of the 17th century.
The place is a convent in Italy.

L'interno di un monastero. La chiesetta e il chiostro. Nel fondo, oltre gli archi di destra, il cimitero; oltre gli archi di sinistra, l'orto. Nel mezzo della scena, cipressi, una croce, erbe e fiori. Nel fondo a sinistra, fra le piante di acòro, una fonte, il cui getto ricadrà in una pila in terra.

LA PREGHIERA

Si apre il velario.
Tramonto di primavera. Un raggio di sole batte al di sopra del getto della fonte. La scena è vuota. Le suore sono in chiesa e cantano.

SUORE (*coro interno*)
   Ave, Maria, piena di grazia,
   il Signore è teco,
   Tu sei benedetta fra le donne,
   benedetta il frutto del ventre tuo, Gesù.

Due Converse, in ritardo per la preghiera, traversano la scena; si soffermano un istante ad ascoltare un cinguettìo che scende dai cipressi, quindi entrano in chiesa.
Suor Angelica, anch'essa in ritardo, esce da destra, si avvia in chiesa, apre la porta, fa l'atto di contrizione delle ritardatarie che le due converse non hanno fatto; si inginocchia e bacia in terra, quindi richiude la porta.

SUORE (*coro interno*)
   Santa Maria, Santa Maria,
   prega per noi peccatori . . .
SUOR ANGELICA (*di dentro*)
   Prega per noi peccatori,
   ora e nell'ora della nostra morte.
SUORE (*coro interno*)
   Prega per noi peccatori,
   ora e nell'ora della nostra morte.
   E così sia.

La preghiera termina. Le monache escono dalla chiesa a due per due. La Badessa si sofferma davanti alla croce. Le suore, passandole innanzi, le fanno atto di reverenza. La Badessa fa il gesto della benedizione e, quando tutte le suore le son passate davanti, si ritira. Le suore non si sciolgono ancora, restano unite formando una specie di semicerchio a piccoli gruppi. La Sorella Zelatrice viene nel mezzo.

LE PUNIZIONI

LA SORELLA ZELATRICE (*alle due converse*)
   Sorelle in umiltà,
   mancaste alla quindéna,
   ed anche Suor Angelica,
   che però fece contrizione piena.
   Invece voi, sorelle,
   peccaste in distrazione,
   e avete perso un giorno di quindéna!

The interior of a convent. The chapel and the cloister. In the rear, beyond the arches on the right: the cemetery; beyond the arches on the left, the vegetable garden. In the middle of the stage: cypresses, a cross, herbs, and flowers. In the rear, at left, among the irises, a fountain, whose jet of water falls into a basin on the ground.

THE PRAYER

The curtains part.

Spring sunset. A ray of sunlight strikes the jet of the fountain. The stage is empty. The nuns are in chapel and are singing.

NUNS (*offstage chorus*)

> Ave, Maria, full of grace,
> the Lord is with thee.
> Blessed art thou among women,
> blessed is the fruit of thy womb, Jesus.

Two lay sisters, late for prayer, cross the stage; they pause for an instant to listen to a chirping that comes down from the cypresses, then they enter the church.

Sister Angelica, also late, comes in at right, heads for the church, opens the door, makes the act of contrition of latecomers that the two lay sisters did not make: she kneels and kisses the ground, then closes the door again.

NUNS (*offstage chorus*)

> Holy Mary, Holy Mary,
> pray for us sinners . . .

SISTER ANGELICA (*inside*)

> Pray for us sinners,
> now and at the hour of our death.

NUNS (*offstage chorus*)

> Pray for us sinners,
> now and at the hour of our death.
> Amen.

The prayer ends. The nuns come from the church, two by two. The Abbess pauses in front of the cross. The sisters, passing before her, bow to her. The sisters do not yet break ranks; they remain together, forming a kind of semi-circle in little groups. Sister Zelatrice comes into the middle.

THE PENANCES

SISTER ZELATRICE (*to the two lay sisters*)

> Sisters in humility,
> you missed quindene,
> and Sister Angelica too,
> who, however, made full contrition.
> You, sisters, on the contrary,
> sinned in distraction,
> and you lost a day of quindene!

UNA CONVERSA M'accuso della colpa
　　　　　　　e invoco una gran pena,
　　　　　　　e più grave sarà
　　　　　　　e più grazie vi dirò,
　　　　　　　sorella in umiltà.
　　　　　　　(*resta in attesa della penitenza*)

LA MAESTRA DELLE NOVIZIE (*alle Novizie, come spiegando*)
　　　　　　　(Chi arriva tardi in coro,
　　　　　　　si prostri e baci terra.)

LA SORELLA ZELATRICE (*alle converse*)
　　　　　　　Farete venti volte
　　　　　　　la preghiera mentale
　　　　　　　per gli afflitti e gli schiavi
　　　　　　　e per quelli che stanno
　　　　　　　in peccato mortale.

UNA CONVERSA Con gioia e con fervore!

LE DUE CONVERSE
　　　　　　　Cristo Signore, Sposo d'amore,
　　　　　　　io voglio sol piacerti,
　　　　　　　ora e nell'ora della mia morte!
　　　　　　　Amen!

　　Si ritirano, compute, sotto gli archi.

LA SORELLA ZELATRICE (*a Suor Lucilla*)
　　　　　　　Suor Lucilla, il lavoro. Ritiratevi.
　　　　　　　E osservate il silenzio.

　　*Suor Lucilla si avvia sotto gli archi di destra, prende la rocca
che è sopra una panca e si mette a filare.*

LA MAESTRA DELLE NOVIZIE (*alle due Novizie, come prima*)
　　　　　　　(Perchè stasera in coro
　　　　　　　ha riso e fatto ridere.)

LA SORELLA ZELATRICE (*a Suor Osmina*)
　　　　　　　Voi, Suor Osmina, in chiesa
　　　　　　　tenevate nascoste nelle maniche
　　　　　　　due rose scarlattine.

SUOR OSMINA (*indocile*)
　　　　　　　Non è vero!

LA SORELLA ZELATRICE (*severa ma senza asprezza*)
　　　　　　　Sorella, entrate in cella.
　　　　　　　(*Suor Osmina scuote le spalle*)
　　　　　　　Non tardate! La Vergine vi guarda!

　　*Suor Osmina si avvia senza far parola. Le suore la seguono
con lo sguardo fino a che non è scomparsa nella sua cella.*

SEI SUORE　　　*Regina Virginum, ora pro ea . . .*

　　Suor Osmina chiude bruscamente la porta della sua cella.

　　　　　　　　　　　　　　　　　LA RICREAZIONE

LA SORELLA ZELATRICE
　　　　　　　Ed or, sorelle in gioia,
　　　　　　　poichè piace al Signore,
　　　　　　　e per tornare

A LAY SISTER I acknowledge my sin,
and I ask for a big penance,
and the harder it is,
the more I will thank you,
sister in humility.
(awaits the penance)

NOVICE MISTRESS *(to the Novices, as if explaining)*
(Anyone who arrives late at choir,
must prostrate herself and kiss the ground.)

SISTER ZELATRICE *(to the lay sisters)*
You will say twenty times
the mental prayer
for the afflicted and for slaves
and for those who are
in mortal sin.

A LAY SISTER With joy and with fervor!

THE TWO LAY SISTERS
Christ our Lord, Bridegroom of love,
I wish only to please Thee,
now and at the hour of my death!
Amen!

They withdraw, demurely, under the arches.

SISTER ZELATRICE *(to Sister Lucilla)*
Sister Lucilla, to work. Withdraw.
And observe silence.

Sister Lucilla goes off beneath the arches at right, takes the distaff that is on a bench, and starts spinning.

NOVICE MISTRESS *(to the two Novices, as before)*
(Because this evening in choir
she laughed and made others laugh.)

SISTER ZELATRICE *(to Sister Osmina)*
You, Sister Osmina, in chapel
kept hidden in your sleeves
two little scarlet roses.

SISTER OSMINA *(rebellious)*
That's not true!

SISTER ZELATRICE *(stern but without harshness)*
Sister, go into your cell.
(Sister Osmina shrugs)
Don't dawdle! The Virgin is watching you!

Sister Osmina goes off without a word. The sisters follow her with their gaze until she has disappeared into her cell.

SIX NUNS *Regina Virginum, ora pro ea . . .*

Sister Osmina slams the door of her cell hard.

RECREATION

SISTER ZELATRICE
And now, sisters in joy,
since it pleases the Lord,
and in order to return

più allegramente
a faticare
per amor Suo,
ricreatevi!

LE SUORE   Amen!

*Le figure bianche delle suore si sparpagliano per il chiostro e
oltre gli archi. Suor Angelica zappetta la terra e innaffia le
erbe e i fiori.*

SUOR GENOVIEFFA (*gaiamente*)
O sorelle, sorelle,
io voglio rivelarvi
che una spera di sole
è entrata in clausura!
Guardate dove batte,
là, là fra la verzura!
Il sole è sull'acòro!
Comincian le tre sere
della fontana d'oro!

ALCUNE SUORE È vero, fra un istante
vedrem l'acqua dorata!

UNA SUORA   È per due sere ancor!

ALCUNE SUORE È maggio! E maggio!
È il bel sorriso di Nostra Signora
che viene con quel raggio . . .
Regina di Clemenza, grazie!
Grazie!

UNA NOVIZIA (*alla Maestra, con fare timoroso*)
Maestra, vi domando
licenza di parlare.

LA MAESTRA DELLE NOVIZIE
Sempre per laudare
le cose sante e belle.

L'A NOVIZIA   Qual grazia della Vergine
rallegra le sorelle?

LA MAESTRA DELLE NOVIZIE
Un segno risplendente
della bontà di Dio!
Per tre sere dell'anno solamente,
all'uscire dal coro,
Dio ci concede di vedere il sole
che batte sulla fonte e la fa d'oro.

LA NOVIZIA   E l'altre sere?

LA MAESTRA DELLE NOVIZIE
O usciamo troppo presto
e il sole è alto,
o troppo tardi
e il sole è tramontato.

ALCUNE SUORE (*con un accento di grande malinconia*)
Un altr'anno è passato! . .

ALTRE SUORE   È passato un altr'anno!

ALCUNE SUORE E una sorella manca!

more gaily
to work
for love of Him,
enjoy yourselves!

NUNS   Amen!

The white figures of the nuns scatter through the cloister and beyond the arches. Sister Angelica hoes the ground and waters herbs and flowers.

SISTER GENOVIEFFA *(gaily)*
O sisters, sisters,
I want to reveal to you
a ray of sunshine
has entered the cloister!
Look where it is striking,
there, there in the greenery!
The sun is on the iris!
The three evenings are beginning
of the golden fountain!

SOME NUNS   It's true: in an instant
we'll see the water gilded!

A NUN   And for two more evenings!

SOME NUNS   It's May! It's May!
It is the lovely smile of Our Lady
that comes with that beam . . .
Queen of Mercy, we thank thee!
We thank thee!

A NOVICE *(to the Mistress, in a shy manner)*
Mistress, I ask of you
leave to speak.

NOVICE MISTRESS
Always to praise
things holy and beautiful.

THE NOVICE   What grace from the Virgin
gladdens the sisters?

NOVICE MISTRESS
A shining sign
of the goodness of God!
For three evenings only of the year,
on coming out of choir,
God allows us to see the sun
striking the fountain and turning it gold.

THE NOVICE   And the other evenings?

NOVICE MISTRESS
Either we come out too early
and the sun is high,
or too late
and the sun has set.

SOME NUNS *(with a tone of great melancholy)*
Another year has passed! . .

OTHER NUNS   Another year has passed!

SOME NUNS   And a sister is gone!

Un silenzio doloroso è nel chiostro; le suore assorte in un atteggiamento di muta preghiera sembrano rievocare l'immagine della sorella che non è più.

SUOR GENOVIEFFA (*improvvisamente, con accento ingenuo e quasi lieto*)

O sorelle in pio lavoro,
quando il getto s'è infiorato,
quando il getto s'è indorato,
non sarebbe ben portato
un secchiello d'acqua d'oro
sulla tomba a Bianca Rosa?

LE SUORE   Sì! La suora che riposa
lo desidera di certo!

SUOR ANGELICA

I desiderî sono i fiori dei vivi,
non fioriscon nel regno delle morte,
perchè la Madre Vergine soccorre,
e in Sua Benignità
liberamente al desiar precorre;
prima che un desiderio sia fiorito,
la Madre delle Madri l'ha esaudito.
O sorella, la morte è vita bella!

LA SORELLA ZELATRICE

Noi non possiamo
nemmen da vive avere desiderî.

SUOR GENOVIEFFA

Se son leggieri e candidi, perchè?
Voi non avete un desiderio?

LA SORELLA ZELATRICE

Io no!

Suor Angelica va verso i fiori a sinistra.

UN'ALTRA   Ed io nemmeno!

UNA NOVIZIA (*timorosa*)

Io no!

SUOR GENOVIEFFA

Io sì. Lo confesso.
(*volgendo lo sguardo in alto*)
Soave Signor Mio,
tu sai che prima d'ora
nel mondo ero pastora . . .
Da cinque anni non vedo un agnellino.
Signore, ti rincresco
se dico che desidero
vederne uno piccino,
poterlo carezzare,
toccargli il muso fresco
e sentirlo belare?
Se è colpa, t'offerisco
il *Miserere mei* . . .
Perdonami, Signore,
tu che sei l'agnus Dei.

SUOR DOLCINA (*grassotella e rubiconda*)

Ho un desiderio anch'io!

*A sorrowful silence is in the cloister; the nuns, pensive, in
an attitude of silent prayer, seem to summon up the image of
the sister who is no more.*

SISTER GENOVIEFFA (*suddenly, in an ingenuous and almost
                    merry tone*)

> O sisters in devout toil,
> when the jet is beflowered,
> when the jet is gilded,
> would it not be well to carry
> a bucket of golden water
> to the grave of Bianca Rosa?
> Yes! The sister who rests
> certainly wishes it!

SISTER ANGELICA

> Wishes are the flowers of the living,
> they do not bloom in the realm of death;
> because the Virgin Mother succors,
> and in her Goodness
> freely anticipates wishing;
> before a wish has blossomed,
> the Mother of Mothers has granted it.
> O sister, death is beautiful life!

SISTER ZELATRICE

> We cannot have wishes
> even when we are alive.

SISTER GENOVIEFFA

> If they are simple and innocent, why not?
> Don't you have a wish?

SISTER ZELATRICE

> Not I!

Sister Angelica goes towards the flowers at left.

ANOTHER   Nor I!

A NOVICE (*shyly*)
> Not I!

SISTER GENOVIEFFA

> I do. I confess it.
>   (*raising her gaze upwards*)
> My Sweet Lord,
> Thou knowest that before now,
> in the world, I was a shepherdess . . .
> For five years I haven't seen a lamb.
> Lord, do I displease Thee
> if I say I wish
> to see a little one,
> to be able to stroke it,
> touch his cool muzzle
> and hear him bleat?
> If it is a sin, I offer Thee
> the *Miserere mei* . . .
> Forgive me, Lord,
> Thou who art the Agnus Dei.

SISTER DOLCINA (*plump and ruddy*)

> I have a wish too!

ALCUNE SUORE Sorella, li sappiamo i vostri desideri!

ALTRE   Qualche boccone buono!

ALCUNE SUORE Della frutta gustosa!

ALTRE   La gola è colpa grave!

ALCUNE SUORE (È golosa!)

ALTRE *(alle Novizie)*
             (È golosa!)

Suor Dolcina resta mortificata e interdetta. Suor Genovieffa si è avvicinata in compagnia di alcune suore a Suor Angelica.

SUOR GENOVIEFFA
             Suor Angelica, e voi?
             Avete desideri?

SUOR ANGELICA *(volgendosi verso le suore)*
             Io? . . . no, sorella, no.

Si volge ancora ai fiori. Le suore fanno gruppo dalla parte opposta e mormorano.

LE SUORE   Che Gesu la perdoni.
             Ha detto una bugia.
             Ha detto una bugia.

UNA NOVIZIA *(avvicinandosi, curiosa)*
             Perchè?

LE SUORE   Noi lo sappiamo,
             ha un grande desiderio.
             Vorrebbe aver notizie
             della famiglia sua!
             Son più di sett'anni,
             da quando è in monastero,
             non ha avuto più nuove!
             E sembra rassegnata,
             ma è tanto tormentata!
                  *(allontanandosi sempre più da
                  Suor Angelica)*
             Nel mondo era ricchissima,
             lo disse la Badessa.
             Era nobile! Nobile! Nobile!
             Principessa!
             La vollero far monaca,
             sembra . . . per punizione.

ALTRE   Perchè? Perchè?

LE SUORE   Chi sa! Mah? Mah?

Si disperdono qua e là.

LA SORELLA INFERMIERA *(accorrendo frettolosa)*
             Suor Angelica, sentite!

SUOR ANGELICA
             O sorella infermiera,
             che cosa accadde, dite!

LA SORELLA INFERMIERA
             Suora Chiara, là nell'orto,
             assettava la spalliera
             delle rose; all'improvviso

SOME NUNS	Sister, we know your wishes!
OTHERS	Some nice morsel!
SOME NUNS	Some tasty fruit!
OTHERS	Greed is a serious sin!
SOME NUNS	(She's greedy!)
OTHERS (*to the Novices*)	
	(She's greedy!

*Sister Dolcina remains mortified and speechless. Sister Gen-
ovieffa, in the company of some nuns, has approached Sister
Angelica.*

SISTER GENOVIEFFA
　　　　　　Sister Angelica, and you?
　　　　　　Do you have wishes?

SISTER ANGELICA (*turning towards the nuns*)
　　　　　　I? . . . No, sister, no.

*She turns again to the flowers. The sisters form a group on
the opposite side and murmur.*

NUNS
　　　　　　May Jesus forgive her.
　　　　　　She told a lie.
　　　　　　She told a lie.

A NOVICE (*approaching, curious*)
　　　　　　Why?

NUNS
　　　　　　We know it:
　　　　　　she has a great wish.
　　　　　　She would like to have news
　　　　　　of her family!
　　　　　　It's more than seven years,
　　　　　　since she's been in the convent,
　　　　　　she's had no more news!
　　　　　　And she seems resigned,
　　　　　　but she is so tormented!
　　　　　　　　(*moving farther and farther away
　　　　　　　　from Sister Angelica*)
　　　　　　In the world she was very rich,
　　　　　　the Abbess said so.
　　　　　　She was noble! Noble! Noble!
　　　　　　A Princess!
　　　　　　They chose to make her a nun,
　　　　　　it seems . . . in punishment.

OTHERS
　　　　　　Why? Why?

NUNS
　　　　　　Who knows? Hm! Hm!

They scatter here and there.

SISTER INFIRMARESS (*running in hastily*)
　　　　　　Sister Angelica, listen!

SISTER ANGELICA
　　　　　　O sister infirmaress,
　　　　　　what's happened. Tell me!

SISTER INFIRMARESS
　　　　　　Sister Chiara, there, in the garden,
　　　　　　was adjusting the trellis
　　　　　　of the roses; suddenly

tante vespe sono uscite,
l'han pinzata qui nel viso!
Ora è in cella e si lamenta;
ah! calmatele, sorella,
il dolor che la tormenta!

ALCUNA SUORE Poveretta! Poveretta!

SUOR ANGELICA
Aspettate! ho un'erba e un fiore!
(*corre cercando fra i fiori e l'erbe*)

LA SORELLA INFERMIERA
Suor Angelica ha sempre
una ricetta buona, fatta coi fiori,
sa trovar sempre un'erba benedetta
per calmare i dolori!

SUOR ANGELICA (*alla Suora Infermiera porgendole alcune
erbe*)
Ecco, questa è calenzóla;
col latticcio che ne cola
bagnate l'enfiagione.
E con questa, una pozione.
Dite a Sorella Chiara
che sarà molto amara,
ma che le farà bene.
E le direte ancora
che punture di vespe
sono piccole pene,
e che non si lamenti,
chè lamentarsi crescono i tormenti.

LA SORELLA INFERMIERA
Le saprò riferire!
Grazie, sorella, grazie.

SUOR ANGELICA (*piegando la testa*)
Son qui per servire.

IL RITORNO DALLA CERCA

*Dal fondo a sinistra entrano due Suore Cercatrici condu-
cendo un ciuchino carico di roba.*

DUE SORELLE CERCATRICI (*entrando*)
Laudata Maria!

LE SUORE   E sempre sia!

*Le Suore si fanno intorno al ciuchino; le cercatrici scari-
cano e consegnano le limosine alla Sorella dispensiera.*

DUE SORELLE CERCATRICI
Buona cerca stasera,
Sorella Dispensiera.

UNA CERCATRICE
Un otre d'olio.

SUOR DOLCINA (*che non può stare*)
Uh! buono!

    many wasps came out,
    and stung her here on the face!
    Now she's in her cell and is moaning;
    ah! sister, relieve
    the pain that is tormenting her!

SOME NUNS   Poor thing! Poor thing!

SISTER ANGELICA
    Wait! I have an herb and a flower!
        (*runs, seeking among the flowers and
        herbs*)

SISTER INFIRMARESS
    Sister Angelica always has
    a good remedy, made with flowers;
    she can always find a blessed herb
    to relieve sufferings!

SISTER ANGELICA (*to the Sister Infirmaress, handing her some
      herbs*)
    Here, this is spurge;
    with the milk that drips from it
    bathe the swelling.
    And with this one, a potion.
    Tell Sister Chiara
    that it will be very bitter,
    but it will do her good.
    And tell her also
    that wasps' stings
    are small sufferings
    and that she mustn't moan,
    for moaning increases the torments.

SISTER INFIRMARESS
    I'll tell her!
    Thank you, sister, thank you.

SISTER ANGELICA (*bowing her head*)
    I am here to serve.

THE RETURN FROM ALMS-COLLECTING

    *From the rear at left enter two sisters, alms-collectors, lead-
ing a little donkey, laden with goods.*

TWO ALMS-COLLECTORS (*entering*)
    Mary be praised!

NUNS   And may she be so forever!

    *The nuns gather around the donkey; the alms-collectors un-
load and deliver the alms to the Sister Procuratrix.*

TWO ALMS-COLLECTORS
    Good collecting this evening,
    Sister Procuratrix.

ONE COLLECTOR
    A skin of oil.

SISTER DOLCINA (*unable to control herself*)
    Mm! Good!

L'ALTRA CERCATRICE
> Nocciòle, sei collane.

UNA CERCATRICE
> Un panierin di noci.

SUOR DOLCINA Buone con sale e pane!

LA SORELLA ZELATRICE (*riprendendola*)
> Sorella!

UNA CERCATRICE
> Qui farina!
> È qui una caciotella
> che suda ancora latte,
> buona come una pasta,
> e un sacchetto di lenti,
> dell'uova, burro e basta.

LE SUORE   Buona cerca stasera,
> Sorella Dispensiera.

L'ALTRA CERCATRICE (*a Suor Dolcina*)
> Per voi, sorella ghiotta . . .
> (*offre un tralcetto di ribes*)
> *La Seconda Cercatrice porta via il ciuchino.*

SUOR DOLCINA (*felice*)
> Un tralcetto di ribes!
> (*vedendo che le altre si scan-
> dalizzano*)
> Degnatene, sorelle!

ALCUNE SUORE Grazie! grazie!

UNA SUORA (*scherzosa*)
> Uh! Se ne prendo un chicco,
> la martorio!

SUOR DOLCINA (*insistendo nell'offrire*)
> No, prendete!

ALTRE SUORE Grazie! Grazie!

*Formano un gruppetto a destra e beccano il ribes, fra risa-
tine discrete.*

UNA CERCATRICE
> Chi è venuto stasera in parlatorio?

LE SUORE   Nessuno. Nessuno. Perchè?

UNA CERCATRICE
> Fuor del portone c'è
> fermata una ricca berlina.

SUOR ANGELICA (*volgendosi alla Sorella Cercatrice, come as-
> salita da un'improvvisa inquietudine*)
> Come, sorella? avete detto?
> Una berlina è fuori?
> Ricca? ricca? ricca?

UNA CERCATRICE
> Da gran signori.
> Certo aspetta qualcuno
> che è entrato nel convento
> e forse fra un momento
> suonerà la campana a parlatorio.

THE OTHER COLLECTOR
> Hazel nuts, six strands.

ONE COLLECTOR
> A little basket of walnuts.

SISTER DOLCINA
> Good with salt and bread!

SISTER ZELATRICE (*reproaching her*)
> Sister!

ONE COLLECTOR
> Flour here!
> And here a little sheep-cheese
> that's still sweating milk,
> good as a cake;
> and a little sack of lentils,
> some eggs, butter, and that's all.

NUNS
> Good collecting this evening,
> Sister Procuratrix.

THE OTHER COLLECTOR (*to Sister Dolcina*)
> For you, greedy sister . . .
> > (*offers her a little bunch of currants*)

The second collector takes away the donkey.

SISTER DOLCINA (*happy*)
> A little bunch of currants!
> > (*seeing that the others are shocked*)
> Help yourselves, please, sisters!

SOME NUNS   Thank you! Thank you!

A NUN (*joking*)
> Hmph! If I take one currant,
> I'm torturing her!

SISTER DOLCINA (*insisting on her offer*)
> No, help yourself!

OTHER NUNS   Thank you! Thank you!

They form a little group at right and pluck at the currants, amid discreet giggles.

A COLLECTOR   Who's come to the parlatory this evening?

NUNS   Nobody. Nobody. Why?

A COLLECTOR   Outside the gate there is
> a sumptuous carriage stopped.

SISTER ANGELICA (*turning to the alms-collector, as if seized by a sudden uneasiness*)
> What did you say, sister?
> A carriage is outside?
> Sumptuous? sumptuous? sumptuous?

A COLLECTOR
> Worthy of great lords.
> Certainly it is awaiting someone
> who has come into the convent
> and perhaps in a moment
> the parlatory bell will ring.

SUOR ANGELICA (*con ansia crescente*)
        Ah! diteme, sorella,
        com'era la berlina?
        Non aveva uno stemma?
        uno stemma d'avorio? . . .
        e dentro tappezzata
        d'una seta turchina
        ricamata in argento?

UNA CERCATRICE (*interdetta*)
        Io non so, sorella, non lo so:
        ho veduto soltanto
        una berlina . . . bella!

LE SUORE (*osservando curiosamente Suor Angelica*)
        È diventata bianca . . .
        Ora è tutta vermiglia!
        Poverina!
        È commossa! È commossa!
        Poverina!
        Spera che sian persone di famiglia!

    Una campanella rintocca; le suore accorrono da ogni parte.

LE SUORE   Vien gente in parlatorio!
        Una visita viene!
        Per chi? Per chi? Per chi?
        Per chi sarà?
        Fosse per me! per me!
        [Fosse mia madre che ci porta
        le tortorine bianche!

ALCUNE SUORE Fosse la mia cugina
        che porta il seme di lavanda buono.]

    *Suor Genovieffa si avvicina alle compagne e quasi inter-
    rompe queste esclamazioni indicando con un gesto pietoso
    Suor Angelica.*

SUOR ANGELICA (*con fervore, volgendo gli occhi al cielo*)
        (O Madre eletta, leggimi nel cuore.
        Volgi per me un sorriso al Salvatore.)

    *Il gruppo delle suore si avvicina in silenzio a Suor Ange-
    lica. Suor Genovieffa esce dal gruppo e si rivolge a Suor An-
    gelica con grande dolcezza.*

SUOR GENOVIEFFA
        O sorella in amore,
        noi preghiam la Stella delle Stelle
        che la visita adesso sia per voi.

SUOR ANGELICA (*commossa*)
        Buona sorella, grazie . . . grazie!

    *Da sinistra entra la Badessa per chiamare la suora che
    dovrà andare al parlatorio. L'attesa è viva. In quell'attimo di
    silenzio tutte le suore fanno il sacrificio del loro desiderio a
    pro della sorella in gran pena. Suor Angelica ha sempre gli
    occhi rivolti al cielo, immobile come se tutta la sua vita fosse
    sospesa.*

LA BADESSA (*chiamando*)
        Suor Angelica!

SISTER ANGELICA (*with mounting anxiety*)
Ah! tell me, sister,
what was the carriage like?
Didn't it have a coat-of-arms?
An ivory coat-of-arms? . . .
and upholstered inside
with pale blue silk,
embroidered in silver?

A COLLECTOR (*dumbfounded*)
I don't know, sister, I don't know:
I saw only
a carriage . . . beautiful!

NUNS (*curiously observing Sister Angelica*)
She's become white . . .
Now she's all crimson!
Poor thing!
She's moved! She's moved!
Poor thing!
She hopes they're people of her family!

A bell rings; the nuns run in from all sides.

NUNS
People are coming into the parlatory!
A visitor is coming!
For whom? For whom? For whom?
For whom will it be?
If it were for me! For me!
If it were my mother bringing us
the white turtle-doves!

SOME NUNS
If it were my girl-cousin
bringing the seed of good lavender.

Sister Genovieffa approaches her fellow-nuns and almost interrupts these exclamations, pointing out, with a pitying gesture, Sister Angelica.

SISTER ANGELICA (*with fervor, raising her eyes to heaven*)
(O elect Mother, read into my heart.
Turn a smile to the Savior for me.)

The group of nuns silently approaches Sister Angelica. Sister Genovieffa steps out of the group and speaks to Sister Angelica with great sweetness.

SISTER GENOVIEFFA
O sister in love,
we pray the Star of Stars
that the visit now may be for you.

SISTER ANGELICA (*moved*)
Good sister, thank you . . . thank you!

From the left the Abbess enters to call the nun who is to go into the parlatory. The waiting is tense. In that moment of silence all the nuns make the sacrifice of their wish in favor of the sister in great suffering. Sister Angelica has her eyes still raised to heaven, motionless as if her whole life were in suspense.

THE ABBESS (*calling*)
Sister Angelica!

LE SUORE   Ah!

*La Badessa fa cenno alle suore che si ritirino; queste si av-
viano, scorgono che la fontana si è fatta d'oro, prendono un
secchiolino d'acqua, si dirigono verso il cimitero e scompaiono.*

SUOR ANGELICA
          Madre, Madre, parlate!
          Chi è? chi è? Madre, parlate!
          Son sett'anni che aspetto,
          che aspetto una parola, uno scritto . . .
          Tutto ho offerto alla Vergine
          in piena espiazione . . .

LA BADESSA (*interrompendola*)
          Offritele anche l'ansia
          che adesso vi scompone!

*Suor Angelica, affranta, si curva lentamente in ginocchio e
si raccoglie. Le voci delle suore arrivano dal cimitero.*

SUORE (*dal cimitero*)
          Requiem aeternam
          dona ei, Domine,
          et lux perpetua
          luceat ei.
          Requiescat in pace. Amen!

SUOR ANGELICA (*alzando gli occhi*)
          Madre, sono serena e sottomessa.

LA BADESSA È venuta a trovarvi
          vosta zia Principessa.

SUOR ANGELICA (*come un sospiro*)
          Ah!

LA BADESSA In parlatorio
          si dica quanto
          vuole ubbidienza,
          necessità.
          Ogni parola è udita
          dalla Vergina Pia.

SUOR ANGELICA
          La Vergine m'ascolti. E così sia.

LA ZIA PRINCIPESSA

*La Badessa si avvia e scompare a sinistra. Suor Angelica si
rialza e si avvia verso gli archi del parlatorio. Guarda ansiosa-
mente verso la porticina. Si ode un rumore di chiavi. La porticina viene aperta in dentro dalla Suora Clavaria che rimarrà a
fianco della porta aperta, nella penombra della stanza. La
Badessa si sofferma davanti alla Suora Clavaria. Le due suore
fanno ala e, fra le due figure bianche che si curvano lievemente in atto di ossequio, passa una figura nera severamente
composta in un naturale atteggiamento di grande dignità aris-
tocratica; è la Zia Principessa. Entra; cammina lentamente
appoggiandosi a un bastoncino d'ebano. Si sofferma: getta per
un attimo lo sguardo sulla nipote, freddamente e senza tradire*

NUNS Ah!

The Abbess motions the nuns to withdraw; they start to go away, notice that the fountain has turned to gold, take a little bucket of water from it, head for the cemetery, and disappear.

SISTER ANGELICA

Mother, Mother, speak!
Who is it? Who is it? Mother, speak!
For seven years I've been waiting,
waiting for a word, a note . . .
I have offered all to the Virgin
in full expiation . . .

THE ABBESS *(interrupting her)*

Offer her also the anxiety
that now makes you lose your composure!

Sister Angelica, distraught, bends slowly on her knees and collects herself. The nuns' voices arrive from the cemetery.

NUNS *(from the cemetery)*

*Requiem aeternam
dona ei, Domine,
et lux perpetua
luceat ei.
Requiescat in pace. Amen!*

SISTER ANGELICA *(raising her eyes)*

Mother, I am calm and submissive.

THE ABBESS Your aunt, the Princess,
has come to visit you.

SISTER ANGELICA *(as if sighing)*

Ah!

THE ABBESS In the parlatory
one says as much
as obedience, necessity
requires.
Every word is heard
by the Blessed Virgin.

SISTER ANGELICA

May the Virgin listen to me. Amen.

THE PRINCESS-AUNT

The Abbess goes off and disappears, at left. Sister Angelica rises and heads for the arches of the parlatory. She looks anxiously towards the little door. A sound of keys is heard. The little door is opened from within by the Sister Janitoress, who then remains beside the open door, in the semi-darkness of the room. The Abbess pauses before the Sister Janitoress. The two nuns step aside, and between the two white forms, who bow slightly in a gesture of respect, a black figure passes, severely composed in a natural attitude of great aristocratic dignity: this is the Princess-Aunt. She enters; she walks slowly, leaning on a little ebony cane. She pauses: she casts her gaze for a moment on her niece, coldly and without be-

nessuna emozione; Suor Angelica invece alla vista della zia è
presa da grande commozione, ma si frena, perchè si scorgono
ancora nell'ombra la Badessa e la Suora Clavaria. La porticina
si richiude sulle due suore. Suor Angelica, commossa, quasi
vacillante, va incontro alla zia, ma la vecchia protende la sin-
istra come per consentire soltanto all'atto sottomesso del ba-
ciamano. Suor Angelica prende la mano che le viene tesa, la
porta alle labbra e, mentre la zia siede, ella cade in ginocchio,
senza poter parlare. Un attimo di silenzio. Suor Angelica, con
gli occhi pieni di lacrime, non toglie mai lo sguardo dal volto
della zia, uno sguardo pietoso,, implorante. La vecchia invece,
ostentatamente, guarda avanti a sè.

LA ZIA PRINCIPESSA
            Il Principe Gualtiero vostro padre,
            la Principessa Clara vostra madre,
            quando ven'anni or sono
            vennero a morte . . .
                  (*si interrompe per farsi il segno*
                  della croce)
            . . . m'affidarono i figli
            e tutto il partrimonio di famiglia.
            Io dovevo dividerlo,
            quando ciò ritenessi conveniente
            e con giustizia piena.
            È quanto ho fatto. Ecco la pergamena.
            Voi potete osservarla, discuterla, firmarla.

SUOR ANGELICA
            Dopo sett'anni . . . son davanti a voi.
            Ispiratevi a questo luogo santo . . .
            È luogo di clemenza,
            è luogo di pietà.

LA ZIA PRINCIPESSA (*come una condanna*)
            Di penitenza.
            Io debbo rivelarvi la ragione
            perchè addivenni a questa divisione.
            Vostra sorella Anna Viola
            anderà sposa . . .

SUOR ANGELICA
            Sposa?! . . .
            Sposa la piccola Anna Viola,
            la sorellina, la piccina?
            Ah! ah! Son sett'anni!
            son passati sett'anni!
            ah! ah!
            O sorellina bionda che vai sposa,
            o sorellina mia, tu sia felice!
            E chi la ingemma?

LA ZIA PRINCIPESSA
            Chi per amore condonò la colpa
            di cui macchiaste il nostro bianco stemma.

SUOR ANGELICA (*con impeto di ribellione*)
            Sorella di mia madre,
            voi siete inesorabile!

traying any emotion; Sister Angelica, on the contrary, at the
sight of her aunt is overcome with great emotion, but she restrains herself, because the Abbess and the Sister Janitoress
can still be discerned in the shadow. The little door is closed
again on the two nuns. Sister Angelica, moved, almost stum-
bling, goes towards her aunt, but the old woman extends her
left hand as if to allow only the submissive act of kissing the
hand. Sister Angelica takes the hand that is held out to her,
raises it to her lips, and as her aunt sits down, she falls to her
knees, unable to speak. A moment of silence. Sister Angelica,
with her eyes filled with tears, never takes her gaze away
from her aunt's face, a pitiful, imploring gaze. The old
woman, on the other hand, deliberately looks straight ahead.

THE PRINCESS AUNT

> Prince Gualtiero, your father,
> Princess Clara, your mother,
> twenty years ago, when
> they came to die . . .
>> (*breaks off, to make the sign of the cross*)
> . . . entrusted to me their children
> and the entire family patrimony.
> I was to divide it
> when I thought it was appropriate
> and with full justice.
> This is what I have done. Here is the parch-
> ment.
> You may observe it, discuss it, sign it.

SISTER ANGELICA

> After seven years . . . I am before you . . .
> Be inspired by this holy place . . .
> It is a place of mercy,
> it is a place of compassion.

THE PRINCESS AUNT (*like a sentence*)

> Of penance.
> I must reveal to you the reason
> why I arrived at this division.
> Your sister Anna Viola
> is to be a bride . . .

SISTER ANGELICA

> Bride?! . . .
> A bride little Anna Viola,
> the little sister, the tiny one?
> Ah! ah! It's been seven years!
> Seven years have passed!
> ah! ah!
> O little blond sister, to be a bride,
> O my little sister, may you be happy!
> And who is to bejewel her?

THE PRINCESS AUNT

> One who out of love forgave the sin
> with which you stained our white escutcheon.

SISTER ANGELICA (*with an access of rebellion*)

> Sister of my mother,
> you are inexorable!

LA ZIA PRINCIPESSA (*scattando*)
          Che dite? E che pensate?
          Inesorabile? Inesorabile?
          Vostra madre invocate
          quasi contro di me? Contro di me!
          Vostra madre invocate
          quasi contro di me?
               (*tornando fredda e composta*)
          Di frequente, la sera,
          là, nel nostro oratorio,
          io mi raccolgo.
          Nel silenzio di quei raccoglimenti,
          il mio spirito par che s'allontani
          e s'incontri con quel di vostra madre
          in colloquì eterei, arcani!
          Com'è penoso, com'è penoso
          udire i morti dolorare e piangere!
          Quando l'estasi mistica scompare,
          per voi ho serbata una parola sola:
          Espiare! Espiare!
          Offritela alla Vergina
          la mia giustizia!

SUOR ANGELICA
          Tutto ho offerto alla Vergine, sì, tutto!
          Ma v'è un'offerta che non posso fare:
          alla Madre soave delle Madri,
          non posso offrire di scordar . . . mio figlio!
          Mio figlio! Mio figlio, figlio mio! Figlio mio!
          La creatura che mi fu, mi fu strappata!
          Figlio mio, che ho veduto e ho baciato
          una sol volta!
          Creatura mia! Creatura mia lontana!
          È questa la parola
          che invoco da sett'anni!
          Parlatemi di lui!
          Com'è, com'è mio figlio?
          Com'è dolce il suo volto?
          Come sono i suoi occhi?
          Parlatemi di lui!
          di mio figlio! . . .
          parlatemi . . . di lui . . .
     La vecchia tace, guardando la madre in angoscia.

SUOR ANGELICA (*con ansia tragica*)
          Perchè tacete? Perchè?
               Perchè?
          Un altro istante di questo silenzio
          e vi dannate per l'eternità!
               (*freddamente*)
          La Vergine ci ascolta e Lei vi giudica!

LA ZIA PRINCIPESSA (*freddamente*)
          Or son due anni
          venne colpito da fiero morbo . . .
          Tutto fu fatto per salvarlo . . .

THE PRINCESS AUNT (*reacting*)

> What are you saying? And what are you think-
> ing?
> Inexorable? Inexorable?
> You call on your mother
> as if against me? Against me!
>
> (*becoming cold and composed again*)
> Often, in the evening,
> There, in our chapel,
> I meditate.
> In the silence of those meditations
> my spirit seems to move off
> and meet that of your mother
> in ethereal, mysterious conversations!
> How painful it is, how painful it is,
> to hear the dead suffer and weep!
> When the mystic ecstasy disappears,
> I have retained for you only one word:
> Expiate! Expiate!
> Offer to the Virgin
> my justice!

SISTER ANGELICA

> I have offered everything to the Virgin, yes,
> everything!
> But there is one offer that I cannot make:
> to the sweet Mother of Mothers,
> I cannot offer to forget . . . my child!
> My child! My child, my child! My child!
> The baby that was, that was torn from me!
> My child, whom I saw and kissed
> only one time!
> My baby! My far-away baby!
> This is the word
> that I have beseeched for seven years!
> Speak to me of him!
> How is he, what is my son like?
> What is his sweet face like?
> What are his eyes like?
> Speak to me of him!
> of my child!
> speak to me . . . of him . . .

The old woman is silent, looking at the mother in anguish.

SISTER ANGELICA (*with tragic anxiety*)

> Why are you silent? Why? Why?
> Another moment of this silence
> and you damn yourself for eternity!
> (*coldly*)
> The Virgin hears us and she judges you!

THE PRINCESS AUNT (*coldly*)

> Two years ago
> he was stricken by a severe illness . . .
> Everything was done to save him . . .

SUOR ANGELICA
        È morto?
        (la zia curva il capo e tace)
        Ah!

Suor Angelica, con un grido, cade di schianto a terra, in avanti, col volto sulle mani. La zia si alza come per soccorrerla, credendola svenuta; ma, al singhiozzare di Suor Angelica, frena il suo movimento di pietà: in piedi, si volge verso un'immagine sacra che è al muro, alla sua destra, e, con le due mani appoggiate al bastoncino d'ebano, la testa curva, in silenzio, prega. Il pianto di Suor Angelica continua soffocato e straziante. Nel parlatorio è già la semioscurità della sera. Si ode la porta aprirsi. Suor Angelica si solleva un poco, restando sempre in ginocchio e col volto coperto. Entra la Suora Clavaria con una lucernina ad olio che pone sul tavolo. La zia Principessa si volge e parla sottovoce con la Suora. La Suora esce e ritorna colla Badessa recando una tavoletta con un calamaio e una penna. Suor Angelica ode entrare le due Suore, si volge, vede, comprende; in silenzio si trascina verso il tavolo e con mano tremante firma la pergamena. Quindi si ritrae di nuovo, sempre ginocchioni, e si ricopre il volto colle mani. Le due suore escono. La zia Principessa prende la pergamena, si avvicina a Suor Angelica, ma questa fa un leggero movimento con tutta la persona come per ritrarsi. Allora la zia procede verso la porta, batte col bastoncino. La Suora Clavaria apre, entra, prende il lume, va avanti; la Principessa la segue; di sulla soglia volge uno sguardo alla nipote; esce, scompare. La Suora Clavaria richiude la porta. La sera è calata; nel cimitero le suore vanno accendendo i lumini sulle tombe. Appena uscita la Principessa, Suor Angelica, rimasta sola, scoppia in un pianto disperato.

LA GRAZIA

SUOR ANGELICA *(sempre in ginocchio, con voce desolata)*
        Senza mamma,
        o bimbo, tu sei morto!
        Le tue labbra,
        senza i baci miei,
        scoloriron
        fredde, fredde!
        E chiudesti,
        o bimbo, gli occhi belli!
        Non potendo
        carezzarmi,
        le manine
        oomponesti in croce!
        E tu sei morto
        senza sapere
        quanto t'amava
        questa tua mamma!

SISTER ANGELICA
> He's dead?
> > (*the aunt bows her head and is silent*)
> Ah!

Sister Angelica, with a cry, falls violently to the ground, prone, her face in her hands. Her aunt rises as if to assist her, believing she has fainted; but, at Sister Angelica's sobbing, she restrains her movement of pity; standing, she turns towards a holy image on the wall, to her right, and with both hands resting on her little ebony cane, her head bowed, in silence, she prays. Sister Angelica's weeping continues, choked and heartrending. In the parlatory there is already the semidarkness of the evening. The door is heard opening. Sister Angelica pulls herself up a little, still remaining on her knees and with her face covered. The Sister Janitoress comes in with a little oil lamp which she sets on the table. The Princess Aunt turns and speaks in a whisper with the nun. The nun goes out and comes back with the Abbess, carrying a little table with an inkwell and a pen. Sister Angelica hears the two nuns come in. She turns, sees, understands; in silence she drags herself towards the table and, with a trembling hand, signs the parchment. Then she draws back again, still on her knees, and covers her face with her hands once more. The nuns go out. The Princess Aunt takes the parchment, approaches Sister Angelica; but the latter makes a slight movement with her whole body, as if to draw away. Then the aunt proceeds towards the door, raps with her cane. The Sister Janitoress opens, comes in, takes the light, and leads the way. The Princess follows her; at the threshold she casts a glance at her niece; she goes out, disappears. The Sister Janitoress closes the door again. Evening has fallen; in the cemetery the sisters are lighting the little votive lights on the graves. As soon as the Princess has gone out, Sister Angelica, remaining alone, bursts into desperate weeping.

GRACE

SISTER ANGELICA (*still on her knees, in a desolate voice*)
> Without your mother,
> O child, you died!
> Your lips
> without my kisses,
> paled,
> cold, cold!
> And you closed,
> O child, your beautiful eyes!
> Not being able
> to caress me,
> you placed
> your little hands in a cross!
> And you died
> without knowing
> how much she loved you,
> this mother of yours!

Ora che sei un angelo del cielo,
ora tu puoi vederla la tua mamma,
tu puoi scendere giù pel firmamento
ed aleggiare intorno a me, ti sento.
Sei qui, sei qui, mi baci e m'accarezzi.

Ah! dimmi, quando in ciel potrò vederti?

Quando potrò baciarti?
Oh! dolce fine d'ogni mio dolore,
quando in cielo con te potrò salire?

Quando potrò morire?
Quando potrò morire, potrò morire?
       (*come in estasi*)
Dillo alla mamma, creatura bella,
con un leggiero scintillar di stella.
Parlami, parlami, amore, amore, amor!

*I lumi del cimitero sono tutti accesi; il chiostro è ormai
quasi oscuro. Le suore escono dal cimitero e si avviano verso
Suor Angelica che è come in estasi. Il gruppo delle suore si
avvicina in silenzio. Nella semioscurità sembra che le figure
bianche, camminando, non tocchino terra.*

SUOR GENOVIEFFA
Sorella, o buona sorella,
la Vergine ha accolto la prece.

ALCUNE SUORE Sarete contenta, sorella,
la Vergine ha fatto la grazia.

*Suor Angelica si leva come in preda ad un'esaltazione mis-
tica.*

SUOR ANGELICA
La grazia è discesa dal cielo,
già tutta, già tutta m'accende,
risplende, risplende!
Già vedo, sorelle, la meta . . .

LE SUORE   E così sia.

SUOR ANGELICA
Sorelle, son lieta, son lieta!
[Cantiamo! Già in cielo si canta!

Lodiamo la Vergine Santa!

LE SUORE   Cantiamo! Già in cielo si canta!]

È così sia.

*Si ode dal fondo a destra il segnale delle tavolette. Le suore
vengono da ogni parte, si raccolgono e tutte in fila si avviano
verso le celle; la teoria bianca entra sotto le arcate di destra;
ciascuna suora apre l'uscio della propria cella, entra e richiude.*

LE SUORE   Lodiamo la Vergine Santa!
[Lodiam, lodiam la Vergine Santa!
Amen!

Now that you are an angel in heaven,
now you can see her, your mother;
you can come down from the firmament
and hover about me, I feel you.
You're here, you're here, you kiss and caress
me.
Ah! tell me: when will I be able to see you in
heaven?
When will I be able to kiss you?
Oh! sweet end of my every sorrow,
when will I be able to come up to heaven with
you?
When will I be able to die?
When will I be able to die, be able to die?
     (*as if in ecstasy*)
Tell your mother, beautiful baby,
with a faint sparkle of a star.
Speak to me, speak to me, my love, love, love!

The lights of the cemetery are all lighted; the cloister is now almost dark. The nuns come from the cemetery and head for Sister Angelica, who is as if in ecstasy. The group of nuns approaches in silence. In the semi-darkness it seems that the white forms, as they walk, do not touch the ground.

SISTER GENOVIEFFA

Sister, O good sister,
the Virgin heard the prayer.

SOME NUNS   You must be happy, sister;
the Virgin has shown her grace.

Sister Angelica stands up as if in the grip of a mystic exaltation.

SISTER ANGELICA

Grace has descended from heaven;
everything, everything already enflames me;
it shines, it shines!
Already, sisters, I see the goal . . .

NUNS   Amen.

SISTER ANGELICA

Sisters, I am happy, I am happy!
Let us sing! Already they are singing in
heaven!
Let us praise the Holy Virgin!

NUNS   Let us sing! Already they are singing in
heaven!
Amen.

From the rear, to the right, the signal of the clappers is heard. The nuns come in from all sides, gather, and all in line head towards the cells; the white line enters under the arches at right; each nun opens the door of her cell, enters, and closes it again.

NUNS   Let us praise the Holy Virgin!
Let us praise, praise the Holy Virgin!
Amen!

SUOR ANGELICA

Ah! . . . Lodiam!]
(*dalla cella*)
La grazia è discesa dal cielo!

La notte avvolge il chiostro. Sulla chiesetta si va illumi-
nando a poco a poco una scintillante cupola di stelle. La luna
dà sui cipressi. Una cella si apre; esce Suor Angelica. Ha
nella mani una ciotola di terra cotta. Si ferma presso la croce
fra i cipressi e depone la ciotola; prende dei sassi e forma con
essi un piccolo fornello; raccoglie sterpi e rami e ne fa un fas-
telletto che depone fra i sassi. Va verso la fonte e riempie
d'acqua la ciotola. Coll'acciarino accende il fuocherello e vi
pone la ciotola a bollire. Quindi si avvia verso la fiorita.

SUOR ANGELICA

Suor Angelica ha sempre una ricetta
buona fatta coi fiori.
Amici fiori, che nel piccol seno
racchiudete le stille del veleno,
Ah! quante cure v'ho prodigate.
Ora mi compensate.
Per voi miei fior io morirò.

Fa un pugnello delle erbe e dei fiori colti e li getta nella
ciotola fumante, guarda un attimo il formarsi del veleno,
prende la ciotola e la posa piè della croce, quindi si volge a
destra verso le celle.

SUOR ANGELICA

Addio, buone sorelle, addio, addio!
Vi lascio per sempre.
M'ha chiamato mio figlio!
Dentro un raggio di stelle
m'è apparso il suo sorriso,
m'ha detto: Mamma, vieni in Paradiso!
Addio! Addio!
Addio, chiesetta! In te quanto ho pregato!

Buona accoglievi preghiere e pianti.
È discesa la grazia benedetta!
Muoio per lui e in cielo lo rivedrò!
Ah!

Esaltata, abbraccia la croce, la bacia, si curva rapidamente,
prende la ciotola e beve il veleno. Quindi si appoggia ad un
cipresso e comprimendosi il petto con la sinistra e abbando-
nando lentamente il braccio destro lascia cadere la ciotola a
terra. L'atto del suicidio ormai compiuto sembra la tolga dalla
esaltazione a cui era in preda e la riconduca alla verità. Un
rapido silenzio. Il suo volto prima sereno e sorridente si atteg-
gia in una espressione angosciosa come se una rivelazione im-
provvisa e tremenda le fosse apparsa. Le nubi coprono adesso
la luna e le stelle; la scene è oscura. Si leva un grido dispe-
rato.

SUOR ANGELICA

Ah! Son dannata!

SISTER ANGELICA

> Ah! . . Let us praise!
> *(from the cell)*
> Grace has descended from heaven!

Night envelops the cloister. Over the chapel, little by little, a sparkling dome of stars is coming alight. A cell opens; Sister Angelica comes out. In her hands she is carrying a terracotta bowl. She stops near the cross among the cypresses and sets down the bowl; she takes some stones and with them forms a little hearth. She collects twigs and boughs and makes a little bundle, which she places among the stones. She goes towards the fountain and fills the bowl with water. With tinder she lights the little fire and sets the bowl to boil. Then she goes towards the flower bed.

SISTER ANGELICA

> Sister Angelica always has a good
> remedy made with flowers.
> Flower-friends, who in your little bosom
> enclose the drops of poison,
> Ah! how much care I've lavished on you.
> Now you reward me.
> Thanks to you, my flowers, I will die.

She makes a little bunch of the herbs and flowers gathered and throws them in the steaming bowl, watches a moment the poison forming, takes the bowl and sets it at the foot of the cross, then turns to the right, towards the cells.

SISTER ANGELICA

> Farewell, good sisters, farewell, farewell!
> I am leaving you forever.
> My son has called me!
> Inside a beam of stars
> his smile appeared to me,
> he said to me: Mamma, come to Paradise!
> Farewell! Farewell!
> Farewell, little church! How much I prayed
> in you!
> You, good, received prayers and tears.
> The blessed grace has descended!
> I die for him and I'll see him again in heaven!
> Ah!

Ecstatic, she embraces the cross, kisses it, bends over rapidly, takes the bowl and drinks the poison. Then she leans against a cypress and, pressing her bosom with her left hand, and slowly dropping her right arm, she lets the bowl fall to the ground.

The act of suicide, now completed, seems to take her out of the exaltation to which she was subject and to bring her back to the truth. A rapid silence. Her face, formerly serene and smiling, now assumes an expression of anguish, as if a terrible and sudden revelation had appeared to her. The clouds now cover the moon and the stars; the scene is dark. A desperate cry rises.

SISTER ANGELICA

> Ah! I am damned!

Mi son data la morte,
mi son data la morte!
Io muoio, muoio in peccato mortale!
        (*si getta disperatamente in
        ginocchio*)
O Madonna, Madonna, salvami! salvami!
Per amor di mio figlio!

IL MIRACOLO

*Già le sembra udire le voci degli angeli imploranti per lei la
Madre della Madri.*

GLI ANGELI   *Regina Virginum, Salve, Maria!*

SUOR ANGELICA
        Ho smarrito la ragione!

GLI ANGELI   *Mater castissima, Salve, Maria!*

SUOR ANGELICA
        Non mi fare morire in dannazione!

GLI ANGELI   *Regina pacis, Salve, Maria!*

SUOR ANGELICA
        Dammi un segno di grazia,
        dammi un segno di grazia,
        Madonna! Madonna!
        Salvami! Salvami!

*A questa invocazione rispondono le voci degli angeli che
levano l'Inno alla Madre delle Madri.*

GLI ANGELI   *O gloriosa Virginum,
        Sublimis inter sidera,
        Qui te creavit, parvulum,
        Lactente nutris ubere.*

SUOR ANGELICA (*supplichevole e disperata*)
        [O Madonna, salvami!
        Una madre ti prega,
        una madre t'implora!

GLI ANGELI   *Quod Heva tristis abstulit,
        Tu reddis almo germine:
        Intrent ut astra flebiles,
        Coeli recludis cardines . . .*]

*Suor Angelica vede il miracolo compiersi: la chiesetta sfol-
gora di mistica luce, la porta si apre: apparisce la Regina del
conforto, solenne, dolcissima e, avanti a Lei, un bimbo biondo,
tutto bianco . . .*

SUOR ANGELICA
        O Madonna, salvami! . .

GLI ANGELI   *Gloriosa Virginum, Salve, Maria!*

*La Vergine, con un gesto dolcissimo, senza toccarlo, sos-
pinge il bimbo verso la moribonda.*

SUOR ANGELICA
        Ah! . .

GLI ANGELI   *Regina Virginum!*

I gave myself death,
I gave myself death!
I die, I die in mortal sin!
   (*flings herself desperately
   on her knees*)
O Madonna, Madonna, save me! save me!
For the love of my son!

THE MIRACLE

*Already she seems to hear the voices of the angels, imploring
the Mother of Mothers for her.*

ANGELS   *Regina Virginum, Salve, Maria!*

SISTER ANGELICA

I have lost my reason!

ANGELS   *Mater castissima, Salve, Maria!*

SISTER ANGELICA

Don't make me die in damnation!

ANGELS   *Regina pacis, Salve, Maria!*

SISTER ANGELICA

Give me a sign of grace,
give me a sign of grace,
Madonna! Madonna!
Save me! Save me!

*To this plea the voices of the Angels reply, raising the
hymn of the Mother of Mothers.*

ANGELS   *O gloriosa Virginum,*
         Sublimis inter sidera,
         Qui te creavit, parvulum,
         Lactente nutris ubere.

SISTER ANGELICA (*imploring and desperate*)
         O Madonna, save me!
         A mother prays you,
         a mother implores you!

ANGELS   *Quod Heva tristis abstulit,*
         Tu reddis almo germine:
         Intrent ut astra flebiles,
         Coeli recludis cardines . . .

*Sister Angelica sees the miracle achieved: the chapel blazes
with mystic light, the door is opened: the Queen of Solace appears, solemn, very sweet, and, in front of her, a blond little
boy, all in white. . . .*

SISTER ANGELICA

O Madonna, save me! . .

ANGELS   *Gloriosa Virginum, Salve, Maria!*

*The Virgin, with a very gentle gesture, without touching
him, urges the child towards the dying woman.*

SISTER ANGELICA

Ah! . . .

ANGELS   *Regina Virginum!*

Suor Angelica, nell'estasi della visione, tende le braccia verso il bimbo.

SUOR ANGELICA
　　　　　Ah!

GLI ANGELI　　*Virgo fidelis!*
　　　　　　　Sancta Maria!
　　　　　　　Gloriosa Virginum! Salve, Maria!

Il bimbo muove il primo passo.

GLI ANGELI　　*Mater purissima! Salve, Maria!*

Il bimbo muove il secondo passo.

GLI ANGELI　　*Turris davidica! Salve, Maria!*
　　　　　　　Ah!

Il bimbo muove il terzo passo. Suor Angelica cade dolcemente riversa e muore. Il miracolo sfolgora.

Sister Angelica, in the ecstasy of the vision, extends her arms towards the child.

SISTER ANGELICA
Ah!

ANGELS   *Virgo fidelis!*
          Sancta Maria!
          Gloriosa virginum! Salve, Maria!

The child takes the first step.

ANGELS   *Mater purissima! Salve, Maria!*

The child takes the second step.

ANGELS   *Turris davidica! Salve, Maria!*
          Ah!

The child takes the third step. Sister Angelica falls back gently, and dies. The miracle shines forth.

Gianni Schicchi

THE PLOT

A large bedroom in the house of Buoso Donati, a rich Florentine, who has just died. The corpse lies in a huge four-poster bed in the background; the bed's curtains are drawn. Buoso's relatives are mourning his death, but then a rumor begins to circulate among them that Buoso's considerable fortune has been left not to his family but to some monks. The relatives break off their laments and search desperately for the will. Young Rinuccio finds it and, before giving it to his aunt Zita, asks her permission to marry his beloved Lauretta, daughter of the upstart Gianni Schicchi. Zita says that if they receive their inheritance, Rinuccio can marry anyone he pleases. But, as a reading of the will quickly reveals, it is indeed the monks who inherit everything. Rinuccio then secretly sends for the shrewd Schicchi, who can save the situation if anyone can, even though the relatives object to this plan. Schicchi arrives with Lauretta, and is ill-received by Zita. Lauretta pleads with her father to help the family anyway, and he agrees. His plan is simple: he will impersonate Buoso, dictate a new will, and leave everything to the relatives, who then, one by one, offer him handsome bribes if he will favor them in the will. The notary arrives and Schicchi dictates the testament, leaving the bulk of the estate to "his good friend Gianni Schicchi." The relatives are helpless, since their — and Schicchi's — deceit is a grave crime. Once the notary has gone, there is a terrible rumpus, whereupon Schicchi chases them all out of the house, which is now his. Only Rinuccio and Lauretta remain, embracing, dreaming of their love. Schicchi, in an aside to the audience, insists that Buoso's money could hardly be used for a more worthy purpose.

GIANNI SCHICCHI

libretto by Giovacchino Forzano

First performed at the Metropolitan Opera House, New York
December 14, 1918

CHARACTERS

Gianni Schicchi, aged fifty	*Baritone*
Lauretta, his daughter, aged twenty-one	*Soprano*
Relatives of Buoso Donati:	
Zita, known as "the old one," cousin of Buoso, aged sixty	*Contralto*
Rinuccio, her nephew, aged twenty-four	*Tenor*
Gherardo, Buoso's nephew, aged forty	*Tenor*
Nella, his wife, aged thirty-four	*Soprano*
Gherardino, their son, aged seven	*Contralto*
Betto di Signa, Buoso's brother-in-law, poor and badly dressed, age undefinable	*Bass*
Simone, Buoso's cousin, aged seventy	*Bass*
Marco, his son, aged forty-five	*Baritone*
La Ciesca, Marco's wife, aged thirty-eight	*Mezzo-soprano*
Maestro Spinelloccio, doctor	*Bass*
Ser Amantio di Nicolao, notary	*Baritone*
Pinellino, cobbler	*Bass*
Guccio, dyer	*Bass*

The time is around the end of the thirteenth century
or beginning of the fourteenth, in Florence.

La camera da letto di Buoso Donati. A sinistra di faccia al pubblico la porta d'ingresso; oltre un pianerottolo e la scala; quindi una finestra a vetri fino a terra per cui si accede al terrazzo con la ringhiera di legno che gira esternamente la facciata della casa. Nel fondo a sinistra un finestrone da cui si scorge la torre di Arnolfo. Sulla parete di destra una scaletta di legno conduce ad un ballatoio su cui trovansi uno stipo e una porta. Sotto la scala un'altra porticina. A destra, nel fondo, il letto. Sedie, cassapanche, stipi sparsi qua e là, un tavolo; sopra il tavolo oggetti d'argento.

Ai lati del letto quattro candelabri con quattro ceri accesi. Davanti al letto, un candelabro a tre candele, spento. Luce di sole e luce di candele: sono le nove del mattino. Le sarge del letto, semichiuse, lasciano intravedere un drappo rosso che ricopre un corpo. I parenti di Buoso sono in ginocchia, con le mani si coprono il volto e stanno molto curvati verso terra. Gherardino è a sinistra vicino alla parete; è seduto in terra, volta la spalle ai parenti e si diverte a far ruzzolare delle palline. I parenti sono disposti in semicerchio; a sinistra del letto la prima è la vecchia, Zita, poi Rinuccio, Gherardo e Nella, quindi Betto di Signa, nel centro, resta un po' isolato perché essendo povero, mal vestito e fangoso, è riguardato con disprezzo dagli altri parenti; a destra, la Ciesca Marco e Simone che sarà davanti alla vecchia.

Da questo gruppo parte il sordo brontolìo di una preghiera. Il brontolìo è interrotto da singhiozzi, evidentemente fabbricati tirando su il fiato a strozzo. Quando Betto di Signa si azzarda a singhiozzare, gli altri si sollevano un po', alzano il viso dalle mani e danno a Betto una guardataccia. Durante il brontolìo si sentono esclamazioni soffocate di questo genere:

ZITA   Povero Buoso!

SIMONE   Povero cugino!

RINUCCIO   Povero zio!

MARCO E CIESCA
             Oh! Buoso!

GHERARDO E NELLA
             Buoso!

BETTO   O cognato! o cognà —

È interrotto perché Gherardino butta in terra una sedia e i parenti, con la scusa di zittire Gherardino, fanno un formidabile sciì sul viso a Betto.

TUTTI (*verso Betto*)
             Scii!

GHERARDO   Io piangerò per giorni
             e giorni.
               (*a Gherardino che si è alzato e lo tira per
               la veste dicendogli qualcosa nell'orecchio*)

Gianni Schicchi © 1918 by G. Ricordi & Co., Milan

The bedroom of Buoso Donati. To the audience's left, the main door with a landing and staircase beyond it. Then a French-window leading to a terrace with a wooden railing that runs around the façade of the house. At left, in the background, a large window through which Arnolfo's tower can be seen. Against the wall, at right, a little wooden stairway leads to a gallery with a cupboard and a door. Under the stairs, another little door. At right, in the background, is the bed. Chairs, chests, cupboards scattered here and there. A table. On the table some silver objects.

At the sides of the bed there are four candelabra, with four lighted candles. Before the bed a candelabrum with three candles, unlighted. Sunlight and candlelight together: it is nine in the morning. The bed curtains are half drawn; we can glimpse a red blanket covering a body. Buoso's relatives are on their knees, their hands covering their faces; they are bent over toward the floor. Gherardino is at left, near the wall. He is sitting on the floor, his back to the relatives, amusing himself by rolling some little balls. The other relatives are in a semi-circle: left of the bed, the first is old Zita, then Rinuccio, Gherardo, and Nella, then Betto di Signa, who remains in the center, somewhat isolated because, being poor, mud-stained and badly dressed, he is regarded with contempt by the other relatives. At right, La Ciesca, Marco, and Simone, who is opposite old Zita.

From the group we hear the dull grumbling of a prayer. The grumbling is broken by sobs, obviously fabricated by drawing breath in a fake choking. When Betto di Signa dares sob, the others straighten up a bit, raise their faces from their hands and give Betto a nasty look. During the mumbling we hear stifled expressions of this sort:

ZITA   Poor Buoso!

SIMONE   Poor cousin!

RINUCCIO   Poor uncle!

MARCO, CIESCA
    Oh! Buoso!

GHERARDO, NELLA
    Buoso!

BETTO   Oh! brother-in-law! Oh brother-in- —

He is interrupted because Gherardino overturns a chair. The relatives, with the pretext of silencing Gherardino, utter a formidable ssshhh in Betto's face.

ALL (*at Betto*)
    Ssshhh!

GHERARDO   I'll weep for days and
days.
        (*to Gherardino, who has stood up and is tugging at his garment whispering something into his ear*)

Sciò!

NELLA   Giorni? Per mesi!
              (*a Gherardino, come sopra*)
           Sciò!

Gherardino va dalla vecchia Zita.

CIESCA   Mesi? Per anni ed anni!

ZITA   Ti piangerò tutta la vita mia!

CIESCA, MARCO
           Povero Buoso!

ZITA (*allontanando Gherardino, seccata si volge a Nella e
              Gherardo*)
           Portatecelo voi, Gherardo, via!

*Gherardo si alza, prende il figliolo per un braccio e, a strat-
toni, lo porta via dalla porticina di sinistra.*

TUTTI   Oh! Buoso, Buoso,
           tutta la vita
           piangeremo la tua dipartita!

CIESCA   Piangerem . . .

RINUCCIO   Piangerem!

ZITA   Buoso! Buoso!

CIESCA   . . . tutta la vita!

*Tutti ripigliano a pregare, meno Betto e Nella che si par-
leranno all'orecchio.*

NELLA   Ma come? Davvero?

BETTO   Lo dicono a Signa.

RINUCCIO (*curvandosi fino a Nella, con voce piangente*)
           Che dicono a Signa?

NELLA   Si dice che . . .
              (*gli mormora qualcosa all'orecchio*)

RINUCCIO (*con voce naturale*)
           Giaaaaa?

BETTO   Lo dicono a Signa.

CIESCA (*curvandosi fino a Betto, con voce piangente*)
           Che dicono a Signa?

BETTO   Si dice che . . .
              (*le mormora qualcosa all'orecchio*)

CIESCA (*con voce naturale, e forte*)
           Nooooo!
           Marco, lo senti
           che dicono a Signa?
           Si dice che . . .
              (*gli mormora qualcosa all'orecchio*)

MARCO   Eeeeeeh!

ZITA (*con voce piagnucolosa*)
           Ma insomma possiamo sapere . . .

BETTO   Lo dicono a Signa.

ZITA   . . . che diamine dicono a Signa?

BETTO   Ci son delle voci . . .
           dei mezzi discorsi . . .
           Dicevan jersera

Scoot!

NELLA   Days? For months!
              (*to Gherardino, as above*)
             Scoot!

Gherardino goes to old Zita.

CIESCA   Months? For years and years!

ZITA   I'll weep for you all my life!

CIESCA, MARCO
             Poor Buoso!

ZITA (*sending away Gherardino, addresses, annoyed, Nella and Gherardo*)
             Gherardo, take him away for us!

Gherardo stands up, takes his son by the arm and, with jerks, takes him away through the little door at left.

ALL   Oh! Buoso, Buoso,
             for all our lives
             we'll weep over your passing!

CIESCA   We'll weep . . .

RINUCCIO   We'll weep!

ZITA   Buoso! Buoso!

CIESCA   . . . all our lives!

All resume praying, except for Betto and Nella, who whisper to each other.

NELLA   What? Really?

BETTO   They're saying it in Signa.

RINUCCIO (*bending toward Nella, in a weeping voice*)
             What are they saying in Signa?

NELLA   It's said that . . .
             (*murmurs something into his ear*)

RINUCCIO (*in a natural voice*)
             Reeeally?

BETTO   They're saying it in Signa.

CIESCA (*bending toward Betto, in a weeping voice*)
             What are they saying in Signa?

BETTO   It's said that . . .
             (*murmurs something into her ear*)

CIESCA (*in a natural voice, and loud*)
             Nooooo!
             Marco, you hear
             what they're saying in Signa?
             It's said that . . .
             (*murmurs into his ear*)

MARCO   Eeeeeh!

ZITA (*in a whimpering voice*)
             In short, may we know . . .

BETTO   They're saying it in Signa.

ZITA   . . . what in the devil are they saying in Signa?

BETTO   There are some rumors . . .
             some half-hinted remarks . . .
             They were saying yesterday evening

dal Cisti fornajo:
"Se Buoso crepa, pei frati è manna!

Diranno: pancia mia, fatti capanna!"
E un altro: "Sì, sì, sì, nel testamento
ha lasciato ogni cosa ad un convento!"

SIMONE (*a metà di questo discorso si è sollevato anche lui ed
          ha ascoltato*)
          Ma che?!?! Chi lo dice?

BETTO   Lo dicono a Signa.

SIMONE   Lo dicono a Signa?

TUTTI   Lo dicono a Signa!

*I parenti sono sempre in ginocchio, ma non pensano più
alle preghiere e si guardano l'un l'altro, sorpresi.*

GHERARDO O Simone?

CIESCA   Simone?

ZITA   Parla, tu se' il più vecchio . . .

MARCO   Tu se' anche stato podestà a Fucecchio . . .

ZITA   Che ne pensi?

MARCO   Che ne pensi?

SIMONE (*riflette un istante, poi dice gravemente*)
          Se il testamento è in mano d'un notajo . . .
          chi lo sa? Forse è un guajo!
          Se però ce l'avesse
          lasciato in questa stanza,
          guajo pei frati, ma per noi: speranza!

TUTTI   Guajo pei frati, ma per noi: speranza!

*Tutti istintivamente si alzano di scatto. Simone e Nella si
dirigono allo stipo nel fondo. La vecchia Zita, Marco, Ciesca
allo stipo che è sul davanti alla parete di destra. Gherardo
torna ora in scena senza il ragazzo e raggiunge Simone e
Nella. Rinuccio si dirige verso lo stipo che è in cima alla
scala.*

RINUCCIO (O Lauretta, amore mio,
           speriam nel testamento dello zio!)

*È una ricerca febbrile. Fruscio di pergamene buttate all'aria.
Betto, scacciato da tutti, vagando per la stanza adocchia sul
tavolo il piatto d'argento col sigillo d'argento e le forbici pure
d'argento. Cautamente allunga una mano. Ma dal fondo si
ode un falso allarme di Simone che crede di aver trovato il
testamento.*

SIMONE   Ah!
           (*Tutti si voltano. Betto fa il distratto. Si-
           mone guarda meglio una pergamena*)

           No. Non è!

*Si riprende la ricerca. Betto agguanta le forbici e il sigillo;
li striscia al panno della manica dopo averli rapidamente ap-
pannati col fiato, li guarda e li mette in tasca. Ora tira al
piatto. Ma un falso allarme della vecchia Zita fa voltare tutti.*

at Cisti the baker's:
"If Buoso gives up the ghost, it's manna for the
    monks!
They'll say: belly of mine, make room!"
And another said: "yes, yes, yes, in his will
he's left everything to a convent!"

SIMONE   (*halfway through this speech he has also risen up and
        has listened*)
        What? Who says it?

BETTO   They're saying it in Signa.

SIMONE   They're saying it in Signa?

ALL   They're saying it in Signa!

*The relatives are still on their knees, but they no longer
think of prayers and look at one another, surprised.*

GHERARDO   Oh, Simone?

CIESCA   Simone?

ZITA   Speak, you're the oldest . . .

MARCO   You've also been mayor at Fucecchio . . .

ZITA   What do you think about it?

MARCO   What do you think about it?

SIMONE   (*reflects a moment, then says gravely*)
        If the will is in a notary's hands . . .
        who knows? Perhaps it's a misfortune!
        If, however, he had
        left it in this room,
        misfortune for the monks, but for us: hope!

ALL   Misfortune for the monks, but for us: hope!

*All instinctively spring to their feet. Simone and Nella head
for the cupboard at the back. Old Zita, Marco, Ciesca go to
the cupboard in the foreground against the right wall. Gherardo now returns to the scene without the boy and joins
Simone and Nella. Rinuccio heads toward the cupboard at the
top of the stairs.*

RINUCCIO   (Oh, Lauretta, my love,
        let us hope in my uncle's will!)

*There is a feverish search. The rustle of parchments thrown
in the air. Betto, cast out by all, wandering around the room,
eyes on the table, with the silver plate, the silver seal, and
scissors, also of silver. Cautiously, he extends one hand. But
from the back a false alarm is heard, from Simone, who thinks
he has found the will.*

SIMONE   Ah!
        (*They all turn. Betto assumes an absent
        air. Simone takes a better look at a parch-
        ment*)
        No. It isn't it!

*The search is resumed. Betto grabs the scissors and the
seal; he rubs them against the cloth of his sleeve after rapidly
breathing on them. He looks at them, puts them in his pocket.
Now he aims at the plate. But a false alarm from old Zita
makes them all turn around.*

ZITA   Ah!
                    (*cacciando la testa nello stipo*)
                No. Non c'è!

    Si riprende più affannosamente la ricerca. I parenti, inferociti, non sanno più dove cercare; buttano all'aria tutto nella camera; rovistano i cassetti, le credenze, le cassapanche, sotto il letto. Le pergamene, le carte volano per l'aria. Betto approfitta di questa confusione per agguantare il piatto e per nasconderlo sotto il vestito, tenendolo assicurato colle mani.

ZITA, CIESCA, NELLA
                No! non c'è . . .

GHERARDO   Dove sia?

MARCO   [Dove sia?

SIMONE, BETTO
                No! non c'è!]

    Rinuccio, che è salito allo stipo in cima alla scala, riesce ad aprirlo. Grida.

RINUCCIO   Salvàti! salvàti!
                Il testamento di Buoso Donati!

    Tutti accorrono con le mani protese per prendere il testamento. Ma Rinuccio mette il rotolo di pergamena nella sinistra, protende la destra come per fermare lo slancio dei parenti.

RINUCCIO (*mentre tutti sono in un'ansia spasmodica*)
                Zia, l'ho trovato io . . . !
                Come compenso, dimmi,
                se lo zio, povero zio!
                m'avesse lasciato bene bene,
                se tra poco si fosse tutti ricchi
                in un giorno di festa come questo,
                mi daresti il consenso di sposare
                la Lauretta figliola dello Schicchi?
                Mi sembrerà più dolce il mio redaggio . . .
                potrei sposarla per Calendimaggio!

BETTO   Ma sì!

GHERARDO   Ma sì!

CIESCA, MARCO, SIMONE
                Ma sì!

NELLA, GHERARDO
                C'è tempo a riparlarne!

RINUCCIO   Potrei sposarla per Calendimaggio!

GHERARDO, MARCO
                Qui, presto il testamento!

CIESCA   Lo vedi che si sta colle spine
                sotto i piedi?

RINUCCIO   Zia!

ZITA   Se tutto andrà come si spera,
                sposa chi vuoi, sia pure la versiera.

    Rinuccio dà a Zita il testamento. Tutti seguono Zita che va al tavolo. Cerca le forbici per tagliare i nastri del rotolo, non trova nè forbici nè piatto; Betto fa una fisionomia incredibile.

ZITA   Ah!
      (*sticking her head into the cupboard*)
    No. It isn't there!

The search is resumed more anxiously. The relatives, en-
raged, no longer know where to hunt; they turn everything in
the room inside out; they rummage in the drawers, the cabi-
nets, the chests, under the bed. Parchments, papers fly through
the air. Betto takes advantage of this confusion to grab the
plate and hide it under his clothes, holding it fast with his
hands.

ZITA, CIESCA, NELLA
    No! It isn't there . . .

GHERARDO Where can it be?

MARCO   Where can it be?

SIMONE, BETTO
    No! It isn't there!

Rinuccio, who has gone up to the cupboard at the top of
the stairs, manages to open it. He shouts.

RINUCCIO Saved! Saved!
    The will of Buoso Donati!

They all run over with hands outstretched to take the will.
But Rinuccio puts the roll of parchment in his left hand, ex-
tends his right hand as if to stop the onrush of the relatives.

RINUCCIO (*while all of them are in spasmodic anxiety*)
    Aunt, I found it . . . !
    As a reward, tell me,
    if my uncle, poor uncle!
    had left me well off
    if in a little while we were all rich,
    on a festive day like this,
    would you give me your consent to marry
    Lauretta, the daughter of Schicchi?
    My inheritance will seem sweeter to me . . .
    I could marry her on May Day!

BETTO   Why, yes!

GHERARDO Why, yes!

CIESCA, MARCO, SIMONE
    Why, yes!

NELLA, GHERARDO
    There's time to talk it over!

RINUCCIO I could marry her on May Day!

GHERARDO, MARCO
    Here, the will, quickly!

CIESCA   Can't you see we're
    on pins and needles?

RINUCCIO Aunt!

ZITA   If all goes as we hope,
    marry whom you like, even the she-devil.

Rinuccio gives Zita the will. All follow Zita, who goes to
the table. She looks for the scissors to cut the ribbons of the
roll, finds neither scissors nor plate; Betto assumes an incred-

Zita strappa il nastro con le mani. Apre. Appare una seconda
pergamena che avvolge ancora il testamento. Zita vi legge
sopra.

RINUCCIO   Ah! lo zio mi voleva tanto bene,
                  m'avrà lasciato colle tasche piene!
                     (*a Gherardino che torna ora in scena*)

                  Corri da Gianni Schicchi,
                  digli che venga qui colla Lauretta:
                  c'è Rinuccio di Buoso che l'aspetta!
                  (*dandogli due monete*)
                  A te, due popolini:
                  comprati i confortini.

     Gherardino corre via.

ZITA   "Ai miei cugini Zita e Simone!"

SIMONE   Povero Buoso!

ZITA   Povero Buoso!

SIMONE   (*in un impeto di riconoscenza accende anche le tre*
                        candele del candelabro spento)
                  Tutta la cera tu devi avere!
                  Insino in fondo si deve struggere!
                  Sì! godi, godi! Povero Buoso!

TUTTI   Povero Buoso!
                  Se m'avesse lasciato questa casa!
                  E i mulini di Signa!
                  Poi la mula . . . !
                  Se m'avesse lasciato . . .

ZITA   Zitti! È aperto!

     La vecchia col testamento in mano; vicino al tavolo ha
dietro a sè un grappolo umano. Marco e Betto sono saliti sopra
una sedia. Si vedranno bene tutti i visi assorti nella lettura. Le
bocche si muoveranno come quelle di chi legge senza emettere
voce. A un tratto i visi si cominciano a rannuvolare . . . arri-
vano ad una espressione tragica . . . finché la vecchia Zita si
lascia cadere seduto sullo sgabello davanti alla scrivania. Si-
mone è il primo, del gruppo impietrito, che si muove; si volta,
si vede davanti le tre candele testé accese, vi soffia su e le
spegne; cala le sarge del letto completamente; spegne poi tutti
i candelabri. Gli altri parenti lentamente vanno ciascuno a
cercare una sedia e vi seggono. Sono come impietriti con gli
occhi sbarrati, fissi; chi qua, chi là.

SIMONE   Dunque era vero! Noi vedremo i frati
                  ingrassare alla barba dei Donati!

CIESCA   Tutti quei bei fiorini accumulati
                  finire nelle tonache dei frati!

MARCO   Privare tutti noi d'una sostanza,
                  e far i frati sguazzar nell'abbondanza!

BETTO   Io dovrò misurarmi il bere a Signa
                  e i frati beveranno il vin di vigna!

NELLA, CIESCA, ZITA
                  Si faranno slargar spesso la cappa,
                  noi schianterem di bile, e loro . . . pappa!

ible expression. Zita rips away the ribbon with her hands. She opens. A second parchment appears, also wrapped around the will. Zita reads it.

RINUCCIO   Ah! uncle was so fond of me,
             he must have left me with my pockets full!
                  (to Gherardino, who now reappears on the scene)
             Run to Gianni Schicchi,
             tell him to come here with Lauretta:
             there's Rinuccio di Buoso waiting for him!
                  (giving him two coins)
             For you, two *popolini:*
             buy yourself sweets.

     Gherardino runs off.

ZITA   "To my cousins Zita and Simone!"

SIMONE   Poor Buoso!

ZITA   Poor Buoso!

SIMONE *(in a burst of gratitude also lights the three candles of the unlighted candelabrum)*
             You must have all the wax!
             It must be burned to the bottom!
             Yes! rejoice, rejoice! Poor Buoso!

ALL   Poor Buoso!
             If he had left me this house!
             And the mills of Signa!
             Then the mule . . . !
             If he had left me . . .

ZITA   Quiet! It's opened!

The old woman, with the will in her hand, is near the table; behind her, a human clump. Marco and Betto have climbed onto a chair. All the faces will be clearly visible, absorbed in the reading. The mouths will move, like those of people reading silently. All of a sudden the faces begin to cloud over . . . they reach a tragic expression . . . until the old Zita sinks into a seated position on the stool in front of the writing desk. Of the petrified group, Simone is the first to move: he turns and sees before him the three candles he just lighted. He blows them out. He draws the curtains of the bed completely, then extinguishes all the candelabra. The other relatives slowly go seeking chairs for themselves; they sit on them. They are as if petrified, with their eyes wide, staring, some here, some there.

SIMONE   So it was true! We'll see the monks
             fattening at the expense of the Donati!

CIESCA   All those beautiful accumulated florins
             ending in the monks' habits!

MARCO   Depriving us all of a substance,
             and making the monks wallow in plenty!

BETTO   I'll have to measure what I drink in Signa
             and the monks will drink wine from the vine-yard!

NELLA, CIESCA, ZITA
             They'll have their robes often made wider,
             we'll burst with bile, and they . . . with grub!

RINUCCIO   La mia felicita sarà rubata
              dall'"Opera di Santa Reparata!"

GHERARDO   Aprite le dispense dei conventi!
              Allegri, frati, ed arrotate i denti!

*A poco a poco l'ira e l'esaltazione dei parenti giunge al
colmo; lasciano i sedili, si aggirano furibondi per la camera,
alzano i pugni imprecando, scoppiano in risa sardoniche che
esplodono come urla di dannati.*

ZITA   Eccovi le primizie di mercato!
              Fate schioccar la lingua col palato!
              A voi, poveri frati: tordi grassi!

SIMONE   Quaglie pinate!

NELLA   Lodole!

GHERARDO   Ortolani!

ZITA   Beccafichi!

SIMONE   Quaglie pinate! Oche ingrassate!

ZITA   Ortolani!

BETTO   E galletti!

TUTTI   Galletti? Gallettini!

RINUCCIO   Galletti di canto tenerini!

ZITA, MARCO, SIMONE, BETTO
              E colle facce rosse ben pasciute,
              ridetevi di noi: ah! ah! ah!
              schizzando dalle gote la salute!
              ah! ah! ah!

CIESCA, NELLA
              Lodole e gallettini!

TUTTI   Eccolo là un Donati! ah! ah! ah!
              Eccolo là! Eccolo là un Donati!
              ah! ah! ah! Eccolo là!
              E la voleva lui l'eredità!
              Ridete, o frati,
              ridete alla barba dei Donati!
              ah! ah! ah! ah!

*L'esasperazione, giunta al colmo, si placa poco a poco e
subentra di nuovo l'abbattimento; qualcuno dei parenti piange
davvero.*

ZITA   Chi l'avrebbe mai detto
              che quando Buoso andava al cimitero,
              si sarebbe pianto per davvero!

*Lentamente ognuno cerca di nuovo una sedia per cadervi
sopra.*

ZITA, CIESCA, NELLA
              E non c'è nessun mezzo . . .

SIMONE, BETTO
              . . . per cambiarlo?

ZITA, MARCO   . . . per girarlo?

GHERARDO   . . . addolcirlo?

MARCO   O Simone, Simone?

ZITA   Tu sei il più vecchio!

MARCO   Tu se' anche stato podestà a Fucecchio!

RINUCCIO   My happiness will be stolen
                     by the "Good Works of Saint Reparata!"

GHERARDO   Open the pantries of the convents!
                     Be merry, monks, and sharpen your teeth!

Little by little the wrath and the excitement of the relatives reach a climax; they leave their seats, roam furiously about the room, raise their fists cursing, burst into sardonic laughs that explode like the screams of the damned.

ZITA   Here are the first fruits from the market!
                     Smack your tongue against your palate!
                     For you, poor monks: fat thrushes!

SIMONE   Firm quail!

NELLA   Larks!

GHERARDO   Ortolans!

ZITA   Warblers!

SIMONE   Firm quail! Fattened geese!

ZITA   Ortolans!

BETTO   And young cockerels!

ALL   Young cockerels? Baby cockerels!

RINUCCIO   Tender little singing cockerels!

ZITA, MARCO, SIMONE, BETTO
                     And with red, well-fed faces,
                     laugh at us: ha! ha! ha!
                     health bursting from your cheeks!
                     ha! ha! ha!

CIESCA, NELLA
                     Larks and little cockerels!

ALL   There, there's a Donati! ha! ha! ha!
                     There he is! There's a Donati!
                     ha! ha! ha! There is he!
                     And he wanted the inheritance himself!
                     Laugh, oh monks,
                     laugh at the expense of the Donati!
                     ha! ha! ha! ha!

Their exasperation, having reached its peak, gradually calms down and again depression takes its place; some of the relatives are really weeping.

ZITA   Who would ever have said
                     that when Buoso went to the cemetery
                     we would have wept really!

Slowly each of them again seeks a chair and falls onto it.

ZITA, CIESCA, NELLA
                     And isn't there any means . . .

SIMONE, BETTO
                     . . . to change it?

ZITA, MARCO   . . . to get around it?

GHERARDO   . . . to soften it?

MARCO   Oh, Simone, Simone?

ZITA   You're the oldest!

MARCO   You've also been mayor at Fucecchio!

Simone fa un cenno come per dire che è impossibile trovare un rimedio.

RINUCCIO   C'è una persona sola
                 che ci può consigliare,
                 forse salvare . . .

TUTTI   Chi?

RINUCCIO   Gianni Schicchi!

Gesto di disillusione dei parenti.

ZITA *(furibonda)*
                 Di Gianni Schicchi, della figliola,
                 non vo' sentirne parlar mai più!
                 E intendi bene!

GHERARDINO *(entrando di corsa, urlando:)*
                 È qui che viene!

TUTTI   Chi?

GHERARDINO   Gianni Schicchi!

ZITA   Chi l'ha chiamato?

RINUCCIO *(accennando il ragazzo)*
                 Io l'ho mandato,
                 perchè speravo . . .

CIESCA, NELLA
                 È proprio il momento
                 d'aver Gianni Schicchi fra i piedi!

ZITA   Ah! bada! se sale,
                 gli fo ruzzolare le scale!

MARCO, SIMONE
                 È proprio il momento
                 d'aver Gianni Schicchi fra i piedi!

GHERARDO *(a Gherardino)*
                 Tu devi obbedire
                 soltanto a tuo padre: là! là!

Sculaccia Gherardino e lo butta nella stanza a destra in cima alla scala.

SIMONE   Un Donati sposare la figlia d'un villano!

ZITA   D'uno sceso a Firenze dal contado!

                 Imparentarsi colla gente nova . . . !
                 Io von voglio che venga! Non voglio!

RINUCCIO   Avete torto! È fine! astuto . . .
                 Ogni malizia di leggi e codici
                 conosce e sa.
                 Motteggiatore . . . ! Beffeggiatore!
                 C'è da fare una beffa nuova e rara?
                 È Gianni Schicchi che la prepara!
                 Gli occhi furbi gli illuminan di riso
                 lo strano viso,
                 ombreggiato da quel suo gran nasone
                 che pare un torracchione per così!
                 Vien dal contado? Ebbene?
                 Che vuol dire?
                 Basta con queste ubbie grette e piccìne!
                 Firenze è come un albero fiorito
                 che in piazza dei Signori ha tronco e fronde,

Simone makes a gesture as if to say that it's impossible to find a remedy.

RINUCCIO There's only one person
      who can advise us,
      perhaps save us . . .

ALL   Who?

RINUCCIO Gianni Schicchi!

Disappointed gesture of the relatives.

ZITA (*furious*)
      I never want to hear any talk
      of Gianni Schicchi, of his daughter ever again!
      Mind me well!

GHERARDINO (*runs in, shouting:*)
      Here he comes!

ALL   Who?

GHERARDINO Gianni Schicchi!

ZITA   Who called him?

RINUCCIO (*nodding toward the boy*)
      I sent him,
      because I hoped . . .

CIESCA, NELLA This is just the moment
      to have Gianni Schicchi underfoot!

ZITA   Ah! mind you! If he comes up,
      I'll make him roll down the stairs!

MARCO, SIMONE
      This is just the moment
      to have Gianni Schicchi underfoot!

GHERARDO (*to Gherardino*)
      You must obey
      only your father: there! there!

He spanks Gherardino and flings him into the room on the right at the top of the stairs.

SIMONE   A Donati marry the daughter of a peasant!

ZITA   Of a man who came down to Florence from the
       country!
      Become related to the new people . . . !
      I don't want him to come! I don't want it!

RINUCCIO You're wrong! He's subtle! astute . . .
      He knows and knows well
      every trick of laws and regulations.
      A joker . . . ! Mocker!
      Must a new, rare joke be played?
      It's Gianni Schicchi who prepares it!
      His sly eyes illuminate with laughter
      his strange face,
      shaded by that great nose of his
      which seems a huge tower set lengthwise!
      He comes from the country? Well?
      What does that mean?
      Enough of these narrow and petty prejudices!
      Florence is like a tree in blossom
      which in the Piazza dei Signori has its trunk and
       branches,

ma le radici forze nuove apportano
dalle convalli limpide e feconde!
E Firenze germoglia ed alle stelle
salgon palagi saldi e torri snelle!
L'Arno, prima di correre alla foce,
canta baciando piazza Santa Croce,
e il suo canto è sì dolce e sì sonoro
che a lui son scesi i ruscelletti in coro!

Così scendanvi dotti in arti e scienze
a far più ricca e splendida Firenze!
E di val d'Elsa giù dalle castella
ben venga Arnolfo a far la torre bella!

E venga Giotto dal Mugel selvoso,
e il Medici mercante coraggioso!
Basta con gli odî gretti e coi ripicchi!
Viva la gente nova a Gianni Schicchi!
    (*si bussa alla porta*)
È lui!

   *Rinuccio apre la porta; entra Gianni Schicchi seguito da
Lauretta.*

GIANNI (*si sofferma sull'uscio: dà un'occhiata ai parenti*)
    (Quale aspetto sgomento e desolato!)
RINUCCIO   (Lauretta!)
LAURETTA   (Rino!)
GIANNI   (Buoso Donati, certo, è migliorato!)
RINUCCIO   Amore mio!
LAURETTA   Perchè sì pallido?
RINUCCIO   Ahimè, lo zio . . .
LAURETTA   Ebbene, parla . . .
RINUCCIO   Amore, amore, quanto dolore!
LAURETTA   Quanto dolore!

   *Mentre Rinuccio e Lauretta stanno in disparte fra il piane-
rottolo e la porta, Gianni lentamente va verso la vecchia Zita
che gli volta le spalle; avanzando vede i candelabri intorno al
letto.*

GIANNI   Ah! Andato?
    (Perchè stanno a lagrimare?
    Ti recitano meglio d'un giullare!)
        (*falso; forte*)
    Ah! comprendo il dolor di tanta perdita . . .
    Ne ho l'anima commossa . . .
GHERARDO   Eh! la perdita è stata proprio grossa!
GIANNI (*come chi dica parole stupide di circostanza*)

    Eh! son cose . . . Mah . . . ! Come si fa . . . !

    In questo mondo una cosa si perde . . .
    una si trova . . .
        (*seccato che facciano la commedia con lui*)
    Si perde Buoso . . .
    ma c'è l'eredità!

but the roots bring new strength
from the limpid and fertile valleys!
And Florence sprouts and to the stars
rise solid buildings and slender towers!
The Arno, before running to its mouth,
sings, kissing Santa Croce square,
and its song is so sweet and so resounding
that the little streams have come down to it in
    chorus!
So descend men learned in arts and sciences
to make Florence richer and more splendid!
And from the castles of the Elsa valley
let Arnolfo come and welcome, to make the
    lovely tower!
And let Giotto come from the wooded Mugello
and Medici, the brave merchant!
Enough of narrow hatreds and spites!
Long live the new people and Gianni Schicchi!
    (*Knocking at the door*)
It's he!

Rinuccio opens the door; Gianni Schicchi enters, followed by Lauretta.

GIANNI (*pauses in the doorway: gives a glance at the relatives*)
    (What a despairing and alarmed appearance!)

RINUCCIO   (Lauretta!)

LAURETTA   (Rino!)

GIANNI   (Buoso Donati, certainly, is better!)

RINUCCIO   My love!

LAURETTA   Why so pale?

RINUCCIO   Alas, my uncle . . .

LAURETTA   Well, speak . . .

RINUCCIO   Love, love, how much sorrow!

LAURETTA   How much sorrow!

As Rinuccio and Lauretta remain to one side between landing and door, Gianni slowly goes towards old Zita, who turns her back on him; as he advances he sees the candelabra around the bed.

GIANNI   Ah! Gone?
    (Why are they crying?
    They play-act better than a buffoon!)
        (*falsely; loud*)
    Ah! I understand the sorrow of such a loss . . .
    My soul is moved by it . . .

GHERARDO   Eh! the loss was really big!

GIANNI (*like a man who says stupid words suited to the occasion*)
    Eh! these are things . . . Ah . . . ! What's to be
    done . . . ?
    In this world you lose one thing . . .
    and you find another . . .
        (*annoyed that they should act for him*)
    You lose Buoso . . .
    but there's the inheritance!

ZITA (*gli si avventa come una bestia feroce*)
Sicuro! Ai frati!

GIANNI   Ah! diseredati?

ZITA   Diseredati! Sì, sì, diseredati!
E perciò ve lo canto:
pigliate la figliola,
levatevi di torno,
io non do mio nipote
ad una senza dote!

RINUCCIO   [O zia, io l'amo, l'amo!

LAURETTA   Babbo, babbo, lo voglio!]

GIANNI   [Figliola, un po' d'orgoglio!

ZITA   Non m n'importa un corno!]

GIANNI   Brava la vecchia! Brava! Per la dote
sacrifichi mia figlia e tuo nipote!
Brava la vecchia! Brava! Vecchia taccagna!
Stillina! sordida! spilorcia! gretta!

LAURETTA   [Rinuccio, non lasciarmi!
L'hai giurato
sotto la luna a Fiesole!
L'hai giurato
quando tu m'hai baciato!

RINUCCIO   Lauretta mia, ricordati!
tu m'hai giurato amore!
E quella sera Fiesole
sembrava tutto un fiore!

ZITA   Anche m'insulta!
Senza la dote
non do, non do il nipote!
       (*tirando Rinuccio a destra*)
Rinuccio, vieni, lasciali andare,
sarebbe un volerti rovinare!
Vieni, vieni, Rinuccio, vieni!

GIANNI (*tirando Lauretta a sinistra*)
Ah! vieni! vieni!
Un po' d'orgoglio!
Vieni, Lauretta, vieni,
rasciuga gli occhi,
sarebbe un parentado di pitocchi!

LAURETTA, RINUCCIO
Addio, speranza bella, speranza bella,
s'è spento ogni tuo raggio;
non ci potrem sposare
per il Calendimaggio!

MARCO, SIMONE, BETTO
Anche le dispute . . .

CIESCA, NELLA
. . . fra innamorati!

*Lauretta sfugge a Schicchi e corre da Rinuccio, che sfugge
alla zia e corre da Lauretta.*

LAURETTA   Babbo, lo voglio!

RINUCCIO   O Zia, la voglio!

ZITA (*hurls herself at him like a fierce beast*)
　　　　Sure! For the monks!

GIANNI　　Ah! disinherited?

ZITA　　　Disinherited! Yes, yes, disinherited!
　　　　And therefore I tell you openly:
　　　　take your daughter,
　　　　get out of here,
　　　　I'm not giving my nephew
　　　　to a girl without dowry!

RINUCCIO　Oh aunt, I love her, I love her!

LAURETTA　Daddy, daddy, I want him!

GIANNI　　Daughter, a bit of pride!

ZITA　　　I don't give a damn!

GIANNI　　Good for you, old woman! Brava! For the dowry
　　　　you sacrifice my daughter and your nephew!
　　　　Good for you, old woman! Brava! Old miser!
　　　　Stingy! sordid! mean! petty!

LAURETTA　Rinuccio, don't leave me!
　　　　You swore it
　　　　under the moon at Fiesole!
　　　　You swore it
　　　　when you kissed me!

RINUCCIO　My Lauretta, remember!
　　　　you swore your love to me!
　　　　And that evening Fiesole
　　　　seemed all one flower!

ZITA　　　He insults me, too!
　　　　Without the dowry
　　　　I won't give, won't give my nephew!
　　　　　　(*drawing Rinuccio to the right*)
　　　　Rinuccio, come, let them go,
　　　　it would mean you wanted to ruin yourself!
　　　　Come, come, Rinuccio, come!

GIANNI (*drawing Lauretta to the left*)
　　　　Ah! come! come!
　　　　A bit of pride!
　　　　Come, Lauretta, come,
　　　　dry your eyes,
　　　　it would mean having misers for relatives!

LAURETTA, RINUCCIO
　　　　Farewell, lovely hope, lovely hope,
　　　　your every ray has been extinguished;
　　　　we will not be able to marry
　　　　on May Day!

MARCO, SIMONE, BETTO
　　　　Even quarrels . . .

CIESCA, NELLA . . . among lovers!

Lauretta eludes Schicchi and runs to Rinuccio, who eludes his aunt and runs to Lauretta.

LAURETTA　Daddy, I want him!

RINUCCIO　Oh, aunt, I want her!

ZITA	Ed io non voglio!
GIANNI	Un po' d'orgoglio!
I PARENTI	Proprio il momento! Pensate al testamento!

GIANNI	Vecchia taccagna, gretta, sordida, spilorcia! Via!
I PARENTI	Pensate al testamento!

ZITA (*a Rinuccio*)
    Ma vieni, vieni!

LAURETTA, RINUCCIO
    Amore!

ZITA	No, no, non voglio, via di qua!
GIANNI	Via di qua! Ah, vieni, vieni! (*trascina Laura verso la porta*)
I PARENTI	Pensate al testamento!

LAURETTA, RINUCCIO
    Amore!

ZITA	No! no! no!
GIANNI	Vien! vien! vien!]

RINUCCIO (*fermando Schicchi*)
    Signor Giovanni,
    rimanete un momento!
        (*a Zita*)
    Invece di sbraitare,
    dategli il testamento!
        (*a Gianni*)
    Cercate di salvarci!
    A voi non può mancare
    un'idea portentosa, una trovata,
    un rimedio, un ripiego, un espediente!

GIANNI (*accennando ai parenti*)
    A pro di quella gente?
    Niente! niente! niente!

LAURETTA (*gli si inginocchia davanti*)
    O mio babbino caro,
    mi piace, è bello, bello;
    vo' andare in Porta Rossa
    a comperar l'anello!
    Sì, sì, ci voglio andare!
    e se l'amassi indarno,
    andrei sul Ponte Vecchio,
    ma per buttarmi in Arno!
    Mi struggo e mi tormento!
    O Dio, vorrei morir!
    Babbo, pietà, pietà!
        (*piangendo*)
    Babbo, pietà, pietà!

GIANNI (*come chi è costretto ad accondiscendere*)
    Datemi il testamento!

ZITA	And I don't want it!
GIANNI	A bit of pride!
THE RELATIVES	Just the moment! Think of the will!
GIANNI	Old miser, petty, sordid, mean! Away!
THE RELATIVES	Think of the will!
ZITA (*to Rinuccio*)	Why, come, come!
LAURETTA, RINUCCIO	Love!
ZITA	No, no, I don't want it; away from here!
GIANNI	Away from here! Ah, come, come! (*drags Lauretta toward the door*)
THE RELATIVES	Think of the will!
LAURETTA, RINUCCIO	Love!
ZITA	No! no! no!
GIANNI	Come! come! come!
RINUCCIO (*stopping Schicchi*)	Signor Giovanni, remain a moment! (*to Zita*) Instead of bawling, give him the will! (*to Gianni*) Try to save us! You can't be lacking for a wondrous idea, a trick, a remedy, a device, an expedient!
GIANNI (*nodding toward the relatives*)	On behalf of those people? Nothing! nothing! nothing!
LAURETTA (*kneels before him*)	Oh, my dear daddy, I like him, he's handsome, handsome; I want to go to via Porta Rossa to buy the ring! Yes, yes, I want to go there! and if I were to love him in vain, I'd go on the Ponte Vecchio, but to throw myself into the Arno! I pine and I'm tormented! Oh God, I would like to die! Daddy, mercy, mercy! (*weeping*) Daddy, mercy, mercy!
GIANNI (*like a man who is forced to comply*)	Give me the will!

Rinuccio glielo dà. Gianni legge e cammina. I parenti lo
seguono con gli occhi, poi inconsciamente finiscono per and-
argli dietro come i pulcini alla chioccia, tranne Simone che
siede sulla cassapanca a destra, e incredulo, scrolla il capo.
Ansia.

GIANNI   Niente da fare!

I parenti lasciano Schicchi e si avviano verso il fondo della
scena; Lauretta e Rinuccio sono appartati, assorti solo nel loro
amore deluso.

LAURETTA, RINUCCIO
                Addio, speranza bella,
                dolce miraggio;
                non ci potrem sposare
                per il Calendimaggio!

Gianni Schicchi riprende a passeggiare, leggendo più atten-
tamente il testamento. S'arresta di botto.

GIANNI   Niente da fare!

I parenti si lasciano cadere sulle sedie.   .

LAURETTA, RINUCCIO
                Addio, speranza bella,
                s'è spento ogni tuo raggio . . .

GIANNI (*tonante*)
                Però!

LAURETTA, RINUCCIO
                (Forse ci sposeremo
                per il Calendimaggio!)

Tutti i parenti si sono alzati di scatto per correre a Gianni.
Schicchi si ferma nel mezzo della scena col viso aggrottato
come perseguendo un suo pensiero, gesticola parcamente
guardando avanti a sé. Tutti sono intorno a lui; ora, anche
Simone; più bassi di lui, con i visi voltati verso il suo viso come
uccellini che aspettino l'imbeccata. Gianni, a poco a poco, si
rischiara, sorride, guarda tutta quella gente . . . alto, dominante,
troneggiante.

TUTTI (*con un filo di voce*)
                Ebbene?

GIANNI (*con voce infantile*)
                Laurettina! va sul terrazzino;
                porta i minuzzolini all'uccellino.
                        (*fermando Rinuccio che vuole seguire*
                        Lauretta)
                Sola.
                        (*appena Lauretta è uscita, Gianni si ri-*
                        volge ai parenti)
                Nessuno sa che Buoso ha reso il fiato?

TUTTI   Nessuno!
GIANNI   Bene! Ancora nessuno deve saperlo!
TUTTI   Nessuno lo saprà!
GIANNI (*assalito da un dubbio*)
                E i servi?

Rinuccio gives it to him. Gianni reads it and paces up and down. The relatives follow him with their eyes, then unconsciousy they end by walking after him like chicks after the hen, except for Simone, who sits on the chest at right and shakes his head, incredulously. Anxiety.

GIANNI   Nothing to be done!

The relatives leave Schicchi and go toward the back of the stage; Lauretta and Rinuccio are off to one side, absorbed only in their disappointed love.

LAURETTA, RINUCCIO

       Farewell, lovely hope,
       sweet mirage;
       we will not be able to marry
       on May Day!

Gianni Schicchi starts pacing up and down again, reading the will more carefully. He stops abruptly.

GIANNI   Nothing to be done!

The relatives sink down onto the chairs.

LAURETTA, RINUCCIO

       Farewell, lovely hope,
       your every ray has been extinguished . . .

GIANNI (*thunderously*)

       However!

LAURETTA, RINUCCIO

       (Perhaps we will be married
       on May Day!)

All the relatives have sprung to their feet to run to Gianni. Schicchi stops in the center of the stage, his face in a frown as if pursuing a thought of his; he gesticulates soberly, looking straight ahead. All of them are around him now, even Simone: lower than he, their faces turned toward his face like little birds waiting to be fed. Gianni, little by little, brightens, smiles. He looks at all those people . . . lofty, dominating, enthroned.

ALL (*in a faint voice*)

       Well?

GIANNI (*in a childish voice*)

       Laurettina! go onto the little terrace;
       take some little crumbs to the little bird.
           (*stopping Rinuccio, who wants to follow
           Lauretta*)
       By yourself.
           (*as soon as Lauretta has gone out, Gianni
           addresses the relatives*)
       Nobody knows that Buoso has given up the
           ghost?

ALL   Nobody!

GIANNI   Good! Nobody must know it yet!

ALL   Nobody will know it!

GIANNI (*assailed by a doubt*)

       And the servants?

ZITA   Dopo l'aggravamento . . .
                in camera . . . nessuno!

GIANNI (*a Marco e Gherardo; tranquillizato, deciso*)
                Voi due portate il morto e i candelabri
                là dentro nella stanza di rimpetto!
                        (*a Ciesca e Nella*)
                Donne! Rifate il letto!

LE DONNE   Ma . . .

GIANNI   Zitte. Obbedite!

*Marco e Gherardo scompaiono fra le sarge del letto e ri-
compaiono con un fardello rosso che portano a destra nella
stanza sotto la scala. Simone, Betto e Rinuccio portano via i
candelabri. Ciesca e Nella ravviano il letto. Si bussa alla porta.*

TUTTI (*si fermano, sorpresi*)
                Ah!

GIANNI (*contrariatissimo, con voce soffocata*)
                Chi può essere? Ah!

ZITA   Maestro Spinelloccio il dottore!

GIANNI   Guardate che non passi!
                Ditegli qualche cosa . . .
                che Buoso è migliorato e che riposa.

*I parenti si affollano alla porta e la schiudono appena, Gianni
si nasconde dietro alle sarge, dalla parte opposta a quella dove
c'è la porta di ingresso. Betto avvicina gli scuri della finestra.*

SPINELLOCCIO (*con voce nasale e accento bolognese*)
                L'è permesso.

TUTTI   Buon giorno, Maestro Spinelloccio!
                Va meglio! va meglio!

NELLA   Va meglio!

SIMONE   Va meglio!

SPINELLOCCIO   Ha avuto il *benefissio?*

TUTTI   Altro che! Altro che!

SPINELLOCCIO   A che *potensa*
                l'è arrivata la *sciensa!*
                Be', vediamo, vediamo!

Maestro Spinelloccio fa per entrare; i parenti lo fermano.

ZITA, MARCO   No! riposa!

SPINELLOCCIO (*insistendo*)
                Ma io . . .

CIESCA, SIMONE
                Riposa!

GIANNI (*seminascosto fra le sarge del letto, contraffacendo la
                voce di Buoso, tremolante*)
                No! No! Maestro Spinelloccio . . . !

*Alla voce del morto i parenti danno un traballone, poi si
accorgono che è Gianni che contraffà la voce di Buoso. Ma
nel traballone a Betto è caduto il piatto d'argento trafugato:
la vecchia lo raccatta e lo rimette sul tavolo minacciando Betto.*

SPINELLOCCIO   Oh! Messer Buoso!

ZITA   After his worsening . . .
in the bedroom . . . nobody!

GIANNI (*to Marco and Gherardo; reassured, determined*)
You two, carry the dead man and the candelabra
in there, in the room opposite!
      (*to Ciesca and Nella*)
Women! Remake the bed!

THE WOMEN   But . . .

GIANNI   Quiet. Obey!

*Marco and Gherardo disappear behind the curtains of the
bed and reappear with a red bundle which they carry to the
right in the room under the stairs. Simone, Betto, and Rinuccio
carry off the candelabra. Ciesca and Nella straighten up the
bed. Someone knocks at the door.*

ALL (*stop, surprised*)
Ah!

GIANNI (*highly vexed, in a stifled voice*)
Who can it be? Ah!

ZITA   Master Spinelloccio, the doctor!

GIANNI   Mind he doesn't come in!
Say something to him . . .
that Buoso is better and that he's resting.

*The relatives crowd to the door and barely open it. Gianni
hides behind the curtains on the side opposite the main door.
Betto closes the shutters at the window.*

SPINELLOCCIO (*in a nasal voice and Bolognese accent*)
May I come in?

ALL   Good day, Master Spinelloccio!
He's better! He's better!

NELLA   He's better!

SIMONE   He's better!

SPINELLOCCIO   Did he have the bowel movement?

ALL   Indeed! Indeed!

SPINELLOCCIO   To what power
has science arrived!
Well, let's see, let's see!

Master Spinelloccio starts to come in; the relatives stop him.

ZITA, MARCO   No! He's resting!

SPINELLOCCIO (*insisting*)
But I . . .

CIESCA, SIMONE
He's resting!

GIANNI (*half hidden in the curtains of bed, imitating the trem-
ulous voice of Buoso*)
No! No! Master Spinelloccio . . . !

*At the voice of the dead man the relatives react with a start,
then they realize it is Gianni imitating Buoso's voice. But in
the start, Betto dropped the silver plate that was stolen: the
old woman picks it up and puts it back on the table, menacing Betto.*

SPINELLOCCIO   Oh! Master Buoso!

GIANNI   Ho tanta voglia di riposare . . .
              potreste ripassare questa sera?
              Son quasi addormentato . . .

SPINELLOCCIO Sì, Messer Buoso!
              Ma va meglio?

GIANNI   Da morto son rinato!
              A stasera.

SPINELLOCCIO A stasera!
                   (*ai parenti*)
              Anche alla voce sento:
              è migliorato!
              Eh! a me non è mai morto un ammalato!
              Non ho delle pretese,
              il merito l'è tutto
              della scuola bolognese!

TUTTI   A stasera, Maestro!

SPINELLOCCIO A questa sera!

*I parenti chiudono la porta e si volgono a Gianni che è
uscito dal suo nascondiglio. Betto va a riaprire le finestre:
entra la luce.*

GIANNI   Era eguale la voce?

TUTTI   Tale e quale!

GIANNI   Ah! Vittoria! vittoria!
              Ma non capite . . . ?

TUTTI   No!

GIANNI   Ah! che zucconi!
              Si corre dal notaio.
                   (*veloce, affannato*)
              "Messer notaio, presto,
              Via da Buoso Donati!
              C'è un gran peggioramento!
              Vuol fare testamento!
              Portate su con voi le pergamene,
              presto, messere, se no è tardi!"
                   (*con voce naturale*)
              Ed il notaio viene.
              Entra: la stanza è semioscura,
              dentro il letto intravede
              di Buoso la figura!
              In testa la cappellina!
              al viso la pezzolina!
              Fra cappellina e pezzolina
              un naso che par quel di Buoso
              e invece è il mio,
              perchè al posto di Buoso ci son io!
              Io, lo Schicchi con altra voce e forma!
              Io falsifico in me Buoso Donati,
              testando e dando al testamento normal!
              O gente! questa matta bizzarria
              che mi zampilla nella fantasia
              è tale da sfidar l'eternità!

*Come strozzati dalla commozione i parenti attorniano Gianni
Schicchi; gli baciano le mani e le vesti.*

GIANNI I have such a desire to rest . . .
    Could you come back this evening?
    I'm almost asleep . . .

SPINELLOCCIO Yes, Master Buoso!
    But are things going better?

GIANNI I've risen from the dead!
    Till this evening.

SPINELLOCCIO Till this evening!
      (to the relatives)
    Even from the voice I can hear:
    he's better!
    Eh! a sick man has never died on me!
    I don't have any pretentions,
    the merit is all
    of the Bolognese school!

ALL Till this evening, master!

SPINELLOCCIO Till this evening!

The relatives shut the door and turn to Gianni, who has come out of his hiding place. Betto goes to reopen the windows: the light comes in.

GIANNI Was the voice the same?

ALL Identical!

GIANNI Ah! Victory! Victory!
    But, don't you understand . . . ?

ALL No!

GIANNI Ah! what pumpkin heads!
    You run to the notary.
      (fast, breathless)
    "Master notary, quickly,
    Away to Buoso Donati!
    There's a great worsening!
    He wants to make a will!
    Take your parchments with you,
    hurry, master, otherwise it's too late!"
      (in his natural voice)
    And the notary comes.
    He enters: the room is half dark,
    in the bed he glimpses
    the form of Buoso!
    The nightcap on his head!
    the kerchief on his face!
    Between nightcap and kerchief
    a nose that seems that of Buoso
    and instead is mine,
    because I am there in Buoso's place!
    I, Schicchi, with another voice and shape!
    In myself I falsify Buoso Donati,
    willing and giving the will regularity!
    Oh people! this mad whimsey
    that springs up in my imagination
    is such to defy eternity!

As if choked with emotion the relatives surround Gianni Schicchi; they kiss his hands and his garments.

TUTTI   [Schicchi! Schicchi! Schicchi!
         Schicchi! Schicchi! Schicchi!

ZITA (*a Rinuccio*)
.   Va, corri dal notaio.

RINUCCIO   Io corro dal notaio!

Rinuccio esce correndo.

SIMONE   Caro Gherardo, Marco, Zita, Ciesca,
          Nella, Gherardo, Zita, Betto ...

BETTO   Ciesca, Marco, Gherardo, Nella,
          caro Gherardo, Marco, Ciesca, Nella ...

GLI ALTRI   Schicchi! Schicchi!

GIANNI   (O quale commozione!)

GHERARDO   Betto, Zita ...

MARCO   Zita, Simone ...

LE DONNE   Nella, Ciesca, Simone. O giorno d'allegrezza!
            La beffa ai frati è bella!

SIMONE, BETTO
            O giorno d'allegrezza!
            La beffa ai frati è bella!

GHERARDO, MARCO
            Schicchi! Schicchi! Schicchi!

GIANNI   (O quale commozione!)

TUTTI   Com'è bello l'amore fra i parenti!
          Com'è bello l'amore fra i parenti!]

I parenti si abbracciano e si baciano con grande effusione.

SIMONE   O Gianni, ora pensiamo un po' alla divisione:

          i fiorini in contanti ...

GLI ALTRI   in parti eguali!

Gianni dice sempre di sì con la testa.

SIMONE   A me i poderi di Fucecchio.

ZITA   A me quelli di Figline.

BETTO   A me quelli di Prato.

GHERARDO   A noi le terre d'Empoli.

MARCO   A me quelle di Quintole.

BETTO   A me quelle di Prato.

SIMONE   E quelle di Fucecchio.

ZITA   Resterebbero ancora: la mula,
          questa casa e i mulini di Signa.

MARCO   Son le cose migliori ...

SIMONE (*falsamente ingenuo*)
          Ah! capisco, capisco!
          perchè sono il più vecchio
          e sono stato podestà a Fucecchio,
          volete darli a me!
          Io vi ringrazio!

ZITA   No, no, no, no! Un momento!
          Se tu se' vecchio, peggio per te!
          peggio per te!

ALL   Schicchi! Schicchi! Schicchi!
      Schicchi! Schicchi! Schicchi!

ZITA (*to Rinuccio*)
      Go, run to the notary.

RINUCCIO I run to the notary!

 Rinuccio goes out, running.

SIMONE   Dear Gherardo, Marco, Zita, Ciesca,
      Nella, Gherardo, Zita, Betto . . .

BETTO   Ciesca, Marco, Gherardo, Nella,
      Dear Gherardo, Marco, Ciesca, Nella . . .

THE OTHERS Schicchi! Schicchi!

GIANNI   (Oh, what emotion!)

GHERARDO Betto, Zita . . .

MARCO   Zita, Simone . . .

THE WOMEN Nella, Ciesca, Simone. Oh, day of happiness!
      The trick on the monks is a beautiful one!

SIMONE, BETTO
      Oh, day of happiness!
      The trick on the monks is a beautiful one!

GHERARDO, MARCO
      Schicchi! Schicchi! Schicchi!

GIANNI   (Oh, what emotion!)

ALL   How beautiful is love among relatives!
      How beautiful is love among relatives!

 *The relatives embrace and kiss one another with great
effusion.*

SIMONE   Oh, Gianni, now let's think a bit about the divi-
        sion:
      the florins in cash . . .

THE OTHERS . . . in equal shares!

 Gianni constantly nods his head: yes.

SIMONE   To me, the farms at Fucecchio.

ZITA   To me, the ones at Figline.

BETTO   To me, the ones at Prato.

GHERARDO To us, the lands at Empoli.

MARCO   To me, the ones at Quintole.

BETTO   To me, the ones at Prato.

SIMONE   And the ones at Fucecchio.

ZITA   There would still remain: the mule,
      this house, and the mills at Signa.

MARCO   They are the best things . . .

SIMONE (*falsely ingenuous*)
      Ah! I understand, I understand!
      because I'm the oldest
      and I have also been mayor at Fucecchio,
      you want to give them to me!
      I thank you!

ZITA   No, no, no, no! One moment!
      If you are old, so much the worse for you!
      so much the worse for you!

GLI ALTRI   Sentilo, sentilo, il podestà,
              vorrebbe il meglio dell'eredità!

GIANNI (*a parte, ridendo*)
              (Quanto dura l'amore fra i parenti!)
              Ah! ah!

TUTTI   La casa, la mula, i mulini di Signa
              toccano a me!
              La casa, la mula, i mulini
              toccano a me, ecc.
              La casa, la mu —

Si odono i rintocchi di una campana che suona a morto.
Tutti i parenti ammutoliscono allibiti.

TUTTI (*con voce soffocata*)
              L'hanno saputo!
              Hanno saputo che Buoso è crepato!

Gherardo si precipita giù dalla scala d'uscita.

GIANNI   Tutto crollato!

LAURETTA (*affacciandosi dal terrazzo*)
              Babbo, si può sapere . . . ?
              L'uccellino non vuole più minuzzoli . . .

GIANNI (*nervoso*)
              Ora dàgli da bere!

Lauretta scompare di nuovo sul terrazzo. Gherardo rientra
affannato; non può parlare, ma ai parenti che lo attorniano fa
segno di no.

GHERARDO   È preso un accidente
              al moro battezzato
              del signor capitano!

TUTTI (*allegramente*)
              Requiescat in pace!

SIMONE (*con autorità*)
              Per la casa, la mula, i mulini
              propongo di rimetterci
              alla giustizia, all'onestà di Schicchi!

TUTTI   Rimettiamoci a Schicchi!

GIANNI   Come volete.
              Datemi i panni per vestirmi.
              Presto! Presto!

Zita, Nella e la Ciesca prendono da una cassapanca la pez-
zolina, la cappellina e una camicia da notte di Buoso e mano
a mano le portano a Gianni Schicchi e lo fanno vestire.

ZITA   Ecco la cappellina!
                  (*a bassa voce a Schicchi*)
              (Se mi lasci la mula,
              questa casa, i mulini di Signa,
              ti do trenta fiorini!)

GIANNI   (Sta bene!)

Zita si allontana fregandosi le mani.

SIMONE (*avvicinandosi con fare distratto a Schicchi; a bassa*
voce)
              (Se lasci a me la casa, la mula
              ed i mulini,

THE OTHERS   Listen to him, listen to him, the mayor,
              he would like the best of the inheritance!

GIANNI (*to one side, laughing*)
              (How long love lasts among relatives!)
              Ha! ha!

ALL   The house, the mule, the mills at Signa
              fall to me!
              The house, the mule, the mills
              fall to me, etc.
              The house, the mu —

*The strokes of a bell are heard, tolling for the dead. All the
relatives fall silent, aghast.*

ALL (*in a stifled voice*)
              They've found out!
              They've found out that Buoso's kicked off!

Gherardo rushes down the stairway of the exit.

GIANNI   Everything's collapsed!

LAURETTA (*looking in from the terrace*)
              Daddy, may I know . . . ?
              The little bird doesn't want any more crumbs...

GIANNI (*nervous*)
              Now give him something to drink!

*Lauretta disappears again onto the terrace. Gherardo comes
back in, breathless; he can't speak, but to the relatives who
surround him he signals: no.*

GHERARDO   The captain's
              baptized Moor
              had an accident!

ALL (*gaily*)
              Requiescat in pace!

SIMONE (*with authority*)
              For the house, the mule, the mills
              I propose we leave it up to
              the justice, the honesty of Schicchi!

ALL   Let's leave it up to Schicchi!

GIANNI   As you wish.
              Give me the clothes to dress myself.
              Quickly! Quickly!

*Zita, Nella, and Ciesca take from a chest the kerchief, the
nightcap, and a nightshirt of Buoso's. One by one, they take
them to Gianni Schicchi and have him dress.*

ZITA   Here's the nightcap!
                    (*in a low voice, to Schicchi*)
              (If you leave me the mule,
              this house and the mills at Signa,
              I'll give you thirty florins!)

GIANNI   (Very well!)

Zita goes off, rubbing her hands.

SIMONE (*approaching Schicchi with a casual manner; in a low
                    voice*)
              (If you leave me the house, the mule
              and the mills

	to do cento fiorini!)

GIANNI   (Sta bene!)

BETTO (*furtivo, a Schicchi*)
          (Gianni, se tu mi lasci
          questa casa, la mula e i mulini
          di Signa, ti gonfio di quattrini!)

GIANNI   (Sta bene!)

Nella, dopo aver presa la pezzolina, parla sottovoce a Gherardo.

NELLA (*a Gianni, forte*)
          Ecco la pezzolina!
          (Se lasci a noi la mula, i mulini
          di Signa e questa casa,
          a furia di fiorini
          ti s'intasa!)

GIANNI   (Sta bene!)

Nella si allontana, va da Gherardo e tutti e due si fregano le mani.

CIESCA   Ed ecco la camicia!
          (Se ci lasci la mula, i mulini
          di Signa e questa casa,
          per te mille fiorini!)

GIANNI   (Sta bene!)

La Ciesca va da Marco, gli parla all'orecchio; si fregano le mani. Tutti sono soddisfatti e si fregano le mani. Intanto Gianni Schicchi si infila la camicia. Quindi con lo specchio in mano si accomoda la pezzolina e la cappellina cambiando l'espressione del viso come per trovare l'atteggiamento giusto. Simone è alla finestra per vedere se arriva il notaio. Gherardo sbarazza il tavolo a cui dovrà sedere il notaio. Marco e Betto tirano le sarge del letto e ravviano la stanza. Zita, Nella e Ciesca guardano Gianni comicamente.

ZITA   [È bello, portentoso!
          Chi vuoi che non s'inganni?
          È Gianni che fa Buoso?
          È Buoso che fa Gianni?
          Il testamento è odioso?
          Un camicion maestoso,
          il viso, il viso dormiglioso,
          il naso poderoso,
          l'accento lamentoso, ah!

CIESCA   Fa' presto, bambolino,
          chè devi andare a letto.
          Se va bene il giochetto
          ti diamo un confortino!
          L'uovo divien pulcino,
          il fior, il fior diventa frutto,
          i frati mangian tutto,
          ma il frate impoverisce,
          la Ciesca s'arricchisce, ah!

NELLA   Spogliati, bambolino,
          chè ti mettiamo in letto.
          E non aver, non aver dispetto,

                I'll give you a hundred florins!)

GIANNI   (Very well!)

BETTO (*furtively, to Schicchi*)
                (Gianni, if you leave me
                this house, the mule, and the mills
                at Signa, I'll stuff you with money!)

GIANNI   (Very well!)

    Nella, after having taken the kerchief, speaks in a whisper to Gherardo.

NELLA (*loud, to Gianni*)
                Here's the kerchief!
                (If you leave us the mule, the mills
                at Signa and this house,
                you'll be choked
                with florins!)

GIANNI   (Very well!)

    Nella moves away, goes to Gherardo, and they both rub their hands.

CIESCA   And here's the nightshirt!
                (If you leave us the mule, the mills
                at Signa and this house,
                a thousand florins for you!)

GIANNI   (Very well!)

    Ciesca goes to Marco, speaks into his ear; they rub their hands. All are content and rub their hands. Meanwhile Gianni Schicchi slips on the nightshirt. Then with the mirror in his hand he adjusts the kerchief and the nightcap, changing the expression of his face as if to find the proper attitude. Simone is at the window to see if the notary is arriving. Gherardo clears the table where the notary is to sit. Marco and Betto draw the curtains of the bed and straighten up the room. Zita, Nella, and Ciesca look at Gianni comically.

ZITA   He's handsome, prodigious!
                Who would not be deceived?
                Is it Gianni who plays Buoso?
                Is it Buoso who plays Gianni?
                Is the will hateful?
                A majestic nightshirt,
                the face, the face sleepy,
                the powerful nose,
                the whining tone, ah!

CIESCA   Hurry up, little baby,
                for you have to go to bed.
                If the game goes well
                we'll give you a sweetmeat!
                The egg becomes chick,
                the flower, the flower becomes fruit,
                the monks eat everything,
                but the monk grows poor,
                Ciesca becomes rich, ah!

NELLA   Undress, little baby,
                for we're putting you to bed.
                And don't, don't be annoyed,

no, no, se cambio il camicino!
Si spiuma il canarino,
la volpe cambia pelo,
il ragno ragnatela,
il cane cambia cuccia,
la serpe cambia buccia,
e il buon Gianni . . .]

ZITA   . . . cambia panni . . .

NELLA   . . . per poterci servir!

CIESCA   Cambia viso . . .

ZITA   . . . muso e naso . . .

CIESCA   . . . per poterci servir!

NELLA   Cambia accento . . .

ZITA   testamento . . .

ZITA, NELLA, CIESCA
                . . . per poterci servir!

GIANNI   Vi servirò a dover!

ZITA, NELLA, CIESCA
                Bravo così!

GIANNI   Contente vi farò!

ZITA, NELLA, CIESCA
                Proprio così! O Gianni, Gianni,
                nostro salvator!

NELLA, CIESCA
                O Gianni Schicchi, nostro salvatore!

ZITA   O Schicchi!

NELLA, CIESCA
                O Schicchi!

ZITA   O Gianni Schicchi, nostro salvatore!

Anche gli uomini attorniano Schicchi.

NELLA, GHERARDO
                È preciso?

GLI ALTRI   Perfetto!

TUTTI   A letto! a letto! a letto!

*Spingono Gianni verso il letto, ma egli li ferma con un gesto
quasi solenne.*

GIANNI   Prima un avvertimento!
                O signori, giudizio!
                Voi lo sapete il rischio?
                "Per chi sostituisce
                se stesso in luogo d'altri
                in testamenti e lasciti,
                per lui e per i complici
                c'è il taglio della mano e poi l'esilio!"

                Ricordatelo bene! Se fossimo scoperti:
                la vedete Firenze?
                        (*accennando la torre di Arnolfo che appare
                        dalla finestra aperta*)
                Addio, Firenze, addio, cielo divino,

no, no, if I change your little shirt!
The canary molts,
the fox changes its coat,
the spider its web,
the dog changes its bed,
the snake changes its skin,
and the good Gianni . . .

ZITA   . . . changes his clothes . . .

NELLA   . . . to be able to serve us!

CIESCA   He changes his face . . .

ZITA   . . . muzzle and nose . . .

CIESCA   . . . to be able to serve us!

NELLA   He changes his tone . . .

ZITA   will . . .

ZITA, NELLA, CIESCA
    . . . to be able to serve us!

GIANNI   I'll serve you properly!

ZITA, NELLA, CIESCA
    Good for you!

GIANNI   I'll make you content!

ZITA, NELLA, CIESCA
    Just so! Oh, Gianni, Gianni,
    our savior!

NELLA, CIESCA
    Oh, Gianni Schicchi, our savior!

ZITA   Oh, Schicchi!

NELLA, CIESCA
    Oh, Schicchi!

ZITA   Oh, Gianni Schicchi, our savior!
       (*The men also surround Schicchi*)

NELLA, GHERARDO
    Is he exact?

THE OTHERS   Perfect!

ALL   To bed! to bed! to bed!

*They push Gianni toward the bed, but he stops them with
an almost solemn gesture.*

GIANNI   First a warning!
    Oh, ladies and gentlemen, discretion!
    Do you know the risk?
    "For him who substitutes
    himself in place of others
    in wills and bequests,
    for himself and for his accomplices
    there is the cutting off of the hand and then
       exile!"
    Remember it well! If we were discovered:
    you see Florence?
       (*nodding towards Arnolfo's tower, which
       appears through the open window*)
    Farewell, Florence, farewell, divine sky,

io ti saluto con questo moncherino,
e vo randagio come un Ghibellino!

TUTTI (*soggiogati, impauriti, guardando verso la finestra*)
Addio, Firenze, addio, cielo divino,
io ti saluto, ecc.

*Si bussa. Gianni schizza a letto; i parenti rendono la stanza
semioscura; mettono una candela sul tavolo dove il notaio deve
scrivere; buttano un mucchio di roba sul letto; aprono.*

RINUCCIO (*entrando*)
Ecco il notaro!

MESSER AMANTIO, PINELLINO, GUCCIO (*entrando*)
Messer Buoso, buon giorno!

GIANNI (*contraffacendo la voce*)
Oh! siete qui?
Grazie, messere Amantio!
O Pinellino calzolaio, grazie!
Grazie Guccio tintore,
troppo buoni, troppo buoni
di venirmi a servir da testimoni!

PINELLINO (*commosso*)
Povero Buoso!
Io l'ho sempre calzato!
vederlo in quello stato . . .
vien da piangere!

*Il Notaio intanto tira fuori da una cassetta le pergamene e i
bolli e mette tutto sul tavolo; si siede nella poltrona e i due
testimoni restano in piedi, ai suoi lati.*

GIANNI   Il testamento avrei voluto scriverlo
con la scrittura mia,
me l'impedisce la paralisia . . .
Perciò volli un notaio,
solempne et leale . . .

AMANTIO   O messer Buoso, grazie!
Dunque tu soffri di paralisia?

*Gianni allunga in alto le mani agitandole tremolanti. Gesto
di compassione di tutti.*

CIESCA, NELLA
Povero Buoso!

ZITA, SIMONE   Povero Buoso!

AMANTIO   Oh! poveretto! Basta!
I testi videro,
testes viderunt!
Possiamo incominciare . . . Ma . . . i parenti . . . ?

GIANNI   Che restino presenti!

AMANTIO   Dunque incomincio:
*In Dei nomini, anno Dei nostri Jesu
Christi ab eius salutifera incarnatione
millesimo ducentesimo nonagesimo nono,
die prima septembris, indictione
undecima, ego notaro Amantio di Nicolao,*

I wave to you with this stump,
and I go off, a stray like a Ghibelline!

ALL (*subdued, frightened, looking toward the window*)
Farewell, Florence, farewell, divine sky,
I wave to you, etc.

*There is a knocking. Gianni darts into bed; the relatives
make the room half dark; they set a candle on the table where
the notary is to write; they throw a pile of things on the bed;
they open the door.*

RINUCCIO (*entering*)
Here's the notary!

MASTER AMANTIO, PINELLINO, GUCCIO (*entering*)
Master Buoso, good day!

GIANNI (*disguising his voice*)
Oh! Are you here?
Thanks, Master Amantio!
Oh, cobbler Pinellino, thanks!
Thanks, dyer Guccio,
too kind, too kind
of you to come and act as witnesses for me!

PINELLINO (*moved*)
Poor Buoso!
I've always shod him!
to see him in that condition . . .
makes we weep!

*The notary in the meanwhile takes the parchments and
seals from a case and puts everything on the table; he sits in
the chair and the two witnesses remaining standing, at either
side of him.*

GIANNI   I would have liked to write the will
with my handwriting,
the paralysis prevents me . . .
Therefore I wanted a notary,
solempne et leale . . .

AMANTIO   Oh, Master Buoso, thanks!
Then you suffer from paralysis?

*Gianni extends his hands upwards, waving them tremulous-
ly. All make a gesture of compassion.*

CIESCA, NELLA   Poor Buoso!

ZITA, SIMONE   Poor Buoso!

AMANTIO   Oh! poor thing! Enough!
The witnesses saw,
testes viderunt!
We can begin . . . But . . . the relatives . . . ?

GIANNI   Let them remain present!

AMANTIO   Then I begin:
*In Dei nomini, anno Dei nostri Jesu
Christi ab eius salutifera incarnatione
millesimo ducentesimo nonagesimo nono,
die prima septembris, indictione
undecima, ego notaro Amantio di Nicolao,*

civis Florentiae, per voluntatem Buosi
Donati scribo hoc testamentum . . .

GIANNI (*mettendo fuori la mano, scandendo ogni parola*)
    Annullans, revocans, et irritans
    omne aliud testamentum!

I PARENTI   Che previdenza! che previdenza!

AMANTIO   Un preambolo: dimmi, i funerali,
    (il più tardi possibile)
    li vuoi ricchi? fastosi? dispendiosi?

GIANNI   No, no, no, pochi quattrini!
    Non si spendano più di due fiorini!

GHERARDO   Oh! che modestia!

MARCO   Oh! che modestia!

CIESCA, NELLA, RINUCCIO
    Povero zio!

ZITA   Che animo!

BETTO   Che cuore!

SIMONE   Gli torna a onore!

GIANNI   Lascio ai frati minori
    e all'opera di Santa Reparata . . .
        (*i parenti si alzano, esterrefatti*)
    . . . cinque lire.

I PARENTI (*tranquillizati*)
    Bravo! Bravo!
    Bisogna sempre pensare alla beneficenza!

AMANTIO   Non ti sembra un po' poco?

GIANNI   Chi crepa e lascia molto
    alle congreghe e ai frati
    fa dire a chi rimane:
    "Eran quattrini rubati!"

NELLA, RINUCCIO, GHERARDO
    Che massime!

CIESCA, MARCO, BETTO
    Che mente!

ZITA, SIMONE   Che saggezza!

AMANTIO   Che lucidezza!

GIANNI   I fiorini in contanti
    li lascio in parti eguali fra i parenti.

CIESCA, NELLA, RINUCCIO
    Oh! grazie, zio!

ZITA   [Grazie, cugino!

SIMONE, BETTO
    Grazie, cognato!]

GIANNI   Lascio a Simone i beni di Fucecchio.

SIMONE   Grazie!

GIANNI   Alla Zita i poderi di Figline.

ZITA   Grazie, grazie!

GIANNI   A Betto i campi di Prato.

BETTO   Grazie, cognato!

> civis Florentiae, per voluntatem Buosi
> Donati scribo hoc testamentum . . .

GIANNI (*thrusting out his hand, stressing each word*)
> Annullans, revocans, et irritans
> omne aliud testamentum!

THE RELATIVES
> What foresight! What foresight!

AMANTIO
> A preamble: tell me, the funeral
> (may it be as late as possible)
> do you want it rich, sumptuous, expensive?

GIANNI
> No, no, no, little money!
> Let no more than two florins be spent!

GHERARDO   Oh! what modesty!

MARCO   Oh! what modesty!

CIESCA, NELLA, RINUCCIO
> Poor uncle!

ZITA   What a soul!

BETTO   What a heart!

SIMONE   It does him honor!

GIANNI
> I leave the friars minor
> and the goods works of Saint Reparata . . .
> > (*the relatives stand up, terrified*)
> . . . five lire.

THE RELATIVES (*reassured*)
> Bravo! Bravo!
> One must always think of charity!

AMANTIO   Does it seem a bit little to you?

GIANNI
> He who dies and leaves much
> to congregations and monks
> makes those who remain say:
> "It was stolen money!"

NELLA, RINUCCIO, GHERARDO
> What maxims!

CIESCA, MARCO, BETTO
> What a mind!

ZITA, SIMONE   What wisdom!

AMANTIO   What lucidity!

GIANNI
> The florins in cash
> I leave in equal shares among the relatives.

CIESCA, NELLA, RINUCCIO
> Oh! thanks, Uncle!

ZITA   Thanks, Cousin!

SIMONE, BETTO
> Thanks, Brother-in-Law!

GIANNI   I leave to Simone the possessions at Fucecchio.

SIMONE   Thanks!

GIANNI   To Zita the farms at Figline.

ZITA   Thanks, thanks!

GIANNI   To Betto the fields at Prato.

BETTO   Thanks, brother-in-law!

GIANNI   A Nella ed a Gherardo i beni d'Empoli.

NELLA, GHERARDO
                    Grazie, grazie!
GIANNI   Alla Ciesca ed a Marco
                    i beni a Quintole.
TUTTI (*fra i denti*)
                    (Ora siamo alla mula, alla casa
                    ed ai mulini.)
GIANNI   Lascio la mula,
                    quella che costa trecento fiorini,
                    che è la migliore mula di Toscana
                    al mio devoto amico . . . Gianni Schicchi.

Rinuccio furtivamente raggiunge Lauretta sul terrazzo.

I PARENTI   Come? Come? Come?

AMANTIO   *Mulam relinquit ejus amico devoto*
                    Joanni Schicchi.
I PARENTI   Ma . . .

SIMONE   Cosa vuoi che gl'importi
                    a Gianni Schicchi di quella mula?
GIANNI   Tienti bono, Simone!
                    Lo so io quel che vuole Gianni Schicchi!
I PARENTI (*brontolando*)
                    Ah! furfante, furfante, furfante!
GIANNI   Lascio la casa di Firenze al mio
                    caro devoto affezionato amico
                    Gianni Schicchi!
I PARENTI (*erompono*)
                    Ah, basta, basta! Un accidente! basta!
                    A Gianni Schicchi, a quel furfante!
                    a quel furfante di Gianni Schicchi!
                    Ci ribelliamo, ci ri . . .
GIANNI   Addio, Firenze . . .
I PARENTI   . . . a quel furfante di Gianni Schicchi
                    ci ribellia . . .

GIANNI   Addio, cielo divino . . .
I PARENTI   Ah!

GIANNI   Io ti saluto . . .
AMANTIO   Non si disturbi
                    del testator la volontà!
GIANNI   Messer Amantio, io lascio a chi mi pare!
                    Ho in mente un testamento e sarà quello,
                    se gridano, sto calmo e canterello . . .
GUCCIO   Ah! che uomo!
PINELLINO   Che uomo!
GIANNI   E i mulini di Signa . . .
I PARENTI   I mulini di Signa?

GIANNI   To Nella and Gherardo the possessions at Em-
                  poli.

NELLA, GHERARDO
                  Thanks, thanks!

GIANNI   To Ciesca and Marco
                  the possessions at Quintole.

ALL (*muttering*)
                  (Now we reach the mule, the house
                  and the mills.)

GIANNI   I leave my mule,
                  the one that costs three hundred florins,
                  which is the best mule in Tuscany
                  to my devoted friend . . . Gianni Schicchi.

Rinuccio furtively joins Lauretta on the terrace.

THE RELATIVES
                  What? What? What?

AMANTIO   *Mulam relinquit ejus amico devoto*
                  Joanni Schicchi.

THE RELATIVES
                  But . . .

SIMONE   What do you think that mule
                  matters to Gianni Schicchi?

GIANNI   Calm yourself, Simone!
                  I know what Gianni Schicchi wants!

THE RELATIVES (*grumbling*)
                  Ah! scoundrel, scoundrel, scoundrel!

GIANNI   I leave the house in Florence to my
                  dear, devoted, affectionate friend
                  Gianni Schicchi!

THE RELATIVES (*exploding*)
                  Ah, enough, enough! My foot! enough!
                  To Gianni Schicchi, to that scoundrel!
                  to that scoundrel of a Gianni Schicchi!
                  We rebel, we re . . .

GIANNI   Farewell, Florence . . .

THE RELATIVES
                  . . . to that scoundrel of a Gianni Schicchi,
                  we reb . . .

GIANNI   Farewell, divine sky . . .

THE RELATIVES
                  Ah!

GIANNI   I wave to you . . .

AMANTIO   Let the wish of the testator
                  not be disturbed!

GIANNI   Master Amantio, I bequeath to whom I please!
                  I have a will in mind and that will be it,
                  if they shout, I remain calm and sing . . .

GUCCIO   Ah! what a man!

PINELLINO   What a man!

GIANNI   And the mills at Signa . . .

THE RELATIVES
                  The mills at Signa?

GIANNI   I mulini di Signa (addio Firenze!)
              li lascio al caro (addio, cielo divino!)
              affezionato amico Gianni Schicchi!
              (e ti saluto con questo moncherino!)
              la, la, la, la, la! Ecco fatto!
                   (*i testi ed il notaio sono un po' sorpresi*)

              Zita, di vostra borsa
              date venti fiorini ai testimoni
              e cento al buon notaio!

AMANTIO   Messer Buoso, grazie!

   *Messer Amantio si avvia verso il letto, ma Gianni lo ferma
con un gesto della mano tremula.*

GIANNI   Niente saluti.
              Andate, andate. Siamo forti . . . !

AMANTIO (*avviandosi per uscire*)
              Ah, che uomo, che uomo!

GUCCIO, PINELLINO (*avviandosi commossi*)
              Che uomo! che perdita!

AMANTIO   Che peccato!

AMANTIO, GUCCIO, PINELLINO
              Che perdita!

GUCCIO (*ai parenti*)
              Coraggio!

PINELLINO   Coraggio!

   *I tre escono. Appena usciti il notaio e i testi, i parenti rest-
ano un istante in ascolto finché i tre si sono allontanati, quindi
tutti, tranne Rinuccio che è con Lauretta sul terrazzino:*

I PARENTI (*a voce soffocata da prima, poi urlando feroci con-
              tro Gianni:*)
              Laadro! ladro! furfante!
              traditore! birbante!
              iniquo! ladro! furfante,
              birbante, traditore!

GIANNI   Gente taccagna!
              Vi caccio via . . .
                   (*salta giù dal letto e, brandendo il bastone
                   di Buoso, mena legnate ai parenti*)

              . . . di casa mia!
              È casa mia!

   *I parenti corrono qua e là rincorsi da Gianni. Saccheggiano
e rubano. Gherardo e Nella salgono a destra e ne tornano carichi con Gherardino carico. Gianni tenta difendere la roba.*

I PARENTI   Saccheggia! saccheggia! saccheggia!
              Le pezze di lino! La roba d'argento!

GIANNI   Via! via!

I PARENTI   La roba d'argento! Le pezze di tela!
              Bottino! bottino! saccheggia! saccheggia!

GIANNI   The mills at Signa (farewell, Florence!)
              I leave to my dear (farewell, divine sky!)
              affectionate friend Gianni Schicchi!
              (and I wave to you with this stump!)
              la, la, la, la, la! That's done!
                      (*the witnesses and the notary are a bit
                      surprised*)
              Zita, from your purse
              give twenty florins to the witnesses
              and a hundred to the good notary!

AMANTIO   Master Buoso, thanks!

*Master Amantio goes toward the bed, but Gianni stops him
with a gesture of his trembling hand.*

GIANNI   No good-bys.
              Go, go. Let us be strong . . . !

AMANTIO (*starting to leave*)
              Ah, what a man, what a man!

GUCCIO, PINELLINO (*going off, moved*)
              What a man! What a loss!

AMANTIO   What a shame!

AMANTIO, GUCCIO, PINELLINO
              What a loss!

GUCCIO (*to the relatives*)
              Courage!

PINELLINO   Courage!

*The three go out. As soon as the notary and the witnesses
have left, the relatives remain listening until the three have
gone away, then all, except Rinuccio, who is with Lauretta
on the terrace:*

THE RELATIVES (*first in a stifled voice, then shouting fiercely
              against Gianni:*)
              Thief! thief! scoundrel!
              traitor! rogue!
              wicked! thief! scoundrel!
              rogue! traitor!

GIANNI   Miserly people!
              I'll drive you away . . .
                      (*he jumps down from the bed and, bran-
                      dishing Buoso's cane, he delivers blows to
                      the relatives*)
              . . . from my house!
              It's my house!

*The relatives run here and there, chased by Gianni. They
sack and steal. Gherardo and Nella climb up on the right and
come back laden with Gherardino, also laden. Gianni tries to
defend the belongings.*

THE RELATIVES
              Plunder! plunder! plunder!
              The linen cloths! The silverware!

GIANNI   Away! away!

THE RELATIVES
              The silverware! The linen cloths!
              Booty! booty! plunder! plunder!

GIANNI   È casa mia!
I PARENTI   Le pezze di tela, ecc.

GIANNI   Via! Via! Via! Via!
                    È casa mia! Vi caccio via!
I PARENTI   Saccheggia, ecc.

Tutti, mano a mano che son carichi, si affollano alla porta, scendono le scale. Gianni li rincorre. La scena resta vuota.

I PARENTI (*dall'interno*)
                    Ladro, furfante, traditore!
GIANNI. (*dall'interno*)
                    Via! Via!
I PARENTI (*allontanandosi*)
                    Ah! ah!
GIANNI   Via! Via!

Dal fondo apre di dentro le impannate del finestrone; appare Firenze inondata dal sole; i due innamorati restano sul terrazzo.

RINUCCIO   Lauretta mia, staremo sempre qui!
                    Guarda . . . Firenze è d'oro!
                    Fiesole è bella!
LAURETTA   Là mi giurasti amore!
RINUCCIO   Ti chiesi un bacio!
LAURETTA   Il primo bacio . . .
RINUCCIO   Tremante e bianca
                    volgesti il viso . . .
LAURETTA, RINUCCIO
                    Firenza da lontano
                    ci parve il Paradiso!

Si abbracciano e restano nel fondo abbracciati. Gianni Schicchi torna risalendo le scale, carico di roba che butta al suolo.

GIANNI   La masnada fuggì!

Di colpo si arresta, vede i due, si pente di aver fatto rumore. Ma i due non si turbano. Gianni sorride; è commosso. Viene alla ribalta e accennando gli innamorati . . . con la berretta in mano:

GIANNI (*licenziando senza cantare*)
                    Diteme voi, signori,
                    se i quattrini di Buoso
                    potevan finir meglio di così?
                    Per questa bizzarria
                    m'han cacciato all'inferno . . . e così sia;
                    ma con licenza del gran padre Dante,
                    se stasera vi siete divertiti,
                    concedetemi voi . . .
                        (*fa il gesto di applaudire*)
                    . . . l'attenuante!
                        (*si inchina graziosamente*)

GIANNI   It's my house

THE RELATIVES

    The linen cloths, etc.

GIANNI   Away! Away! Away! Away!

    It's my house! I'll drive you away!

THE RELATIVES

    Plunder, etc.

All of them, gradually as they become laden, crowd to the door, descend the steps. Gianni chases them. The stage remains empty.

THE RELATIVES (*from within*)

    Thief, scoundrel, traitor!

GIANNI (*from within*)

    Away! Away!

THE RELATIVES (*going off*)

    Ah! ah!

GIANNI   Away! Away!

From the background the window curtains open in; Florence appears, bathed in sunshine. The two lovers remain on the terrace.

RINUCCIO   My Lauretta, we'll be here always!

    Look . . . Florence is golden!

    Fiesole is beautiful!

LAURETTA   There you swore your love to me!

RINUCCIO   I asked you for a kiss!

LAURETTA   The first kiss . . .

RINUCCIO   Trembling and white

    you turned your face . . .

LAURETTA, RINUCCIO

    Florence, from the distance,

    seemed paradise to us!

They embrace and remain in the background, embracing. Gianni Schicchi comes back up the stairs, laden with belongings which he throws on the ground.

GIANNI   The band fled!

Suddenly he stops, sees the two, regrets having made any noise. But the couple are undisturbed. Gianni smiles; he is moved. He comes to the footlights and nodding toward the lovers . . . with his cap in hand:

GIANNI (*taking his leave, without singing*)

    You tell me, ladies and gentlemen,

    if Buoso's money

    could end in a better way than this?

    For this whimsey

    they stuck me in hell . . . and so be it;

    but with permission of great father Dante,

    if this evening you've been amused,

    grant me . . .

      (*makes the gesture of applauding*)

    . . . the extenuating circumstances . . .

      (*bows gracefully*)

Turandot

After the completion of the *Trittico* Puccini wrote no music for more than two years. The frantic search for a new libretto went on, Forzano suggested subjects, and so did Giuseppe Adami (the librettist of *La rondine* and *Il tabarro*), but none of their ideas struck the magic spark. Finally, in the summer of 1920, Puccini had lunch in Milan with Adami and with another prospective librettist, Renato Simoni, playwright, drama critic, and then editor of *La lettura* (whose former editor had been Giacosa). In the course of the meeting, someone — apparently Puccini himself — mentioned the eighteenth century Venetian writer Carlo Gozzi, proposing his colorful, fantastic play *Turandotte*. The play had already served as libretto for Ferruccio Busoni and, earlier, for Antonio Bazzini, Puccini's old teacher at the Milan Conservatory. The play had also been adapted by Schiller in German in 1803, and it was an Italian retranslation of this German version that Puccini and Simoni first used as a basis for discussion.

For some time Puccini had been saying that he wanted, with his next opera, to attempt something new, and with *Turandot,* he knew that he had a golden opportunity. This time the writing and rewriting were more tormented than ever, and the novelty of the subject also seemed to cause more than the usual number of ups and downs in Puccini's mood. At one point, in the late autumn of 1920, he wrote to Adami: " . . . I fear that *Turandot* will never be finished . . . When the fever abates, it ends by disappearing altogether, and without fever there is no creation; because emotional art is a kind of malady, an exceptional state of mind, an over-excitation of every fiber, of every atom of one's being . . ."

A year later the first act was virtually finished, but the rest of the opera — and especially the love duet at the end — was causing difficulties. The librettists tried and tried again, but Puccini could not be satisfied and, about that time, he contemplated abandoning the opera in favor of a new idea of Forzano's. Then, after further delays, he got back to work on *Turandot* in the summer of 1923. By the fall of 1924 all that remained to be composed was the love duet and the last act finale. The premiere of the opera was tentatively scheduled for the ing of 1925 at La Scala, with Toscanini as the conductor. The composer was already thinking about the cast, up the young Beniamino Gigli for the tenor part.

ber 22, 1924, the composer wrote to Adami: *thi*h a most terrible time. That trouble in my *with him* more morally than physically. I am going a famous specialist. . . . Will they oper- red? Or condemned to death? I cannot And then there is *Turandot* . . ."

now it, the "trouble in his throat" er 29, after an operation which d in the Brussels hospital. The ve duet, which he had taken ly with his body.

On the basis of those sketches, the composer Franco Alfano — commissioned by Toscanini — completed the opera, which was then given at La Scala seventeen months after Puccini's death. On the opening night Toscanini ended the performance after the death of Liù, turning to the audience to announce that it was at this point that Puccini laid down his pen. The reviews — as might be expected — were all favorable, and many critics recognized the new quality of Puccini's last work. For once, the public was slower than the press to hail the opera, and until recently *Turandot* — like Verdi's *Falstaff* — was more respected than loved. Lately, however, it has been heard much more widely and more frequently; and now the icy Princess is almost as popular as the warm-blooded Tosca or the pathetic Mimì.

THE PLOT

ACT ONE

In Peking, in legendary times. The cold and beautiful Princess Turandot is destined, by a sacred oath, to be the bride of the royal suitor who can successfully answer three riddles which the Princess asks him. So far all of Turandot's suitors have failed; and for failure the punishment is death, by beheading. In fact, as the opera begins, the Imperial City is preparing for the execution of the latest unlucky aspirant, the Prince of Persia. In the milling crowd appears Timur, the defeated Tartar king, old and blind, led by his faithful slave girl, Liù. As the guards roughly handle the mob, the old man falls to the ground. A stranger helps him up and recognizes him. The stranger, the Unknown Prince, is Timur's son, who was believed killed in battle. As they exchange glances, Timur describes Liù's affectionate care, and the prince asks her why she has voluntarily shared such hardship. In a voice filled with love, Liù answers, "because, one day, you smiled at me." The moon rises: the hour for the execution has come. The crowd begs for mercy for the young victim, but Turandot orders the executioners to proceed. The crowd follows the executioner and the victim, leaving Timur, Liù, and the Prince alone. At his first sight of the icy Turandot, the Prince has fallen madly in love and is eager to try his luck. Timur and Liù try to dissuade him, and so do the three grotesque ministers, Ping, Pang, and Pong, who appear just as the Prince is about to strike the gong, signaling that a new suitor has appeared. All pleas are ineffectual and, calling Turandot's name, the Prince strikes the gong.

ACT TWO

Ping, Pang, and Pong meet to lament th[e]
Peking, where beheadings are becomin[g]

quent. Each minister speaks nostalgically of his native region, to which he longs to return. But it is time for the Prince to face the supreme trial. The aged Emperor tries also to dissuade him, but the Prince is adamant. Turandot herself appears and vows that no one shall ever possess her, since she is avenging the cruel murder of her ancestress at the hand of the Tartars long ago. One by one, Turandot asks the riddles, and each time the Prince guesses the correct answer. Defeated, Turandot begs her father not to give her to the stranger, but the Emperor says that the sacred vow must be fulfilled. Finally, Turandot turns to the Prince and asks him if he wants to have her by force. He answers that he wants her love, and offers to release her from the vow if she can discover his name before dawn.

ACT THREE

No one is sleeping in Peking since the Princess has commanded that the stranger's name be discovered by dawn. Otherwise heads will roll. The three ministers try to lure the Prince with offers of lovely maidens, wealth, glory; he refuses all of them. Then guards drag in Timur and Liù. Turandot appears and orders Liù to be tortured. But Liù explains that her love gives her the strength to resist, and when she feels herself weakening, she seizes a dagger and commits suicide. The crowd is aghast and, with Timur, all follow the poor girl's body as it is carried off. Left alone with Turandot, the Prince reproaches her and, at the same time, insists that love can make her human. He kisses her. Turandot returns the kiss, but is then overcome with shame at her own weakness. She admits that she loves the Prince, but begs him to go away. Instead, he places his life in her hands, revealing that his name is Calaf, son of Timur. Dawn comes at last. The court and the crowd gather to hear Turandot's defeat or victory. She announces that she does indeed know the stranger's name, but then, vanquished, she murmurs: "His name . . . is love!" Calaf rushes to her, as the crowd cheers.

TURANDOT

libretto by Giuseppe Adami and Renato Simoni

First performed at the Teatro alla Scala, Milan
April 25, 1926

CHARACTERS

Princess Turandot	*Soprano*
The Emperor Altoum	*Tenor*
Timur, exiled Tartar king	*Bass*
The Unknown Prince (Calaf), his son	*Tenor*
Liù, a slave girl	*Soprano*
Ping, Grand Chancellor	*Baritone*
Pang, Grand Purveyor	*Tenor*
Pong, Grand Cook	*Tenor*
A Mandarin	*Baritone*

The Prince of Persia, the executioner, servants,
handmaidens, etc.

In Peking, in legendary times.

ATTO PRIMO

Le mura della grande Città Violetta: la Città Imperiale. Gli spalti massicci chiudono quasi tutta la scena in semicerchio. Soltanto a destra il giro è rotto da un grande loggiato tutto scolpito e intagliato a mostri, a liocorni, a fenici, coi pilastri sorretti dal dorso di massicce tartarughe. Ai piedi del loggiato, sostenuto da due archi, è un gong di sonorissimo bronzo.

Sugli spalti sono piantati i pali che reggono i teschi dei giustiziati. A sinistra e nel fondo, s'aprono nelle mura tre gigantesche porte. Quando si apre il velario siamo nell'ora più sfolgorante del tramonto. Pekino, che va digradando nelle lontananze, scintilla dorata. Il piazzale è pieno di una pittoresca folla cinese, immobile, che ascolta le parole di un Mandarino. Dalla sommità dello spalto, dove gli fanno ala le guardie tartare rosse e nere, egli legge un tragico decreto.

MANDARINO	Popolo di Pekino!
	La legge è questa: Turandot, la Pura,
	sposa sarà di chi, di sangue regio,
	spieghi i tre enigmi ch'ella proporrà.
	Ma chi affronta il cimento e vinto resta,
	porga alla scure la superba testa.
LA FOLLA	Ah! Ah!
MANDARINO	Il Principe di Persia
	avversa ebbe fortuna:
	al sorger della luna,
	per man del boia
	muoia!

Il Mandarino si ritira e la folla rompe la sua immobilità con crescente tumulto.

LA FOLLA	Muoia! Sì, muoia!
	Noi vogliamo il carnefice!
	Presto, presto! Muoia! muoia!
	Al supplizio! Muoia, muoia!
	Presto, presto!
	Se non appari, noi ti sveglierem!
	Pu-Tin-Pao! Pu-Tin-Pao! Pu-Tin-Pao!
	(e cercando d'invadere lo spalto)
	Alla reggia! Alla reggia! Alla reggia!

Le guardie respingono la folla. Nell'urto molti cadono. Confuso vociare di gente impaurita. Urla. Proteste. Invocazioni.

LE GUARDIE	Indietro, cani! Indietro, cani!
LA FOLLA	Oh, crudeli! Pel cielo, fermi!
	O madre mia! Ahi! I miei bimbi!
	[Crudeli, ecc.

ACT ONE

The walls of the great Violet City: the Imperial City. The massive ramparts enclose almost the whole stage in a semicircle. Their movement is broken only on the right by a great loggia, all sculptured and carved with monsters, unicorns, phoenixes, its columns supported by the backs of massive tortoises. At the foot of the loggia, held up by two arches is a gong of very sonorous bronze.

Some poles are set in the ramparts, which bear the skulls of the executed. At left and in the background three gigantic gates open in the walls. When the curtain goes up we are in the most dazzling hour of sunset. Peking, which slopes away in the distance, sparkles, golden. The square is filled with a picturesque Chinese crowd, motionless, listening to the words of a mandarin. From the top of the rampart, where the red and black Tartar guards flank him, he reads a tragic decree.

MANDARIN   People of Peking!
                 This is the law: Turandot, the pure,
                 will be the bride of the man, of royal blood,
                 who solves the three riddles that she will propose.
                 But he who faces the trial and remains defeated,
                 must offer his haughty head to the ax.

THE CROWD   Ah! Ah!

MANDARIN   The Prince of Persia
                 had luck against him:
                 at the rise of the moon,
                 by the executioner's hand
                 let him die!

The mandarin retires and the crowd breaks its immobility with mounting tumult.

THE CROWD   Let him die! Yes, let him die!
                 We want the executioner!
                 Quickly, quickly! Let him die, die!
                 To the torture! Let him die, die!
                 Quickly, quickly!
                 If you don't appear, we'll waken you!
                 Pu-Tin-Pao! Pu-Tin-Pao! Pu-Tin-Pao!
                 (and, trying to invade the rampart)
                 To the palace! To the palace! To the palace!

The guards thrust back the crowd. In the shoving many people fall. Confused voices of frightened people. Shouts. Protests. Invocations.

THE GUARDS   Back, dogs! Back, dogs!

THE CROWD   Oh, cruel ones! Stop, for heaven's sake!
                 Oh, my mother! Ahi! My babies!
                 Cruel ones, etc.

LE GUARDIE   Indietro, cani!

LIÙ (*disperatamente*)
                Il mio vecchio è caduto!

LA FOLLA   Crudele! Siate umani!
                Non fateci male!]

LIÙ   Chi m'aiuta?
                Chi m'aiuta a sorreggerlo?
                Il mio vecchio è caduto ...
                Pietà, pietà!

   E volge intorno lo sguardo supplichevole. D'improvviso un giovine accorre, si piega sul vecchio, e prorompe in un grido.

IL PRINCIPE IGNOTO
                Padre! Mio padre!

LE GUARDIE   Indietro!

IL PRINCIPE IGNOTO
                O padre, sì, ti ritrovo!

LA FOLLA   Crudeli!

IL PRINCIPE IGNOTO
                Guardami! Non è sogno!

LA FOLLA   [Perchè ci battete? ahimè!
                Pietà! Pietà!

LIÙ   Mio signore!]

IL PRINCIPE IGNOTO (*con crescente angoscia e commozione*)
                Padre! Ascoltami! Padre ... ! Son io! ...
                E benedetto sia ...
                E benedetto sia il dolor
                per questa gioia che ci dona
                un Dio pietoso.

TIMUR (*rinvenendo, apre gli occhi, fissa il suo salvatore, quasi non crede alla realtà, gli grida:*)
                O mio figlio! tu! vivo?

IL PRINCIPE IGNOTO (*con terrore*)
                Taci!
                        (*e, aiutato da Liù, trascinando Timur in
                        disparte, sempre piegato su di lui, con
                        voce rotta, con carezze, con lagrime:*)
                Chi usurpò la tua corona
                me cerca e te persegue!
                Non c'è asilo per noi, padre, nel mondo!

TIMUR   T'ho cercato, mio figlio,
                e t'ho creduto morto!

IL PRINCIPE IGNOTO
                T'ho pianto, padre ...
                e bacio queste mani sante!

TIMUR   O figlio ritrovato ... !

LA FOLLA (*che nel frattempo s'è raggruppata presso gli spalti,
            ora ha un urlo di ebbrezza feroce*)

                Ecco i servi del boia!
                Muoia! Muoia! Muoia! Muoia!

THE GUARDS   Back, dogs!

LIÙ (*desperately*)

    My old one has fallen!

THE CROWD   Cruel ones! Be human!
    Don't hurt us!

LIÙ   Who will help me?
    Who will help me lift him up?
    My old one has fallen . . .
    Pity, pity . . . !

And she casts an imploring glance around. Suddenly a young man runs up, bends over the old man, and bursts out with a cry.

THE UNKNOWN PRINCE

    Father! My father!

THE GUARDS   Back!

THE UNKNOWN PRINCE

    Oh, father, yes, I find you again!

THE CROWD   Cruel ones!

THE UNKNOWN PRINCE

    Look at me! It isn't a dream!

THE CROWD   Why are you striking us? Alas!
    Pity! Pity!

LIÙ   My lord!

THE UNKNOWN PRINCE (*with mounting anguish and emotion*)
    Father! Listen to me! Father . . . ! It is I!
    And blessed be . . .
    And blessed be grief
    for this joy that a pitying God
    gives us.

TIMUR (*coming to, opens his eyes, stares at his savior, almost doesn't believe the reality, cries to him:*)
    Oh, my son! You! Alive?

THE UNKNOWN PRINCE (*with terror*)
    Be silent!
        (*and, assisted by Liù, drawing Timur to one side, still bent over him, in a broken voice, with caresses, with tears:*)
    He who usurped your crown
    is seeking me and pursuing you!
    There is no refuge for us, Father, in the world!

TIMUR   I sought you, my son,
    and I believed you dead!

THE UNKNOWN PRINCE

    I wept for you, Father . . .
    and I kiss these sainted hands!

TIMUR   Oh, refound son!

THE CROWD (*which has gathered in the meanwhile near the ramparts, now emits a cry of fierce intoxication*)
    Here are the executioner's servants!
    Let him die! Die! Die! Die!

Infatti sulla sommità delle mura, vestiti di luridi cenci in-
sanguinati, appariscono, grottescamente tragici, i servi del car-
nefice trascinando l'enorme spada, che affilano su una immensa
cote.

TIMUR (*sempre a terra, al figlio curvo su lui, sommessamente*)

> Perduta la battaglia, vecchio re
> senza regno e fuggente,
> una voce sentii che mi diceva:
> "Vien con me, sarò tua guida . . ."
> Era Liù!

IL PRINCIPE IGNOTO
> Sia benedetta!

TIMUR
> Ed io cadeva affranto,
> e m'asciugava il pianto,
> mendicava per me . . .

IL PRINCIPE IGNOTO (*fissando la fanciulla, commosso*)
> Liù . . . chi sei?

LIÙ   Nulla sono . . . una schiava, mio Signore . . .

LA FOLLA   Gira la cota! Gira la cota!

IL PRINCIPE IGNOTO
> E perchè tanta angoscia hai diviso?

LIÙ (*con dolcezza estatica*)
> Perchè un dì . . . nella Reggia,
> mi hai sorriso.

LA FOLLA (*aizzando i servi del boia*)
> Gira la cote! Gira! ecc.

Allora due servi, che han detersa la lama, la fanno passare e
stridere sulla cote che vertiginosamente gira. E sprizzano scin-
tille, e il lavoro si anima ferocemente accompagnato da un
canto sguaiato cui la folla fa eco.

SERVI DEL BOIA
> Ungi! Arrota! Che la lama
> guizzi, sprizzi fuoco e sangue!
> Il lavoro mai non langue,
> mai non langue . . .

LA FOLLA   Mai non langue . . .

SERVI DEL BOIA
> . . . dove regna, dove regna Turandot!

LA FOLLA   . . . dove regna Turandot!

SERVI DEL BOIA
> Ungi! Arrota!

TUTTI   Fuoco e sangue!

LA FOLLA   Dolci amanti, avanti, avanti!

SERVI DEL BOIA
> Cogli uncini e coi coltelli
> noi siam pronti a ricamar le vostre pelli!

LA FOLLA   Dolci amanti, ecc.
> Chi quel gong percuoterà,
> apparire la vedrà!

SERVI DEL BOIA
> Apparire la vedrà,
> bianca al pari della giada . . .

In fact, at the top of the walls, dressed in lurid, bloodstained rags, there appear, grotesquely tragic, the executioner's servants, dragging the enormous sword, which they sharpen on an immense whetstone.

TIMUR (*still on the ground, to his son bent over him, in a low voice*)

> The battle lost, an old king
> without kingdom and in flight,
> I heard a voice that said to me:
> "Come with me, I'll be your guide . . ."
> It was Liù!

THE UNKNOWN PRINCE

> Bless her!

TIMUR

> And I would fall, exhausted,
> and she would dry my tears,
> she begged for me . . .

THE UNKNOWN PRINCE (*staring at the girl, moved*)

> Liù . . . who are you?

LIÙ   I am nothing . . . a slave, my lord . . .

THE CROWD   Turn the whetstone! Turn the whetstone!

THE UNKNOWN PRINCE

> And why have you shared such anguish?

LIÙ (*with ecstatic sweetness*)

> Because one day . . . in the Palace,
> you smiled at me.

THE CROWD (*inciting the executioner's servants*)

> Turn the whetstone! Turn! etc.

Then two servants, who have cleaned the blade, make it pass and clank on the whetstone which turns dizzyingly. And sparks fly, and the work becomes fiercely animated, accompanied by a raucous song which the crowd repeats, echo-like.

THE EXECUTIONER'S SERVANTS

> Oil! Sharpen! Let the blade
> flash, spurt fire and blood!
> Work never languishes,
> never languishes . . .

THE CROWD   Never languishes . . .

THE EXECUTIONER'S SERVANTS

> . . . where reigns, where reigns Turandot!

THE CROWD   . . . where reigns Turandot!

THE EXECUTIONER'S SERVANTS

> Oil! Sharpen!

ALL   Fire and blood!

THE CROWD   Forward, forward, sweet lovers!

THE EXECUTIONER'S SERVANTS

> With hooks and with knives
> we are ready to embroider your skins!

THE CROWD   Sweet lovers, etc.
>   He who will strike that gong
>   will see her appear!

THE EXECUTIONER'S SERVANTS

> He will see her appear,
> white as jade . . .

TUTTI	Fredda come quella spada . . .
SERVI DEL BOIA	
	. . . è la bella Turandot!
LA FOLLA	È la bella Turandot!
	Dolci amanti, avanti, avanti!
	Quando rangola il gong
	gongola il boia!
SERVI	Quando rangola il gong
	gongola il boia.
	Ungi! Arrota!
	La morte è una!
	[Quando rangola il gong, ecc.
LA FOLLA	Vano è l'amore se non c'è fortuna!
	Gli enigmi sono tre, la morte è una!
	Sì, gli enigmi sono tre, la morte è una!
	Chi quel gong percuoterà?
TUTTI	Ungi! Arrota! ecc.
	Il lavoro mai non langue
	dove regna Turandot! Ah!]

E mentre i servi si allontanano per portare al carnefice la spada, la folla si raggruppa qua e là, pittorescamente, sugli spalti e scruta con impazienza feroce il cielo che a poco a poco s'è oscurato.

LA FOLLA	Perchè tarda la luna? Faccia pallida!
	Mostrati in cielo! Presto! Vieni! Spunta!
	O testa mozza! O squallida!
	Vieni! Spunta! Mostrati in cielo!
	O testa mozza! O esangue!
	O esangue, o squallida!
	O taciturna! O amante smunta dei morti!
	Come aspettano il tuo funereo lume
	i cimiteri! O esangue, o squallida!
	O testa mozza!
	(*e come a poco a poco un chiarore lunare*
	si diffonda)
	Ecco laggiù un barlume!
	Vieni, ecc.
	Ecco laggiù un barlume,
	dilaga in cielo la sua luce smorta!
	Pu-Tin-Pao! La luna è sorta!
	Pu-Tin-Pao, ecc.

L'oro degli sfondi s'è tramutato in un livido colore di ar-gento. La gelida bianchezza della luna si diffonde sugli spalti e sulla città. Sulla porta delle mura appariscono le guardie vestite di lunghe tuniche nere. Una lugubre nenia si diffonde. Il corteo si avanza, preceduto da una schiera di ragazzi che cantano:

I RAGAZZI	Là sui monti dell'Est
	la cicogna cantò.
	Ma l'april non rifiorì,
	ma la neve non sgelò.
	Dal deserto al mar — non odi tu
	mille voci sospirar:
	"Principessa, scendi a me!

ALL   Cold as that sword . . .

THE EXECUTIONER'S SERVANTS
                 . . . is the beautiful Turandot!

THE CROWD   Is the beautiful Turandot!
                 Sweet lovers, forward, forward!
                 When the gong clangs
                 the executioner rejoices!

SERVANTS   When the gong clangs
                 the executioner rejoices.
                 Oil! Sharpen!
                 Death is one!
                 When the gong clangs, etc.

THE CROWD   Love is vain if there is no luck!
                 The riddles are three, death is one!
                 Yes, the riddles are three, death is one!
                 Who will strike that gong?

ALL   Oil! Sharpen, etc.
                 Work never languishes
                 where reigns Turandot! Ah!

And as the servants go off to take the sword to the execu-
tioner, the crowd forms groups here and there, picturesquely,
on the ramparts and examines with fierce impatience the sky,
which little by little has grown dark.

THE CROWD   Why does the moon delay? Wan face!
                 Show yourself in the sky! Quickly! Come! Rise!
                 Oh, severed head! Oh, bleak one!
                 Come! Rise! Show yourself in the sky!
                 Oh, severed head! Oh, bloodless one!
                 Oh, bloodless, oh, bleak!
                 Oh, taciturn! Oh, pale lover of the dead!
                 How the cemeteries await your funereal
                 light! Oh, bloodless, oh, bleak!
                 Oh, severed head!
                      (and, as little by little a lunar light spreads)

                 There's a glimmer down there!
                 Come, etc.
                 There's a glimmer down there,
                 which spreads in the sky its pallid light!
                 Pu-Tin-Pao! The moon has risen!
                 Pu-Tin-Pao, etc.

The gold of the background has changed into a livid silver
color. The icy whiteness of the moon spreads over the ram-
parts and over the city. At the gate in the walls the guards
appear, dressed in long black tunics. A lugubrious dirge
spreads. The procession advances, preceded by a group of
boys who sing:

THE BOYS   There, on the mountains of the East
                 the stork sang.
                 But April did not reflower,
                 but the snow did not thaw.
                 From the desert to the sea — don't you hear
                 a thousand voices sigh:
                 "Princess, come down to me!

Tutto fiorirà,
tutto splenderà! Ah!"

S'avanzano i servi del boia, seguiti dai sacerdoti che recano
le offerte funebri. Poi i Mandarini e gli alti dignitari. E final-
mente, bellissimo, quasi infantile, appare il Principino di Per-
sia. Alla vista della vittima che procede smarrita, trasognata,
il bianco collo nudo, lo sguardo assente, la ferocia della folla
si tramuta in indicibile pietà. Quando il Principino di Persia è
in scena, appare, enorme, gigantesco, tragico il carnefice, re-
cando sulla spalla lo spadone immenso.

LA FOLLA   O giovinetto! Grazia! Grazia!
                Com'è fermo il suo passo! Grazia!
                Com'è dolce, come è dolce il suo volto!
                Ha negli occhi l'ebbrezza! Pietà!
                Ha negli occhi la gioia!
                Ah! la grazia! Pietà di lui!
                Principessa! Pietà! Grazia!
                Pietà di lui, pietà, pietà!

IL PRINCIPE IGNOTO
                Ah! la grazia!
                Ch'io ti veda e ch'io ti maledica!
                Crudele, ch'io ti maledica!

Ma il grido si spezza sulle sue labbra, perchè dall'alto della
loggia imperiale si mostra Turandot. Un raggio di luna la
illumina. La Principessa appare quasi incorporea, come una
visione. Il suo atteggiamento dominatore e il suo sguardo al-
tero fanno cessare per incanto il tumulto. La folla si prostra,
faccia a terra. In piedi rimangono soltanto il Principino di
Persia, il carnefice e il Principe Ignoto.

IL PRINCIPE IGNOTO
                O divina bellezza, o meraviglia!
                O sogno, o divina bellezza, ecc.

E si copre il volto con le mani, abbacinato. Turandot ha un
gesto imperioso: è la condanna, il carnefice piega il capo,
annuendo. La lugubre nenia riprende. Il corteo si muove, sale
le mura, sparisce oltre gli spalti, e la folla lo segue.

I SACERDOTI BIANCHI DEL CORTEO
                O gran Koung-tzè!
                Che lo spirto del morente
                giunga fino a te!

Le loro voci si perdono. Turandot non c'è più. Nella pe-
nombra del piazzale deserto, restano soli Timur, Liù e il
Principe Ignoto. Il Principe è tuttora immobile, estatico come
se la inattesa visione di bellezza lo avesse fatalmente inchio-
dato al suo destino. Timur gli si avvicina, lo richiama, lo
scuote.

TIMUR   Figlio! Che fai?

IL PRINCIPE IGNOTO
                Non senti? Il suo profumo
                è nell'aria! è nell'anima!

TIMUR   Ti perdi!

> Everything will bloom,
> everything will shine! Ah!"

*The executioner's servants advance, followed by the priests,
who carry the funeral offerings. Then the mandarins and the
high dignitaries. And finally, very handsome, almost childish,
appears the young Prince of Persia. At the sight of the victim,
who comes forward, dazed, dreaming, his white neck bared,
his gaze absent, the crowd's ferocity is changed into ineffable
pity. When the young Prince of Persia is on the stage, there
appears, enormous, gigantic, tragic, the executioner, carrying
his immense sword on his shoulder.*

THE CROWD Oh, youth! Mercy! Mercy!
    How steady is his step! Mercy!
    How sweet, how sweet is his face!
    He has intoxication in his eyes! Pity!
    He has joy in his eyes!
    Ah! mercy! Pity on him!
    Princess! Pity! Mercy!
    Pity on him, pity, pity!

THE UNKNOWN PRINCE
    Ah! mercy!
    Let me see you and let me curse you!
    Cruel one, let me curse you!

*But the cry breaks off on his lips, because from the height
of the imperial balcony Turandot shows herself. A ray of
moonlight illuminates her. The Princess seems almost incor-
poreal, like a vision. Her masterful attitude and her haughty
gaze make the tumult cease magically. The crowd prostrates
itself, face to the ground. Only the Prince of Persia, the executioner, and the Unknown Prince remain standing.*

THE UNKNOWN PRINCE
    Oh, divine beauty, oh, wonder!
    Oh, dream, oh, divine beauty, etc.

*And he covers his face with his hands, dazzled. Turandot
makes an imperious gesture: it is the death sentence. The executioner bows his head, assenting. The lugubrious dirge resumes. The procession moves, climbs the walls, disappears
beyond the ramparts, and the crowd follows it.*

THE WHITE PRIESTS OF THE PROCESSION
    O great Kung-tze!
    May the spirit of the dying man
    come to you!

*Their voices die away. Turandot is no longer there. In the
half light of the deserted square remain only Timur, Liù, and
the Unknown Prince. The Prince is still motionless, ecstatic, as
if the unexpected vision of beauty had fatally riveted him to
his destiny. Timur approaches him, calls him, stirs him.*

TIMUR Son! What are you doing?
THE UNKNOWN PRINCE
    Don't you feel it? Her fragrance
    is in the air! It's in my soul!
TIMUR You are lost!

IL PRINCIPE IGNOTO

O divina bellezza, o meraviglia!
Io soffro, padre, soffro!

TIMUR

No! No! Stringiti a me!
Liù, parlagli tu! Qui salvezza non c'è!
Prendi nella tua mano la sua mano!

LIÙ   Signore! Andiam lontano!

TIMUR   La vita c'è laggiù!

IL PRINCIPE IGNOTO

Quest'è la vita, padre!

TIMUR   La vita c'è laggiù!

IL PRINCIPE IGNOTO

Io soffro, padre, soffro!

TIMUR   Qui salvezza non c'è!

IL PRINCIPE IGNOTO

La vita, padre, è qui!
            (*svincolandosi si precipita verso il gong
            che risplende di una luce misteriosa, e
            grida:*)
Turandot! Turandot! Turandot!

IL PRINCIPE DI PERSIA (*interno, coma ad invocazione suprema*)
Turandot!
            (*poi, l'urlo della folla, rapido e violento
            come una vampata*)

TIMUR   Vuoi morire così?

IL PRINCIPE IGNOTO

Vincere, padre, nella sua bellezza!

TIMUR   Vuoi finire così?

IL PRINCIPE IGNOTO

Vincere gloriosamente nella sua bellezza!

*E si slancia contro il gong. Ma d'improvviso fra lui e il
disco luminoso tre misteriose figure si frappongono. Sono Ping,
Pang, Pong, tre maschere grottesche, i tre ministri dell'Imperatore, e precisamente: il grande Cancelliere, il gran Provve-
ditore, il gran Cuciniere. Il Principe Ignoto arretra. Timur e
Liù si stringono insieme, paurosamente, nell'ombra. Il gong
s'è oscurato.*

I MINISTRI (*incalzando e attorniando il Principe*)
Fermo! Che fai? T'arresta!
Chi sei? Che fai? Che vuoi? Va' via!

Va', la porta è questa
della gran beccheria!
Pazzo, va' via!

PING   Qui si strozza!

PONG E PANG   Si trivella!

PING   Si sgozza!

PONG E PANG   Si spella!

PING   Si uncina e scapitozza!

PONG E PANG   Va' via!

THE UNKNOWN PRINCE
        Oh, divine beauty, oh, wonder!
        I suffer, Father, suffer!

TIMUR   No! No! Cling to me!
        Liù, you speak to him! There's no safety here!
        Take his hand in your hand!

LIÙ   Lord! Let us go far away!

TIMUR   Life is down there!

THE UNKNOWN PRINCE
        This is life, Father!

TIMUR   Life is down there!

THE UNKNOWN PRINCE
        I suffer, Father, suffer!

TIMUR   There's no safety here!

THE UNKNOWN PRINCE
        Life, Father, is here!
             (*freeing himself, he rushes toward the
             gong, which glows with a mysterious light,
             and shouts:*)
        Turandot! Turandot! Turandot!

THE PRINCE OF PERSIA (*within, as if in a supreme invocation*)
        Turandot!
             (*then, the shout of the crowd, rapid and
             violent as a burst of flame*)

TIMUR   You wish to die thus?

THE UNKNOWN PRINCE
        To conquer, Father, in her beauty!

TIMUR   You wish to end thus?

THE UNKNOWN PRINCE
        To conquer gloriously in her beauty!

*And he rushes toward the gong. But suddenly between him
and the luminous disk three mysterious figures place themselves. They are Ping, Pang, Pong, three grotesque masks, the
Emperor's three ministers, respectively: the Grand Chancellor,
the Grand Purveyor, the Grand Cook. The Unknown Prince
steps back. Timur and Liù huddle together, fearfully, in the
shadow. The gong has become dark.*

THE MINISTERS (*pursuing and surrounding the Prince*)
        Stand still! What are you doing? Stop!
        Who are you? What are you doing? What do
            you want? Go away!
        Go, this is the gate
        to the great butcher's shop!
        Madman, go away!

PING   Here they garrote you!

PONG AND PANG
        They impale you!

PING   They cut your throat!

PONG AND PANG
        They skin you alive!

PING   They sink hooks into you and behead you!

PONG AND PANG
        Go away!

PING	Si sega e si sbudella!
	[Sollecito, precipite,
	al tuo paese torna
	in cerca d'uno stipite
	per romperti le corna!
	Ma qui no!
PONG E PANG	Va' via! Al tuo paese torna!
	Che vuoi? Chi sei?
	Va' via! Va' via!]

I MINISTRI	Ma qui no!
	Pazzo, va' via! va' via!

IL PRINCIPE IGNOTO (*con impeto*)
        Lasciatemi passare!
            (*i ministri gli sbarrano il passo*)

PONG	Qui tutti i cimiteri sono occupati!
PANG	Qui bastano i pazzi indigeni!
PING	Non vogliam più pazzi forestieri!
PONG E PANG	O scappi, o il funeral per te s'appressa!

IL PRINCIPE IGNOTO (*con crescente vigore*)
        Lasciatemi passar!

PONG E PANG	Per una Principessa! Peuh!

PONG	Che cos'è?
PANG	Una femmina colla corona in testa!
PONG	E il manto colla frangia!
PING	Ma se la spogli nuda . . .
PONG	. . . è carne!
PANG	È carne cruda!
I MINISTRI	È roba che non si mangia!
	Ah, ah, ah!

IL PRINCIPE IGNOTO
        Lasciatemi passare! Lasciatemi!

PING	Lascia le donne! O prendi cento spose,
	che, in fondo, la più sublime
	Turandot del mondo ha una faccia —
	due braccia — e due gambe — sì — belle,
	imperiali — sì, sì, belle, sì —
	ma sempre quelle!
	Con cento mogli, o sciocco,
	avrai gambe a ribocco!
	Duecento braccia! E cento dolci petti
	sparsi per cento letti!
PONG E PANG	Cento petti . . .

I MINISTRI	. . . per cento letti! Ah, ah, ah!
	(*e sghignazzano, stringendo sempre più da presso al Principe*)

PING   They saw you up and disembowel you!
Promptly, hastily
go back to your country
to look for a doorpost
to break your head on!
But not here!

PONG AND PANG
     Go away! Go back to your country!
What do you want? Who are you?
Go away! Go away!

THE MINISTERS
     But not here!
Madman, go away! Go away!

THE UNKNOWN PRINCE (*with vehemence*)
     Let me pass!
         (*the ministers block his way*)

PONG   Here all the cemeteries are occupied!

PANG   Here the native madmen suffice!

PING   We don't want any more foreign madmen!

PONG AND PANG
     Either you flee, or your funeral is drawing near!

THE UNKNOWN PRINCE (*with mounting vigor*)
     Let me pass!

PONG AND PANG
     For a princess! Phew!

PONG   What is she?

PANG   A female with a crown on her head!

PONG   And a cloak with fringe!

PING   But if you strip her naked . . .

PONG   . . . she's flesh!

PANG   She's raw flesh!

THE MINISTERS
     It's inedible stuff!
Ha! ha! ha!

THE UNKNOWN PRINCE
     Let me pass! Let me go!

PING   Give up women! Or take a hundred brides,
for, after all, the most sublime
Turandot in the world has a face —
two arms — and two legs — yes — beautiful,
imperial ones — yes, yes, beautiful, yes —
but still legs!
With a hundred wives, oh foolish man,
you'll have a surplus of legs!
Two hundred arms! And a hundred soft bosoms
scattered in a hundred beds!

PONG AND PANG
     A hundred bosoms . . .

THE MINISTERS
     . . . in a hundred beds! Ha! ha! ha!
         (*and they snicker, pressing closer and closer
to the Prince*)

IL PRINCIPE IGNOTO (*con violenza*)
          Lasciatemi passar!
I MINISTRI   Pazzo, va' via! Pazzo, ecc.

Alcune fanciulle chiarovestite — le Ancelle di Turandot — si affacciano alla balaustra della loggia imperiale, e bisbigliando ammoniscono:

LE ANCELLE DI TURANDOT
          Silenzio, olà! Laggiù chi parla?
          Silenzio! Silenzio!
          È l'ora dolcissima del sonno!
          Il sonno sfiora gli occhi di Turandot!
          Si profuma di lei l'oscurità!
PING   Via di là, femmine ciarliere!
I MINISTRI   Via di là!
               (*con improvvisa preoccupazione, perchè
               s'avvedono d'aver lasciato libero per un
               momento il Principe*)
          Attenti al gong! Attenti al gong!

Le Ancelle sono sparite. Il Principe, assente, ripete:

IL PRINCIPE IGNOTO
          Si profuma di lei l'oscurità!
PANG   Guardalo, Pong!
PONG   Guardalo, Ping!
PING   Guardalo, Pang!
PANG   È insordito!
PONG   Intontito!
PING   Allucinato!
TIMUR (*in disparte, a Liù*)
          Più non li ascolta, ahimè!
I MINISTRI (*decisi*)
          Su! Parliamogli in tre!
               (*si aggruppano intorno al Principe in pose
               grottesche*)
PANG   Notte senza lumicino . . .
PONG   . . . gola nera d'un camino . . .
PING   . . . son più chiare degli enigmi di Turandot!
PANG   Ferro, bronzo, muro, roccia . . .
PONG   . . . l'ostinata tua capoccia . . .
PING   . . . son men duri degli enigmi di Turandot!
PANG   Dunque va'! Saluta tutti!
PONG   Varca i monti, taglia i flutti!
PING   Sta alla larga dagli enigmi di Turandot!

Il Principe non ha quasi più forza di reagire. Ma ecco richiami incerti, non voci ma ombre di voci, si diffondono dall'oscurità degli spalti. E qua e là, appena percettibili prima, poi di mano in mano, più lividi e fosforescenti, appariscono i fantasmi. Sono gli innamorati di Turandot che, vinti nella tragica prova, hanno perduta la vita.

THE UNKNOWN PRINCE (*with violence*)
>   Let me pass!

THE MINISTERS
>   Madman, go away! Madman, etc.

Some maidens dressed in white — Turandot's handmaidens — look over the balustrade of the imperial balcony and whispering, they admonish:

TURANDOT'S HANDMAIDENS
>   Silence! Hola! Who's talking down there?
>   Silence! Silence!
>   It is the very sweet hour of sleep!
>   Sleep is grazing Turandot's eyes!
>   The darkness is scented with her perfume!

PING   Away from there, chattering females!

THE MINISTERS
>   Away from there!
>   (*with sudden concern, because they real-
>   ize that they have left the Prince free for a
>   moment*)
>   Watch out for the gong! Watch out for the gong!

The handmaidens have vanished. The Prince, absently, repeats:

THE UNKNOWN PRINCE
>   The darkness is scented with her perfume!

PANG   Look at him, Pong!

PONG   Look at him, Ping!

PING   Look at him, Pang!

PANG   He's deafened!

PONG   Stunned!

PING   Dazzled!

TIMUR (*aside, to Liù*)
>   He's no longer listening to them, alas!

THE MINISTERS (*determined*)
>   Come! Let's speak to him, all three together!
>   (*they gather around the Prince in grotesque
>   poses*)

PANG   Night without a little lamp . . .

PONG   . . . black flue of a chimney . . .

PING   . . . are clearer than Turandot's riddles!

PANG   Iron, bronze, wall, rock . . .

PONG   . . . your stubborn head . . .

PING   . . . are less hard than Turandot's riddles!

PANG   So go! Say good-by to all!

PONG   Cross the mountains, ford the streams!

PING   Keep clear of Turandot's riddles!

The Prince almost no longer has the strength to react. But then vague calls, not voices but shadows of voices, spread out from the darkness of the ramparts. And here and there, barely perceptible at first, then gradually more livid and phosphorescent, the ghosts appear. They are those who were in love with Turandot and who, defeated in the tragic trial, have lost their lives.

LE VOCI DELLE OMBRE

Non indugiare! Se chiami, appare
quella che, estinti, ci fa sognare!
Fa' ch'ella parli! Fa' che l'udiamo!
Io l'amo! Io l'amo! Io l'amo!

E i fantasmi vaniscono.

IL PRINCIPE IGNOTO (*con un grido*)

No! No! Io solo l'amo!

I MINISTRI (*sgambettandogli intorno*)

L'ami? Che cosa? Chi?
Turandot? Ah! Ah! Ah!

PONG   O ragazzo demente!

PANG   Turandot non esiste!

PING   Non esiste che il Niente,
nel quale ti annulli . . . !

PONG E PANG   Turandot non esiste, non esiste!

PING   Turandot, come tutti quei citrulli
tuoi pari! L'uomo! Il Dio!
Io! I popoli! I sovrani!
[Pu-Tin-Pao . . . !
Non esiste che il Tao!

PONG E PANG   Tu ti annulli come quei citrulli
tuoi pari, ecc.]

IL PRINCIPE IGNOTO (*divincolandosi dalle maschere*)

A me il trionfo! A me l'amore!

Fa per slanciarsi verso il gong, ma il boia appare in alto sul bastione colla testa mozza del Principe di Persia.

I MINISTRI   Stolto! Ecco l'amore!
Così la luna bacerà il tuo volto!

Allora, Timur, con impeto disperato, aggrappandosi al figlio, esclama:

TIMUR   O figlio, vuoi dunque ch'io solo,
ch'io solo trascini pel mondo
la mia torturata vecchiezza?
Aiuto! Non c'è voce umana
che muova il tuo cuore feroce?

LIÙ (*avvicinandosi al principe, supplicante, piangente*)

Signore, ascolta! Ah, Signore, ascolta!
Liù non regge più!
Si spezza il cuor! Ahimè, ahimè, quanto cammino

col tuo nome nell'anima,
col nome tuo sulle labbra!
Ma se il tuo destino
doman sarà deciso,
noi morrem sulla strada dell'esilio!
Ei perderà suo figlio . . .

THE VOICES OF THE SHADOWS
        Don't delay! If you call, she appears,
        who makes us, dead men, dream!
        Make her speak! Make us hear her!
        I love her! I love her! I love her!

And the ghosts vanish.

THE UNKNOWN PRINCE (*with a cry*)
        No! No! I alone love her!

THE MINISTERS (*prancing around him*)
        You love her? What? Who?
        Turandot? Ha! Ha! Ha!

PONG   Oh, insane youth!

PANG   Turandot doesn't exist!

PING   There exists only the Nothingness
        in which you annihilate yourself . . . !

PONG AND PANG
        Turandot doesn't exist, doesn't exist!

PING   Turandot, like all simpletons
        like yourself! Man! God!
        I! Peoples! Sovereigns!
        Pu-Tin-Pao . . . !
        There exists only the Tao!

PONG AND PANG
        You annihilate yourself like those simpletons
        like yourself, etc.

THE UNKNOWN PRINCE (*freeing himself from the masks*)
        For me, the triumph! For me, love!

He starts to hurl himself toward the gong, but the executioner appears high on the bastion with the severed head of the Prince of Persia.

THE MINISTERS
        Fool! There's love!
        Thus the moon will kiss your face!

Then, Timur, in a desperate impulse, clutching his son, exclaims:

TIMUR   Oh, Son, do you then want me, alone,
        alone, to drag about the world
        my tortured old age?
        Help! Is there no human voice
        that can move your fierce heart?

LIÙ (*approaching the prince, imploring, weeping*)
        Lord, listen! Ah, Lord, listen!
        Liù can stand no more!
        Her heart is breaking! Alas, alas, what a long
           way
        with your name in my soul,
        with your name on my lips!
        But if your fate
        is decided tomorrow,
        we'll die on the road of exile!
        He will lose his son . . .

io l'ombra d'un sorriso!
Liù non regge più! Ah, pietà!
(*e si piega a terra, sfinita, singhiozzando*)

IL PRINCIPE IGNOTO (*avvicinandosele, con commozione*)
Non piangere, Liù!
Se in un lontano giorno
io t'ho sorriso,
per quel sorriso, dolce mia fanciulla,
m'ascolta: Il tuo Signore
sarà, domani, forse solo al mondo . . .
Non lo lasciare, portalo via con te!

LIÙ   Noi morrem sulla strada dell'esilio!

TIMUR   Noi morrem!

IL PRINCIPE IGNOTO
Dell'esilio addolcisci a lui le strade!
Questo . . . questo . . . o mia povera Liù,
al tuo piccolo cuore che non cade
chiede colui che non sorride più . . .
che non sorride più!

TIMUR   Ah! per l'ultima volta!

LIÙ   Vinci il fascino orribile!

I ministri, che s'erano appartati, ora si riavvicinano al Principe, pregando, insistendo.

I MINISTRI   La vita è così bella!

TIMUR   Abbi di me pietà!

LIÙ   Abbi di Liù pietà!

I MINISTRI   La vita è così bella!

TIMUR   [Abbi di me pietà!
Non posso staccarmi da te!
Non voglio staccarmi da te!
Pietà! Pietà!
Mi getto ai tuoi piedi gemente!
Abbi pietà! non voler la mia morte!

IL PRINCIPE IGNOTO
Son io che domando pietà!
Nessuno più ascolto!
Io vedo il suo fulgido volto!
La vedo! Mi chiama! Essa è là!
Il tuo perdono chiede
colui che non sorride più!

LIÙ   Signore, pietà! Abbi di Liù pietà!
Pietà di noi, ecc.

I MINISTRI
Non perderti così!
Afferralo! Portalo via!
Trattieni quel pazzo furente!
Su, porta via quel pazzo!]
Folle tu sei! La vita è così bella!

           I, the shadow of a smile!
           Liù can stand no more! Ah, pity!
           (*and she bends to the ground, exhausted,*
             sobbing)

THE UNKNOWN PRINCE (*approaching her, with emotion*)
           Don't cry, Liù!
           If, on one far-off day
           I smiled at you,
           for that smile, my sweet girl,
           listen to me: your Lord
           will be, tomorrow, perhaps alone in the world...
           Don't leave him, take him away with you!

LIÙ   We'll die on the road of exile!

TIMUR   We'll die!

THE UNKNOWN PRINCE
           Make gentle the roads of exile for him!
           This . . . this . . . Oh, my poor Liù,
           of your little heart that doesn't fail
           he asks who smiles no more . . .
           who smiles no more!

TIMUR   Ah! for the last time!

LIÙ   Overcome the horrible spell!

*The ministers, who had moved to one side, now approach
the Prince again, praying, insisting.*

THE MINISTERS
           Life is so beautiful!

TIMUR   Have pity on me!

LIÙ   Have pity on Liù!

THE MINISTERS
           Life is so beautiful!

TIMUR   Have pity on me!
           I can't separate myself from you!
           I don't want to separate myself from you!
           Pity! Pity!
           I cast myself moaning at your feet!
           Have pity! Don't wish my death!

THE UNKNOWN PRINCE
           I'm the one who asks for pity!
           I no longer listen to anyone!
           I see her radiant face!
           I see her! She calls me! She's there!
           He asks your pardon
           who smiles no more!

LIÙ   Lord, pity! Have pity on Liù!
           Pity on us, etc.

THE MINISTERS
           Don't ruin yourself thus!
           Seize him! Take him away!
           Restrain that raving madman!
           Come, take away that madman!
           You're mad! Life is so beautiful!

I ministri aiutano il vecchio e tentano con ogni sforzo a trascinar via il Principe.

PING   Su, un ultimo sforzo,
              portiamolo via!

I MINISTRI   Portiamolo via!

IL PRINCIPE IGNOTO
              [Lasciatemi: ho troppo sofferto!
              La gloria m'aspetta, m'aspetta laggiù!
                  (*il gong si illumina*)

TIMUR   Tu passi su un povero cuore
              che sanguina invano,
              che sanguina invano per te!

I MINISTRI   Il volto che vedi è illusione!
              La luce che splende è funesta!]

IL PRINCIPE IGNOTO
              [Forza umana non c'e che mi trattenga!
              Io seguo la mia sorte!
              Son tutto una febbre, son tutto un delirio!
              Ogni senso è un martirio feroce!

TIMUR   Nessuno ha mai vinto, nessuno!
              Su tutti la spada, la spada piombò!

LIÙ   Ah! Pietà! Pietà di noi!
              Se questo suo strazio non basta,
              Signore, noi siamo perduti! Con te!

I MINISTRI   Tu giochi la tua perdizione, la testa!

              . . . è illusione funesta!
              La morte, la morte, la morte!
              C'è l'ombra del boia,
              C'è l'ombra del boia laggiù!

LA FOLLA (*interno*)
              La fossa già scaviam per te
              che vuoi sfidar l'amor!]
              [Nel buio c'è segnato, ahimè,
              il tuo crudel destin!

LIÙ   Ah! fuggiamo, Signore! Ah! fuggiamo!

TIMUR   Mi getto ai tuoi piedi!
              Non voler la mia morte!

I MINISTRI   Tu corri alla rovina!

              La vita non giocar!

IL PRINCIPE IGNOTO
              Ogni fibra dell'anima ha una voce
              che grida:] Turandot!

TUTTI   La morte!

IL PRINCIPE IGNOTO
              Turandot!

TUTTI   La morte!

The ministers assist the old man and try, with every effort, to drag away the Prince.

PING
Come, a final effort,
let's take him away!

THE MINISTERS
Let's take him away!

THE UNKNOWN PRINCE
Let go of me: I've suffered too much!
Glory awaits me, awaits me over there!
(*the gong becomes luminous*)

TIMUR
You pass over a poor heart
that bleeds in vain,
that bleeds in vain for you!

THE MINISTERS
The face you see is an illusion!
The light that gleams is dire!

THE UNKNOWN PRINCE
There's no human strength that can restrain me!
I follow my destiny!
I'm all a fever, I'm all a delirium!
Every sense is a fierce torment!

TIMUR
No one has ever won, no one!
On all the sword, the sword swooped down!

LIÙ
Ah! Pity! Pity on us!
If this torment of his isn't enough,
Lord, we are lost! With you!

THE MINISTERS
You risk your destruction, your head!
. . . it's a dire illusion!
Death, death, death!
There is the shadow of the executioner,
there is the shadow of the executioner over there!

THE CROWD (*within*)
We are already digging the grave for you
who want to challenge love!
In the darkness is sealed, alas,
your cruel fate!

LIÙ
Ah! let us flee, Lord! Ah! let us flee!

TIMUR
I cast myself at your feet!
Don't wish my death!

THE MINISTERS
You are running to your ruin!
Don't risk your life!

THE UNKNOWN PRINCE
Every fiber of my soul has a voice
that cries: Turandot!

ALL
Death!

THE UNKNOWN PRINCE
Turandot!

ALL
Death!

IL PRINCIPE IGNOTO
                    Turandot!
TUTTI   La Morte!

Il Principe si precipita verso il gong. Afferra il martello.
Batte, come forsennato tre colpi. Liù e Timur si stringono in-
sieme disperati. I tre ministri inorriditi tendendo alte le brac-
cia, fuggono, esclamando:

I MINISTRI   [E lasciamolo andar!

                    Inutile è gridar
                    in sanscrito, in cinese, in lingua mongola!

                    Quando rangola il gong la morte gongola!
                    Ah, ah, ah, ah!

LA FOLLA (*interno*)
                    La fossa già scaviam per te
                    che vuoi sfidar l'amor!]

Il Principe è rimasto estatico ai piedi del gong.

ATTO SECONDO

Quadro primo

Appare un padiglione formato da una vasta tenda tutta
stranamente decorata da simboliche e fantastiche figure cinesi.
La scena è in primissimo piano ed ha tre aperture: una cen-
trale e due laterali. Ping fa capolino dal centro. E rivolgendosi
prima a destra, poi a sinistra, chiama i compagni. Essi entrano
seguiti da tre servi che reggono ciascuno una lanterna rossa,
una lanterna verde e una lanterna gialla, che poi depongono
simmetricamente in mezzo alla scena sopra un tavolo basso,
circondato da tre sgabelli. I servi quindi si ritirano nel fondo,
dove rimangono accovacciati.

PING   Olà, Pang! Olà, Pong!
                         (*e misteriosamente*)
                    Poichè il funesto gong
                    desta la Reggia e desta la città,
                    siam pronti ad ogni evento:
                    se lo straniero vince, per le nozze,
                    e s'egli perde, pel seppellimento.

PONG (*gaiamente*)
                    Io preparo le nozze!

PANG (*cupamente*)
                    Ed io le esequie!

PONG   Le rosse lanterne di festa!

PANG   Le bianche lanterne di lutto!

PONG   Gli incensi e le offerte . . .

PANG   Gli incensi e le offerte . . .

PONG   Monete di carta, dorate . . .

PANG   Thè, zucchero, noci moscate!

THE UNKNOWN PRINCE
> Turandot!

ALL   Death!

The Prince rushes toward the gong. He seizes the hammer. He strikes, like a madman, three blows. Liù and Timur huddle together in despair. The three ministers, horrified, holding their arms up, flee, exclaiming:

THE MINISTERS
> And we'll let him go!
> Shouting is useless
> in Sanskrit, in Chinese, in the Mongolian language!
> When the gong clangs, the executioner rejoices!
> Ha, ha, ha, ha!

THE CROWD (*within*)
> We are already digging the grave for you
> who want to challenge love!

The Prince has remained, ecstatic, at the foot of the gong.

ACT TWO

Scene One

A pavilion appears, shaped like a vast tent all strangely decorated with symbolic and fantastic Chinese figures. The set is very much in the foreground and has three openings: one in the center and one at either side. Ping peers in from the center. And, turning first to the right, then to the left, he calls his companions. They enter, followed by three servants, each carrying a red lantern, a green lantern, and a yellow lantern, which they then place symmetrically in the center of the stage on a low table surrounded by three stools. Then the servants withdraw to the background, where they remain, crouching.

PING   Hola! Pang! Hola, Pong!
> (*and mysteriously*)
> Since the dire gong
> is wakening the palace and wakening the city,
> let us be ready for every event:
> if the foreigner wins, for the wedding,
> and if he loses, for the burial.

PONG (*gaily*)
> I'll prepare the wedding!

PANG (*gloomily*)
> And I, the obsequies!

PONG   The red festival lanterns!

PANG   The white mourning lanterns!

PONG   The incenses and the offerings . . .

PANG   The incenses and the offerings . . .

PONG   Paper coins, gilded . . .

PANG   Tea, sugar, nutmegs!

PONG	Il bel palanchino scarlatto!
PANG	Il feretro, grande, ben fatto!
PONG	I bonzi che cantano . . .
PANG	I bonzi che gemono . . .
PONG E PANG	E tutto quanto il resto,

secondo vuole il rito . . .
minuzioso, infinito!

PING (*tendendo alte le braccia*)
O Cina, o Cina,
che or sussulti e trasecoli
inquieta!

Come dormivi lieta,
gonfia dei tuoi settantamila secoli!

I MINISTRI   Tutto andava secondo

L'antichissima regola del mondo . . .
Poi nacque . . . poi nacque . . .
poi nacque Turandot . . . !

PING   E sono anni che le nostre feste
si riducono a gioie come queste:

PONG   . . . tre battute di gong . . .

PANG   . . . tre indovinelli . . .

PING   e giù teste!

PONG   e giù teste!

PING   e giù teste!

*Siedono tutt' e tre presso il piccolo tavolo sul quale i servi
hanno deposto dei rotoli. E di mano in mano che enumerano,
sfogliano or l'uno or l'altro volume.*

PANG   L'anno del Topo furon sei.

PONG   L'anno del Cane furon otto!

I MINISTRI   Nell'anno in corso

il terribile anno della Tigre,
siamo già . . .
    (*contando sulle dita*)
siamo già al tredicesimo
con quello che va sotto!
Che lavoro! Che lavoro!
Che noia! Che noia!
A che siamo ridotti?
I ministri del boia!
Ministri del boia!

*Lasciano cadere i rotoli e si accasciano comicamente nos-
talgici.*

PING (*assorto in una visione lontana*)
Ho una casa nell'Honan
con il suo laghetto blu
tutto cinto di bambù . . .
E sto qui a dissipar la mia vita,
a stillarmi il cervel sui libri sacri . . .

PONG E PANG   . . . sui libri sacri . . .

PONG	The handsome scarlet palanquin!
PANG	The big, well-made bier!
PONG	The bonzes who sing . . .
PANG	The bonzes who groan . . .

PONG AND PANG

And all the rest,
as the ritual demands . . .
minute, infinite!

PING (*holding his arms up*)

O China, O China,
who now leap and start
restlessly!

How happy you slept,
swollen with your seventy-thousand centuries!

THE MINISTERS

Everything went according
to the very ancient rule of the world . . .
then was born . . . then was born . . .
then was born Turandot!

PING	And for years our holidays are reduced to joys like these:
PONG	. . . three strokes of the gong . . .
PANG	. . . three riddles . . .
PING	and off with heads!
PONG	and off with heads!
PING	and off with heads!

All three sit down near the little table on which the servants have set some scrolls. And, as they enumerate, they unroll one or the other volume.

PANG	The year of the rat there were six.
PONG	The year of the dog there were eight!

THE MINISTERS

In the current year,
the terrible year of the tiger,
we are already . . .
        (*counting on their fingers*)
we are already up to the thirteenth,
counting the one who is going under!
What work! What work!
What boredom! What boredom!
To what have we been reduced?
The ministers of the executioner!
Ministers of the executioner!

They drop the scrolls and sink down, comically nostalgic.

PING (*absorbed in a distant vision*)

I have a house in Honan
with its little blue lake
all girdled with bamboo . . .
And I am here wasting my life,
racking my brain over the sacred books . . .

PONG AND PANG

. . . over the sacred books . . .

PING	. . . sui libri sacri . . .
	E potrei tornar laggiù . . .
PANG E PONG	Tornar laggiù!

PING	. . . presso il mio laghetto blu . . .
PANG E PONG	Tornar laggiù!

PING	. . . tutto cinto di bambù!
PONG	[Ho foreste, presso Tsiang,
	che più belle non ce n'è,
	che non hanno ombra per me.
	Ho foreste che più belle non ce n'è.
PANG	Ho un giardino presso Kiù
	che lasciai per venir qui
	e che non rivedrò, non rivedrò mai più!
PING	. . . e potrei tornar laggiù
	presso il mio laghetto blu!]
	Tutto cinto di bambù!
I MINISTRI	E stiam qui . . . a stillarci il cervel
	sui libri sacri!

PONG	E potrei tornare a Tsiang . . .
PING	E potrei tornar laggiù . . .
PANG	E potrei tornar a Kiù . . .
PING	. . . a godermi il lago blu . . .
PONG	Tsiang . . .
PANG	Kiù . . .
PING	Honan . . .
	[tutto cinto di bambù!
PONG	E potrei tornare a Tsiang!
PANG	E potrei tornare a Kiù!]

Si risollevano, e con gesto largo e sconfortato esclamano:

I MINISTRI	O Mondo, o mondo pieno
	di pazzi innamorati!

PONG E PANG	Ne abbiam . . . ne abbiam visti
	arrivar degli aspiranti!

PING	O quanti!
PONG	O quanti!
PING	Ne abbiam visti
	arrivar degli aspiranti!
PANG	O quanti, o quanti!
PONG	O quanti!
PING	O mondo pieno di pazzi innamorati!
	Vi ricordate il principe
	regal di Samarcanda?
	Fece la sua domanda!
	E lei, con quale gioia,
	gli mandò il boia!
	Il boia!

PING   . . . over the sacred books . . .
And I could go back down there . . .

PANG AND PONG
Go back down there!

PING   . . . to my little blue lake . . .

PANG AND PONG
Go back down there!

PING   . . . all girdled with bamboo!

PONG   I have forests, near Tsiang,
than which none is more beautiful,
which have no shade for me.
I have forests than which none is more beautiful.

PANG   I have a garden near Kiù
which I left to come here
and which I'll never see, never see again!

PING   . . . and I could go back down there
to my little blue lake!
All girdled with bamboo!

THE MINISTERS
And we are here . . . racking our brains
over the sacred books!

PONG   And I could go back to Tsiang . . .

PING   And I could go back down there . . .

PANG   And I could go back to Kiù . . .

PING   . . . to enjoy my blue lake . . .

PONG   Tsiang . . .

PANG   Kiù

PING   Honan . . .
all girdled with bamboo!

PONG   And I could go back to Tsiang!

PANG   And I could go back to Kiù!

They rise and with a broad, disconsolate gesture exclaim:

THE MINISTERS
O world, O world full
of mad lovers!

PONG AND PANG
We have . . . we have seen
plenty of suitors arrive!

PING   Oh, how many!

PONG   Oh, how many!

PING   We have seen plenty
of suitors arrive!

PANG   Oh how many, oh how many!

PONG   Oh how many!

PING   O world full of mad lovers!
Do you remember the royal
Prince of Samarkand?
He made his request!
And she, with what joy,
sent him the executioner!
The executioner!

VOCI INTERNE   Ungi, arrota,
                che la lama
                guizzi, sprizzi
                fuoco e sangue . . .
                fuoco e sangue!

PONG   E l'indiano gemmato Sagarika,
                cogli orecchini come campanelli?
                Amore chiese, fu decapitato!
PANG   Ed il Birmano?
PONG   E il prence dei Kirghisi?
PONG E PANG   Uccisi! Uccisi! Uccisi! Uccisi!

PING   E il tartaro dall'arco di sei cubiti,
                [di ricche pelli cinto?
VOCI INTERNE   Ungi, arrota, ecc.
                Dove regna Turandot,
                il lavoro mai non langue!

PONG   Estinto!
PANG   Estinto!
PING   E decapita . . .
PANG   Uccidi e estingui . . .
PONG   Ammazza . . . ammazza!
PING   Uccidi! Ammazza!]
I MINISTRI   Addio, amore . . . ! addio, razza!

                Addio, stirpe divina!
                Addio, amore, ecc.
                E finisce la Cina!
                Addio, ecc.

   *Tornano a sedere. Solo Ping rimane in piedi, quasi a dar
più valore alla sua invocazione.*
PING (*tendendo alte le braccia*)
                O Tigre! O Tigre! O grande Marescialla
                [del Cielo! Fa' che giunga
                la gran notte attesa,
                la notte della resa . . .
PONG E PANG   O grande Marescialla del cielo!

                Fa che giunga, ecc.]
PING   Il talamo le voglio preparare!
PONG (*con gesto evidente*)
                Sprimaccerò per lei le molli piume!
PANG (*come spargesse aromi*)
                Io l'alcova le voglio profumare!
PING   Gli sposi guiderò reggendo il lume!
I MINISTRI   Poi tutt'e tre, in giardino,
                noi canterem . . .

VOICES WITHIN

> Oil, sharpen,
> let the blade
> flash, spurt
> fire and blood . . .
> fire and blood!

PONG

> And the bejeweled Indian Sagarika,
> with earrings like little bells?
> He asked for love, he was decapitated!

PANG   And the Burmese?

PONG   And the Prince of the Kirghiz?

PONG AND PANG

> Killed! Killed! Killed! Killed!

PING

> And the Tartar with the six-cubit bow,
> girdled with rich hides?

VOICES WITHIN

> Oil, sharpen, etc.
> Where reigns Turandot
> work never languishes!

PONG   Executed!

PANG   Executed!

PING   And decapitate . . .

PANG   Kill and execute . . .

PONG   Slaughter . . . slaughter!

PING   Kill! Slaughter!

THE MINISTERS

> Farewell, love . . . ! farewell, breed!
> Farewell, divine race!
> Farewell, love, etc.
> And China ends!
> Farewell, etc.

They sit down again. Only Ping remains standing, as if to give more value to his invocation.

PING (*holding his arms up*)

> O Tigress! O Tigress! O great she-marshal
> of heaven! Grant that it arrive,
> the great, awaited night,
> the night of surrender . . .

PONG AND PANG

> O great she-marshal of heaven!
> Grant that it arrive, etc.

PING   I want to prepare the nuptial bed for her!

PONG (*with an obvious gesture*)

> I'll plump up the soft feathers for her!

PANG (*as if scattering perfumes*)

> I want to perfume her bedchamber!

PING   I'll lead the bridal pair, carrying the light!

THE MINISTERS

> Then, all three, in the garden,
> we'll sing . . .

PONG   . . . canteremo d'amor fino al mattino . . .
PING   Così . . .
PANG   Così . . .

Ping in piedi sullo sgabello, gli altri due seduti ai suoi piedi.

I MINISTRI   Non v'è in Cina, per nostra fortuna,
                donna più che rinneghi l'amor!

                Una sola ce n'era e quest'una
                che fu ghiaccio, ora è vampa ed ardor!
                Principessa, il tuo impero si stende
                dal Tse-Kiang all'immenso Jang-Tse!
PING   Ma là, dentro alle soffici tende,
                c'è uno sposo che impera su te!
I MINISTRI   Tu dei baci già senti l'aroma,
                già sei doma, sei tutto languor!

PONG E PANG   Gloria, gloria alla notte segreta
                che il prodigio ora vede compir!

PING E PANG   Gloria, gloria! alla notte segreta!

PONG   Alla gialla coperta di seta
                testimone dei dolci sospir!
I MINISTRI   Nel giardin sussurran le cose
                e tintinnan campanule d'or . . .

                Si sospiran parole amorose . . .
PING   . . . di rugiada s'imperlano i fiori!
I MINISTRI   Gloria, gloria al bel corpo discinto
                che il mistero ignorato ora sa!

                Gloria all'ebbrezza e all'amore che ha vinto,
                e alla Cina la pace ridà,
                alla Cina la pace ridà . . .

Ma dall'interno il rumore della Reggia che si risveglia, richiama i tre ministri alla triste realtà. E allora Ping, balzando a terra, esclama:

PING   Noi si sogna! E il Palazzo già formicola
                di lanterne, di servi e di soldati!
                Udite: il gran tamburo
                del Tempio Verde! Già stridon le infinite
                ciabatte di Pekino!
PONG   Udite le trombe! altro che pace!
PANG   Ha inizio la ceremonia!
I MINISTRI   Andiamo a goderci l'ennesimo supplizio!

Se ne vanno mogi mogi.

PONG   . . . we'll sing of love till morning . . .

PING   Like this . . .

PANG   Like this : . .

Ping, standing on the stool, the other two are seated at his feet.

THE MINISTERS

                No longer in China, to our good luck,
                is there a woman who rejects love!
                There was only one and this one
                who was ice now is flame and ardor!
                Princess, your empire stretches
                from the Tse-Kiang to the immense Yangtze!

PING   But there, within the soft draperies,
                there is a husband who rules over you!

THE MINISTERS

                You already smell the aroma of kisses,
                already you are tamed, you are all languor!

PONG AND PANG

                Glory, glory to the secret night
                which now sees the wonder accomplished!

PING AND PANG

                Glory, glory to the secret night!

PONG   To the yellow coverlet of silk,
                witness to the sweet sighs!

THE MINISTERS

                Everything whispers in the garden
                and golden campanulas tinkle . . .
                They whisper amorous words to one another . . .

PING   . . . the flowers are beaded with dew!

THE MINISTERS

                Glory, glory to the beautiful, unclad body
                which now knows the mystery it was ignorant
                    of!
                Glory to the ecstasy and to love which has won,
                and restores peace to China,
                restores peace to China . . .

But from within the sound of the palace reawakening recalls the three ministers to the sad reality. And then Ping, leaping to the ground, exclaims:

PING   We're dreaming! And the palace already teems
                with lanterns, with servants and with soldiers!
                Hear: the great drum
                of the Green Temple! Already the infinite
                slippers of Peking are clattering!

PONG   Hear the trumpets! Peace, indeed!

PANG   The ceremony is beginning!

THE MINISTERS

                Let us go to enjoy the umpteenth torture!
    They go off, crestfallen.

ATTO SECONDO

Quadro secondo

Appare il vasto piazzale della Reggia. Quasi al centro è un'enorme scalèa di marmo, che si perde nella sommità fra archi triforati. La scala è a tre larghi ripiani. Numerosi servi collocano in ogni dove lanterne variopinte. La folla, a poco a poco, invade la piazza. Arrivano i Mandarini, colla veste azzurra e d'oro. Sul sommo della scala, altissimi e pomposi si presentano gli otto sapienti. Sono vecchi, quasi eguali, enormi e massicci. Il loro gesto è lentissimo e simultaneo. Hanno ciascuno tre rotoli di seta sigillati in mano. Sono i rotoli che contengono la soluzione degli enigmi di Turandot.

LA FOLLA (*commentando l'arrivo dei vari dignitari*)

> Gravi, enormi ed imponenti
> col mister dei chiusi enigmi
> già s'avanzano i Sapienti . . .
> col mister, ecc.

Incensi cominciano a salire dai tripodi che sono sulla sommità della scala. Tra gli incensi si fanno largo i tre ministri che indossano, ora, l'abito giallo di ceremonia.

LA FOLLA   Ecco Ping! Ecco Pong! Ecco Pang!

Tra le nuvole degli aromi si vedono apparire gli stendardi gialli e bianchi dell'Imperatore. Lentamente l'incenso dirada, e allora, sulla sommità della scala appare, seduto sull'ampio trono d'avorio, l'Imperatore Altoum. È vecchissimo, tutto bianco, venerabile, ieratico. Pare un dio che apparisca di tra le nuvole.

LA FOLLA   Diecimila anni al nostro imperatore!

Tutta la folla si prosterna a terra in attitudine di grande rispetto.

LA FOLLA   Gloria a te!

Il piazzale è avvolto in una calda luce. Il Principe Ignoto è ai piedi della scala. Timur e Liù a sinistra, confusi tra la folla.

L'IMPERATORE (*lento, con voce esile e lontana*)

> Un giuramento atroce mi costringe
> a tener fede al fosco patto. E il santo
> scettro ch'io stringo, gronda
> di sangue! Basta sangue!
> Giovine, va'!

IL PRINCIPE IGNOTO (*con fermezza*)

> Figlio del cielo, io chiedo
> d'affrontar la prova!

L'IMPERATORE (*quasi supplichevole*)

> Fa' ch'io possa morir senza portare
> il peso della tua giovine vita!

ACT TWO

Scene Two

The vast square of the royal palace appears. Almost in the center there is a vast marble stairway, which is lost at its summit among triple arches. The stairway has three broad landings. Numerous servants set varicolored lanterns on all sides. The crowd, little by little, invades the square. The mandarins arrive, in their blue and gold garments. At the top of the steps, very tall and pompous the eight sages appear. They are old, almost exactly alike, enormous, and massive. Their gestures are very slow and simultaneous. Each has three silk scrolls, sealed, in his hand. These are the scrolls that contain the solution to Turandot's riddles.

THE CROWD (*commenting on the arrival of the various dignitaries*)

> Grave, enormous, and imposing
> with the mystery of the sealed riddles
> already the sages advance . . .
> with the mystery, etc.

Incense begins to rise from the tripods that are set at the top of the stairs. Amid the clouds of incense the three ministers make their way, now wearing their yellow ceremonial dress.

THE CROWD   There's Ping! There's Pong! There's Pang!

Amid the clouds of perfume the yellow and white standards of the Emperor are seen arriving. Slowly the incense clears away, and then, at the top of the steps, appears, seated on a broad ivory throne, Emperor Altoum. He is very old, all white, venerable, hieratic. He seems a God who appears from among the clouds.

THE CROWD   Ten thousand years to our emperor!

The whole crowd prostrates itself on the ground in an attitude of great respect.

THE CROWD   Glory to you!

The square is wrapped in a warm light. The Unknown Prince is at the foot of the steps. Timur and Liù, at left, mixed with the crowd.

THE EMPEROR (*slow, in a faint and distant voice*)

> An atrocious oath forces me
> to keep faith with the grim pact. And the holy
> scepter that I clasp streams with
> blood! Enough of blood!
> Young man, go!

THE UNKNOWN PRINCE (*firmly*)

> Son of Heaven, I ask
> to face the trial!

THE EMPEROR (*almost imploring*)

> Allow me to die without bearing
> the weight of your young life!

IL PRINCIPE IGNOTO (*con maggiore forza*)
Figlio del cielo! Io chiedo
d'affrontar la prova!

L'IMPERATORE Non voler, non voler che s'empia ancor
d'orror la Reggia, il mondo!

IL PRINCIPE IGNOTO (*con forza crescente*)
Figlio del cielo! Io chiedo
d'affrontar la prova!

L'IMPERATORE (*con ira, ma con grandiosità*)
Straniero ebbro di morte! E sia!
Si compia il tuo destino!

LA FOLLA Diecimila anni al nostro Imperatore!
Diecimila anni al nostro Imperatore!

*Un chiaro corteo di donne appare dalla Reggia e si distende
lungo la scalèa: sono le Ancelle di Turandot. Fra il generale
silenzio, il Mandarino si avanza.*

IL MANDARINO Popolo di Pekino!

La legge è questa: Turandot, la Pura,
sposa sarà di chi, di sangue regio,
spieghi gli enigmi ch'ella proporrà.

Ma chi affronta il cimento e vinto resta,
porga alla scure la superba testa!

RAGAZZI (*interno*)
Dal deserto al mar
non odi mille voci sospirar:
Principessa, scendi a me!
Tutto splenderà, splenderà, splenderà!

*S'avanza Turandot che va a porsi davanti al trono. Bellissi-
ma, impassibile, guarda con freddissimi occhi il Principe, il
quale, abbacinato sulle prime, a poco a poco riacquista il
dominio di sè stesso e la fissa con ardente volontà. Timur e
Liù non sanno staccare gli occhi e l'anima dal Principe. Fra
un solenne silenzio Turandot dice:*

TURANDOT In questa Reggia, or son mill'anni e mille,
un grido disperato risonò.
E quel grido, traverso stirpe e stirpe,

qui nell'anima mia si rifugiò!
Principessa Lo-u-Ling,
ava dolce a serena, che regnavi
nel tuo cupo silenzio, in gioia pura,
e sfidasti inflessibile e sicura
l'aspro dominio, oggi rivivi in me!

LA FOLLA (*sommessamente*)
Fu quando il Re dei Tartari
le sette sue bandiere spiegò!

TURANDOT (*come cosa lontana*)
Pure, nel tempo che ciascun ricorda,
fu sgomento e terrore e rombo d'armi!

Il Regno vinto! Il Regno vinto!
E Lo-u-Ling, la mia ava, trascinata

THE UNKNOWN PRINCE (*more strongly*)
> Son of Heaven! I ask
> to face the trial!

THE EMPEROR Don't wish, don't wish that again
> the palace, the world be filled with horror!

THE UNKNOWN PRINCE (*with mounting strength*)
> Son of Heaven! I ask
> to face the trial!

THE EMPEROR (*with wrath, but with grandeur*)
> Foreigner, drunk with death! So be it!
> Let your destiny be fulfilled!

THE CROWD Ten thousand years to our emperor!
> Ten thousand years to our emperor!

A white procession of women appears from the palace and spreads out along the stairs: they are Turandot's handmaidens. Amid the general silence the mandarin advances.

THE MANDARIN
> People of Peking!
> This is the law: Turandot, the Pure,
> will be the bride of the man, of royal blood,
> who solves the three riddles that she will pro-
>   pose.
> But he who faces the trial and remains defeated,
> must offer his haughty head to the ax!

BOYS (*within*)
> From the desert to the sea
> don't you hear a thousand voices sigh:
> Princess, come down to me!
> Everything will shine, shine, shine!

Turandot advances and places herself before the throne. Very beautiful, impassive, she looks with very cold eyes at the Prince, who, dazzled at first, gradually regains his self-control and stares at her with ardent determination. Timur and Liù cannot take their eyes, their souls from the Prince. In the solemn silence Turandot says:

TURANDOT In this Palace, a thousand, thousand years ago,
> a desperate cry resounded.
> And that cry, through descendant and descend-
>   ant,
> took refuge here in my soul!
> Princess Lo-u-Ling,
> sweet and serene ancestress, who reigned
> in your dark silence, in pure joy,
> and who defied, inflexible and sure,
> bitter domination, you relive in me today!

THE CROWD (*softly*)
> It was when the King of the Tartars
> unfurled his seven flags!

TURANDOT (*like something remote*)
> Still, in the time that everyone remembers,
> there was alarm, and terror and the rumble of
>   arms!
> The kingdom defeated! The kingdom defeated!
> And Lo-u-Ling, my ancestress, dragged away

da un uomo come te, come te, straniero,
là nella notte atroce,
dove si spense la sua fresca voce!

LA FOLLA (*mormora reverente:*)
Da secoli Ella dorme
nella sua tomba enorme!

TURANDOT
O Príncipi che a lunghe carovane
d'ogni parte del mondo
qui venite a gettar la vostra sorte,
io vendico su voi, su voi quella purezza,
quel grido e quella morte!
Quel grido e quella morte!
Mai nessun m'avrà! Mai nessun,
nessun m'avrà!
L'orror di chi l'uccise
vivo nel cor mi sta!
No, no! Mai nessun m'avrà!
Ah, rinasce in me l'orgoglio
di tanta purità!
        (*e minacciosa, al Principe:*)
Straniero! Non tentar la fortuna!
"Gli enigmi sono tre, la morte è una!"

IL PRINCIPE IGNOTO
No, no! Gli enigmi sono tre,
una è la vita!

TURANDOT
No! No!
[Gli enigmi sono tre, la morte è una!

IL PRINCIPE IGNOTO
Gli enigmi sono tre, una è la vita!]

LA FOLLA
Al Principe straniero
offri la prova ardita,
o Turandot! Turandot!

Squillano le trombe. Silenzio. Turandot proclama il primo enigma.

TURANDOT
Straniero, ascolta! "Nella cupa notte
vola un fantasma iridiscente. Sale
e dispiega l'ale
sulla nera, infinita umanità.
Tutto il mondo l'invoca
e tutto il mondo l'implora!
Ma il fantasma sparisce con l'aurora
per rinascere nel cuore!
Ed ogni notte nasce
ed ogni giorno muore . . ."

IL PRINCIPE IGNOTO (*con improvvisa sicurezza*)
Sì! Rinasce! Rinasce! E in esultanza
mi porta via con sè, Turandot,
"La Speranza."

I SAPIENTI (*si alzano e ritmicamente aprono insieme il primo rotolo*)
La speranza! La speranza! La speranza!

Poi tornano, insieme, a sedere. Nella folla corre un mormorio, subito represso dal gesto d'un dignitario.

by a man like you, like you, foreigner,
there in the atrocious night,
where her fresh voice was extinguished!

THE CROWD (*murmurs reverently:*)
For centuries she has slept
in her enormous tomb!

TURANDOT
O Princes who in long caravans
from every part of the world
come here to try your fate,
I avenge upon you, upon you that purity,
that cry and that death!
That cry and that death!
No one will ever possess me! No one ever,
no one will possess me!
The horror of him who killed her
is alive in my heart!
No, no! No one will ever possess me!
Ah, in me is reborn the pride
of such purity!
(*and, threatening, to the Prince:*)
Stranger! Don't tempt fate!
"The riddles are three, death is one!"

THE UNKNOWN PRINCE
No, no! The riddles are three,
one is life!

TURANDOT
No! No!
The riddles are three, death is one!

THE UNKNOWN PRINCE
The riddles are three, one is life!

THE CROWD
Offer the bold trial
to the foreign prince,
Oh, Turandot! Turandot!

The trumpets blare. Silence. Turandot proclaims the first riddle.

TURANDOT
Stranger, listen! "In the gloomy night
an iridescent ghost flies. It rises
and spreads its wings
over the black, infinite mankind.
All the world invokes it,
and all the world implores it!
But the ghost vanishes with the dawn
to be reborn in the heart!
And every night it is born
and every day it dies . . ."

THE UNKNOWN PRINCE (*with sudden confidence*)
Yes! It is reborn! It is reborn! And in triumph
it carries me away with itself, Turandot,
"Hope."

THE SAGES (*stand up and rhythmically open together the first scroll*)
Hope! Hope! Hope!

Then, together, they sit down again. A murmur runs through the crowd, repressed promptly by a dignitary's gesture.

TURANDOT (*gira gli occhi fierissimi. Ha un freddo riso. La sua
           altera superiorità la riprende*)
           Sì! la speranza che delude sempre!
                    (*E allora, quasi per affascinare e stordire
                    il Principe, scende rapida fino a metà della
                    scala. E di là propone il secondo enigma*)

           "Guizza al pari di fiamma, e non è fiamma!
           È talvolta delirio! È febbre
           d'impeto e ardore!
           L'inerzia lo tramuta in un languore!
           Se ti perdi o trapassi, si raffredda!
           Se sogni la conquista avvampa, avvampa!
           Ha una voce che trepido tu ascolti,
           e del tramonto il vivido baglior . . ."

*Il Principe esita. Lo sguardo di Turandot sembra smarrirlo.
Egli cerca. Egli non trova. La Principessa ha un'espressione di
trionfo.*

L'IMPERATORE Non perderti, straniero!

LA FOLLA   È per la vita!
              E per la vita! Parla!
              Non perderti, straniero!
              Parla! Parla!

LIÙ   È per l'amore

IL PRINCIPE IGNOTO (*perde ad un tratto la dolorosa atonìa del
                    viso. E grida a Turandot:*)
           Sì, Principessa! Avvampa e insieme langue,
           se tu mi guardi, nelle vene. "Il Sangue!"

I SAPIENTI (*aprendo il secondo rotolo*)
           Il sangue! Il sangue! Il sangue!

LA FOLLA (*prorompendo gioiosamente*)
           Coraggio, scioglitore degli enigmi!

TURANDOT (*raddrizzandosi come colpita da una frustata, urla
           alle guardie:*)
           Percuotete quei vili!

*E così dicendo corre giù dalla scala. Il Principe cade in gi-
nocchio. Ed ella si china su di lui, e, ferocemente, martellando
le sillabe, quasi con la bocca sul viso di lui, dice il terzo
enigma.*

TURANDOT   "Gelo che ti dà foco! E dal tuo foco
              più gelo prende! Candida ed oscura!
              Se libero ti vuol, ti fa più servo!
              Se per servo t'accetta, ti fa Re!"

*Il Principe Ignoto non respira più. Non risponde più. Tu-
randot è su di lui, curva come sulla sua preda.*

TURANDOT (*sogghigna*)
           Su, straniero! Ti sbianca la paura!
           E ti senti perduto! Su, straniero,
           il gelo che dà foco, che cos'è?

TURANDOT (*turns her very proud eyes. She laughs a cold laugh. Her haughty superiority grips her again*)

Yes! Hope, which always disappoints!

(*And then, as if to bewitch and daze the Prince, she rapidly comes halfway down the stairs. And, from there, she asks the second riddle*)

"It darts like a flame, and is not a flame!
At times it is delirium! It's a fever
of impulse and ardor!
Inertia transforms it into languor!
If you are lost or die, it grows cold!
If you dream of conquest, it flames, it flames!
It has a voice that you listen to in fear
and the vivid glow of the sunset . . ."

The Prince hesitates. Turandot's gaze seems to confound him. He seeks. He doesn't find. The Princess assumes an expression of triumph.

THE EMPEROR

Don't destroy yourself, foreigner!

THE CROWD

It's for your life!
It's for your life! Speak!
Don't destroy yourself, foreigner!
Speak! Speak!

LIÙ

It's for love!

THE UNKNOWN PRINCE (*loses suddenly the painful, lost expression. And he cries to Turandot:*)

Yes, Princess! It flames and also languishes,
in my veins, if you look at me. "Blood!"

THE SAGES (*opening the second scroll*)

Blood! Blood! Blood!

THE CROWD (*bursting out, joyously*)

Courage, solver of riddles!

TURANDOT (*stiffening, as if struck by a lash, shouts to the guards:*)

Strike those wretches!

And, saying this, she runs down the steps. The Prince falls to his knees. And she bends over him, and, fiercely, hammering out the syllables, her mouth almost on his face, she asks the third riddle.

TURANDOT

"Frost that sets you afire! And from your fire
gains more frost! Candid and dark!
If it wants you free, it makes you more enslaved!
If it accepts you for slave, it makes you king!"

The Unknown Prince is no longer breathing. He no longer answers. Turandot is upon him, bent as if over her prey.

TURANDOT (*sneering*)

Come, foreigner! Fear makes you blanch!
And you feel yourself lost! Come, foreigner,
the frost that gives fire — what is it?

IL PRINCIPE IGNOTO (*desolato ha piegato la testa fra le mani.
                     Ma è un attimo. Un lampo di gioia lo illumi-
                     na. Balza in piedi, magnifico d'alterigia e di
                     forza. Esclama:*)

               La mia vittoria ormai t'ha data a me!
               Il mio fuoco ti sgela: "Turandot!"

*Turandot vacilla, arretra, rimane immobile ai piedi della
scala impietrita dallo sdegno e dal dolore.*

I SAPIENTI (*che hanno svolto il terzo rotolo, esclamano:*)
               Turandot! Turandot! Turandot!

LA FOLLA   Turandot! Turandot!
               Gloria, gloria, O vincitore!
               Gloria, gloria, O vincitore!
               Ti sorrida la vita!
               Ti sorrida l'amor!
               Diecimila anni al nostro Imperatore!
               Luce, Re di tutto il mondo!

TURANDOT (*al primo grido s'è scossa. Risale affannosamente la
           scala. È presso il trono dell'Imperatore. Pro-
           rompe:*)
               Figlio del cielo! Padre augusto! No!
               Non gettar tua figlia nelle braccia
               dello straniero!

L'IMPERATORE (*solenne*)
               È sacro il giuramento!

TURANDOT (*con impeto, con ribellione*)
               No! Non dire! Tua figlia è sacra!
               Non puoi donarmi a lui come una schiava!
               Ah! No! Tua figlia è sacra!
               Non puoi donarmi a lui come una schiava
               morente di vergogna!
                  (*al Principe*)
               Non guardarmi così!
               Tu che irridi al mio orgoglio,
               non guardarmi così!
               Non sarò tua! No, no, non sarò tua!
               Non voglio, non voglio!
               No, no, non sarò tua!

L'IMPERATORE (*ergendosi in piedi*)
               È sacro il giuramento!

LA FOLLA   È sacro il giuramento!

TURANDOT   No, non guardarmi così, non sarò tua!

LA FOLLA   Ha vinto, Principessa!
               Offrì per te la vita!

TURANDOT   Mai nessun m'avrà!

LA FOLLA   Sia premio al suo ardimento!
               Offrì, ecc.

TURANDOT (*rivolta ancora al Principe*)
               Mi vuoi nelle tue braccia a forza
               riluttante, fremente?

IL PRINCIPE IGNOTO (*con impeto audacissimo*)
               No, no, Principessa altera!
               Ti voglio tutta ardente d'amor!

THE UNKNOWN PRINCE (*desolate, he has bowed his head in his hands. But it is only for a moment. A flash of joy illuminates him. He springs to his feet, magnificent in pride and strength. He exclaims:*)
My victory now has given you to me!
My fire thaws you: "Turandot!"

Turandot staggers, steps back, remains motionless at the foot of the steps, numbed by contempt and by grief.

THE SAGES (*who have unrolled the third scroll, exclaim:*)
Turandot! Turandot! Turandot!

THE CROWD   Turandot! Turandot!
Glory, glory, O victor!
Glory, glory, O victor!
May life smile upon you!
May love smile upon you!
Ten thousand years to our emperor!
Light, king of all the world!

TURANDOT (*has stirred at the first cry. She breathlessly climbs the steps. She is near the Emperor's throne. She cries out:*)
Son of Heaven! August Father! No!
Don't cast your daughter into the arms
of the foreigner!

THE EMPEROR (*solemnly*)
The oath is sacred!

TURANDOT (*with vehemence, with rebellion*)
No! Don't say so! Your daughter is sacred!
You can't give me to him like a slave girl.
Ah no! Your daughter is sacred!
You can't give me to him like a slave girl,
dying of shame!
        (*to the Prince*)
Don't look at me like that!
You who mock my pride,
don't look at me like that!
I won't be yours! No, no, I won't be yours!
I don't want to, I don't want to!
No, no, I won't be yours!

THE EMPEROR (*rising to his feet*)
The oath is sacred!

THE CROWD   The oath is sacred!

TURANDOT   No, don't look at me like that, I won't be yours!

THE CROWD   He's won, Princess!
He offered his life for you!

TURANDOT   No one will ever possess me!

THE CROWD   Be the reward of his daring!
He offered, etc.

TURANDOT (*again addressing the Prince*)
Do you want me in your arms by force,
reluctant, shuddering?

THE UNKNOWN PRINCE (*with bold impetuousness*)
No, no, haughty princess!
I want you all ardent with love!

LA FOLLA   Coraggioso! Audace! Coraggioso!
                  O forte!

IL PRINCIPE IGNOTO
                  Tre enigmi m'hai proposto! e tre ne sciolsi!
                  Uno soltanto a te ne proporrò:
                  il mio nome non sai! Dimmi il mio nome,
                  dimmi il mio nome, prima dell'alba!
                  E all'alba morirò!

*Fra l'attesa più intensa Turandot piega il capo annuendo.
Allora il vecchio Imperatore si erge e con accorata commozione
dice:*

L'IMPERATORE
                  Il cielo voglia che col primo sole
                  mio figliolo tu sia!

*La Corte si alza. Squillano le trombe. Ondeggiano le ban-
diere. Il Principe, a testa alta, con passo sicuro, sale la scalèa;
mentre l'inno imperiale erompe solenne, cantato da tutto il
popolo.*

LA FOLLA   Ai tuoi piedi ci prostriam,
                  Luce, Re di tutto il mondo!
                  Per la tua saggezza,
                  per la tua bontà,
                  ci doniamo a te,
                  lieti, in umiltà!
                  A te salga il nostro amor!
                  Diecimila anni al nostro Imperatore!
                  A te, erede di Hien Wang,
                  noi gridiam:
                  Diecimila anni al nostro Imperatore!
                  Alte, alte le bandiere!
                  Gloria a te! Gloria a te!
                  Gloria a te! Gloria a te!

ATTO TERZO

Quadro primo

*Il giardino della Reggia, vastissimo, tutto rialzi ondulati, ces-
pugli e profili scuri di divinità in bronzo, lievemente illuminate
dal basso in alto dal riflesso degli incensieri. A destra sorge
un padiglione a cui si accede per cinque gradini, e limitato da
una tenda riccamente ricamata. Il padiglione è l'avancorpo
d'uno dei palazzi della Reggia, dal lato delle stanze di Turandot.
È notte. Dalle estreme lontananze giungono voci di Araldi che
girano l'immensa città intimando il regale comando. Altre voci,
vicine e lontane, fanno eco. Adagiato sui gradini del padiglione è il Principe. Nel grande silenzio notturno egli ascolta i
richiami degli Araldi, come se quasi più non vivesse nella
realtà.*

LE VOCI DEGLI ARALDI
                  Così comanda Turandot:
                  "Questa notte nessun dorma in Pekino!"

THE CROWD   Brave one! Bold! Brave!
             Oh, strong one!

THE UNKNOWN PRINCE
             You asked me three riddles, and three I solved!
             I'll ask you only one:
             you don't know my name! Tell me my name,
             tell me my name, before the dawn!
             And, at dawn, I'll die!

Amid intense expectancy Turandot bows her head, assenting. Then the old Emperor rises and, with heartbroken emotion, says:

THE EMPEROR
             May heaven will that, at the first sunlight,
             you be my son!

The court rises. The trumpets blare. The flags sway. The Prince, his head high, with firm step, climbs the staircase, while the imperial anthem bursts forth, solemn, sung by the whole populace.

THE CROWD   At your feet we prostrate ourselves,
             Light, King of all the world!
             For your wisdom,
             for your goodness,
             we give ourselves to you,
             happy, in humility!
             Let our love rise to you!
             Ten thousand years to our emperor!
             To you, heir of Hien Wang,
             we cry:
             Ten thousand years to our emperor!
             High, high the flags!
             Glory to you! Glory to you!
             Glory to you! Glory to you!

ACT THREE

Scene One

The garden of the royal palace, very vast, all rolling slopes, bushes, and the dark outlines of bronze divinities, faintly illuminated from below by the reflection from the incense braziers. At right rises a pavilion which is reached by five steps and bound by a richly embroidered hanging. The pavilion is the forepart of one of the buildings of the palace, on the side toward the rooms of Turandot. It is night. From the farthest distances come voices of heralds who are going through the immense city issuing the royal command. Other voices, near and far, echo these. Lying on the steps of the pavilion is the Prince. In the great nocturnal silence he listens to the cries of the heralds, as if he were almost no longer living in reality.

THE VOICES OF THE HERALDS
             Thus commands Turandot:
             "This night let no one sleep in Peking!"

VOCI LONTANE
>Nessun dorma! Nessun dorma!

LE VOCI DEGLI ARALDI
>"Pena la morte, il nome dell'Ignoto
>sia rivelato prima del mattino!"

VOCI LONTANE
>Pena la morte! Pena la morte!

LE VOCI DEGLI ARALDI
>"Questa notte nessun dorma in Pekino!"

VOCI LONTANE
>Nessun dorma! Nessun dorma!

IL PRINCIPE IGNOTO
>Nessun dorma! Nessun dorma . . . !
>Tu pure, O Principessa,
>nella tua fredda stanza
>guardi le stelle
>che tremano d'amore e di speranza!
>Ma il mio mistero è chiuso in me,
>il nome mio nessun saprà!
>No, no, sulla tua bocca lo dirò
>quando la luce splenderà!
>Ed il mio bacio scioglierà il silenzio
>che ti fa mia . . . !

VOCI DI DONNE (*misteriose e lontane*)
>Il nome suo nessun saprà . . .
>E noi dovrem, ahimè, morir, morir . . . !

IL PRINCIPE IGNOTO
>Dilegua, o notte . . . ! Tramontate, stelle!
>Tramontate, stelle!
>All'alba vincerò! Vincerò! Vincerò!

Ed ecco alcune ombre appariscono strisciando fra i ces-
pugli: figure confuse col buio della notte, che si fanno sempre
più numerose e finiranno col diventare una folla. I tre ministri
sono alla testa.

PING (*si accosta al Principe*)
>Tu che guardi le stelle, abbassa gli occhi,
>[abbassa gli occhi!

PONG   La nostra vita è in tuo potere!

PANG   La nostra vita!]

PING   Udiste il bando? Per le vie di Pekino

>ad ogni porta batte la morte
>e grida: il nome!

I MINISTRI   Il nome o sangue!

IL PRINCIPE IGNOTO
>Che volete da me?

PING   Di' tu, che vuoi! Di' tu, che vuoi!

PONG   Di' tu, che vuoi!

PING   È l'amore che cerchi?

PANG   Di' tu, che vuoi?

PING   Di' tu, che vuoi?
>Ebbene: prendi!

DISTANT VOICES
>Let no one sleep! Let no one sleep!

THE VOICES OF THE HERALDS
>"Under pain of death, the stranger's name
>must be revealed before morning!"

DISTANT VOICES
>Under pain of death! Under pain of death!

THE VOICES OF THE HERALDS
>"This night let no one sleep in Peking!"

DISTANT VOICES
>Let no one sleep! Let no one sleep!

THE UNKNOWN PRINCE
>Let no one sleep! Let no one sleep . . . !
>You too, O Princess,
>in your cold room
>are looking at the stars
>that tremble with love and with hope!
>But my mystery is locked in me,
>no one will know my name!
>No, no, upon your mouth I'll say it
>when the light shines!
>And my kiss will break the silence
>that makes you mine . . . !

WOMEN'S VOICES (*mysterious and remote*)
>No one will know his name . . .
>And we, alas, shall have to die, to die . . . !

THE UNKNOWN PRINCE
>Dissolve, O Night . . . ! Set, stars!
>Set, stars!
>At dawn I'll win! I'll win! I'll win!

And there, some shadows appear, gliding among the bushes, forms confused in the darkness of the night, who become more and more numerous and finally turn into a crowd. The three ministers are at its head.

PING (*sidles up to the prince*)
>You who look at the stars, lower your eyes,
>lower your eyes!

PONG
>Our life is in your power!

PANG
>Our life!

PING
>Did you hear the proclamation? Through Pe-
>king's streets
>death raps at every door
>and cries: the name!

THE MINISTERS
>The name, or blood!

THE UNKNOWN PRINCE
>What do you want of me?

PING
>You say what you want! You say what you want!

PONG
>You say what you want!

PING
>Is it love you seek?

PANG
>You say: what do you want?

PING
>You say: what do you want?
>Very well: take!

E sospinge un gruppo di fanciulle bellissime, seminude, procaci, ai piedi del Principe.

PING   Guarda . . . ! son belle!
                        Son belle fra lucenti veli!

PONG E PANG   Corpi flessuosi!

PING   Tutte ebbrezze e promesse
                        d'amplessi prodigiosi!

LE FANCIULLE   (*circondando il Principe*)
                        Ah, ah! Ah, ah!

IL PRINCIPE IGNOTO   (*con un movimento di ribellione*)
                        No . . . ! No . . . !

PONG E PANG   Che vuoi?

I MINISTRI   Ricchezze? Tutti i tesori a te!
                        A te! a te . . . !

Ad un cenno di Ping vengono portati davanti al Principe sacchi, cofani, canestri ricolmi d'oro e di gemme. E i tre ministri fanno scintillare questi splendori davanti agli occhi abbagliati del Principe.

PING   Rompon la notte nera . . .

PONG   Fuochi azzurri!

PING   . . . queste fulgide gemme!

PANG   Verdi splendori!

PONG   Pallidi giacinti!

PANG   Le vampe rosse dei rubini!

PING   Sono gocciole d'astri!

PONG E PANG   Fuochi azzurri!

PING   Prendi! È tutto tuo!

PONG E PANG   Vampe rosse!

IL PRINCIPE IGNOTO   (*ribellandosi ancora*)
                        No! Nessuna ricchezza! No!

I MINISTRI   Vuoi la gloria? Noi ti farem fuggir!

PONG E PANG   E andrai lontano con le stelle
                        verso imperi favolosi!

LA FOLLA   Fuggi! Fuggi! Va' lontano!
                        Va' lontano! Fuggi, ecc.
                        e noi tutti ci salviam!

IL PRINCIPE IGNOTO   (*tendendo le braccia al cielo*)
                        Alba, vieni! Quest'incubo dissolvi . . . !

Allora i tre ministri si stringono intorno a lui con crescente minacciosa disperazione.

PING   Straniero, tu non sai, tu non sai
                        di che cosa è capace la Crudele,
                        tu non sai . . .

And he thrusts a group of very beautiful, half-naked, provocative maidens at the Prince's feet.

PING   Look . . . ! They are beautiful!
              They are beautiful amid shining veils!

PONG AND PANG
              Supple bodies!

PING   All ecstasies and promises
              of wondrous embraces!

THE MAIDENS (*surrounding the Prince*)
              Ah, ah! Ah, ah!

THE UNKNOWN PRINCE (*with a movement of rebellion*)
              No . . . ! No . . . !

PONG AND PANG
              What do you want?

THE MINISTERS
              Riches? All treasures for you!
              For you! For you . . . !

At a sign from Ping before the Prince are carried sacks, coffers, baskets brimming with gold and gems. And the three ministers make these splendors flash before the dazzled eyes of the Prince.

PING   They break the black night . . .

PONG   Blue fires!

PING   . . . these bright gems!

PANG   Green splendors!

PONG   Pale hyacinths!

PANG   The rubies' red flames!

PING   They are stars' drops!

PONG AND PANG
              Blue fires!

PING   Take! It's all yours!

PONG AND PANG
              Red flames!

THE UNKNOWN PRINCE (*rebelling again*)
              No! No riches! No!

THE MINISTERS
              Do you want glory? We'll have you escape!

PONG AND PANG
              And you'll go far off with the stars
              toward fabulous empires!

THE CROWD   Flee! Flee! Go far off!
              Go far off! Flee, etc.
              and all of us will be saved!

THE UNKNOWN PRINCE (*holding his arms up to heaven*)
              Dawn, come! Dissolve this nightmare . . . !

Then the three ministers huddle around him with mounting, threatening despair.

PING   Foreigner, you don't know, you don't know
              what the Cruel One is capable of,
              you don't know . . .

PONG E PANG   Tu non sai quali orrendi martiri
              la Cina inventi
              se tu rimani e non ci sveli il nome!

MINISTRI E FOLLA
              L'Insonne non perdona!
              Siam perduti! Siam perduti!
              Sarà martirio orrendo!
              I ferri aguzzi! L'irte ruote!
              Il caldo morso delle tenaglie!
              La morte a sorso a sorso!
              Non farci morire! Non farci morir!

IL PRINCIPE IGNOTO (*con suprema fermezza*)
              Inutili preghiere! Inutili minacce!
              Crollasse il mondo, voglio Turandot!

*Allora la folla perde ogni ritegno, ed urla selvaggiamente
attorniando il Principe:*

LA FOLLA   Non l'avrai! No, non l'avrai!
              Morrai prima di noi! Tu maledetto!
              Morrai prima di noi, tu spietato!
              Crudele! Il nome! Parla! Il nome! Il nome!

*Si tendono alti e minacciosi i pugnali verso il Principe, stret-
to nella cerchia feroce e disperata. Ma d'un tratto s'odono
grida tumultuose dal giardino e tutti s'arrestano.*

GLI SGHERRI   Eccolo il nome! È qua! È qua!
              Eccolo il nome! È qua! È qua!

*Un gruppo di sgherri trascina il vecchio Timur e Liù, logori,
pesti, affranti, insanguinati. La folla ammutolisce nell'ansia
dell'attesa. Il Principe si precipita, gridando:*

IL PRINCIPE IGNOTO
              Costor non sanno . . . ! Ignorano il mio nome!

Ma Ping, che riconosce i due, ebbro di gioia ribatte:

PING   Sono il vecchio e la giovane
              che iersera parlavano con te!

IL PRINCIPE IGNOTO
              Lasciateli!

PING   Conoscono il segreto!
                  (*agli sgherri*)
              Dove li avete colti?

GLI SGHERRI   Mentre erravano là, presso le mura!

I MINISTRI (*correndo al padiglione*)
              Principessa!

MINISTRI, FOLLA
              Principessa!

*Turandot appare sul limite del padiglione. Tutti si proster-
nano a terra. Solo Ping, avanzando con estrema umiltà, dice:*

PING   Principessa divina! Il nome dell'ignoto
              sta chiuso in queste bocche silenti.
              E abbiamo ferri per schiodar quei denti,
              e uncini abbiamo per strappar quel nome!

PONG AND PANG

> You don't know what horrible tortures
> China may invent
> if you remain and don't reveal your name to us!

MINISTERS AND CROWD

> The Sleepless One doesn't forgive!
> We're lost! We're lost!
> It will be horrible torture!
> The sharp irons! The bristling wheels!
> The hot grip of the pincers!
> Death in little sips!
> Don't make us die! Don't make us die!

THE UNKNOWN PRINCE (*with supreme firmness*)

> Useless prayers! Useless threats!
> Should the world collapse, I want Turandot!

Then the crowd loses all restraint, and it yells savagely, surrounding the Prince:

THE CROWD

> You won't have her! No, you won't have her!
> You'll die before us! You, accursed!
> You'll die before us, you, pitiless!
> Cruel! The name! Speak! The name! The name!

High and menacing, daggers are stretched out toward the Prince, enclosed in the fierce and desperate circle. But suddenly tumultuous cries are heard from the garden, and all stop.

THE GUARDS

> Here's the name! It's here! It's here!
> Here's the name! It's here! It's here!

A group of hired assassins drags in old Timur and Liù, worn, beaten, exhausted, bloodstained. The crowd falls silent in the anxiety of waiting. The Prince rushes over, shouting:

THE UNKNOWN PRINCE

> They don't know . . . ! They don't know my name!

But Ping, who recognizes the two, drunk with joy, replies:

PING

> They are the old man and the young girl
> who were talking with you yesterday evening!

THE UNKNOWN PRINCE

> Let them go!

PING

> They know the secret!
>   (*to the guards*)
> Where did you catch them?

THE GUARDS   While they wandered there, near the walls!

THE MINISTERS (*running to the pavilion*)

> Princess!

MINISTERS, CROWD

> Princess!

Turandot appears at the edge of the pavilion. All prostrate themselves on the ground. Only Ping, advancing with extreme humility, says:

PING

> Divine Princess! The stranger's name
> is closed in these silent mouths.
> And we have irons to wrench out those teeth,
> and we have hooks to tear out that name!

*Il Principe che s'era dominato per non tradirsi, ora, a udir
lo scherno crudele e la minaccia, ha un movimento di impe-
tuosa ribellione. Ma Turandot lo ferma con uno sguardo pieno
d'impero e d'ironia.*

TURANDOT   Sei pallido, straniero!

IL PRINCIPE IGNOTO (*alteramente*)
                Il tuo sgomento
                vede il pallor dell'alba sul mio volto!
                Costor non mi conoscono!

TURANDOT   Vedremo!
                    (*e rivolgendosi a Timur, con fermissimo
                    commando*)
                Su! Parla, vecchio!

*Attende sicura, quasi indifferente. Ma il vecchio tace. In-
tontito dal dolore, scompigliata la sua veneranda canizie,
pallido, lordo, pesto, guarda la Principessa muto, con gli occhi
sbarrati e un'espressione di supplica disperata.*

TURANDOT (*con furore, ai ministri*)
                Io voglio ch'egli parli!
                Il nome!

*Timur è riafferrato, ma prima che il Principe abbia tempo
di muoversi per buttarsi avanti e difenderlo, Liù si avanza
rapidamente verso Turandot.*

LIÙ   Il nome che cercate
                io sola la so.

LA FOLLA   La vita è salva! L'incubo svanì!

IL PRINCIPE IGNOTO (*con fiero rimprovero a Liù*)
                Tu non sai nulla, schiava!

LIÙ (*guarda il Principe con infinita tenerezza, poi volgendosi a
        Turandot:*)
                Io so il suo nome . . .
                M'è suprema delizia
                tenerlo segreto e possederlo io sola!

LA FOLLA (*che vede sfuggire la sua speranza, irrompe verso
            Liù, gridando*)
                Sia legata! sia straziata!
                Perchè parli! Perchè muoia!

IL PRINCIPE IGNOTO (*ponendosi davanti a Liù*)
                Sconterete le sue lagrime!
                Sconterete i suoi tormenti!

TURANDOT (*violenta, alle guardie*)
                Tenetelo!

*Il Principe è afferrato dagli sgherri e tenuto fermo, legato.
Allora Turandot riprende la sua attitudine ieratica, quasi assente, mentre Liù, ghermita dai suoi torturatori, è caduta a
terra in ginocchio.*

LIÙ (*con fermezza, al Principe*)
                Signor, non parlerò!

PING (*curvo su di lei*)
                Quel nome!

LIÙ   No!

PING   Quel nome!

The Prince, who had controlled himself not to give himself away, now, at hearing the cruel contempt and the menace, makes a movement of impetuous rebellion. But Turandot stops him with a look full of imperiousness and of irony.

TURANDOT You're pale, foreigner!

THE UNKNOWN PRINCE (*haughtily*)
　　　　　Your alarm
　　　　　sees dawn's pallor on my face!
　　　　　They don't know me!

TURANDOT We'll see!
　　　　　　　　(*and, addressing Timur, with very firm command*)
　　　　　Come! Speak, old man!

She waits, sure, almost indifferent. But the old man is silent. Dazed with grief, his venerable hair disheveled, pale, dirty, bruised, he looks mutely at the Princess, his eyes wide, with an expression of desperate imploration.

TURANDOT (*with fury, to the ministers*)
　　　　　I want him to speak!
　　　　　The name!

Timur is seized again, but before the Prince has time to move, to hurl himself forward and defend him, Liù advances rapidly toward Turandot.

LIÙ　　　　The name that you seek
　　　　　only I know.

THE CROWD Our life is saved! The nightmare's vanished!

THE UNKNOWN PRINCE (*with haughty reproof, to Liù*)
　　　　　You know nothing, slave!

LIÙ (*looks at the Prince with infinite tenderness, then, turning to Turandot*)
　　　　　I know his name . . .
　　　　　It is a supreme delight for me
　　　　　to keep it a secret and to possess it, alone!

THE CROWD (*which sees its hope vanishing, bursts toward Liù, shouting*)
　　　　　Let her be bound! Let her be tortured!
　　　　　That she may speak! That she may die!

THE UNKNOWN PRINCE (*placing himself before Liù*)
　　　　　You'll pay for her tears!
　　　　　You'll pay for her torments!

TURANDOT (*violent, to the guards*)
　　　　　Hold him!

The Prince is seized by the guards and held fast, bound. Then Turandot resumes her hieratic attitude, almost absent, as Liù, gripped by her torturers, has sunk to the ground on her knees.

LIÙ (*firmly, to the Prince*)
　　　　　Lord, I won't speak!

PING (*bent over her*)
　　　　　That name!

LIÙ　　　　No!

PING　　　That name!

LIÙ   La tua serva chiede perdono,
             ma obbedir non può!

A un cenno di Ping gli sgherri l'afferrano, le torcono le braccia. Liù grida.

LIÙ   Ah!

TIMUR (*si scuote dal suo terribile silenzio*)
             Perchè gridi?

IL PRINCIPE IGNOTO
             Lasciatela!

LIÙ   No ... no ... Non grido più! Non mi fan male!

             No, nessun mi tocca ...
                  (*agli sgherri*)
             Stringete ... ma chiudetemi la bocca
             ch'ei non mi senta!
                  (*poi, sfibrata*)
             Non resisto più!

LA FOLLA   Parla! Il suo nome!

TURANDOT   Sia lasciata! Parla!

Liù è liberata.

LIÙ   Piuttosto morrò!

E cade accasciata presso i gradini del padiglione.

TURANDOT (*fissando Liù, quasi a scrutarne il mistero*)
             Chi pose tanta forza nel tuo cuore?

LIÙ   Principessa, l'amore!

TURANDOT   L'amore?

LIÙ (*sollevando gli occhi pieni di tenerezza*)
             Tanto amore segreto, e inconfessato,
             grande così che questi strazî sono
             dolcezze per me, perchè ne faccio dono
             al mio Signore ...
             Perchè, tacendo, io gli do il tuo amore ...
             Te, gli do, Principessa, e perdo tutto!
             e perdo tutto! persino l'impossibile speranza!
                  (*e rivolta agli sgherri*)
             Legatemi! Straziatemi!
             Tormenti e spasimi
             date a me!
             Ah! Come offerta suprema del mio amore!

TURANDOT (*che è rimasta per un momento turbata e affascina-
             ta dalle parole di Liù, ora ordina ai ministri:*)
             Strappatele il segreto!

PING   Chiamate Pu-Tin-Pao!

IL PRINCIPE IGNOTO (*dibattendosi rabbiosamente*)
             No, maledetto! Maledetto!

LA FOLLA   Il boia! Il boia! Il boia!

PING   Sia messa alla tortura!

LA FOLLA (*selvaggiamente*)
             Alla tortura! Sì! il boia!
             Parli! Alla tortura!

LIÙ   Your servant asks forgiveness,
                      but she cannot obey!

At a sign from Ping, the assassins seize her, twist her arms. Liù screams.

LIÙ   Ah!

TIMUR (*stirs from his terrible silence*)
                      Why are you crying?

THE UNKNOWN PRINCE
                      Let her go!

LIÙ   No . . . no . . . I won't cry any more! They aren't
                      hurting me!
                      No, no one is touching me . . .
                         (*to the guards*)
                      Twist harder . . . but close my mouth
                      so that he won't hear me!
                         (*then, exhausted*)
                      I can stand no more!

THE CROWD   Speak! His name!

TURANDOT   Free her! Speak!

Liù is released.

LIÙ   I'd rather die!

And she sinks down near the steps of the pavilion.

TURANDOT (*staring at Liù, as if to gaze into her mystery*)
                      Who placed such strength in your heart?

LIÙ   Princess — love!

TURANDOT   Love?

LIÙ (*raising her eyes, filled with tenderness*)
                      Such love — secret and unconfessed,
                      so great that these tortures are
                      sweetnesses for me, because I present them
                      to my Lord . . .
                      Because, remaining silent, I give him your love . . .
                      I give him you, Princess, and I lose all!
                      and I lose all! even impossible hope!
                       (*and, addressing the guards*)
                      Bind me! Torture me!
                      Give me
                      torments and pains!
                      Ah! as the supreme offering of my love!

TURANDOT (*who, for a moment, has remained upset and fascin-
                ated by Liù's words, orders the ministers:*)
                      Tear the secret from her!

PING   Call Pu-Tin-Pao!

THE UNKNOWN PRINCE (*struggling angrily*)
                      No, accursed! Accursed!

THE CROWD   The executioner! The executioner! The execu-
                      tioner!

PING   Let her be put to torture!

THE CROWD (*savagely*)
                      To torture! Yes! The executioner!
                      Let her speak! To torture!

Ed ecco il gigantesco Pu-Tin-Pao con i suoi aiutanti appare nel fondo, immobile e spaventoso. Liù ha un grido disperato, s'aggira come pazza cercando, inutilmente, di aprirsi un varco, implorando, supplicando.

LIÙ   Più non resisto!
                Ho paura di me!
                Lasciatemi passare . . . !

LA FOLLA (*sbarrandole il passo*)
                Parla! Parla!

LIÙ (*disperatamente, correndo presso Turandot*)
                Sì, Principessa . . . ! Ascoltami!
                Tu che di gel sei cinta,
                da tanta fiamma vinta
                l'amerai anche tu!
                l'amerai anche tu!
                Prima di questa aurora
                io chiudo stanca gli occhi,
                perchè Egli vinca ancora . . . ei vinca ancora . . .

                Per non . . . per non vederlo più!
                Prima di questa aurora, di questa aurora
                io chiudo stanca gli occhi
                per non vederlo più!

Strappa con mossa repentina dalla cintola di un soldato un acutissimo pugnale e so lo pianta nel petto. Gira intorno gli occhi perduti, guarda il Principe con dolcezza suprema, va, barcollando, presso di lui e gli stramazza ai piedi, morta.

LA FOLLA   Ah! Parla! Parla! Il nome! Il nome!
IL PRINCIPE IGNOTO
                Ah! Tu sei morta, tu sei morta,
                o mia piccola Liù . . . !

Si fa un grande silenzio, pieno di terrore. Turandot fissa Liù stesa a terra; poi con gesto pieno di collera strappa ad un aiutante del boia che le è vicino una verga e percuote con essa in pieno viso il soldato che si è lasciato strappare il pugnale da Liù. Il soldato si copre il volto e arretra tra la folla. Il Principe è liberato. Allora il vecchio Timur, come impazzito, si alza. Si accosta barcollando alla piccola morta. Si inginocchia.

TIMUR   Liù . . . ! Liù . . . !
                Sorgi . . . ! sorgi! È l'ora chiara
                d'ogni risveglio!
                È l'alba, o mia Liù . . .
                Apri gli occhi, colomba!

C'è in tutti un senso di pietà, di turbamento, di rimorso. Sul volto di Turandot passa una espressione di tormento. Se ne avvede Ping, che va rudemente verso il vecchio per allontanarlo. Ma quando gli è vicino la sua naturale crudeltà è vinta e la durezza del suo tono attenuata.

PING   Alzati, vecchio! È morta!
TIMUR (*come un urlo*)
                Ah! Delitto orrendo! L'espieremo tutti!
                L'anima offesa, l'anima offesa si vendicherà!

And there, the gigantic Pu-Tin-Pao with his assistants appears in the background, immobile and frightful. Liù emits a desperate cry, wanders about like a madwoman, trying in vain to force her way out, imploring, pleading.

LIÙ   I can stand no more!
     I'm afraid of myself!
     Let me pass . . . !

THE CROWD (*blocking her way*)
     Speak! Speak!

LIÙ (*desperately, running over to Turandot*)
     Yes, Princess . . . ! Listen to me!
     You who are girded with frost,
     overcome by such flame,
     you also will love him!
     You also will love him!
     Before this dawn
     I close, weary, my eyes,
     that he may win again . . . that he may win
     again . . .
     To not . . . to not see him any more!
     Before this dawn, this dawn
     I close, weary, my eyes
     to not see him any more!

With a sudden movement she tears from a soldier's belt a very sharp dagger and plunges it into her bosom. She casts her lost eyes about, looks at the Prince with supreme sweetness, goes staggering over to him and falls at his feet, dead.

THE CROWD Ah! Speak! Speak! The name! The name!

THE UNKNOWN PRINCE
     Ah! You are dead, you are dead,
     Oh, my little Liù . . . !

A great silence, filled with terror, falls. Turandot stares at Liù, lying on the ground; then with a gesture full of rage she seizes a lash from one of the executioner's assistants standing near her and strikes full in the face with it the soldier who allowed Liù to seize his dagger. The soldier covers his face and steps back amid the crowd. The Prince is freed. Then old Timur, as if crazed, stands up. He goes over, staggering, to the little dead girl. He kneels.

TIMUR   Liù . . . ! Liù . . . !
     Rise . . . ! rise! It is the bright hour
     of every awakening!
     It's dawn, Oh my Liù . . .
     Open your eyes, dove!

In all there is a feeling of pity, of dismay, of remorse. On Turandot's face there passes an expression of torment. Ping notices it, and goes roughly toward the old man to send him away. But when he is near him his natural cruelty is overcome and the harshness of his tone attenuated.

PING   Get up, old man! She's dead!

TIMUR (*like a cry*)
     Ah! Horrible crime! We'll all expiate it!
     The offended spirit, the offended spirit will
     avenge itself!

*Allora un terrore superstizioso prende la folla: il terrore che
quella morta, divenuta spirito malefico perchè vittima di una
ingiustizia, sia tramutata, secondo la credenza popolare, in
vampiro. E, mentre due Ancelle coprono il volto di Turandot
con un velo bianco trapunto d'argento, la folla, supplice, dice:*

LA FOLLA   Ombra dolente, non farci del male!
               Ombra sdegnosa, perdona! perdona!

*Con religiosa pietà il piccolo corpo viene sollevato, tra il
rispetto profondo della folla. Il vecchio si avvicina, stringe
teneramente una mano della morta e cammina vicino a lei.*

TIMUR   Liù . . . ! bontà Liù . . . ! dolcezza!
               Ah! camminiamo insieme un'altra volta
               così, con la tua mano nella mia mano . . .
               Dove vai ben so . . .
               Ed io ti seguirò
               per posare a te vicino
               nella notte che non ha mattino!
PING   [Ah! Per la prima volta
               al vedere la morte non sogghigno!
PONG   Svegliato s'è qui dentro il vecchio ordigno
               il cuore, e mi tormenta!
PANG   Quella fanciulla spenta
               pesa sopra il mio cuor come un macigno!]

Mentre tutti si avviano, la folla riprende:

LA FOLLA   Liù, bontà, perdona, perdona!
               Liù, bontà, Liù, dolcezza, dormi!
               Oblia! Liù! Poesia!

*Le voci si vanno perdendo lontano. Tutti, oramai, sono
usciti. Rimangono soli, l'uno di fronte all'altra, il Principe e
Turandot. La Principessa, rigida, statuario sotto l'ampio velo,
non ha un gesto, non un movimento.*

IL PRINCIPE IGNOTO
               Principessa di morte!
               Principessa di gelo!
               Dal tuo tragico cielo
               scendi giù sulla terra . . . !
               Ah! Solleva quel velo . . .
               Guarda . . . guarda, crudele,
               quel purissimo sangue
               che fu sparso per te!

E si precipita verso di lei, strappandole il velo.

TURANDOT (*con fermezza ieratica*)
               Che mai osi, straniero!
               Cosa umana non sono . . .
               Son la figlia del cielo
               Libera e pura . . . ! Tu
               stringi il mio freddo velo,
               ma l'anima è lassù!

IL PRINCIPE IGNOTO (*che è rimasto per un momento come af-
                   fascinato, indietreggia. Ma si domina. E con
                   ardente audacia esclama:*)

Then a superstitious terror grips the crowd: the terror that the dead girl, having become a maleficent spirit because the victim of an injustice, may be changed — according to the popular belief — into a vampire. And, as two handmaidens cover Turandot's face with a white, silver-embroidered veil, the crowd says, supplicating:

THE CROWD   Grieving shade, don't hurt us!
                Disdainful shade, forgive! forgive!

With religious piety the little body is raised up, amid the profound respect of the crowd. The old man approaches, tenderly clasps a hand of the dead girl and walks along beside her.

TIMUR   Liù . . . ! goodness! Liù . . . ! sweetness!
                Ah! let us walk together one more time
                like this, with your hand in my hand . . .
                I know well where you are going . . .
                And I'll follow you
                to rest beside you
                in the night that has no morning!

PING   Ah! For the first time
                I don't sneer at seeing death!

PONG   Here inside me the old mechanism, my heart,
                has awakened and is tormenting me!

PANG   That dead girl
                weighs upon my heart like a block of stone!

As all go off, the crowd resumes:

THE CROWD   Liù, goodness, forgive, forgive!
                Liù, goodness, Liù, sweetness, sleep!
                Forget! Liù! Poetry!

The voices are being lost in the distance. All, now, have gone off. Alone, the one facing the other, remain the prince and Turandot. The princess, rigid, statuesque beneath the broad veil, makes not a gesture, not a movement.

THE UNKNOWN PRINCE
                Princess of death!
                Princess of frost!
                From your tragic sky
                descend, down upon the earth . . . !
                Ah! Lift that veil . . .
                Look . . . look, cruel one,
                at that purest of blood
                that was shed for you!

And he rushes toward her, tearing the veil from her.

TURANDOT *(with rigid firmness)*
                What are you daring, foreigner!
                I am no human thing . . .
                I am the daughter of heaven,
                free and pure . . . ! You
                clasp my cold veil,
                but my soul is on high!

THE UNKNOWN PRINCE *(who has remained for a moment as if
                fascinated, steps back. But he recovers him-
                self. And with ardent boldness he exclaims:)*

La tua anima è in alto!
Ma il tuo corpo è vicino.
Con le mani brucianti
stringerò i lembi d'oro
del tuo manto stellato!
La mia bocca fremente
premerò su di te!

E si precipita verso Turandot tendendo le braccia.

TURANDOT (*arretrando sconvolta, spaurita, disperatamente mi-
                      nacciosa*)
Non profanarmi!

IL PRINCIPE IGNOTO (*perdutamente*)
Ah! Sentirti viva!

TURANDOT   Indietro!

IL PRINCIPE IGNOTO
Sentirti viva! Sentirti viva!

TURANDOT   Indietro! Non profanarmi! Non profanarmi!

IL PRINCIPE IGNOTO
Il gelo tuo è menzogna!

TURANDOT   Indietro!

IL PRINCIPE IGNOTO
È menzogna!

TURANDOT   No! Mai nessun m'avrà!

IL PRINCIPE IGNOTO
Ti voglio mia!

TURANDOT   Dell'ava lo strazio
non si rinnoverà! Ah, no!

IL PRINCIPE IGNOTO
Ti voglio mia!

TURANDOT   Non mi toccar, straniero . . . !
È un sacrilegio!

IL PRINCIPE IGNOTO
No, il bacio tuo mi dà l'eternità!

TURANDOT   Sacrilegio!

*Il Principe, in così dire, forte della coscienza del suo diritto
e della sua passione, rovescia nelle sue braccia Turandot e
freneticamente la bacia. Turandot — sotto tanto impeto — non
ha più resistenza, non ha più voce, non ha più forza, non ha
più volontà. Il contatto incredibile l'ha trasfigurata. Con accento di supplica quasi infantile, mormora:*

TURANDOT   Che è mai di me? perduta!

IL PRINCIPE IGNOTO
Mio fiore!
Oh! Mio fiore mattutino!
Mio fiore, ti respiro!
I seni tuoi di giglio,
ah! treman sul mio petto!
Già ti sento mancare di dolcezza,
tutta bianca nel tuo manto d'argento!

> Your soul is on high!
> But your body is near.
> With burning hands
> I'll clasp the golden edges
> of your spangled mantle!
> My trembling mouth
> I'll press upon you!

And he rushes toward Turandot, holding out his arms.

TURANDOT (*stepping back, distraught, frightened, desperately threatening*)
> Don't profane me!

THE UNKNOWN PRINCE (*wildly*)
> Ah! To feel you alive!

TURANDOT   Back!

THE UNKNOWN PRINCE
> To feel you alive!
> To feel you alive!

TURANDOT   Back! Don't profane me!
> Don't profane me!

THE UNKNOWN PRINCE
> Your iciness is falsehood!

TURANDOT   Back!

THE UNKNOWN PRINCE
> It's falsehood!

TURANDOT   No! No one will ever possess me!

THE UNKNOWN PRINCE
> I want you mine!

TURANDOT   The torment of my ancestress
> will not be renewed! Ah, no!

THE UNKNOWN PRINCE
> I want you mine!

TURANDOT   Don't touch me, foreigner . . . !
> It's a sacrilege!

THE UNKNOWN PRINCE
> No, your kiss gives me eternity!

TURANDOT   Sacrilege!

The prince, in saying this, strong in the knowledge of his right and in his passion, throws Turandot back into his arms and kisses her frenziedly. Turandot — against such impetuousness — has no more resistance, no more voice, no more strength, no more will. The incredible contact has transfigured her. With a tone of almost childish pleading she murmurs:

TURANDOT   What has become of me? Lost!

THE UNKNOWN PRINCE
> My flower!
> Oh! My morning flower!
> My flower, I breathe you in!
> Your breasts of lily,
> ah!, they tremble beneath my chest!
> Already I feel you fainting with sweetness,
> all white in your silver mantle!

TURANDOT (*con gli occhi velati di lagrime*)
   Come vincesti?

IL PRINCIPE IGNOTO (*con tenerezza estatica*)
   Piangi?

TURANDOT (*rabbrividendo*)
   È l'alba! È l'alba! È l'alba!
   Turandot tramonta!

VOCI LONTANE L'alba! Luce e vita!

   Tutto è puro! Tutto è santo!
   Che dolcezza nel tuo pianto!

IL PRINCIPE IGNOTO
   È l'alba! È l'alba!
   E amor . . . e amor nasce col sole!

TURANDOT Che nessun mi veda . . .
    (*e con rassegnata dolcezza*)
   La mia gloria è finita!

IL PRINCIPE IGNOTO (*con impetuoso trasporto*)
   No! Essa incomincia!

TURANDOT Onta su me!

IL PRINCIPE IGNOTO
   Miracolo! La tua gloria risplende
   nell'incanto del primo bacio,
   del primo pianto.

TURANDOT (*esaltata, travolta*)
   Del primo pianto . . . Ah . . .
   Del primo pianto . . . sì . . .
   straniero, quando sei giunto,
   con angoscia ho sentito
   il brivido fatale
   di questo mal
   supremo!
   Quanti ho visto morire
   per me!
   E li ho spregiati
   ma ho temuto per te!
   C'era negli occhi tuoi
   la luce degli eroi!
   C'era negli occhi tuoi
   la superba certezza . . .
   E t'ho odiato per quella . . .
   E per quella t'ho amato,
   tormentata e divisa
   fra due terrori uguali:
   vincerti o esser vinta . . .
   E vinta son . . . Ah! vinta
   più che dall'alta prova
   da questa febbre
   che mi vien da te!

IL PRINCIPE IGNOTO
   Sei mia! mia!

TURANDOT Questo, questo chiedevi . . .
   ora lo sai. Più grande

TURANDOT (*with her eyes veiled with tears*)
How did you conquer?

THE UNKNOWN PRINCE (*with ecstatic tenderness*)
Are you weeping?

TURANDOT (*shuddering*)
It's dawn! It's dawn! It's dawn!
Turandot's sun is setting!

DISTANT VOICES
Dawn! Light and life!
All is pure! All is holy!
What sweetness in your weeping!

THE UNKNOWN PRINCE
It's dawn! It's dawn!
And love . . . love is born with the sun!

TURANDOT
Let no one see me . . .
(*and with resigned sweetness*)
My glory has ended!

THE UNKNOWN PRINCE (*with impetuous transport*)
No! It's beginning!

TURANDOT
Disgrace upon me!

THE UNKNOWN PRINCE
Miracle! Your glory shines
in the spell of the first kiss,
of the first weeping.

TURANDOT (*exalted, overcome*)
Of the first weeping . . . Ah . . .
Of the first weeping . . . yes . . .
foreigner, when you arrived,
with anguish I felt
the fatal shudder
of this supreme
illness!
How many men have I seen die
for me!
And I scorned them
but I feared for you!
There was in your eyes
the light of heroes!
There was in your eyes
the proud certainty . . .
And I hated you for that . . .
And for that I loved you,
tormented and torn
between two equal terrors:
to conquer you or to be conquered . . .
And I am conquered . . . Ah! conquered
more than by the supreme trial
by this fever
that comes to me from you!

THE UNKNOWN PRINCE
You're mine! mine!

TURANDOT
This, this you asked . . .
now you know. Don't desire

vittoria non voler . . .
Parti, straniero . . .
col tuo mister!

IL PRINCIPE IGNOTO (*con caldissimo impeto*)
Il mio mistero? Non ne ho più! Sei mia!
Tu che tremi se ti sfioro!
Tu che sbianchi se ti bacio,
puoi perdermi se vuoi.
Il mio nome e la vita insiem ti dono.
Io son Calaf, figlio di Timur!

TURANDOT   So il tuo nome! So il tuo nome!

CALAF   La mia gloria è il tuo amplesso!

TURANDOT   Odi! Squillan le trombe!

CALAF   La mia vita è il tuo bacio!

TURANDOT   Ecco! È l'ora!
È l'ora della prova!

CALAF   Non la temo!

TURANDOT (*ergendosi tutta, regalmente, dominatrice*)
Ah! Calaf, davanti al popolo con me!

CALAF   Hai vinto tu!

ATTO TERZO

Quadro secondo

*L'esterno del palazzo imperiale, tutto bianco di marmi tra-
forati, sui quali i riflessi rosei dell'aurora s'accendono come
fiori. Sopra un'alta scala, al centro della scena, l'Imperatore
circondato dalla corte, dai dignitari, dai sapienti, dai soldati.
Ai due lati del piazzale, in vasto semicerchio, l'enorme folla
che acclama.*

LA FOLLA   Diecimila anni al nostro imperatore!

*I tre ministri stendono a terra un manto d'oro mentre Tu-
randot ascende la scala. D'un tratto è il silenzio. E in quel
silenzio la Principessa esclama:*

TURANDOT   Padre augusto . . . conosco il nome
dello straniero!
(*e fissando Calaf che è ai piedi della scalèa,
finalmente, vinta, mormora quasi in un sospiro dolcissimo:*)
Il suo nome è Amor!

*Calaf sale d'impeto la scala, e i due amanti si trovano avvinti
in un abbraccio, perdutamente, mentre la folla tende le braccia, getta fiori, acclama gioiosamente.*

LA FOLLA   Amor! O sole! Vita! Eternità!
Luce del mondo è amore!
Ride e canta nel Sole
l'infinita nostra felicità!
Gloria! Gloria a te! Gloria!

a greater victory . . .
Leave, foreigner . . .
with your mystery!

THE UNKNOWN PRINCE (*with very warm impetuousness*)
My mystery? I no longer have any? You're mine!
You who tremble if I touch you!
You who pale if I kiss you,
can destroy me if you wish.
I give you together my name and my life.
I am Calaf, son of Timur.

TURANDOT   I know your name! I know your name!

CALAF   My glory is your embrace!

TURANDOT   Hear! The trumpets blare!

CALAF   My life is your kiss!

TURANDOT   Lo! It is the hour!
The hour of the trial!

CALAF   I don't fear it!

TURANDOT (*drawing herself up to her full height, regally, dominating*)
Ah! Calaf, before the people with me!

CALAF   You have conquered!

ACT THREE

Scene Two

The exterior of the imperial palace, all white with perforated marbles, on which the rosy lights of dawn are kindled like flowers. Above a high staircase, in the center of the stage, is the Emperor, surrounded by the court, by the dignitaries, by the sages, by the soldiers. At the two sides of the square, in a vast semicircle, the enormous, acclaiming crowd.

THE CROWD   Ten thousand years to our emperor!

The three ministers spread on the ground a golden mantle as Turandot climbs the stairs. Suddenly there is silence. And in that silence the Princess exclaims:

TURANDOT   August father . . . I know the name
of the foreigner!
(*and, staring at Calaf, who is at the foot of the stairs, she murmurs, finally, conquered, as if in a very soft sigh:*)
His name is love!

Calaf impetuously climbs the stairs, and the two lovers are clasped in an embrace, wildly, as the crowd holds out its arms, throws flowers, joyously acclaims.

THE CROWD   Love! O Sun! Life! Eternity!
Light of the world is love!
Our infinite happiness
laughs and sings in the sun!
Glory! Glory to you! Glory!